THE ARMS DYNAMIC IN WORLD POLITICS

Barry Buzan & Eric Herring

LYNNE
RIENNER
PUBLISHERS

BOULDER
LONDON

Published in the United States of America in 1998 by
Lynne Rienner Publishers, Inc.
1800 30th Street, Boulder, Colorado 80301

and in the United Kingdom by
Lynne Rienner Publishers, Inc.
3 Henrietta Street, Covent Garden, London WC2E 8LU

Library of Congress Cataloging-in-Publication Data
Buzan, Barry.
    The arms dynamic in world politics / by Barry Buzan and Eric
Herring.
    Successor to Buzan's An introduction to strategic studies :
military technology and international relations.
    Includes bibliographical references and index.
    ISBN 1-55587-573-4 (hardcover : alk. paper)
    ISBN 1-55587-596-3 (pbk. : alk. paper)
    1. World politics—1989–   2. Armaments—Political aspects.
I. Herring, Eric. II. Title.
D860.B89   1998
320.9'04—dc21   97-48486
                                                                 CIP

British Cataloguing in Publication Data
A Cataloguing in Publication record for this book
is available from the British Library.

Printed and bound in the United States of America

    The paper used in this publication meets the requirements
 ∞ of the American National Standard for Permanence of
    Paper for Printed Library Materials Z39.48-1984.

5 4 3 2 1

To Deborah, who wisely doesn't let the grass grow under her feet, and whose partnership happily prevents me from letting it grow too much under mine.

—B. B.

To my foul-weather friends—Christine, Désirée, Hannah, Helen, Nick, Sean, Susanne, and Vernon.

—E. H.

CONTENTS

TABLES AND FIGURES

Tables

Figures

PREFACE

This book is designed as a successor to Barry Buzan's 1987 work *An Introduction to Strategic Studies: Military Technology and International Relations* (hereafter *ISS*), published by Macmillan for the International Institute for Strategic Studies (IISS). *ISS* was a Cold War book. It reflected the heavy emphasis of strategic studies at that time on the military rivalry between the superpowers, and in particular on the centrality of nuclear deterrence. It also tried to present a coherent interpretation of strategic studies as being essentially about the impact of military technology on relations between states. By the early 1990s, however, *ISS*, like much else in international relations theory, was badly out of date.

In line with the sectoral approach to international relations theory that he has been developing, Buzan thought that the basic approach of looking at world politics through the military lens was worth preserving. In 1993 he approached Eric Herring with the idea of their jointly rewriting *ISS*. Once we decided to abandon the idea that the new book would try specifically to be an introduction to strategic studies, we were able to find plenty of common ground on which to make the project work. We agreed that it would be aimed at scholars and students of not only strategic studies, but also of peace studies, reflecting the narrowing of differences between the two fields in the past decade. Attention also would be paid to the emergent field of critical security studies. Our strategy was to pursue the subtitle of *ISS* while reorienting the discussion toward the post–Cold War strategic environment. The focus on nuclear weapons was broadened to weapons of mass destruction in general, and more scope was given to other levels of force.

After we sorted out the general principles for the rewrite, Herring had first cut, taking whatever material was useful from the text of *ISS* and writing a complete first draft. Buzan then commented on and wrote into Herring's drafts; and the chapters continued to be batted back and forth until we both were satisfied. It was striking that there were no major disagreements between us and only a few secondary issues to be sidestepped due to actual or potential differences.

As our work progressed, we decided not to highlight changes to the text when we made them. Although this meant a full rereading every time another draft was looked at, we wanted the manuscript to become fully a jointly written one, rather than some bits being one's own and some bits the other's. This process sometimes had amusing consequences: on one occasion one of us was scathing about a particular line of argument, only to have the other e-mail him gleefully, "I didn't write that bit—you did!"

We agreed that the military technology theme needed to be broadened even while its basic categories remained largely the same. It had to reflect not only the increasingly blurred boundary between military and civil technology, but also the radical shift of emphasis in the actors and issues defining the military security agenda. This shift meant, among other things, loosening the rather rigid neorealist state-centrism of *ISS* and opening up to the fact that the domestic arena had become the primary military forum in some parts of the world, while in other parts the international arena had matured into security communities in which hostile military interplay was virtually ruled out. The most drastic change is reflected in Part 3, which has been developed from a Cold War discussion of nuclear deterrence into a much broader assessment of the use of force, threats, and symbols.

We also agreed that although we would continue to focus on the narrow logic of military security, the linking of that view to the wider international political, economic, and normative context needed to be strengthened. Such links were already a feature of *ISS*, but even so, some readers interpreted that book as an exercise in technological determinism (Reppy 1990). We were determined to prevent such misinterpretation this time and have emphasized the interaction of choice, politics, and values with technology. Furthermore, we see technology not only as a means by which states deal with state or nonstate opponents, but also as an instrument of struggles between nonstate actors or by nonstate actors against states. Hence, the title of this book refers to the broad field of world politics, rather than to international relations, which traditionally has been almost totally state-centric (although this has been less the case recently).

To summarize briefly the final result of our collaboration, *The Arms Dynamic in World Politics* focuses on three themes: ways in which the political and military impacts of technological revolutions spread; explanations of the arms dynamic; and the political, economic, and military implications of various regulatory approaches. While we recognize that the arms dynamic does not determine directly what happens in world politics, we do intend to demonstrate how it shapes in dramatic ways the context and possibilities of world politics.

* * *

We would like to express our gratitude to the following for their assistance: the University of Bristol for a one-year research fellowship and for two terms of study leave, parts of which were used by Herring to work on this book; Theo Farrell and Patrick Morgan for very generously taking the time to comment on the entire manuscript; Theo Farrell and Anne Jewell for providing a steady stream of material; David Campbell, Terrell Carver, Ian Douglas, Nick Rengger, Richard Shapcott, Lene Hansen, Ole Wæver, and Michael Williams for their comments on Chapter 11; Bjørn Møller for his comments on Chapter 14; Patricia Owens for her swift and accurate work in compiling the index; Christine Davis for support and encouragement; and Nick Rengger for organizing what we hope was a dialogue of uncertainties rather than a clash of certainties between Herring and David Campbell based on Chapter 11 at a University of St. Andrews seminar.

Barry Buzan
Eric Herring

1

INTRODUCTION

In this book we offer a particular perspective on military security. Our approach to the subject is through technology, but we also place military security firmly within the wider context of world politics. Technology is not the only possible point of entry to this subject. One might, for example, start with morality or violence. But since students of military security are so often preoccupied with technology, we felt that it would be useful to provide an analysis that went far beyond a narrow weapon systems or bombs-and-bullets hardware approach. The aim is to offer a framework that links the diverse issues involved with military security, technology, and world politics into a coherent whole. We hope that this will encourage those who think about military technology to do so politically more than technically, and in terms of ideas more than hardware. Before explaining the structure of the book, we must indicate what we mean by military security, technology, and world politics.

Perspectives on Military Security

Defining the scope of military security is not a straightforward task. Approached in the traditional objectivist way, it might be defined as the pursuit of actual or perceived freedom of threat from organized political violence. Achievement of such freedom, or the perception of it, would mean that military security was no longer an issue. With a bit more nuance, a condition of military security can be thought of as one where threats exist, but where the countermeasures against them are thought to be adequate. If one takes a constructivist view, then military security is about the way in which states or other actors securitize (or desecuritize, as with the end of the Cold War) other actors or situations by defining them as existential threats requiring exceptional countermeasures (Buzan, Wæver, and de Wilde 1998).

1

Military security contains a diverse set of topics. The study of it has been divided principally between peace studies and strategic studies, although that division has fortunately been eroding in recent years. Military security has elements that make it distinct, but it is connected to world politics in myriad ways that severely limit the extent to which the two can be disconnected without risking potentially fatal misunderstanding. The study of military security detached from the study of world politics would be in constant danger of seeing only the conflict and taking it as the whole reality. This is where the integration of peace studies and strategic studies, the general move toward a broader understanding of security, and the development of what is called "critical security studies" (Krause and Williams 1997), is helping to provide the study of military security with the balance it needs.

The distinctive identity of strategic studies as an approach to military security stems in part from its focus on military strategy (for discussion of other features, see Groom 1988). Strategy can be broadly defined as "the art or science of shaping means so as to promote ends in any field of conflict" (Bull 1968: 593). For military strategy, the means to be shaped are armed forces, the field of conflict is the international system, and the ends are the political objectives of actors large enough to register as significant in the international context. Since states command the overwhelming bulk of military power and command the resources to influence intellectual inquiry, the study of military security is mostly about the study of the use of force within and between states. Some substate entities, like separatist or national liberation movements or terrorist revolutionary groups, are substantial enough to register, but the main actors are states, and those nonstate actors are mostly studied as problems to be dealt with by states. The preeminence of states is underlined by the fact that most of the substate entities deploying force do so either to capture an existing state, like the successful case of the African National Congress (ANC), or to create a new one, like the partly successful case of the Palestine Liberation Organization (PLO).

Military strategy has been defined as: "the art of distributing and applying military means to fulfil ends of policy" (Liddell Hart 1967: 335); "exploiting military force so as to attain given objects of policy" (Bull 1968: 593); "the relationship between military power and political purpose" (Gray 1982b: 1); and "the art of the dialectic of two opposing wills using force to resolve their dispute" (Beaufre 1965: 22). From these definitions it is clear that they present the essence of military strategy as being about "force, or the threat of force" (Gray 1982a: 3). The advent of nuclear weapons and other weapons of mass destruction (WMD) plus effective long-range delivery systems has greatly raised the relative importance of threats to use force, while at the same time increasing the restraints on the actual use of force in combat. Because of this development, the study of strategy since 1945 has developed a strong emphasis on the instruments of force themselves, on the use of threats, and on the problem of how to prevent the use of WMD, especially nuclear weapons. The study of strategy in terms of warfighting aimed at decisive military victories faltered in the nuclear realm but was by no means abandoned, and it is still highly relevant to the extensive array of military relations that are not subject to paralysis by WMD. However, there has been a very important shift toward the study of civil wars and collective state attempts to use force or threats to influence those civil wars for ostensibly humanitarian purposes.

The Fuzzy Boundary Between
Military Security and World Politics

At first glance, the ideas of strategy, force, and threats seem to provide a clear basis for those in the strategic studies tradition for distinguishing military security from world politics (though less so for the peace studies or conflict research traditions, which have rather different starting points). World politics covers a broad spectrum that includes political, economic, social, legal, and cultural interactions, as well as military ones. One can thus see military security in the same light as international law, simply as a subfield specializing in one aspect of a larger whole. Unfortunately, this enticingly simple view does not stand up to a searching examination. The problem is that many crucial elements of strategy are hard to understand if they are disentangled from the political and economic parts of the international system. One might think, for example, that the subject of war belonged clearly to military security. It is true that states may threaten each other with war on the purely military grounds that each is a potential attacker of the other, but the threat and use of force usually bespeak grounds for rivalry rooted in considerations of power, status, ideology, and wealth. It is therefore difficult to study the causes of and cures for war without ranging deeply into the broader subject matter of international relations. Similarly, the currently most common form of war, civil war, also needs to be understood in terms of these broader considerations. Those in peace studies would also resist vigorously a definition that allocated war exclusively to strategic studies (Groom 1988; Booth and Herring 1994: 120–132).

Other well-established subjects such as alliance, "arms racing," coalition, and crisis management also straddle any attempt to draw a crude boundary between military security and world politics on the basis of strategy and the use of force. In one sense all four subjects seem to be part of military security. Alliances, "arms races," and coalitions are central mechanisms in military relations, and crisis is often a critical stage in the process by which actors move toward, or away from, the use of force. But all four just as clearly belong in the domain of political relations between actors, and therefore to world politics. Alliances and coalitions reflect common or at least compatible political interests, and "arms races" and crises are forms of political process that should be seen as reflecting political interests as much as, or more than, military ones. The difficulty of deciding what falls into one field and what into the other is even more problematic at the level of day-to-day events and policies, where their entanglement is thickest. Who can say where the line between military security and world politics runs in relation to diverse events like the Iran–Iraq War, the impact of French nuclear testing in the South Pacific, or sales of landmines?

Technology in Military and Political Context

The concept of technology has had a wide range of meanings. In the seventeenth century, it was used with reference to grammar, and its connotations were and are of use and control (Bush 1977: 12; Spufford and Uglow 1996). Critical theorists, interpretivists, poststructuralists, and postmodernists use it in terms of the use and control involved in their collapsing the distinction between words and actions. They come up with phrases like "technologies of the self" (Martin, Gutman, and Hutton 1988) or "the eight technologies of otherness" (Golding 1997), the latter being curiosity, noise, cruelty, appetite, skin, nomadism, contamination, and dwelling. Technology is often seen in the study of military security as just hardware. However, it is helpful to see technology as more than hardware, and the same can be said of military technology, which is hardware intended for organized political violence combined with the wide range of skills needed to create, adapt, reproduce, operate, and maintain it (cf. Krause 1992). The distinction between military and civil technology is becoming harder to maintain.

Technology is a major factor in determining the scope of military options; the character of military force, threats, and symbols; and the shape of world politics. The nature of technology sets a basic condition of strategy, and one that has been subject to frequent change ever since the industrial revolution. Strategy is going down yet another path of change as information age technology emerges. Changes in military technology should be understood not only in themselves but also in terms of their impact on prevailing strategic theories and policies. This book seeks to offer such a perspective. In addition, while there is much highly specialized literature on military technology, there is much less literature that places military technology within the broader context of military security and, beyond that, world politics. The specialized literature on technology as it relates to military security mostly reflects an intense, short-term policy orientation that is closely tied to the agenda of government decisionmaking on military procurement issues. Such a literature dates quickly. Although it does have underlying continuities, these are often buried under the details of an ever shifting technological and political context. The mass of detail is a barrier to those seeking entry to the subject. It confronts them with an unassembled jigsaw puzzle of parts with little guide as to how they fit together. A random sampling of parts can mislead more than it informs. Most of the literature on technology as it affects military security does not clearly reveal the essentials of the subject, and therefore does not serve the needs of the many nonexperts who rightly feel that they want to understand what is going on. Even for experts, excessive surrender to the specializing demands of the subject does not, in the long run, serve the goal of better understanding.

The Structure of the Book: Tracing, Explaining, Using, and Controlling the Arms Dynamic

Part 1 traces what we call the *arms dynamic*—that is, the entire set of pressures that make actors (usually states) both acquire armed forces and change the quantity and quality of the armed forces they possess. The discussion is built around two themes: (1) the revolutions in technology that have accompanied the industrial age (and now the information age) and (2) the processes by which the military and political impact of those revolutions have spread, and are still spreading, around the planet. The arms trade and proliferation of WMD receive particular attention as part of that spread. In addition, the close relationship between civil and military technology and the implications of this for military security are analyzed.

The argument underlying Part 1 is that the technological aspect of the global strategic environment is partway through a centuries-long process of transformation. The twin elements of that transformation are technological innovation and the diffusion of advanced technology. Before the process took off during the nineteenth century the standard of military technology in most parts of the globe was similar and the pace of change was slow. The industrial revolution accelerated the pace of technological innovation and created marked disparities in the quality and quantity of military technology held by different countries. The latest information age technology has added a new dimension to the arms dynamic. The two elements of innovation and diffusion interact powerfully. The play between them and the particular stage of development they have reached are major factors affecting military security and world politics.

Actors in world politics face a central security worry not only about the quantity and quality of military technology in the hands of potential and actual opponents, but also about the pace and direction of change in these variables. This concern leads directly to Part 2 on explaining the arms dynamic, and Part 3 on using the products of the arms dynamic. The arms dynamic is perhaps the most important phenomenon arising in world politics as a direct consequence of the application of technology to military security, and the main attempts to explain it are examined at length. The phenomenon of arms racing is mostly not well understood. The use of the term is often undisciplined and polemical, and the literature remains disjointed and incomplete. We set the concept clearly into the context of an overarching arms dynamic and fill in some of the gaps in the literature. In this way we construct the foundations for the discussion in Parts 3 and 4.

Part 3 examines the main uses to which the products of the arms dynamic have been put. In strategic studies and peace studies, these uses are usually taken to be force and threats of force. We have separate chapters for each of these. The chapter on the use of force explores the reasons for the relative infrequency of the use of force between states and the relative frequency of the use of force within them in civil war and domestic repression. The chapter on the use of threats focuses primarily, but by no means solely, on conventional and nuclear deterrence. On the nuclear issue, the question of whether nuclear deterrence of nuclear attack is easy or difficult is used to provide a means of organizing what is an inordinately complex literature. Part 3 makes something of a break from the vast bulk of the literature on the uses of military means by including a chapter on their uses as symbols.

Part 4 examines the main concepts that have arisen in response to military technology seen not primarily as a problem in the hands of others, as in Parts 2 and 3, but more as a creator of security problems in itself. The view that military means create problems in themselves stems from the increasing destructiveness of war that has accompanied the innovation in and diffusion of modern military technology. The fear of war means that the arms dynamic and the uses of military means take on a paradoxical role. They are solutions if the problem is military means in the hands of others, but causes of insecurity if the problem is military means in themselves. The old concept of disarmament and the newer ones of arms control and nonoffensive defense (NOD) are all tested against the full measure of the problem they seek to redress. Each is examined in terms of its political, economic, and military implications.

Part 5 considers whether and in what ways regulatory approaches (that is, arms control, NOD, and disarmament) can be combined to deal with the problems caused by military means. We also consider the relative merits of regulation versus laissez-faire approaches to military security and point out that laissez-faire approaches have predominated.

PART 1

TRACING
THE ARMS DYNAMIC

2

REVOLUTIONS IN MILITARY TECHNOLOGY

Technology defines much of the contemporary agenda of military security and generates much of the language in which security is discussed. Many of the acronyms and abbreviations for which strategic discourse is notorious—PGM, ASAT, ASW, CBW, ECM, and many more—are directly descriptive of military technology. Technology is most usefully seen in broad terms. As Andrew L. Ross (1993: 110–111) argues: "Military technology, like technology generally, encompasses both hardware and software. It includes not only the actual instruments or artefacts of warfare, but the means by which they are designed, developed, tested, produced, and supplied—as well as the organizational capabilities by which hardware is absorbed and employed." That military technology should not be equated with military hardware can be illustrated simply: without software, a modern aircraft is just pieces of metal and other components rather than a usable weapon system. The element of skilled human beings (sometimes called "wetware") is also required. The trend is for the software element of military technology to be increasingly important in order to make weapons smarter. Just as we have moved from manual typewriters to computers, so we have moved from primarily mechanical tank guns to increasingly electronic ones that would be useless without their on-board acquisition, tracking, aiming, and firing computers. This trend is part of a broader process of adding information age technology to the weapons characteristic of older industrial age technology. It indicates a general period of transition that can be captured in several different perspectives. Some distinguish between Fordism (after Henry Ford, the inventor of assembly line production) and post-Fordism, industrialism, and postindustrialism, and modernity and postmodernity (Toffler and Toffler 1993; Amin 1995; Bell 1974; Rose 1991; Sarup 1993). These perspectives all argue that great social and technological upheaval is under way.

This chapter looks first at the idea of revolutionary change in military technology. It then examines the nature, foundations, and consequences of

9

the industrial revolution in military technology that has been going on since the middle of the nineteenth century, and that shows little sign of ending. It concludes with an examination of the idea that this ongoing revolution is itself now undergoing a qualitative shift into a third wave of information-based technology.

The Idea of Revolutionary Change in Military Technology

The idea of "revolutionary change" in military technology lacks agreed defining criteria. For Robert Jervis (1989: 15), nuclear weapons in large numbers combined with long-range aircraft and missile delivery systems were revolutionary due to their implications for statecraft: they produced "a change that turns established truths about the relationships between force and statecraft on their heads." Specifically, before the advent of high-performance, long-range air power, a society could not be destroyed without first being defeated militarily. This fundamental strategic equation does not apply if the opponent is armed with a large enough nuclear delivery capability. Furthermore, in the nuclear context, Jervis argues, a conflict of interest cannot be total, because both sides have a shared interest in avoiding mutually disastrous all-out war. In the conventional context, total war could be won as well as lost. Nevertheless, in a nuclear war, both sides would have strong incentives for restraint, and so there could still be a winner and a loser.

From another perspective, military technology may be revolutionary in terms of a vast leap in technical performance, such as firepower, protection, mobility, and communications: these performance criteria are discussed in this chapter, while their implications for military security are considered in Parts 2 and 3. Nuclear weapons, many argue, can be seen as revolutionary both in terms of firepower performance and strategic implications. Before the industrial age, military technology changed slowly and revolutionary changes were rare (but not absent). Important aspects of modern warfare emerged in Europe as early as the sixteenth century (Eltis 1995; Ayton and Price 1995), but the nature and dating of military revolution in Europe is irresolvably disputed (Rogers 1995). What we would argue is that the industrial age, which was well under way by the late eighteenth century, resulted in a revolution of frequent change in military technology. This process of frequent change greatly increased the salience of technological issues for military security. There is also a broader sense of military technological revolution: "A revolution in military affairs occurs when new technologies (internal combustion engines) are incorporated into a militarily significant number of systems (tanks, troop carriers, aircraft) which are then combined with innovative operational concepts (Blitzkrieg [lightning war] tactics) and new organisational adaptations

(Panzer divisions) to produce quantum improvements in military effectiveness" (*Strategic Survey 1995–96* 1996: 30; Toffler and Toffler 1993: 31). In the following discussion, it is worth keeping in mind all of these conceptions of what is revolutionary: all three are summarized in Figure 2.1. All in all, there is no right way to distinguish between significant change and revolution, and one should not get hung up on the labels (Gray 1997). What matters more is the task of identifying change and its implications.

From Occasional to Frequent Change in Military Technology

Technological change has been an important factor in war and strategy throughout prehistory and recorded history (Keeley 1996; Brodie 1973; Howard 1976b; McNeill 1982; Pearton 1982; Skolnikoff 1993; Smith 1985; van Creveld 1989). A host of classical cases illustrate the strategic significance of changes in military technology. The ancient Egyptians, who used weapons made of bronze, were defeated by enemies equipped with harder iron swords. The ancient Greeks were able to defeat larger numbers of Persians, partly because the Greeks' generalized use of body armor for troops allowed them to develop close-formation fighting tactics: success required all three elements of hardware, software (in terms of doctrine and organization), and skilled human "wetware." The development of the stirrup around the sixth century A.D. enormously increased the power of mounted warriors. The development of the longbow, the crossbow, and the pike ended the supremacy of the mounted and armored knight in medieval Europe. During the fourteenth century, the coming of primitive cannon made the existing construction of high, thin-walled fortifications highly vulnerable. By the late 1850s, developments in shipbuilding, steam engines, and gun design were making it suicidal to go to war in the wooden sailing ships that had formed the backbone of naval power for the previous three centuries.

Figure 2.1   Technological Revolutions

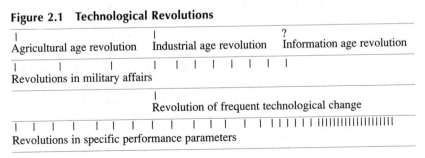

Note: | indicates a revolutionary change.
? indicates a tentative classification.

The historical record demonstrates clearly the long-standing importance of technology to military strategy. But the significance of modern military technology is defined more by recent changes than by any long-standing patterns of continuity. The historical norm has reflected a pace of technological innovation so slow that the continuity of weapons systems has been more conspicuous than their transformation: revolutionary changes in military technology did occur, as indicated above, but these were the exception rather than the rule. The military technology of the Roman legions changed little in the six centuries between the conquest of Greece and the fall of Rome. The galleys used by the Ottomans and the Christians during their Mediterranean wars as late as the sixteenth century were quite similar to those used by the Greeks against Xerxes in 480 B.C. The ships of the line (that is, the large ships in the front line of battle) that fought at Trafalgar in 1805, and even as late as the Crimean War (1853–1856), were easily recognizable as the same class of ship pioneered by Henry VIII in the first half of the sixteenth century. In other words, revolutionary changes like the shift from oars to sail at sea in the sixteenth century and the development of giant siege cannon in the late fourteenth century were infrequent before the nineteenth century. Evolutionary changes, like the 300-year development of the modern repeating rifle out of the sixteenth-century harquebus, proceeded so slowly that they seldom created upheavals in the conditions of strategy (cf. Perrin 1979). Napoleon's astonishing victories at the end of the eighteenth century were based almost wholly on innovative use of existing types of weapons, and scarcely at all on innovations in the weapons themselves.

By the middle of the nineteenth century, a fundamental transformation in military technology was under way. The industrial revolution, with its ever expanding use of energy and machinery in the process of production, had by this time developed such momentum that major changes in technology began to occur frequently. From around the middle of the nineteenth century, a new norm of frequent change asserted itself. That norm still prevails. It shows little sign of weakening, though it is beginning to assume a new form. The mid-nineteenth century is therefore a major historical boundary in the relationship between technology and strategy. On both sides of it technology is important. On the older side the main theme is continuity measured in centuries, and the minor theme is change. On the more recent side, a high degree of change in terms of capability and cost between earlier versions of weapon systems (like the bombers of the 1920s) and later ones (like the B-2 "Stealth") is dominant. Nevertheless, there are recognizable continuities in, for example, ballistic missiles, strategic bombers, tanks, jet fighters, aircraft carriers, and so on.

Although the possibility of a future in which there is a return to occasional rather than frequent technological innovation cannot be ruled out, the trend in the opposite direction appears durable. The revolution in technology was quantitative in two senses: first, the number and frequency of changes were large, and second, the ability to produce huge numbers of new items increased dramatically. It was qualitative in the sense that each new innovation either improved an old capability substantially, like the machine gun, or opened up a capability never before possessed, like the submarine, the airplane, and the reconnaissance satellite. Given the rapid pace of change, these qualitative improvements quickly added up to an enormous expansion of technological capabilities for both military and civil purposes. Changes occurred on a broad front and affected every aspect of society. They were both manifestations and movers of profound changes in human knowledge and social organization. The changes were not solely, or even mainly, motivated by the desire to improve military instruments, but such improvement was one of their major effects. Indeed, it sometimes produced such dysfunctional, "baroque" innovations as swing-wing jet fighters, which displayed technical changes that were innovations but that degraded the fighters' military utility (Kaldor 1982).

The principal effects of this technological revolution in terms of military performance parameters can be organized into five categories: firepower, protection, mobility, communications, and intelligence.

Firepower

The technological revolution made an early and dramatic impact on firepower, which has remained perhaps its principal effect down to the present day, especially in the form of nuclear weapons. Earlier innovations often made only marginal differences in capability: there was not all that much to choose from, for example, between the firepower performance of a medieval crossbow or longbow and that of a seventeenth-century smoothbore musket (cf. Perrin 1979). Firepower began to increase in the 1840s, with the widespread replacement of muzzle-loading muskets by much faster firing breech-loading rifles. The arrival of qualitatively superior weapons meant that firepower could be increased more effectively by improving weapons than by the traditional method of increasing the number of soldiers in the field. Ten soldiers each able to fire thirty rounds per minute were, in terms of their weight of fire, three times more powerful than twenty soldiers each able to fire five rounds per minute. Higher rates of fire, together with improved accuracy, steadily multiplied the killing power of the individual soldier.

Advancing knowledge in chemistry, metallurgy, and engineering thenceforth opened the floodgates to enormous increases in firepower. Higher rates of fire were accompanied by longer ranges, greater accuracy, better reliability, and more powerful destructive effects on the target. Machine guns first appeared in combat use in the U.S. Civil War, and by 1883 were capable of firing up to 650 rounds per minute. The contrast between that number and the three or four shots per minute of which the most skilled musketeer was capable indicates the magnitude and pace of change at this time. Artillery also improved apace. Better steel allowed bigger and more powerful cannon. Better engineering allowed breech loading, which in turn allowed rifled barrels. Such artillery had longer range, faster rates of fire, and better accuracy than the old smoothbore muzzle loaders. The new guns quickly grew to many times the size of even the largest naval guns of the preindustrial era. Heavy naval cannon during the Napoleonic Wars fired solid shot weighing 32 pounds, but during the mid-nineteenth century explosive shells replaced solid shot, and by 1914 there were guns capable of firing shells more than 1 ton in weight. The battlefield consequences of increasing firepower were suggested by the 600,000 dead of the U.S. Civil War. This lesson did not register on either elite or public awareness in the main world power center of Europe until the awful carnage of World War I.

The increase in firepower has continued down to the present, though some technologies have peaked, either because further expansion of capability is hard to achieve or because it has no compelling use. Rates of fire have nearly reached their mechanical limits, and any further increases are less of a priority than greater reliability and accuracy. Nuclear weapons can be made with an explosive potential far larger than is called for by any military mission: there are few targets, other than exceptionally deep underground bunkers (Ball and Toth 1990), that cannot be destroyed more efficiently by several 1-megaton warheads than by a single 60-megaton device. Indeed, as one writer has argued: "For thousands of years before [1945], firepower had been so scarce a resource that the supreme test of generalship lay in conserving it for application at the crucial time and place. Suddenly, it promised to become so abundant that it would be madness ever to release more than the tiniest fraction of the total quantity available" (Brown 1977: 153). The point about the tiniest fraction is not merely rhetorical.

Raw firepower has also been enhanced by increases in the range and accuracy of delivery systems. Heavy bombers and intercontinental missiles have achieved the maximum strike range that can be of use on this planet, and accuracy is perhaps the most dynamic remaining area of innovation in firepower. Against static targets precision-guided munitions (PGMs), such as cruise missiles and laser-guided bombs, are steadily approaching the goal of "single shot equals kill," even at long ranges. As PGMs do so, they reduce the need for both volume of fire and weight of destructive capability delivered to the target. If targets are mobile, accuracy is more problematic, especially against very fast moving ones such as ballistic missiles, where currently affordable ballistic missile defense (BMD) technologies are still almost totally ineffective.

This surplus capacity of destructive power is a unique historical condition that has shaped much of contemporary strategic thinking. However, its implications are limited by a number of important factors. First, very few states—Russia, the United States, Britain, France, and increasingly China—possess this vast surplus of nuclear firepower. Most are still in the business of increasing their (usually nonnuclear) firepower. Second, because of the political implications of causing casualties through the use of excessive firepower, or because of fear of escalation, or because using more firepower would not help achieve their objectives, states often use only a fraction of the firepower at their disposal. Third, the greater accuracy arising from information age military technology involves a higher priority being given to finding ways of using very limited, focused firepower rather than finding ways of using more firepower. The latest trend is toward exploration of the value of minimal firepower with low-lethality weapons (LLWs).

Protection

The revolution in firepower was for a time accompanied by a revolution in the capability of self-protection. The knowledge of higher quality steels that made possible improvements in cannon also made possible improvements in armor plate. In the early phases of the technological revolution armor occasionally outperformed firepower: the most famous instance was the stalemate between the warships *Monitor* and *Merrimac* during the U.S. Civil War. However, although armor still provides useful protection in an absolute sense, the victory of firepower has been complete. Nothing can be armored so effectively that it cannot be destroyed, a fact that underlay the unease of the early 1980s about the vulnerability of ICBMs based in fixed silos (heavily reinforced holes in the ground). Self-protection is now best pursued by concealment. This can be achieved by disrupting the opponent's means of detection with electronic countermeasures (ECM), or rendering the means ineffective by the adoption of stealth technologies, or by locating one's targets in ways that make detection difficult, such as by making them mobile or putting them into submarines. A kind of armoring can also be achieved by dispersing military capabilities throughout the civil population, though the effectiveness of such measures depends on the attacker's sensitivity to either inflicting civilian casualties or alienating those in other societies observing the conflict through the news media.

Ironically, the revolution in firepower has progressed so far that it is beginning to provide one of the most effective countermeasures against itself. Small, fast, accurate, powerful missiles have become the scourge of larger weapon platforms like tanks, aircraft, and surface warships. The most sophisticated of these PGMs can even be used (not yet very effectively) against other missiles in antimissile mode, as can (more effectively) modern multibarreled machine guns firing 6,000 rounds per minute. Enthusiasm for BMD that would stop hitherto unstoppable weapons has waxed and waned. President Reagan's Strategic Defense Initiative (SDI) has been superseded by a shift in emphasis toward theater missile defense (TMD), while research into defense against long-range ballistic missiles continues. The Clinton administration allocated $2 billion to TMD for the 1996 fiscal year but only $.5 billion for national missile defense (NMD), although the administration is under pressure from Congress to emphasize NMD (*Military Balance 1996–97* 1996: 18–19). Less than 10 percent of U.S. missile defense spending goes toward dealing with cruise missile attack as opposed to ballistic missile attack (*Strategic Survey, 1996–97* 1997: 16, 27–31), but this may change as concern over cruise missile proliferation intensifies in the United States, its allies, and other states wealthy enough to consider building or buying defense systems. As it is, NATO and Russia have already begun preliminary talks on cooperating on missile defense. Although normally presented as contributions to defense, such protective measures may actually serve offensive as well as defensive purposes. Anyway, until such technologies are effective, which may be a long time, if ever, direct protection will have to rely on concealment (the race between stealth and detection technologies). The only other alternative is reducing the probability of being attacked, which might be pursued either by deterrence or by the development of more general normative constraints on the use of force that make deterrence unnecessary (i.e., more stable political relations).

Mobility

A revolution in mobility also began in the middle of the nineteenth century. At sea, this took the form of a rapid replacement of wooden, sail-powered ships by iron, steam-powered ones. In 1850 the old ships of the line were still completely dominant, but by the early 1870s an extraordinary period of innovation had produced the first all-steam-powered modern battleship, HMS *Devastation*. Iron ships could be built much larger than wooden ones, and by the time of World War I battleships weighed more than six times as much as the largest wooden warships ever built. Given frequent improvements in firepower and armor, each new model of these ships was more powerful than its immediate predecessor. Perhaps the most famous development took place in 1906, with the launching of the all-big-gun battleship HMS *Dreadnought*. This ship contained many technological innovations, including steam turbine engines and telephones, and was based on the design innovation of carrying ten identical heavy guns. Previous types of battleship had carried four heavy guns and a mixture of medium guns. A dreadnought-type battleship had such an advantage in the weight of its long-range firepower that it was reckoned to be equal to at least three of the older types.

On land, the revolution in strategic mobility started with railways, which spread rapidly throughout the latter half of the nineteenth century.

As first demonstrated in the U.S. Civil War, railways enabled enormous numbers of troops to be moved and supplied with hitherto undreamed of speed. Like firepower, the technology of mobility multiplied the effectiveness of military forces possessing it in relation to those without it. Not only could they mobilize faster than opponents, they could be shifted en masse from one scene of battle to another. The effect of railways on the speed with which armies could be deployed and supplied was so crucial that railway capabilities became the centerpiece of war planning in Europe before World War I (Pearton 1982: 64–76, 117–139). The whole German plan was based on using superior mobilization speeds to crush France in the few weeks available before the slow-moving Russians could bring their forces into play. The era was characterized by deeply held beliefs in the superiority of offensive over defensive strategies and in the value of war as a means of testing a society's vigor and worthiness (Howard 1983: 9; Snyder 1984; Van Evera 1984). War was likely in such circumstances even without the effect of railways on mobilization rates (Rosen 1982), but this technological condition helped to further destabilize an already unstable strategic environment.

With the manufacture of reliable internal combustion engines at the end of the nineteenth century, the revolution in mobility broadened in scope. Road and cross-country vehicles added greatly to the flexibility of the mass transportation already created by railways. Developments of such vehicles soon began to give armies not only the independence of movement typical of today's motorized divisions, but also highly mobile firepower in the form of tanks. The internal combustion engine also made possible powered flying machines and efficient submarines. These technologies enabled military activity to move on a large scale into two dimensions that could previously be reached only by the use of hazardous and unreliable devices. Submarines quickly developed into a major new element of naval power—and given the increasing vulnerability of surface ships to PGMs, submarines may one day be the only reliable constituent of naval power in many circumstances.

Aircraft started out in reconnaissance during World War I but they quickly graduated to ground attack and aerial combat, where they easily outperformed the lumbering and vulnerable zeppelins. Major strides in aircraft technology between the world wars transformed the air arm into a much more potent weapon of war. Aircraft made naval vessels of all kinds easier to detect and destroy and resulted in the replacement of the battleship by the aircraft carrier as the key to naval power and sea control. Air power enabled states to inflict massive damage on each other at long ranges without first defeating each other's armies. Aircraft further multiplied the mobility of troops and the combination of land mobility and air power made possible the blitzkrieg tactics employed so effectively by the German armed forces during the early years of World War II. Increases in speed, altitude, endurance, and carrying capacity have in recent years been less sought after than improvements in terms of efficiency, agility, versatility, weapon systems, and electronics. Aircraft remain the most effective way of performing many missions, but missiles have usurped some of their functions and pose a threat to their ability to survive in combat (Welch 1989; Harvey 1992).

In the past few decades, the revolution in mobility has begun to move into what may be the last and biggest dimension available: space. So far, the presence of human beings in space has been on a small scale and in very temporary conditions. But a permanent presence in the form of orbiting space stations is not far off, and, as many a science fiction writer has suggested, the potential for expansion of the technological revolution in space is unlimited (Langford 1979). To date, however, space has been of relevance mainly to the revolutions in communications and intelligence.

Communications

The revolution in communications began in the mid-nineteenth century with the invention of the telegraph. Like the railways, the telegraph spread rapidly, adding instant long-distance communication to the revolution in mobility. The development of radio communications ("wireless telegraphy") at the end of the nineteenth century added flexibility to the rigid telegraph system. With radio, mobile units on land and ships at sea could be kept in constant touch with central control. This revolution has traveled into space with satellites, which enable huge increases in the range and flow of communications to be achieved easily. Its effect has been to enhance central command and control of military forces on a scale unimaginable even in the early nineteenth century, when the speed of a horse or a clipper ship measured the number of days or weeks it would take to transmit a complex message between two distant points. Centralized communications of course create new targets, and become new vulnerabilities for those dependent on them.

Intelligence

The revolution in intelligence is closely linked to improved communications. The same links that enabled the center to exercise command and control over widely scattered forces also served to feed information about local conditions into the central command. Without such information, command authorities would not have an adequate basis on which to make decisions about strategy. In addition, the electronics technology that spawned radio communication also gave rise to detection devices like radio location, radar and sonar, and later to information-processing computers of enormous power. The Battle of Britain was an early example in which the use of radar as a force multiplier helped the numerically smaller British air force to defeat the larger German one. Superior knowledge of the location of enemy forces enables smaller numbers to concentrate against individual sections of a larger opposing force, and so defeat it piecemeal. Detection devices not only increase the flow of information into the command and decisionmaking process, but also play a large role in the improvement of accuracy that has been a major part of the firepower revolution over the past decades.

The revolution in intelligence technology is now dominated by space-based systems and by computers. The former allow the countries possessing them to observe each other in astonishing detail (Jasani and Barnaby 1984), while the latter make it possible to handle the vast amount of incoming data that result. Computers have become so important now that the abbreviation C3I (command, control, communications, and intelligence) has been changed to C4I (command, control, communications, computers, and intelligence). Appropriately equipped states can monitor others constantly right across the radio and light spectra and can detect missile launches at the point of ignition; satellite cameras have become so powerful that they can take pictures of the earth's surface in which human faces are recognizable (Tsipis 1985: 245). Satellites and other intelligence-gathering technologies (such as seabed listening arrays) have made surprise invasions by land or sea much more difficult, and can even give some (brief) warning of missile attack. The technologies' deployment and the huge resources put into them ensure that the major powers have built regular surveillance reports into their decisionmaking processes, and provide antagonists with reassurance about the activities of potential attackers. The transparency created by these technologies has also become an important part of confidence-building measures (CBMs) and arms control verification.

However, such capabilities do not guarantee against the sort of surprise attacks that Hitler was able to launch against the Soviet Union and Japan against the United States in 1941. Although information about the imminent German and Japanese attacks was available to the Soviet Union and United States, respectively, it was not taken seriously by the top decisionmakers. This could happen again. Intelligence is inherently ambiguous, and this allows decisionmakers to interpret the intelligence in ways that fit their preconceptions (in the case of unmotivated or cognitive bias) or that fit what they want to hear (in the case of motivated bias) (Jervis 1976; Lebow 1987b; Lebow and Stein 1994; Herring 1995). The multiplication of satellites controlled by more and more states and commercial organizations means that there will be more opportunity to challenge claims of what satellites show. (The United States used satellite information to "show" Saudi Arabia that Iraqi forces were massing for an invasion, even though the information could have been interpreted differently.) Satellites are important both for reassurance and arms control and for gathering information to fight wars (Der Derian 1992: 32–33). But there is no guarantee that more information will reduce hostilities: due to inherent ambiguity, even the most peacelike gesture can be interpreted as a trick to lull the opponent into a false sense of security. In a sense, more information does not get us closer to reality but simply creates more subjectively constructed material (Der Derian 1992: 27–28, 59).

Satellites have also created a revolution in navigation through the global positioning system (GPS), which enables ships, tanks, or individuals to determine their location to within a few meters using receivers costing only a few hundred dollars. GPS technology is even available to those who go hill walking for recreation. By using such precision, ballistic missile submarines can target their missiles with much greater accuracy than was previously possible. Only the deep oceans have resisted effective penetration by detection technology. Water absorbs electromagnetic radiation and plays innumerable tricks with the one energy that moves easily through it: sound.

The Civil Foundations of Revolutions in Military Technology

It is easy to think of revolutions in military technology as independent processes, somehow separable from human activity in nonmilitary spheres. That cast of mind is encouraged by the ill-disciplined use of terms like "arms race" to describe the process of frequent improvements in weaponry, and "militarism" to imply military interests dominating the rest of society. There is value in assuming that there is a definable military sector in society, but much can be gained from thinking in terms of the extensive and fundamental links that connect that sector to technology in the civil sector. Despite its distinctive elements, the revolution of frequent change in military technology needs to be seen not as a thing apart, but as an integrated element of a broader revolution in science, technology, and the human condition as a whole due to the emergence of the industrial age and now the arrival of information age technology.

There are a number of perspectives on what the driving force is behind the revolution of frequent change. Some see technological advance as an expression of human intelligence; some see it as a historical manifestation of Western civilization; some see it as a product of the competitive, materialist, and profit-oriented ethic of capitalism; and some see it as a result of the revolution in thinking unleashed by the discovery of the scientific method. Whatever the answer, the point is that the process of technological advance now has a momentum that is deeply rooted in human society. Just as this process cannot be implanted in less industrialized societies without transforming their indigenous cultures, so it cannot be stopped where it already exists without destroying much of the social structure that generated it and that now depends on its continuance. The revolution of frequent technological change has both challenged and reinforced the state system in a variety of dimensions, of which the military is one. Just as the growth of military power has seemed to undermine the state as a meaningful unit of defense (Herz 1957), so the expansion of a world industrial economy has outgrown the state as an economic unit, and the spread of ideas has eroded it as an autonomous political and cultural unit (Keohane and Nye [1977] 1989). At the same time as technology appears to transcend the state, it also bolsters the state by providing an immense increase in the size and variety of resources available to support the purposes of government. Highly organized societies are able to extract much more productive energy of all sorts from their populations than had hitherto been possible. This organizational factor contributed as much to the power of the state possessing it as did the hardware of the industrial age.

For the foreseeable future, we are locked into a process of frequent, and probably quite rapid, technological change. Since it took off during the nineteenth century, this process has had a profound impact on all aspects of society, including the military, and there is little reason to expect that this pattern will not continue. In all eras, civil and military technology are closely linked (Shapley 1978: 1102–1105; Väyrynen 1983a: 150–152; Toffler and Toffler 1993). The closeness of civil and military technologies during the nineteenth century is evident in terms of both the common body of knowledge underlying them and the numerous overlaps between civil and military applications of technology. During the nineteenth century, the knowledge of metallurgy, engineering technique, and design that generated the revolution in firepower was the same knowledge that produced ever more efficient steam engines for mining, shipping, railways, and industry in the civil sector. Similarly, the knowledge of chemistry that produced more effective explosives was intimately related to the knowledge that underlay the burgeoning industry in chemicals for civil applications ranging from fertilizers to pharmaceuticals. In these two cases, as well as many others, the knowledge and skills that produced the revolutions in military technology were almost indistinguishable from those that served the development of civil technology. The existence of a single body of knowledge underlying the revolution of frequent change as a whole is evident from any general study of the phenomenon. A number of studies (Landes 1969; Brodie 1973: especially chapters 5–9; Pearton 1982; Toffler and Toffler 1993) explore in detail the specific linkages between military technological developments and the overall advance of scientific and technological knowledge.

The essential wholeness of the industrial revolution is even more obvious in terms of overlapping applications of technology. The railways and the telegraphs that so transformed the conditions of warfare in the nineteenth century were technologies that would have been developed even if they had no military use. In several areas, developments in civil technology preceded, and laid the foundations for, later military applications. This is known as "spin-on" (as opposed to "spin-off," where civil applications are found for military technologies). Such a sequence was true of iron-built ships, where the civil sector was years in advance of the military. Vessels like Brunel's *Great Britain* (1845) led the way in integrating iron construction and steam propulsion, a combination that was not fully adopted by the Royal Navy until the late 1850s. The civil sector also led in the development of aircraft and motor vehicles. Only the pressure of World War I aroused military interest in these devices, both of which had been manufactured in the civil sector for more than a decade. The airplanes that had been successfully developed since the Wright brothers' triumph in 1903 and the motor vehicles that had been developed for commercial and private use were only adapted and developed seriously for military use after 1914.

Similarity of function between the military and civil sectors means that many civil technologies will always have military applications in mobility, communications, and intelligence. Transport aircraft, trucks, computers, and telecommunications equipment are clear examples. Many other elements of military technology are superficially quite distinct from the civil sector, especially those associated with firepower. Few civil applications can be found for machine guns, large cannon, small missiles, and nuclear warheads. Even here, however, the difference between the military and civil sectors is more one of degree than of kind. A civil economy capable of manufacturing advanced steam engines could build machine guns quite easily. One capable of making large passenger aircraft could also make bombers. One capable of exploring space will be able to make military missiles. And one capable of making nuclear power plants to generate electricity has nearly all the knowledge, material, and skill necessary to build nuclear explosives. Where military requirements demand high performance at the expense of economy, then branches of largely military development can evolve. This has been the case for high-performance jet engines and stealth aircraft and submarines. Military research and development priorities and funding may favor some technological developments (notably nuclear) over others, and accelerate some (e.g., computers, aircraft) that would have occurred anyway (Buzan and Sen 1990). But even the most distinctively military technologies are just variations on the main themes of whatever knowledge and skill is available to society as a whole.

On this basis, it can be argued that any civil industrial society contains a latent military potential (Schaerf and Carlton 1995). This potential lies in its stock of knowledge, equipment, material, technique, and capital. Depending on the character and extent of that stock, the society will have the capacity to turn itself almost immediately to some kinds of arms production, and with various measures of delay to others. Military potential cannot be removed from industrial society even if it is not actually expressed in the manufacture of weapons. Some civil equipment can be turned directly to military use, like transport aircraft and poisonous chemicals. Manufacturing facilities for a wide range of civil goods involving engineering, chemicals, aerospace, and electronics can quite quickly be converted to military production. As will be seen in Chapter 4, perhaps the clearest example of this latent potential in today's world is the civil nuclear power industry. Most of the concern about the proliferation of nuclear weapons over the past three decades has focused on the spread of civil nuclear technology. Long-standing efforts to separate the civil from the military applications of nuclear technology have had only limited success. The fundamental similarity is inescapable and leads to persistent worries that countries mastering civil technology give themselves an option to produce nuclear weapons within a short time of their decision to do so. Quite a few countries, notably India, Pakistan, Iran, North Korea, South Korea, and Taiwan, are pursuing civil nuclear technology with a military option in mind. This was also the case with South Africa under apartheid, and Argentina and Brazil under military governments. Japan uses its possession of advanced civil nuclear and space technologies to signal a capability to go militarily nuclear if necessary, even though it is clear that the country strongly prefers not to do so.

Technological options emerge from the general advance of human knowledge, and, because they are in many ways independent of specific military demand, they put constant pressure on the formulation of military strategy. The advent of steam propulsion, for example, made irrelevant much of the tactical and strategic wisdom accumulated during the age of sail. As the debate about an as yet nonexistent BMD option (whether tactical or strategic) illustrates, the pressure from technological options has now become so great that it shapes much of the strategic debate. That debate is moving into a new phase as it focuses on the implications of developments in information technology.

The Information Age: The Potentially Revolutionary Acceleration of the Industrial Age

There is a strand of thought that argues that the older industrial centers of the world (Western Europe and North America) and the newer industrial centers (particularly in East and Southeast Asia) are going through the upheavals that will take them into a postindustrial age based on information economies. This will, it is claimed, bring with it a shift from primarily industrial-based to primarily information-based military security and warfare (Toffler and Toffler 1993). This shift—which would be revolutionary— would in part be fueled by the revolution of frequent technological change that is not only a phenomenon of material objects but also one of social organization. Although we have adopted the agricultural-industrial-information taxonomy, it should be noted that the category "industrial" is difficult to see as beginning before the late eighteenth century and so comes considerably later than the sociopolitical developments in Europe (especially the modern state) that are generally accepted as dividing the modern from the premodern (ancient and classical) at around 1500 A.D.

The main purpose here is to consider the arguments that contrast the industrial age with the information one, but before we do that it is worth recalling briefly the agricultural age to remind ourselves that radical change in the social, economic, and political conditions of civilization are a recurrent, if infrequent, characteristic of the human condition (Mann 1986; Gellner 1988; Buzan and Segal 1998). The agricultural age (from about 8000 B.C. on) shifted the human condition from nomadic hunting-gathering to a more territorially fixed, and more numerous, human population. This revolution was the basis of the many great empires and city-states of classical history. During classical times, weapons and warfare reflected civil technologies and organization. Farming civilizations generated infantry armies equipped with weapons derived from agricultural implements (swords, spears). Nomadic herders (barbarians) became charioteers and light cavalry and specialized in archery. Sea traders like the Greeks and Carthaginians developed navies. What was striking about this prolonged period of human history was its strong resistance to technological innovation. Although some notable military advances did take place (in metallurgy, siege equipment, and shipbuilding), the rigid sociopolitical hierarchies of classical civilization generally resisted technological innovation. The whole mind-set of society was profoundly different between the hunter-gatherers of prehistory and the agrarian civilizations of classical antiquity. A similar gulf exists between classical antiquity and the industrial age, with the latter embracing technological and social change as much as the former resisted it. Just as it would have been difficult for someone in the agricultural age to foresee the nature of the industrial age, so it is impossible from the perspective of the late industrial age to see with clarity the contours of the information age.

Some of that change and some of the contrasts between industrial age and information age characteristics posited by Toffler and Toffler, among others, are summarized in Table 2.1.

We are a long way from being in an information age: what we are currently experiencing is an industrial age with information age elements. There is a lot of life in the industrial age yet, and the trends are contradictory and ambiguous. Multinational corporations (MNCs) are accounting for an ever increasing share of world production, and the largest MNCs have assets worth more than the gross national product (GNP) of many states. Ownership of the news media is also concentrating. Rupert Murdoch, through his News Corporation, has developed an enormous global media

Table 2.1   Contrasts Between Industrial Age and Information Age Technology

Industrial age characteristics	Information age characteristics
Types of society	
Mass—mass production, consumption, education, society, media, conscription, and destruction	Fragmentation—niche (i.e., small-scale, cheap, highly specialized, ultimately individualized) production, etc.
World politics dominated by a large number of similar units (states)	Nonstate actors increasingly powerful
Dominant technologies	
Hardware	Software
Stupid machines	Smart machines
Large machines	Tiny machines (e.g., nanomachines)
Oil, gasoline, diesel	Electricity
Standardization	Diversification
Quantification and concreteness	Quality and abstractness
Styles of perception	
Public perception of events as "real"	Public perception of blurring of real and fictional
Styles of organization	
Secrecy	Openness
Indiscriminate gathering of vast amounts of information	Specialized gathering of small amounts of information
Moderately skilled, interchangeable labor and military personnel	Highly skilled, highly specialized, hard-to-replace personnel
Humans in direct economic and military control	Automation and robot control
Top-down, centralized civilian and military command of organizations	Bottom-up, bottom-across organizations
Stockpiling	Just-in-time (i.e., for immediate use)
Styles of warfare	
Control of territory	Use of speed
Maximum lethality, high casualties, little weight attached to combatant/noncombatant distinction	Minimum/nonlethality, low casualties, strong combatant/noncombatant distinction
Humans in combat	Automated and robotic combat
Total war	Very limited niche war
Mechanized war	Electronic war
Brute force	Skill
Attrition	Precision
Hard kill (the physical destruction of targets)	Soft kill (prevention of people/objects from fulfilling their purpose without physically destroying them)
Gunpowder, high explosives, nuclear explosives	Electricity

empire worth $8.4 billion in 1995. To a great extent the media are provid-
ing a standard product for mass audiences and consumers—while much of
the world is still industrializing. However, the potential for fragmentation
is developing with the growth in the number of television channels available due to satellite and cable technology, and the number of highly specialized information sources is expanding exponentially through the Internet. The issue of realization and projection of trends is central to this kind
of discussion. Information age technology is resulting in the collection of
staggering amounts of information of dubious value: although it is possible that in an information age techniques will be developed so that the
amount of useful and used information increases in proportion to the
amount of the useless and unused, our impression is that the trend is not
yet going in that direction.

In many respects, an information age would represent the acceleration
(or, to put it differently, intensification) of the characteristics of the industrial age, as can be suggested by a range of examples drawn from Table
2.1:

- Emphasis on the value of time is very much part of the industrial
  age (e.g., "time is money," time-and-motion analysis), but the acceleration is much more part of information age technology.
- Electricity generation was and is a core element of industrialization, but information age technology emphasizes the importance of
  electricity over other sources of power, and with potentially enormous implications. For example, if vehicles ran on electricity rather
  than the internal-combustion engine, oil companies and oil-producing states would have to change radically or suffer the economic
  consequences.
- Miniaturization has been a standard industrial age objective,
  whether it be with radios, bombs, computers, or watches. Information age technology is showing signs of carrying that process to a
  qualitatively new level in terms of extraordinarily small machines—including nanotechnology constructed atom by atom, a
  process that already exists (Drexler 1990).
- The combatant/noncombatant legal distinction was contradicted by
  total war but was still developed in the industrial age: its possible
  implementation in an information age would in a sense be the realization of an industrial age ideal.

This lack of a sharp discontinuity between each era is not surprising.
The arrival of the industrial age did not obliterate the legacy of classical
civilization. Although agriculture has been largely industrialized, all of the
major world religions, and most of the great cultural and civilizational
identities that dominate our time stem from the classical era. The arrival of

the information age will likewise overlay what exists without destroying all of it. Industry will still be required, though almost certainly not all of the social and political structures that it generated during the nineteenth and twentieth centuries. Some industrial age ideas that seem likely to survive are the state, the market, nationalism, science, and the belief that all-out war between advanced societies is fundamentally irrational (Buzan 1995d). The transition to an information age will take decades or even centuries—and may not happen at all if we have misunderstood the dominant trends. In addition, the entire world is not entering the information age in the same way or at the same pace. Instead, a mix of levels of development will continue to exist and to evolve in an extraordinarily complex fashion. Even now, a few people can still be found living in essentially prehistoric conditions. Toffler and Toffler see it as a shift from a largely bisected world (agricultural and industrial) to a trisected world (agricultural, industrial, and information based). However, the trisection will not primarily be geographical, although there will be some geographical concentration of elements of the information age. In some parts of Latin America and South Asia, for example, that are still making the transition from the agricultural age into the industrial age, there are also nodes of the information age where people are fully integrated into the worldwide electronic information economy. Agricultural age military characteristics are very diverse and not easily codified in the simple way we might like. Somalia and Afghanistan, for example, have clearly agrarian age political and societal characteristics in terms of tribes (nomadic sheep, goat, and cattle herders and warriors organized into clans) but their weapons are of the industrial age. The Zapatista rebels in the Chiapas region of Mexico are from an agricultural background, but they have conducted a lively information age propaganda battle against the government via the Internet. In the former Yugoslavia there were some parallels to medieval warlordism, but the main features were industrial age—nationalism, conscription, and large-scale destruction.

For military security, what are the consequences of adding information age elements to the industrial age? The most obvious impact this process is already having is that new generations of weapon systems are emerging. Increasingly, remotely piloted vehicles (RPVs) or drones are being used for reconnaissance: these go back to the attempts in the 1950s by the United States to monitor the Chinese nuclear weapons program and have now evolved into $10 million stealth reconnaissance vehicles (Rich and James 1995). There are even plans for pilotless submarines and vessels called "arsenal ships"—crewless, stealthy, highly automated vessels with a wide-ranging armory of missiles. Research into automated weapons that decide, based on their programming, whether or not to open fire have been the cause of serious ethical and political concern. With regard to nuclear weapons, it was decided to keep human beings "in the loop" of decisionmaking even though this ran the risk of a decapitating attack on those human decisionmakers—which would destroy the ability to retaliate. Now the concern has shifted to what would be killer robots (De Landa 1991). Information age technologies are also having a big impact on conceptions of the tactics and strategies involved with using those weapon systems. For example, at present, a weapon platform such as a ship can only fire a missile at a target if its on-board detection systems have spotted it. With networking, a weapon platform will be able to have its missile guided to its target by the sensors of other platforms. Improved information (as opposed to increases in mobility for maneuver or increases in production for attrition) is at the heart of this kind of tactical and strategic change.

Whether the current revolutions in specific performance parameters will add up to an overall revolution in military affairs (RIMA) is a hotly contested point, with many vested interests at stake (Campden 1992; *Strategic Survey 1995–96* 1996: 29–40; Gray 1997). So far it has been variations on the industrial theme, but so much may end up changing that there may in the end be an information-based RIMA. As Stephen Biddle (1996) argues, the victory of the U.S.-led UN forces in Kuwait against Iraq was not solely based on the coalition's vastly superior performance capabilities in hardware and software, but on the synergy of that hardware and software with vastly superior skill (both in terms of individual and organizational performance). Maintaining skill levels is at least as important as keeping up with narrowly defined technological developments. The United States in particular is investing heavily in research into all aspects of information warfare (infowar). Information age weapons or strategies will not inevitably defeat industrial weapons or strategies—just as the primarily industrial United States was unable to defeat primarily agricultural Vietnam. Nor are states or nonstate actors that invest heavily in the information age necessarily more secure militarily: in particular, the software is potentially vulnerable to complete devastation by computer viruses. Instead, they will have a different mix of strengths and vulnerabilities. Furthermore, the emphasis by the Zapatistas on the use of the Internet is as much a sign of military weakness as tactical skill.

An awareness of this complexity is an important corrective to simplistic claims that we are now in the information age, postindustrial age, postmodern age, or whatever. Such claims are commonplace in characterizations of the U.S.-led war against Iraq in 1990–1991. If anything, we are entering a period of increasing complexity, with tangled interconnections at all levels. The world is trisected neatly only in tables and diagrams, not "out there." Information societies will not necessarily be more peaceful or ethically more desirable than industrial ones. Indeed, it may be that the information age war form will be added to others so that the overall level of violence and conflict is increased. Those discussions will come later: first we wish to trace in more depth the global development of the arms dynamic.

3

THE GLOBAL SPREAD OF MILITARY TECHNOLOGY

This chapter examines the relationship between the qualitative advance of technology and its spread, as well as the processes by which the spread of military capability has occurred. The theme from Chapter 2 of the close relationship between civil and military technology continues to be central, and it ties into the argument that the process of spread is uneven and incomplete. Particularly important is the point that although arms production capabilities have spread, the military products of the revolution of frequent change in military technology have been much more widely diffused by the arms trade than has the capability to produce them.

The Interaction Between Spread and Qualitative Advance

The unequal distribution of military capability was a normal feature of the international system before (as well as after) the beginning of the revolution of frequent change in military technology. That technological capabilities were a part of this unequal distribution is a fact illustrated by the European successes in empire building against more numerous but more primitively equipped peoples during the sixteenth, seventeenth, and eighteenth centuries, most notably in North and South America. In addition to technology, differences in population, resources, immunity to disease, political and economic organization, and geography also ensured that the military power of states was very unevenly distributed. Once the revolution of frequent technological change took hold, however, it greatly amplified the relative importance of technology in the distribution of military power and consequently enlarged the range of difference between states. In its early stages, this revolution meant that the few states in possession of its products gained an enormous advantage over the rest. As Hilaire Belloc wrote of the late-nineteenth-century colonial wars: "Whatever happens we have got / The Maxim gun, and they have not" (quoted in Sampson

1991: 50). Although this smacks of technological determinism, it still summarizes a valid point (Raudzens 1990).

As the influence and the products of the revolution of frequent technological change spread, the absolute distinction between "haves" and "have nots" became less important. The have nots might still be unable to produce modern weapons themselves, but the increasing trade in modern infantry weapons meant that there would be no major recurrence of situations in which the wielders of modern arms would face opponents armed only with bows, clubs, and spears. The diffusion of the technological revolution and its products thus tended to restore the weight of other factors such as population and wealth. Despite the leveling effect of the spread of modern military technology, a major element of qualitative distinction remains because the process of diffusion occurs in parallel with continued qualitative advance. The trade in arms works to redress the imbalance between haves and have nots, but qualitative advance continues to open up new distance between those states at the forefront of the ongoing revolution and the rest. For the small group of states able to ride the crest of technological innovation, a qualitative edge remains a critical ingredient of military strength.

The relationship between spread and qualitative advance is more complicated than the simple one of leaders and followers: each process actively promotes the other. The process of spread stimulates that of advance, because only by staying ahead in quality can some states maintain their power position and/or their military security. The leading powers in the system have to keep close to the front edge of technological advance unless they want to fall back into the second rank of power. Realization of this was a vital motivating factor in former Soviet leader Mikhail Gorbachev's program of perestroika and in the support he received from leading figures in the Soviet armed forces. Aspirants to first-rank power status must acquire the capability to compete at the leading edge of technological innovation. The twentieth-century rise of Japan and Russia (and then the Soviet Union) to first-rank status can be seen in these terms, as can the post-1945 consolidation of the Soviet Union's status as a military superpower under Stalin, Khrushchev, and Brezhnev. As can be seen in the relationship between India and Pakistan, and among the various rival states in the Middle East, the same logic applies to regional power struggles.

The leading edge of technological advance sets the standard for the international system and its continuous forward movement exerts pressure on the whole process of spread. As the leading edge creates ever higher standards of military capability, followers either have to upgrade the quality of their weapons or else decline in capability relative to those who do. States at the leading edge have political and economic reasons for pumping qualitative advances back into the pipeline through the mechanism of arms aid and sales. Competition between the states can become so intense that they may even find it difficult to reserve all of the latest innovations for their own armed forces. By diffusing the products of qualitative advance, the leading-edge states inexorably raise the standard of military power in the lower ranks. This process adds to the states' incentives to find further lines of technological advance with which to maintain their military advantage. The irony is a strong one: the U.S. government spent vast sums of money to develop the most advanced fighter aircraft such as the F-15E, allowed their sale abroad to states such as Saudi Arabia and Israel for political or economic reasons, and then asked the taxpayer for more, vast sums of money to maintain a technological lead by developing a new aircraft such as the F-16ES or F-16XL (Lumpe 1995: 12). The consequences of this process can be seen in the enormous effort that the world's leading military power (the United States) had to make to defeat a middle-rank regional power (Iraq) in 1990–1991. The days are long gone when the Spanish conquistador Pizarro was able to overthrow the Inca Empire with 164 men, sixty-two horses, and two cannon. Whether proposals for arms control, NOD, or disarmament offer ways out of the vicious circle that connects the spread of weapons and the process of technological advance will be discussed in Parts 4 and 5.

Where rivalries exist between states, the level of technology between them becomes a high priority (although, in itself, the level of technology is not enough to determine which rival wins or loses the competition). At the leading edge, rivals generally believe that they have to guard against their opponents' making some decisive technological breakthrough, and consequently see themselves as always being under pressure to maintain high levels of innovation. Much of the controversy about the SDI was based on the fear that unequal capability in strategic nuclear defense might create a major imbalance in military potency between the two superpowers, and would create perceptions that one superpower had lost status as an equal of the other. The Soviet fear of the SDI greatly exceeded any practical prospect that it could alter the strategic balance fundamentally, because if even 1 or 2 percent of Soviet warheads had reached their targets, the damage would have been truly immense. In other words, it was not the actual technology that had the political effect. Rather, it was exaggerated perceptions of its potential and more accurate perceptions of it as a potent symbol of U.S. willingness to engage in an accelerated and massively expensive high-technology arms competition that would deny the Soviet Union its hard-earned status as an equal. In the lower ranks the relative level of technology is no less important. The states on both sides of the Arab-Israeli and the Indian-Pakistani rivalries have been extremely sensitive to the quality of their opponent's weapons. Both Israel and Pakistan have consistently sought to offset their inferior size by acquiring superior weapons, and the same logic can be seen at work between Iran and Iraq and Taiwan and China.

In one sense, the qualitative pressure created by the arms trade is no different from the general upward qualitative pressure that trade creates in the civil sectors of technology. In a trading environment, any state that fails to keep pace with international standards will be unable to sell its goods abroad, and only able to sell them at home if it restricts imports of cheaper and/or better quality goods. The process is similar, and the consequences of technological weakness in either sector can be severe. Leaders of states have generally been more concerned with technological weakness in the military sector than in the civilian sector because military weakness can more obviously contribute to the overthrow or destruction of the state through war. However, Gorbachev's gamble to try to transform the Soviet economy was driven by concern for Soviet technological backwardness more in the civil than the military sector. He feared that the declining civil economy would soon no longer be able to support its oversized military cousin. As it turned out, the political forces unleashed by his actions brought about the collapse of the Soviet Union. Some states are located in "security communities," in which they do not expect, or prepare for, military attacks by or militarized disputes with the other states in the community, and in which they share common institutions (Deutsch et al. 1957). For those states, concern with civil technology may well begin to outweigh traditional concerns with staying at the military leading edge. Where states and societies expect peace, concern about economic capability can displace the military priorities that feed on fear of possible attack.

The arms trade helps to even out the military differences between states, but it does so only at the cost of setting a high and continually rising global standard of military technology. The standard is high because it is set by the quality of the leading edge, and it is upwardly mobile because it is driven along at the pace of qualitative advance in the top-rank military producers. Since the pace of advance is itself pushed in part by military rivalry among the top-rank powers, the technological consequences of their power rivalry are quite quickly imposed on the rest of the international system. States that can afford to buy modern weapons will do so either to match, or gain an edge on, their rivals. States that cannot afford modern weapons, but see their security needs as requiring them, may have to make political arrangements with a supplier state in which allegiance, bases, or economic assets are traded for arms aid. The relationship between Somalia and the Soviet Union during the 1970s can be seen in this light, as can the more long-standing one between the United States and Pakistan. Others will make do with the offerings on the secondhand market, keeping pace with the forward qualitative movement of the leading edge, but only at some distance behind it.

During the Cold War, this pumping effect of new military technology from the leading-edge states to the periphery worked particularly strongly. Rivalry between the superpowers both kept their own levels of military innovation high and encouraged them to distribute advanced weapons to their allies and clients in every region of the world. Now that the Cold War is over, and in the absence of any other great-power military rivalry to replace it, one might safely predict that this dynamic will operate at a lower level of intensity. Innovation at the center should be slower. Russia cannot afford to sustain the high military expenditures of its Soviet predecessor. The United States is committed to maintaining its military research-and-development (R&D) base, but at a slower pace, and with fewer systems brought into mass production. However, the advanced industrial states are still determined to maintain a qualitative edge over potential and lesser opponents to limit the casualties and destruction that decisionmakers fear may cause public opposition to the use of force, whether unilaterally or as part of multinational interventions in civil wars. Furthermore, as Patrick Morgan suggests, continuing qualitative advance creates incentives to export in order to recover R&D costs and pay for the new qualitative advances in the pipeline.

As far as the dynamics of diffusion are concerned, there has been a temporary "end-of-war" effect of the great powers' disposing of surplus weapons, but for the longer term the political reasons for extravagant supplies of arms to the periphery have largely dried up. Arms sales are becoming more commercial, which tends to raise the price and restrict the number of recipients. Another possible influence on this dynamic is the shift from industrial to information age military technologies. Many of the information age technologies (computers, software, sensors, communication systems) are just as strongly rooted in the civil as in the military sector. Such dual-use technologies blur the distinction between civil and military (Schaerf and Carlton 1995; Leitner 1995), and may signal a return to the conditions of the nineteenth century when civil developments defined much of the technological leading edge. If the hard products of the industrial age (weapons and delivery systems) are going to lose ground in the calculus of military power to the soft, dual-use, products of the information age, then the whole concept of the arms dynamic seems likely to become much more diffuse.

The Mechanisms Behind the Spread of Military Technology

Advanced military technology has spread throughout the international system in three ways: by the physical and political expansion of those states possessing it; by the transfer of weapons from those capable of manufacturing them to those not; and by the spread of manufacturing capability to ever more centers of control. In historical terms, these three mechanisms of diffusion have operated simultaneously, but not evenly. The mechanism of direct physical expansion was prominent during the colonial period, and has declined in importance since 1945. It is now relevant principally in the form of the overseas deployments and bases of a few great powers, and the end of the Cold War has brought about the closure and scaling down of many of these (*Conversion Survey*, annual). Conversely, the spread of independent centers of manufacture has been increasing in importance, especially in the period since decolonization (Brzoska and Ohlson 1986; Looney 1995; Sköns and Gill 1996). The mechanism of the arms trade has been steadier than either of the other two. It has been central to the diffusion of military technology throughout the period from the late nineteenth century to the present day, and it has been increasingly important as the number of states has increased.

The key to understanding the apparent permanence of the arms trade is the powerful constellation of vested interests that support it: "supply push" from producers, and "demand pull" from consumers. Supplier interests can be both political and economic. Possession of an arms industry serves the basic security value of self-reliance, and also supports the pursuit of power and influence. Traditionally, any state seeking to attain a leadership position in the international power hierarchy has needed its own arms industry. If there is a significant possibility of military conflict, one important aspect of great-power status is the independent ability to wage war: hence a substantial measure of domestic arms production is an essential requirement. Once attained, an arms industry can add to the tools of influence at a government's disposal. Arms supply is one of the classical ways in which great powers compete for the allegiance of lesser powers. States in control of their own arms industry can supply arms to others for political purposes like supporting allies, winning friends, opposing the influence of rivals, or helping recipients eliminate domestic opposition (Stanley and Pearton 1972: chapter 4; McKinlay and Mughan 1984; Pierre 1982: part 1; Chomsky 1994). Experience has shown that supplying another actor with arms is no guarantee of influence (Handel 1982; Nachmias 1988). Weapons supplied to Iraq by the United States to help it counterbalance fundamentalist Iran were redirected against Kuwait. The United States ended up waging a war to undo Iraq's actions. Some supplier states do not care much about the domestic consequences of arms in the recipient. This indifference is exemplified by arms supplies to Indonesia notwithstanding that country's brutal colonizations of West Papua and East Timor (Budiardjo 1991). Others actively seek to influence the outcomes of domestic conflict, as in the many instances of U.S. supplies to anti-Communist regimes (and Soviet supplies to anti-Western ones), often regardless of the openly authoritarian, repressive, and violent character of those regimes (Wolpin 1972; Klare 1977; Fitch 1979; Herman and Chomsky 1988; Klare and Arnson 1979; George 1991; Chomsky 1994).

Political motives for states to acquire arms production capabilities are entangled with economic ones. In a trading environment, the market has some impact on setting standards of both quality and price that determine whether the pursuit of self-reliance by any state is a viable or desirable policy. The economic motives for states to spend money on domestic arms production are to save the cost of importing weapons and to improve the balance of payments by exporting them (Brzoska and Ohlson 1986: 279–280). Once an arms industry exists, it generates vested interests in profits and jobs and in preserving high-technology capabilities, and these interests can lead to pressure to export in order to sustain the companies concerned. States are effectively subsidizing private profit through public taxation and engaging in military Keynesianism, that is, the spending of public money on arms to stimulate the economy (Melman 1985; Chomsky 1994: 100–113). In the Cold War, arms spending for economic motives was justified by reference to external military threats. Now state expenditure on technological innovation is increasingly being represented as a necessary part of industrial policy.

Another potent pressure to export is the fact that only states with large domestic requirements for arms have any hope of achieving economies of scale in their own production. Longer production runs lower the unit cost of the items produced. If the number of sophisticated items like tanks and aircraft required for domestic consumption is small, then home production will result in high unit costs unless exports can be found to lengthen the production run. Long production runs are especially necessary to amortize investment in advanced technology items where R&D accounts for a high proportion of total cost. Very few states have domestic requirements large enough to achieve economies of scale. Consequently, nearly all arms producers have strong incentives to export in order to achieve reasonable costs for that part of their production that they wish to buy for their own use. Second-rank powers like Britain and France are the most vulnerable to this squeeze because they are just big enough to be arms producers but have small requirements for arms. The need to export between one-third and almost half of their production is one reason why they have been aggressive in seeking export markets (Kolodziej 1987; Anthony 1992; Jones and Rees 1994; Bittleston 1990: 25; Cooper 1993–1994). Small arms and antipersonnel weapons such as landmines, grenades, and cluster bombs are easy to produce in economic quantities and so do not produce the same questions about economies of scale as do large weapons platforms. They can be sold simply for profit (Boutwell, Klare, and Reed 1994; Prokosch 1995) or they can be withheld from sale on political grounds, without much affecting the ability of a state to produce arms economically for itself. The need to guarantee economically attractive production runs for expensive modern weapon systems explains why the Western European arms producers are increasingly attempting multinational arms production projects like the Jaguar, the Tornado, and the Eurofighter aircraft (Bittleston 1990; Brzoska and Lock 1992). However, arms production in Western

Europe and around the world is still very much dominated by national production for national consumption or export. The United States had led the way, through a combination of government subsidy and market forces and in mergers and acquisitions in arms production, while West European arms production is very fragmented. Between 1991 and 1995, the United States also led the way in terms of value of major conventional weapons exported ($62 billion), followed by the Soviet Union/Russia ($16 billion), Germany ($10 billion), Britain ($7 billion), France ($6 billion), China ($5 billion), the Netherlands ($2 billion), Italy ($2 billion), Czechoslovakia/Czech Republic ($2 billion), and Israel ($1 billion) (Anthony, Wezeman, and Wezeman 1996).

Even the United States has not been, and the Soviet Union was not, immune from the need to achieve economies of scale despite their starting advantage of large domestic arms purchases. The process of qualitative advance means that the unit cost of sophisticated modern weapons is usually higher than the cost of the previous generation. This cost, which tends to outrun the general rate of inflation, and the fact that the newer weapons are more capable than the older ones they replace create pressure to acquire smaller numbers. This process is likely to accelerate now that the Cold War can no longer be used to justify large deployments. Shrinking domestic demand in terms of numbers of weapons in turn raises the incentives to lengthen production runs by finding export markets. The United States will increasingly find itself faced with difficult choices between maintaining its technological lead by keeping leading edge weapons to itself (e.g., stealth bombers, cruise missiles, BMD systems) or exporting them. Not exporting will mean bearing the extremely high unit costs of small production runs. Exporting them will mean loss of U.S. leverage (whether with potential foes or dependent allies).

The desire of producers to transfer arms is complemented by the assertion of the right to receive arms mounted by those countries unable to manufacture some or all of their own weapons. They might support the denial of the right to buy as a policy against a special case like South Africa (due to the apartheid system) or Yugoslavia (supposedly to prevent escalation and save lives) (Cigar 1995; Herring 1997b). However, the nonproducers have opposed as an assault on their sovereignty, dignity, independence, and equality any general attempt to restrict the supply of arms. The principle that nonproducers have the right to buy technologies they cannot make themselves is as strong a feature of the trade in conventional weapons as it is of the trade in civil nuclear technology. Without such a right, the nonproducer states argue, they would become second-class states, unable to match the military forces of producers and relegated to a politically unacceptable category of those judged incapable of being allowed to manage their own affairs. Protestations of this "right" often mask a reality of states' buying weapons to subjugate their own populations and/or spending extravagantly on weapons for status purposes. However, regardless of the motive, the key fact is that the arms trade is maintained by a combination of supply push and demand pull.

There is thus a potent shared interest between suppliers and recipients in maintaining the arms trade. Because that shared interest is backed by strong incentives on the part of suppliers to sell and strong motives on the part of recipients to maintain their access to the market, the arms trade will be difficult to challenge or reshape. Governments and arms manufacturers argue that ordinary citizens also share an interest in the arms trade in that jobs are supported by it and profits that can be taxed by the state to support social spending generated by it. These points are true, but ignore broader issues. First, the creation of jobs is an incidental issue for arms manufacturers: like other industries they are primarily interested in profits and will not hesitate to sacrifice jobs for profits if they can. Second, tax receipts from profits from the arms trade are not usually tallied against the subsidies to arms manufacturers provided by taxpayers.

The Historical Process of the Spread of Military Technology

During the nineteenth century, only a handful of states managed to acquire the capability for sustained industrial development that was the key to manufacturing modern weapons. Britain was the leader in the early stages, but Germany, France, the United States, and some smaller European countries quickly caught up. Russia and Japan constituted the tail end of this first wave of industrialization. Among the members of this group, trade and investment provided a major mechanism for the transfer of technology. Technological leaders were generally more than willing to sell their products, and investment from Europe underpinned the industrialization of the United States and Russia. The later entrants to the group were able to use this transfer of finance and technology to bring their own process of industrialization up to the point at which it became self-sustaining. All of these countries fairly quickly attained sufficient command of basic industry to develop and manufacture weapons up to the leading technological standard of the day. As they did so their dependence on arms purchases declined, and some of them entered the market as sellers.

The leaders of the first wave, particularly Britain and Germany, did good business selling such military products of industrialization as artillery, machine guns, and warships to countries unable to manufacture them. Late industrializers, such as Japan, purchased major weapon systems like battleships until they developed the capacity to manufacture their own. Many countries, like Brazil and the Ottoman Empire, were not at this time serious entrants in the industrialization process. Others, like Belgium and the Netherlands, were industrializing, but did not command the scale of industry or markets necessary to make domestic production of the whole range of modern arms an economic proposition. Both types of country were forced to depend on the arms trade in order to keep pace with progress in military technology. Under these conditions of unequally distributed capability to manufacture modern weapons, notorious arms sellers like Basil Zaharoff set the model for "the merchants of death" by selling modern weapons to both sides of rivalries between nonproducers: submarines to Greece and the Ottoman Empire and battleships to Argentina, Chile, and Brazil (Noel-Baker 1936; Sampson 1991: chapter 2).

The industrialized group contained most of the states that were already established as imperial powers—Britain, France, and Russia—and some—Germany, Belgium, Japan, and the United States—that became imperial powers during the last rounds of empire building. In their imperial roles, these powers spread elements of the revolution of frequent technological change all through the areas of the planet over which they exercised control, including most of Africa and large parts of Asia. They created local economies geared to their own resource needs. They built transportation networks of ports and railways both to serve those economies and to strengthen their military control. They deployed the military products of industrialization to seize and maintain occupation of vast colonial areas. In these areas, there was little in the way of transfer of technology comparable to that among the first wave of industrializing countries. Since the local peoples were not independent, neither was there any arms trade on a scale comparable to that between the industrialized powers and the independent countries in the Balkans, the Far East, and Latin America. Then, as now, political and economic motives ensured that arms almost always found their way to areas of high demand. Within their own empires, each colonial power as a rule made available only selected products of industrialization, and not the process of industrialization itself. Most of the industrial products that were transferred to colonial areas remained under the control of the colonizing powers, especially those associated with military capability.

The diffusion of military capability remained very much in this quite concentrated pattern until World War II, especially in terms of the capability for producing advanced weapons. Europe and the United States continued to be the focus of qualitative innovation in technology, and Japan and the Soviet Union caught up in terms of independent production capability. Technology was taken to the areas under colonial control, but seldom implanted there. Independent non–arms producers like the Latin American countries mostly made little progress toward industrialization, and so their rulers remained dependent on the arms trade.

After World War II, and in no small measure as a result of it, the spread of military capability picked up speed across the planet. This acceleration was closely linked to the vast process of decolonization and involved both political and technological factors. When Portugal surrendered the last of its empire in the mid-1970s the process of formal decolonization was virtually complete. In three decades, the number of states in the international system tripled as more than half of humankind moved from direct foreign rule to government by domestic elites, some of them elected.

The end of empires ruled directly by Western states increased the spread of military capability in two ways. First, it increased the level of political organization among the local populations, making them harder to dominate and easier to mobilize for armed resistance. Guerrilla warfare came to symbolize the potency of political mobilization as a weapon for peoples unable to match the weapons of their opponents. The spread of a will for independence among colonized peoples became a central element in the spread of military capability. Second, decolonization added enormously to the number of nonproducing countries whose rulers needed to get their military equipment via the arms trade. Instead of being denied modern arms, the new rulers were treated as legitimate customers. Their need arose not only from the domestic order requirements of self-rule, but also from the complex pattern of relations with neighbors that replaced the simpler and often more coherent patterns of colonial rule. Where India and Pakistan and the smaller states of South Asia now worry about each other, Britain formerly worried about maintaining its control over the subcontinent as a whole. Decolonization thus facilitated the spread of military capability both by creating many new independent or semi-independent centers of political power, and by providing a new focus for a host of local disputes and rivalries.

Because most of the new states had little or no industrial base, decolonization initially just increased the number of non–arms producers in the system. Some of these countries had never had any industrial base. Others, such as Egypt and India, had been major premodern centers of technology and production, but had been subordinated to, and in some ways deliberately deindustrialized by, colonial powers to eliminate them as economic competitors and reduce them to the status of suppliers of raw materials. In contrast, Japanese colonialism, especially in Taiwan and Korea, was more of a motor (although a violent and oppressive one) for state-led industrialization (Chomsky 1994: 113–120; Kiernan 1995: especially 56–69). The military imbalance between the producers and the newly independent nonproducers was rectified to the extent that arms were now available rather than denied, but it was maintained inasmuch as the nonproducers remained dependent on a small number of suppliers for their weapons. Nonproducers of arms in both the newly independent areas of Africa and Asia, and the older ex-colonial area of Latin America, were not satisfied to remain economically and industrially dependent. Many of them actively set about acquiring industrial economies of their own. In several of the less industrialized countries—India, Egypt, and China, and later Argentina, Brazil, Iran, and South Africa—acquiring the capability for at least some military production was a priority (Brzoska and Ohlson 1986; Väyrynen 1992; Singh 1997). Some of these industrialization projects have made scant progress. Others, most spectacularly in Iran under the shah, have destroyed the political structures that promoted them. In the case of Brazil, short-term success was followed by the near collapse of its military R&D and military production due to the demands of the Brazilian military and the global pressures on the Brazilian economy (Conca 1997). But some have succeeded, albeit in varying degrees and with varying, sometimes very high, costs. This industrialization resulted by the 1970s in a broadening group of countries able to supply some of their own military needs. In a few of these, most notably India, Israel, South Africa, and China, the quality and quantity of production were high enough to enable them to compete in some of the lower technology sectors of the arms trade, and thereby multiply the sources of armaments within the international system.

The mechanisms by which arms production capabilities have spread to these countries are similar to those that created the first group of producers. Straight transfers of arms do not assist development of production capability unless a sufficient industrial base already exists to enable local copies to be made. As argued in the previous chapter, civil industrial capability carries military potential, and so some of the new production capability simply reflects spin-ons from a broader process of economic development. But in many cases, the development of arms production has also been stimulated by the direct transfer of manufacturing capability from producer to nonproducer countries, though even here the success of the transplant depends on the existence of a civil industrial base (Klare 1983; Brzoska and Ohlson 1986: especially chapter 10; Bitzinger 1994). The Soviet Union played this role in China during the 1950s and in Eastern Europe up to 1989. Several Western suppliers were doing the same in Iran up to 1979, and both East and West have done so in India.

Such transfers reflect economic and political competition among the supplier states. After World War II, the arms trade was dominated initially by the United States and Britain. The small number of suppliers created a seller's market. As other industrial states such as France, the Soviet Union, Germany, Czechoslovakia, Belgium, and Italy recovered from the war, the number of arms suppliers increased. This trend has been reinforced by the development of arms industries in some less industrialized countries (LICs), especially China, which has become a very significant arms supplier (Bitzinger 1992; Gill 1992; Sköns and Gill 1996: 437–444). As the number of suppliers increases, competition among them for the export market becomes more intense, with the result that buyers have more leverage. In the buyer's market that the increase in the number of suppliers has now created, many states have used that leverage to get production facilities and knowledge as part of their major arms purchases. India, for example, has negotiated many such deals with the Soviet Union, Britain, and France. From being almost solely a purchaser during the 1950s, India has steadily built up an indigenous arms production capability of some sophistication (Sköns and Gill 1996: 445–447).

Licensing production arrangements seldom transfer technology quickly, and do not represent a short path from dependence to independence. Typically, they start with assembly of imported components, which leaves the importers only marginally more independent, and possibly less well off financially, than if they imported completed weapons. Despite the well-established view that licensing does not lead to independent production (Brzoska and Ohlson 1986: 283–285), India has demonstrated that over the years such arrangements can promote the development of local component suppliers as well as capability for maintenance and design. India has built up some independent capability in the less technologically advanced areas of military production and some foundations on which to rest advantageous licensed production arrangements for more sophisticated weapons. Its partial success in this development would not have been possible at all without possession of a broadly based industrial economy, and even so has been expensive and not very efficient (Smith 1994). Without devoting the much larger resources necessary to bring its own R&D up to the pace and standard of the leading edge of qualitative advance, even a country like India will not be able to achieve more than semi-independence in arms supply. Although it will be able to produce a variety of less sophisticated weapons independently, it will remain partly dependent on more advanced suppliers if it wishes to deploy weapons close to the highest standard of technology available (Brzoska and Ohlson 1986: chapter 7).

The end of the Cold War has brought about renewed interest in conversion of much of the military sector to civil uses. Conversion involves not just conversion of industries but also financial restructuring, redirection of R&D, demobilization and reintegration of personnel, closing and redeveloping bases, and selling, destroying, or mothballing surplus weapons (Chatterji and Forcey 1992; Sandler and Hartley 1995; *Conversion Survey*, annual). In the United States, subsidies to ailing arms industries made under the fig leaf of protecting the defense-industrial base are under great pressure (Leitner 1995). Conversion efforts are also under way in Russia and Eastern Europe (Renner 1992; de Andreis and Calogero 1995; Gaddy 1996; Kiss 1996). The conversion program in China is under particular strain. There, decisionmakers are trying simultaneously to modernize and shrink the military-industrial base, and convert some military industries to civil production, while limiting social dislocation—and to do all this for as little money as possible (Brömmelhörster and Frankenstein 1996; Shambaugh and Yang 1997).

The Hierarchy of Arms-Producing States

The result of the spread of military technology to date has been to create a hierarchy of states defined in terms of their capabilities for military production, as shown in Table 3.1 (Neuman 1984; Krause 1992; Mussington 1994; Pearson 1994; Sköns and Gill 1996). At the top are those capable of producing the whole spectrum of modern weapons. These need to import little or no military technology from abroad and can act as suppliers to states further down the hierarchy. Membership in this top class is defined not only by possession of a complete arms-manufacturing industry, but also by the fielding of a sufficient R&D capability to keep the products of that industry at the leading edge of technological quality. Britain, Germany, the United States, and France were members of this class before 1914. Japan and the Soviet Union joined it during the interwar years, but by the 1960s, only the United States and the Soviet Union could claim full first-rank status. With the collapse of the Soviet Union, the United States was the sole remaining full-spectrum arms producer. Furthermore, in terms of arms exports, as indicated earlier, the United States stands head and shoulders above the rest. However, with even military industries now subject to the globalization that has so strongly affected most of the civilian economy, there is a real prospect that soon there will be no states producing a full range of leading-edge weapons (Moran 1990; Bitzinger 1994). As Patrick Morgan (personal correspondence) suggests, rapid diffusion of information-based military technologies will further flatten the hierarchy, whereas slow diffusion will accentuate it.

At the bottom of the hierarchy are those states with little or no capability for independent military production. This group expanded as a result of the influx of the African and Asian states into the international system. Many of these new states lacked either or both the industrial capability and the economies of scale necessary to produce modern weapons. Some, like Nigeria, Indonesia, and Egypt, might hope one day to supply a good proportion of their own arms needs. Small, less industrialized states such as Sierra Leone, Guyana, and Laos are unlikely ever to develop a significant level of arms production. To the extent that they seek modern weapons to preserve or symbolize their independence, the larger, less industrialized states are temporarily, and the small ones permanently, dependent on the arms trade.

The middle range of the hierarchy is occupied by several strata of what can be called "part-producers." Part-producers have a significant enough arms production capability to distinguish them from nonproducers, but they do not match the scope and/or the quality of a full producer. In the lowest stratum of part-producers are countries like Mexico that have barely struggled up from the ranks of nonproducers and can only produce undemanding items like small arms and coastal patrol vessels. Next up are

Table 3.1   Hierarchy of Arms-Producing States

Full producers	Full range of production at leading edge	United States, but slipping due to globalization of arms industries
Part-producers	Nearly full range of production, at leading edge in some areas, and close to leading edge in many	Russia; France, Britain, and Germany, but increasingly relying on coproduction
	Nearly full range of production, but not close to leading edge	China, and to a lesser extent India
	Substantial range of production, but often dependent on imported components	For example, Brazil, Israel, Italy, Sweden, South Africa, Argentina, North and South Korea, Taiwan, Czech Republic, Slovakia
	Narrow range of production	For example, Pakistan, Spain, Indonesia, Egypt, Chile, Canada, Belgium
	Small amount of undemanding production (e.g., small arms only)	For example, Mexico, Philippines, Thailand, Peru
Nonproducers	Possible short-term	For example, Nigeria, Iran, Turkey
	Probable long-term	For example, Laos, Sierra Leone, Guyana, Papua New Guinea, Ethiopia

countries such as Pakistan and Spain that have the beginnings of more sophisticated production capabilities. Higher still are those like Israel, Sweden, South Africa, Brazil, and Argentina that can produce a fair range of military goods, some capable of competing in the international market. This stratum blends into a more ambitious one, typified by India, and even more so China, where foundations for a broadly based arms industry are being developed. China has achieved virtually a full range of production, and a high level of independence, but does not have the industrial or R&D sophistication to produce weapons of leading-edge quality.

The middle range also contains lapsed first-rank powers. Some of these, like France, Britain, and Germany, are capable of independent competition at the leading edge in some, but not all, areas of advanced military technology. These countries undertake sufficient R&D to keep up with the leading edge in some areas, and not to fall too far behind it in many. They compete with the leading edge but they may be dependent not only for whole types of weapons that they do not produce themselves, but also for sophisticated components for weapons that they do produce. Britain, for example, relied on the United States for Trident submarine-launched missiles (while building its own submarines and strategic nuclear warheads), but at the same time competed with it in the international market for tanks, tactical missiles, and fighter-bombers. France, which produces a nearly complete range of high-technology military equipment, relies on the United States for such items as in-flight refueling and early-warning aircraft. Other lapsed first-rank powers, most notably Japan, choose not to turn their formidable industrial capability to the broad-spectrum production of weapons, and not to export those that they do produce. Germany formerly took this position, but since the 1970s, and even more so since the end of the Cold War, has expanded its role as both producer and supplier (Lucas 1985; Bittleston 1990: 25; Anthony, Wezeman, and Wezeman 1996: 471–472). All of these countries are increasingly reliant on collaborative production to stay in the game (Kapstein 1991–1992; Cornish 1995). Russia is probably now best classified in this group, but the chaos in its economy and R&D and the uncertainty of its politics make it very unclear where it will end up (Anthony, Wezeman, and Wezeman 1996: 469–471; Gaddy 1996; Anthony 1997).

Part-producer countries can only achieve independence in arms by one of two routes. Either they can engage in R&D at the leading edge, as the Soviet Union did after World War II, or they can pursue independence at a level of technology lower than that set by the leading edge, as China did after its break with the Soviet Union. Matching the leading edge requires a size of economy and a level of industrialization possessed by very few states. Given the huge resources devoted to R&D by the superpowers and then by the United States alone after the Soviet collapse, the leading edge of technology has moved rapidly away from aspirant arms producers. The impact of R&D on technological advance in weapons has thus become the key to maintaining a qualitative hierarchy of arms producers. The respective drawbacks of the paths to independence (high cost and inferior armaments) are sufficiently compelling to ensure that most middle-rank states will stay in a position of semidependence.

In addition, the globalization of military industries, combined with the commercialization of high technology, now under way, makes leading-edge independence look less and less possible in the future, even for the United States (Moran 1990; Sköns and Gill 1996; Sedaitis 1997). As long as the leading powers continue to form a security community, and to perceive a low risk of world war, they are likely to allow the logic of economic efficiency to continue eroding their national capacities for independent arms production. This unprecedented development suggests that in future there will only be part-producers and nonproducers of arms. Once the arms industry becomes detached from immediate questions of national survival and gets treated as any other industry, economic logic will follow the pattern of civil industry and produce a global stratification. In such a system, the advanced countries will still dominate R&D and the high-technology end of the industry, but lower technology production will move out to those countries that can do it more cheaply.

As long as top-quality producers pass on the higher levels of military technology for economic or political reasons, either through production licenses or finished products, a degree of dependence does not pose unacceptable vulnerabilities on the military policies of recipient states. In this sense, the existence of a buyer's market is already an economically attractive and politically acceptable substitute for domestic manufacture of arms for many states, and may soon be so for nearly all. Because of the arms trade, nonproducers like Libya, Ethiopia, and Papua New Guinea, and part-producers like India, Australia, Argentina, and Israel, can maintain modern military forces proportional to the size of their economies in a way that would be impossible if they had to rely solely on their own manufacturing capability.

Most of the part-producer countries are both buyers and sellers in the arms trade. The logic of stratification suggests that more and more states will adopt niche strategies, specializing in areas where they have a comparative advantage, or wish to support an industry (such as aircraft or ship building), and importing the rest of their requirements. Israel and Belgium are good examples of states that have developed successful niche strategies. Some, like China and India—and for quite different reasons South Africa under apartheid—pursue or pursued quite broad independent production capability to reduce reliance on arms imports, and therefore minimize their political vulnerability to supplier pressure. Others, like Sweden, Switzerland, and Austria, strove as part of their policy of formal diplomatic neutrality to maintain the maximum self-reliance compatible with their economic base—a policy whose costs are now under question given that there is no Cold War about which to be neutral. The leaders of these countries value independence but have small home markets, and so face strong pressures to export in order to maintain the breadth and reduce the costs of their domestic production base. It remains to be seen whether this approach will be maintained now that some of these states have joined the European Union.

The expanding ranks of part-producers and the globalization of arms industries make increasingly difficult any attempt to sustain the simple distinction from the pre–World War II era between producer/suppliers and nonproducer/recipients of arms. Even the superpowers, which came closest to the pure producer/supplier model, chose to import some arms from other producers. The part-producers, like Britain, Israel, and Germany, are often simultaneously producers, suppliers, and recipients. Only the still large group of nonproducers occupies an unmixed role at present, and it divides between those who are nonproducers for the long term or for the short term.

The spread of military technology to date has thus been very uneven. The military products of the revolution of frequent technological change

are, with some important exceptions like nuclear weapons, long-range missiles, and heavy bombers, easily available and widely distributed. But the
ability to produce advanced weapons is much more restricted, even though
it has spread significantly since World War II. For the most part, the diffusion of arms production capability follows closely the general spread of
industrialization, which is itself very uneven. This linkage supports the
general argument about the close relationship between military and civil
technology made in Chapter 2. Some exceptions to the rule occur when
political considerations override economic ones. Because of defeat in
World War II, Japan, and to a lesser extent Germany and Italy, are less
prominent as arms producers than might be expected from their industrial
capabilities. Conversely, China, South Africa under apartheid, and Israel,
because of the intense military and political pressure to which they have
been subjected, are more prominent as arms producers than their industrial
base would warrant.

Controversies over the Arms Trade

The term "arms trade" refers not just to international sales of weapons, but
also to transfers of weapons on a political basis and to the international
workings of the arms industry. A number of survey works give good
overviews of the history and the workings of the arms trade, and look at
the interests, motives, and policies of both suppliers and recipients (Stanley and Pearton 1972; Cannizzo 1980; Neuman and Harkavy 1980; Pierre
1982; Sampson 1991; Krause 1992; Kramer 1992). Comprehensive and
up-to-date information on the trade is hard to come by. Even routine arms
purchases are often considered sensitive by governments, and there is a
whole world of covert transfers, much of which never surfaces into the
public domain. Two independent annual publications provide valuable reg-
isters of known deals (*Military Balance*, *SIPRI Yearbook*) and there is now
a UN Register of Conventional Arms that monitors the arms trade. Increasing attention is being paid to the idea of trying to control the trade in
weapons and weapon-making technology (Cornish 1995; Forsberg 1996).
    Despite the strong support for it from both suppliers and recipients,
the arms trade arouses intense controversy. This controversy in part reflects that which generally attaches to the role of the instruments of violence in society. It also reflects the very problematic mix of commercial
interests with large-scale means of destruction captured by the phrase
"merchants of death." In the early decades of the revolution of frequent
technological change—up to World War I—the arms trade was dominated
by mostly private companies, like Krupp and Vickers, that were the leading producers and innovators of weapons. The freewheeling activities of
these companies up to 1914 caused a reaction against the arms trade during the years between World Wars I and II.

The solution adopted in those countries where the manufacturing companies remained in the private sector was to bring the trade under government control, or at least supervision, by a system of export licensing (Stanley and Pearton 1972: chapter 3). In this way, the foreign policy interests of the state would supposedly filter out the undesirable political effects of an arms trade conducted for purely commercial motives. But at this time the rising capital demands of the arms industry, and the increasing importance of high technology for military security, were anyway leading to a situation of increasing state involvement in the arms industry as monopoly or dominant buyer. The rising resource requirement for the development and production of modern weapons was also concentrating arms production into an ever smaller number of large companies. By the end of World War II, there was thus close government involvement with the arms industry even where the industry was not formally nationalized (Stanley and Pearton 1972: chapter 1; Pearton 1982: 177–258).

When states took control over the arms trade, they inherited responsibility for all the pressures in the trade that had led to the "merchants of death" image. State control did not eliminate these pressures. Instead, it ensured that the interests and objectives of the leaders of states interacted more directly with the interests of individual companies. The result has been an awkward mix of economic and political interests. Although governments are more inclined than companies to consider the political consequences of their actions, they are by no means immune from the economic temptations of the arms trade in terms of employment, export earnings, and maintaining their own arms industries at a tolerable cost. Both East and West supplied arms to both Iran and Iraq while they were at war and have supplied both Greece and Turkey, although the latter have been and still are rivals.

The arms trade thus still attracts criticism no less intense, and perhaps more widely ranging, than that during the years between the world wars. The imposition of state control on the arms trade has not removed the suspicion that it stimulates military competition, though it has changed the form of the problem. In addition to buyers being manipulated into arms purchases by unscrupulous economic interests, recipients also get caught up in arms dynamics fed by political competition among supplier states, particularly the superpowers during the Cold War. The classic example here is the Middle East, where an intense local rivalry between Israel and the Arab states became militarized to a very high level, partly as a result of competitive support for clients by the United States and the Soviet Union.

Particular attention has been paid to the impact of the arms trade on LICs for quite some time (Benoit 1973; McKinlay and Mughan 1984; Gilks and Segal 1985; Graham 1994; Conca 1997). This subject has almost become a distinct subfield. It connects to the literatures on military government (Wolpin 1972, 1978; Kennedy 1974; McKinlay and Cohan 1975; Sarkesian 1978), intervention (Ayoob 1980; Girling 1980), the supposed diplomatic leverage provided by arms sales (Nachmias 1988; Hartung 1994), and development (Albrecht et al. 1975; Luckham 1977a, 1977b; Deger and West 1987; Mullin 1987; Graham 1994). Through and frequently within these literatures, concern about the arms trade to the LICs ties into the critical, and often radical, body of thought that sees the arms trade as a major disease of the international system. However, conditions in LICs cover a wide range. Military spending does not necessarily and everywhere impede economic development (Benoit 1973). Military governments do not always perform much differently from or worse than civilian ones (McKinlay and Cohan 1975; Sarkesian 1978; cf. Mazrui 1977). The arms trade does not always put the military into a stronger or more disruptive position in weak states than it would be anyway. And modern weapons are sometimes well suited to achieving the objectives pursued by the leaders of LICs—regardless of whether or not one approves of their purposes. Afghanistan, India, Iran, Vietnam, Egypt, Morocco, and Ethiopia have made effective use of modern weapons. Without the arms trade there would be, as in the late nineteenth century, a tremendous disparity in military power between those states able to produce modern weapons and those not.

Nevertheless, the negative case raises telling points (Ball 1978, 1989). In a broader sense, criticism of the arms trade reflects not just concern about the stimulation of specific military rivalries, but also about the way in which the whole planet was drawn into the Cold War rivalry in the past and the way in which they are still tied into the global arms dynamic. States with virtually no industrial base, like Libya, Saudi Arabia, and Syria, were nonetheless lavishly equipped with the most modern weapons. They found themselves in a security environment defined not only by the technological standards of the leading powers, but also in which those powers actively promote the diffusion of military technology through the arms trade. Looked at from this perspective, the arms trade cannot be seen simply as serving the right to equality of nonproducers. It also puts pressure on them to participate in a military system that is often beyond their economic means, damaging to their political structures, and disproportionate to the security needs arising from their local environment. To some extent, pressure to participate exists because states that do not keep up with the prevailing military standards may make themselves vulnerable to those that do. Some critics use the term "the world military order" to describe this situation (Kaldor and Eide 1979; Kaldor 1982: chapter 5). However, it is also a matter of acculturation to a substantial degree. Some states might be able to achieve security through a broader, more militia-based, less high-technology approach. However, they are tied into the world military order by a military culture in which high-technology weapons operated by professional armed forces are treated as normal and best (Wendt and Barnett 1993).

Entanglement in the world military order adds to the already difficult economic and political problems of LICs. On the economic side, expenditures on modern arms clash with both the immediate welfare needs of poor populations and with the investment needs of less industrialized economies (Benoit 1973; Report of the Secretary General 1977; Harris, Kelly, and Pranowo 1998; Mintz and Chan 1992). Establishing and maintaining a modernized military sector draws not only capital but also skilled labor out of struggling economies where both are in short supply (Neuman and Harkavy 1980: chapter 15). The need to finance arms purchases can distort the whole economy away from development priorities toward exports geared to earning hard currency, especially since weapons have to be replaced periodically if the country is to maintain its military standing (Luckham 1977a, 1977b).

On the political side, it contributes to the domination of national politics by the military in many LICs (Wendt and Barnett 1993: 342) and to interference by supplier states in the politics of clients. In states where government does not have well-developed social foundations, modernized armed forces can easily become the most powerful organization in the country. From such a position the armed forces face constant temptation to intervene in politics, either to pursue their own interests or to replace inefficient, weak, or corrupt civilian governments. By encouraging development of the armed forces in weak states the world military order may encourage the tendency toward military rule. The arms trade also provides suppliers with a channel into the armed forces of clients that may be politically significant if the armed forces are active in politics. Because modern weapons require training contacts between suppliers and recipients, many officers will have spent extensive periods in the supplier country, which therefore has a chance to shape both their attitudes and their personal contacts (Neuman and Harkavy 1980: chapters 14, 16; Wendt and Barnett 1993: 338–340).

In military terms, the world military order presents LICs with an integrated package of military technology, doctrine, and organization that was evolved to meet the needs of substantially different societies and that may be in many respects wholly unsuited to the actual military needs of LICs (Kaldor and Eide 1979: 7–12). Weapons and doctrines designed to fight European-style wars are difficult to maintain in the low-technology environment of many LICs; can heighten tensions by posing threats to neighbors; and, when war does occur, may make the war more intense and contribute to escalation (Pearson, Brzoska, and Crantz 1992; Brzoska and Pearson 1994). Those weapons and doctrines are sometimes of little use against the domestic-level threats that are frequently the main security problem facing governments in the LICs: this may be no bad thing if those domestic threats are movements that are less repressive than those they oppose.

The Technological Imperative

The arms trade takes place in the broader context of the technological imperative that helps drive the global spread of modern technology. The technological imperative exists in the sense that decisionmakers have to consider how to respond to actual and potential technological change. However, as will be emphasized in the discussion of organizational theory, it is not simply that technology exists or is invented and then decisionmakers respond rationally to it. Instead, states often initiate technological advance: in crucial ways they shape the development of the technological imperative through their actions and interactions. Indeed, whereas one decisionmaker may see a particular piece of technology as requiring a response, others may not. It is possible that varied responses to the same piece of technology are rational responses to different structural issues. For example, an actor may not respond to a particular technological development because that actor lacks the resources to respond, is not in a sufficiently intense rivalry to make a response worthwhile, or is in thrall to a set of internal interests that makes a response unfeasible.

The linking and indeed blurring of the civil and military spheres of technology discussed in Chapter 2 creates technology "creep" (Shapley 1978): a large element of the pressure for qualitative technological advance is not located in the military sector, and the military sector cannot escape the implications of a relentless qualitative advance over which it has only partial control. One way of looking at the technological imperative as a main input into the arms dynamic is in terms of the idea raised in Chapter 2 that all industrial societies have a latent military potential. If we assume a disarmed major industrial country in which no military sector exists, there would still be a powerful industrial technology and an institutionalized process of qualitative advance. If that country had to arm itself for some reason, a set of military applications would quickly come forth from the existing technological and industrial base. One can approach this exercise by imagining the disarmed country first with a technological level similar to that of the industrial countries in the 1920s, and then with a level similar to the present. At the 1920s level, the civil base would easily give rise to a whole array of chemical weapons, both poisonous and explosive, and probably to the idea of aircraft as a delivery system, but it would not generate thoughts of nuclear weapons, lasers, or precision-guided munitions. With the knowledge and technology base of the present, the idea of nuclear weapons would be unavoidable, as would the idea of using rockets to deliver them. Japan provides a partial example of this latter case. Although it is by no means disarmed, Japan does not have a large arms industry. No one doubts, however, that Japan could rapidly convert its impressive R&D and productive capacity to military purposes should its political consensus on the issue change (Drifte 1986; Ikegami-Andersson

1992; Chinworth 1993; Matthews and Matsuyama 1993; Samuels 1994). The term coined by Daniel Deudney for a deliberate strategy of creating military potential is "recessed" deterrence. Then again, Japan's political consensus against developing a large and offensively capable military establishment is very deep-seated: it would take a powerful change in circumstances to overturn it (Buzan 1995a; Halloran 1994). There is a general process of technological advance that is only partly driven by the military but that has profound military implications. This process is probably strongest in capitalist societies because of their commitment to technological innovation as an engine of economic growth. Sustained growth not only means higher profits, but also makes easier the job of managing politics in the presence of a markedly unequal distribution of wealth. Even in noncapitalist industrial societies, however, there is a deeply embedded commitment to the pursuit of technological innovation for civil purposes.

The action-reaction process and the assortment of factors that make up the domestic structure of states, and that are explored in Part 2, cannot explain all of the qualitative advance that is such a major feature of the arms dynamic. The stimulus of international rivalry and the permanent organization of military R&D certainly contribute to the process of technological advance. They increase the amount of resources available to fuel the process and they select areas of military utility for intensive development. These are important considerations that make a major impact on the whole pattern. Their contribution is easily sufficient to justify the other two models, but they need to be set in context. A substantial amount of the behavior that is commonly identified as arms racing (but which, as we explain in Part 2, may turn out to be something less than that) stems from the underlying process of technological advance. When countries compete with each other in armaments (whether as potential opponents in war or competitors in the arms trade), they must also compete with a standard of technological quality that is moving forward. When they institutionalize military R&D, countries are seeking to exploit, and not be left behind by, a process that is already under way in society as a whole.

Conclusion

The arms trade moderates the huge power imbalances that would otherwise exist between producers and nonproducers of weapons. Whether one regards this as a good thing or not will depend on one's objectives and values. Looked at in detail, the trade raises serious questions about the economic, political, cultural, and military consequences for LICs. Looked at in broader perspective, it is a manifestation of the arms dynamic, and the technological imperative identifies an important element of the arms dynamic that is not captured fully by the action-reaction and domestic structure explanations of the arms dynamic. Adding a massive current of independent technological advance to the analysis creates a sense of continuous process that is more deeply institutionalized even than that of the domestic structure model. This depth stems from the technological imperative being global rather than being based within single states, and from the way it relates to the totality of technology rather than to the military sector alone.

4

THE PROLIFERATION OF WEAPONS OF MASS DESTRUCTION

The proliferation of weapons of mass destruction (WMD) is a prominent contemporary case of the diffusion of military capability. By WMD we mean weapons of which small numbers can destroy life and/or inanimate objects on a vast scale very quickly. Although massive numbers of people were killed in Rwanda with machetes, the killing took time and large numbers of the weapon. Extremely powerful conventional weapons, notably fuel–air explosives (FAE), which create a widely dispersed and very violently combustible aerosol, can be as destructive as small nuclear weapons and thus in a sense are WMD. However, they have not generally penetrated the public, academic, or even military consciousness thus far and have not yet been deployed in very large numbers. They are not regarded as being as horrifying or repulsive as nuclear, chemical, biological, and toxin weapons, perhaps because their method of killing is a more familiar one in war and they are not associated (as are nuclear weapons) with potential escalation to global holocaust. Having said that, it is also worth noting that concern over category of WMD does not flow simply from the objective technological characteristics of the weapons but is socially constructed (Price and Tannenwald, 1996). As the significance of WMD is strongly influenced by their capability to reach their targets, we will also consider delivery systems in this chapter. In discussions on this subject, there is a standard distinction between vertical and horizontal proliferation. Vertical proliferation is the increase in stockpiles of weapons by states already holding them. Horizontal proliferation is the spread of weapons to states not previously possessing them, and this is what is usually meant by proliferation. Acquisition of nuclear WMD by nonstate actors has not yet occurred. Less commonly, vertical proliferation also refers to the positioning of weapons in additional locations outside the territory of the state itself. Such external positioning can be in overseas bases, like those of the United States in Western Europe and East Asia, or in naval vessels or aircraft that patrol outside the state's territory. Cold War rivalry produced a sprawling global infrastructure for nuclear weapons research, development, production, testing, deployment, and control (Arkin and Fieldhouse 1985; IPPNW 1991), but since the end of the Cold War both types of vertical proliferation have gone substantially, though by no means completely, into reverse.

For two reasons the main focus in this chapter will be on horizontal proliferation. First, the political significance of a spread of control is higher than that of a spread of numbers. The acquisition of one nuclear warhead by, say, South Korea, would attract much more attention than the addition of another several hundred warheads to the Chinese arsenal. Second, although the point is contested (Waltz 1981; Sagan and Waltz 1995; Hagerty 1995–1996; Karl 1996–1997), the spread of WMD is widely thought to have important negative implications for deterrence and strategic stability (Sagan 1994; Simpson 1994; Fetter 1996). Despite this focus, something needs to be said first about the acquisition of enormous nuclear arsenals by East and West during the Cold War, because this was the context in which horizontal nuclear proliferation first took place.

Vertical Nuclear Proliferation During the Cold War

In the case of nuclear weapons, the firmest trend until recently was vertical proliferation by the existing nuclear states. At their peak in 1985, if one counts the total number of warheads in all categories (smallest to largest in explosive power, and on very short-range to intercontinental delivery systems) stockpiled by the declared nuclear weapon states, the figures were 24,898 for the United States, between 22,000 and 33,000 for the Soviet Union, 686 for Britain, 514 for France, and about 250 for China (Arkin and Fieldhouse 1985: 38). About half of the warheads were strategic in that they were aimed at targets in the homelands of possible opponents: the other half were for use at sea, in the air, or on the battlefield (Arkin and Fieldhouse 1985: 37–63).

There are a number of other ways of counting nuclear weapons. One measure is explosive yield. At first the United States built up the explosive yield of its arsenal and then rapidly cut it as it concentrated on using a larger number of smaller weapons. The cut in explosive yield did not mean that nuclear war would be less destructive. Indeed, the opposite was the case because, for example, three smaller warheads allow destruction to be spread over a much wider area than one large one. The United States concentrated on developing much more accurate and reliable devices so that smaller warheads would yield a higher probability of kill (PK), that is, a higher probability that each warhead would destroy its target. For a long time the Soviet Union relied more on large warheads than on accuracy, but by the 1980s was combining high accuracy with less of a cut in explosive yield than the United States.

Hawkish circles in the United States feared that the Soviet Union had what they saw as a potentially very threatening advantage in "throw weight"—its large missiles were capable of carrying many more warheads, which might be secretly produced and deployed and then used to destroy fixed U.S. targets, especially land-based intercontinental ballistic missiles (ICBMs). To see this as a serious threat required one to assume that the Soviet Union would not be deterred by potential retaliation from U.S. submarine-launched ballistic missiles (SLBMs) and bombers armed with gravity bombs and cruise missiles, which together made up 70 percent of the U.S. strategic arsenal, not to mention its tactical and theater nuclear weapons and any land-based ICBMs that survived the first-strike attempt. Neither side ever had confidence that it had a counterforce first-strike capability, that is, an ability to destroy the other side's strategic nuclear weapons through direct hits in one massive attack to the extent that the damage caused by any surviving nuclear weapons launched in retaliation would be acceptable. Both sides worried about their vulnerability to a countercommand first strike in which nuclear forces are paralyzed due to the destruction of command and control systems: for obvious reasons this is known as a "decapitation" attack. Such an attack would still be an enormous gamble because the local commanders might still launch their weapons even without central authority. Indeed, both sides moved towards a "launch-on-warning" (LOW) posture, in which counterattacks would commence before either weapons or command systems began to be destroyed by the other side's incoming warheads (Blair 1993). LOW doctrine created the potential for nuclear war through misperception: the warnings could turn out to be wrong, but it would be too late.

The nuclear destructive power accumulated by the mid-1980s was quite staggering. In some respects decisionmakers would have incentives to try to keep nuclear war limited rather than use all their forces, but even taking this into account, a war involving only a fraction of the nuclear arsenals of the United States and Soviet Union would have resulted in enormous casualties (Daugherty, Levi, and von Hippel 1986; Levi, von Hippel, and Daugherty 1987–1988). This is illustrated in Tables 4.1 and 4.2.

The figures for counterforce first strike refer to an attack on the opponent's missile silos, strategic bomber and tanker bases, nuclear navy bases, nuclear weapons storage facilities, missile launch control facilities, national command posts and alternative headquarters, early-warning radars, navy and other strategic radio transmitters, and satellite command transmitters. Real U.S. target lists for strategic nuclear forces have been much longer than this: the same may also have been true for the Soviet Union.

A number of conclusions with which we concur are drawn by Daugherty, Levi, and von Hippel. First, a limited attack would have been difficult to distinguish from an all-out attack. Second, an attack on military targets would have looked very similar to an attack intended to wipe out cities

Table 4.1   Estimated Consequences of Soviet Strategic Nuclear Attacks on the United States

	Immediate casualties	Short-term casualties
Counterforce first strike[a]		
1,215 targets		
2,839 warheads		
1,342 megatons	13–34 million dead	25–64 million dead or injured
Countercity attack[b]		
100 1-megaton warheads[c]	25–66 million dead	36–71 million dead or injured

Sources: Based on figures in Daugherty, Levi, and von Hippel (1986) and Levi, von Hippel, and Daugherty (1987–1988).

Notes: Casualty figures are only for those resulting from radiation, blast, and fire. The figures could at least double if indirect environmental and social consequences (e.g., exposure, starvation, disease) are taken into account.

a. Approximately 33 percent of warheads and 25 percent of megatonnage on Soviet strategic delivery vehicles (excluding reloads).

b. The figures assume that the warheads are aimed at the 100 largest population area targets (as opposed to, say, the centers of the 100 largest cities—a large enough city that can be divided into a number of population area targets). They also assume that there will not have been large-scale evacuation and other civil defense measures instituted. Even with such measures, many survivors would become casualties due to the short-term effects of radiation, blast, and fire and due to indirect environmental, economic, and social consequences.

c. Approximately 1 percent of warheads and 2 percent of megatonnage on Soviet strategic delivery vehicles (excluding reloads).

because military targets are often located in or close to cities. Third, damage on an incredible scale could have been inflicted with only about 2 percent of the strategic arsenal of either side. This is particularly alarming when viewed in the context of Bruce Blair's (1993) conclusion that the LOW policies of the United States and Soviet Union tied the two states to operational plans and organizational routines that would have made it extremely difficult for decisionmakers to use their nuclear arsenals in a limited way: everything was geared to massive, early use in spite of some elements of strategic nuclear doctrine that called for limited nuclear options (LNOs). Fourth, on the basis of potential casualties, there was clear scope to reduce strategic nuclear arsenals to a small fraction of what they were. This process has begun with the Strategic Arms Reduction Talks (START) agreements. Fifth, a counterforce first strike would still have left the opponent with a capability to wipe out the society of the attacker many times over: this is what became known as "overkill" capacity. Sixth, even a near-perfect system of ballistic missiles defense (BMD) with 98 percent reliability would have been disastrously inadequate. There is every reason to think that the logic of this analysis would apply to any similar nuclear buildup in the future: in this sense there was something unreal about the

Table 4.2   Estimated Consequences of U.S. Strategic Nuclear Attacks on the Soviet Union

	Immediate casualties	Short-term casualties

Counterforce first strike[a]
  1,740 targets
  4,108 warheads
  844 megatons
	12–27 million dead	25–54 million dead or injured

Countercity attack[b] 100 1-megaton warheads[c]	45–77 million dead	73–93 million dead or injured

Sources: Based on figures in Daugherty, Levi, and von Hippel (1986) and Levi, von Hippel, and Daugherty (1987–1988).

Notes: Casualty figures are only for those resulting from radiation, blast, and fire. The figures could at least double if indirect environmental and social consequences (e.g., exposure, starvation, disease) are taken into account.

a. Approximately 30 percent of warheads and 17 percent of megatonnage on U.S. strategic delivery vehicles (excluding reloads).

b. The figures assume that the warheads are aimed at the 100 largest population area targets (as opposed to, say, the centers of the 100 largest cities—a large enough city that can be divided into a number of population area targets). They also assume that there will not have been large-scale evacuation and other civil defense measures instituted. Even with such measures, many survivors would become casualties due to the short-term effects of radiation blast and fire and due to indirect environmental, economic, and social consequences.

c. Approximately 1 percent of warheads and 2 percent of megatonnage on U.S. strategic delivery vehicles (excluding reloads).

size of the U.S. and Soviet nuclear arsenals. What those arsenals did do was symbolize the superpower status of the United States and Soviet Union. Indeed, the Soviet Union was more a nuclear superpower than it ever was an economic, ideological, or even conventional military one (Herring 1992).

The Process of Horizontal Proliferation

Against this extraordinary background, the proliferation of WMD in general and related delivery systems has proceeded much more slowly.

Nuclear Weapons

In most basic respects, the horizontal proliferation of nuclear weapons shows the same pattern of slow and uneven spread as that of military technology in general. It also shows the same linkage between civil and military technology. However, in one respect, nuclear proliferation follows a distinctive pattern. The leading-edge states have shown a much greater reluctance to allow the spread of nuclear weapons than has been the case with any previous military technology. So far as is known, there has never been any direct trade in nuclear weapons. There have been rumors that Iran has bought four tactical nuclear weapons from Kazakhstan in the wake of the collapse of the Soviet Union, but the rumors appear to be without foundation (Reiss 1995: 143–144). The closest approximations to such trade have been the cooperation between the United States and Britain (Simpson 1983) and to a lesser extent France (Ullman 1989), and between the Soviet Union and China (Garthoff 1966: chapters 5, 6, 8). The cooperation between Britain and the United States started during World War II, but flourished only after both states had independently achieved nuclear status. The brief cooperation between the Soviet Union and China during the 1950s ended when the two countries fell out politically. More noteworthy than these two exceptions is the fact that the United States and Soviet Union (and, after its collapse, Russia) have devoted considerable effort, some of it cooperative, to instituting and maintaining a nuclear non-proliferation regime. However, although the nuclear weapon states were strict about forbidding transfers of nuclear weapons, most of them were happy to trade in civil nuclear technology, much of which could be adapted to military purposes.

The established nuclear powers oppose nuclear proliferation for three reasons. First, they see the spread of such powerful weapons as a threat to their own power and security, as they believe it is to their advantage to have a nuclear monopoly vis-à-vis potential adversaries. Second (especially in the cases of the United States and the Soviet Union/Russia), they think that proliferation will in some sense undermine their symbolic status in the international system. Third, they think that the spread of nuclear weapons to more states will make the world more dangerous for everyone because they believe that more fingers on more triggers will increase the probability of nuclear weapons being used either deliberately or by accident, that the leaders of the states that get them might be fanatical or irrational, or that the nuclear weapons will be deployed in organizations that are either accident prone or vulnerable to attack. However, they are sometimes unwilling to provide security guarantees or other incentives to prevent proliferation.

The magnitude of the issues raised by nuclear proliferation means that the issue has spawned an extensive literature of its own. This literature relates to deterrence and to arms control, especially in terms of the Nonproliferation Treaty (NPT) of 1968, the International Atomic Energy Agency (IAEA), and the various other national and international instruments devised to support the nonproliferation regime. It also relates to technological issues (Kokoski 1996), especially those involving the links between civil and military applications of nuclear power; and it concerns political and technological developments in those countries seen to have interests in acquiring either nuclear weapons or a short-term option on the capability to manufacture them. This literature is rather isolated from thinking about the spread of military capability in general. Because the issue of nuclear proliferation has developed almost as a subject in its own right, it has helped to mask awareness of the broader process of which it is a part. From reading the literature, it is easy to get the impression that nuclear proliferation is a unique problem of the post-1945 era, rather than a contemporary manifestation of a long-standing and deeply rooted process of diffusion of military technology. It is, however, precisely the character of that broader process that makes the specific problem of nuclear proliferation so difficult.

Because there has been no direct trade in nuclear weapons, diffusion of them has taken place as a result of states acquiring the necessary knowledge, technology, and material to undertake independent manufacture. This absence of direct trade in weapons between producers and nonproducers highlights the strong linkage between the civil and military sides of nuclear technology. In the nuclear field, the civil-military linkage lies primarily in the availability of fissile material (that is, material the atoms of which split in a chain reaction to produce energy): usually uranium 235 (U235) or plutonium 239 (Pu239). Neither of these materials is easy to manufacture. U235 has to be separated from the much more common uranium isotope U238, a process called "enrichment," which cannot be achieved chemically and which so far requires extremely costly and sophisticated technology. Pu239 does not exist naturally, but is a product of the irradiation of U238 inside a nuclear reactor. It can be chemically extracted from the leftovers of the fission process within a nuclear reactor. This extraction is not as demanding a task as enrichment, but it does require a reactor, control over a supply of uranium, and the ability to build and run a chemical separation plant capable of handling materials that are radioactive, poisonous, corrosive, and inflammable.

U235 and Pu239 can serve either as reactor fuels or as fissile material for nuclear weapons. The basic design principles of nuclear weapons long ago passed into public knowledge as a result of the quite phenomenal advances in the understanding of physics made since World War II. Getting possession of weapons-grade fissile material is thus the principal technical obstacle to building one's own nuclear weapons. Most, though not all, nuclear reactors use partly enriched uranium. The technology of enrichment is therefore part of the technology of civil nuclear power even though the level of enrichment required for weapons is much higher than that generally used for reactors. The main exception to this rule is the naval propulsion reactor, which needs to be small, and therefore uses weapons-grade enriched uranium. All reactors that burn natural or low-enriched uranium produce substantial quantities of plutonium as a by-product. Because U238 is over 100 times more plentiful than U235, it is possible to design reactors, called "fast breeders," which produce more fuel than they consume by converting nonfissile U238 into fissile Pu239. These reactors pose more severe technological problems than ones using uranium and are not yet in widespread use. The prospect of them nevertheless makes recovery of Pu239 attractive (whether as reactor fuel or warhead material), especially since the alternative is to treat it as permanent waste, which poses difficult long-term problems of disposal. The technology of reprocessing is thus also firmly embedded in the development of civil nuclear power (Gardner 1994: chapters 1–3).

This close connection between the civil and military elements of nuclear technology has made trade in civil nuclear technology a possible mechanism for the proliferation of nuclear weapons (Kokoski 1996). Without the civil trade, many of those countries that now possess all or part of the equipment for generating nuclear power would not be in the nuclear game at all. Nuclear technology is still not far from the leading edge of current capabilities in an advanced industrial society. Purely indigenous development of it requires an industrial base of a size and sophistication possessed by relatively few countries. Because trade in civil nuclear technology has generally been seen as legitimate, it has served to spread widely the knowledge, skills, technologies, and materials that provide the necessary foundation for a military nuclear option. Although direct trade in nuclear weapons has not occurred, the trade in civil nuclear technology, both legal and illegal, has successfully transplanted varying degrees of production capability into many countries.

The trade in civil nuclear technology boomed after 1973, when the quadrupling of oil prices by the Middle Eastern oil-producing countries made nuclear energy seem both economically and politically attractive (Burn 1978). Civil energy requirements provided a powerful independent justification for trade in nuclear technology and, like the arms industry, they generated a buyer's market. Major suppliers like the United States, France, and West Germany, and minor ones like Canada and Switzerland, competed fiercely to meet demand from a wide variety of countries hit hard by the leap in oil prices. Because supply was in excess of demand, again like the arms industry, transfer of production capability often became a way of winning contracts. The most spectacular example of this tendency was the 1975 deal in which West Germany agreed to equip Brazil with a complete nuclear industry, including technology for enrichment and reprocessing (Gall 1976). The case of Pakistan illustrates an equally interesting aspect of the civil-military link through trade. Denied the right to purchase a reprocessing plant directly from France, Pakistan organized the covert piecemeal purchase of component parts for an enrichment facility. The ruse worked well enough before it was discovered to give Pakistan the makings of a limited enrichment capability (Kapur 1987; Albright 1987; Reiss 1995). Pakistan's ploy was later copied by Iraq, with a degree of success revealed in detail by the post–Gulf War UN inspections (Ekeus 1993; Dallmeyer 1995).

Trade in civil nuclear power technology transformed the whole problem of nuclear proliferation. Prior to the 1970s, the problem had been seen primarily in terms of decisions to acquire nuclear weapons by countries such as West Germany, Japan, and Sweden, which already possessed an advanced industrial economy. Such countries were capable of making their decision on the basis of their own resources. The dominant model of proliferation at this time reflected the existing history, which showed a record of states proceeding directly to military applications of nuclear energy. In all of the early nuclear powers—the United States, the Soviet Union, Britain, France, and China—military developments preceded civil ones. After 1973, the problem came to be seen much more in terms of LICs using civil nuclear technologies as the basis for a military option. The defining example for this model was India, which possessed the most long-standing, advanced and best domestically rooted civil nuclear programs outside the industrialized states. The testing of a nuclear device by India in 1974 (plus more tests in 1998) showed how easy it was for a civil nuclear program to act as the foundation for a military option. The fact that the Indian government labeled the 1974 device a "peaceful nuclear explosive" (PNE) underlined the connection between civil and military nuclear technology that was at the heart of the proliferation problem (Marwah 1977; Chellaney 1991; Smith 1994; Reiss 1995).

The civil route to military nuclear status quite changed the character of nuclear proliferation. Open deployment of fully developed weapons on delivery systems became less important than it had been for the first five nuclear powers. Instead, attention focused on shrinking the lead time: that is, the length of time between the decision to acquire nuclear weapons and the ability to test or deploy them. The way to achieve such shrinkage was to acquire those elements of civil nuclear technology—particularly enrichment or reprocessing—that could provide fissile material for military applications. By doing so, a state could achieve the status of a "threshold" nuclear power: not possessing nuclear weapons, but clearly in a position to do so quickly (Spector 1988; Karp 1992: chapter 8; Fortmann 1992–1993). Threshold nuclear status, also labeled "virtual" nuclear status (see Mazarr 1995b), has been attractive to several states. It enabled them to get some of the perceived benefits of nuclear weapon status without either violating nonproliferation norms openly or paying the cost of deployment. Some states—Pakistan (until 1998), India (until 1998), Israel, and (until apartheid ended) South Africa—are or were "opaque" nuclear weapon states in that they have tested or acquired nuclear weapons but have not openly deployed them or admitted to having them (Frankel 1991; Fortmann 1992–1993).

Although nuclear proliferation clearly deserves its status as a special case of the spread of military technology, it has produced results not markedly different from that of military technology in general. In nuclear technology, a hierarchy of full producers, part-producers, and nonproducers exists that is similar in form to that for conventional armaments and that appears to share the same future of a trend toward expansion of the middle ranks. Although the horizontal spread of nuclear weapons has so far been quite limited, the diffusion of the technology necessary for their production has kept pace with that in the conventional weapons sector. It can thus be said that the nuclear weapons potential of the international system has increased markedly. Whether the spreading capability for making nuclear weapons will actually be translated into military hardware remains an open question.

Chemical Weapons and Biological and Toxin Weapons

Chemical weapons (CWs) and biological and toxin weapons (BTWs) deserve to be classified as weapons of mass destruction because small numbers of them can destroy life on a vast scale. Unlike nuclear and conventional weapons they do not destroy through blast and heat. As a result they are physically much less destructive: after their use, buildings, machines, and bodies are left more or less intact. In 1918, during World War I, 20 percent of shells fired were filled with chemical agents but these produced only 15 percent of casualties (i.e., deaths and injuries) and only 1.4 percent of deaths caused by artillery fire (Roberts 1992: 6). However, under the right circumstances against an unprotected urban population of around 1 million people, a chemical weapon attack with eight F-16 aircraft could inflict up to 50 percent casualties: no conventional weapon can match this (Roberts 1992: 79). Biological warfare agents are "living micro-organisms (e.g., bacteria, rickettsiae, viruses, or fungi) that infect a human, animal, or plant host to [cause] a debilitating or fatal illness" (Tucker 1993: 231). One aircraft that dispensed 50 kilograms of anthrax in aerosol form could cause hundreds of thousands of deaths (Tucker 1993: 232). In contrast, toxins are "non-living poisons manufactured by biological organisms." One ten-thousandth of a milligram of botulinum toxin is fatal (Tucker 1993: 232).

Peaceful and military chemical, biological, and toxin technologies overlap heavily (Tucker 1994). Simple CWs such as chlorine gas are basic products of the chemical industry. Just as a country acquires the capacity to manufacture conventional weapons when it acquires an engineering industry, and nuclear weapons if it acquires the full fuel cycle for a civil nuclear industry, so the ability to build CWs comes along with the acquisition of a chemical industry. Since chemicals are more basic to industrialization than nuclear power, the spread of industrial development carries with it the option for acquiring a poor state's atom bomb in the form of CWs, a strategy again illustrated by Saddam Hussein's Iraq. The dual-use dimension is also true for BTW agents because they are developed by commonplace biotechnology commercially available worldwide. In May 1995, a white supremacist in Ohio used the certification of the well and septic company for which he worked to acquire freeze-dried cultures of bubonic plague by post (Associated Press 1995b). Due to the ambiguity of the technology, efforts at control will focus on monitoring of civil chemical, biological, and toxin activities for possible diversions to military uses: even if it cannot be prevented technically, increased likelihood of exposure, condemnation, and punishment might help prevent it politically (Lundin 1991; Geissler and Woodall 1994; see also *Strategic Survey 1996–97* 1997: 31–41).

Delivery Systems for Weapons of Mass Destruction

Concern about the spread of WMD has been heightened by the spread of means of delivering such weapons to targets over long ranges. Both aircraft and missiles can be used for long-range delivery of WMD. However, although suitable aircraft are widely available, the main concern has focused on ballistic missiles, which are initially powered by rocket motors but then fall in an arc onto their target (Welch 1989; Fetter 1991: 9–12; Harvey 1992; Karp 1996). Ballistic missiles are widely perceived to be the most effective delivery system for WMD because they are much faster and much harder to shoot down than aircraft. However, aircraft and cruise missiles are much more effective when it is necessary to release the agents over a wide area, as in the case of BTWs (*Strategic Survey 1996–97* 1997: 18). For shorter range delivery of WMD, artillery shells are sufficiently accurate and much cheaper than ballistic missiles. Cruise missiles (jet-powered pilotless aircraft that fly horizontally at a low altitude and guide themselves by reference to the contours of the terrain they fly over) are roughly similar to aircraft in terms of speed and vulnerability to being shot down (cruise missiles being generally slightly slower but more able to penetrate air defenses due to their small radar cross-section). They have the added advantages of being extremely accurate and not having to put human pilots at risk. They are a very expensive means of delivering weapons: cruise missiles are destroyed in the attack, whereas aircraft are reusable. However, for heavily defended high-value targets against which only stealthy aircraft (that is, those with a very small radar cross-section) have any chance of success, they are more cost-effective. Proliferation of long-range cruise missiles has lagged far behind the proliferation of ballistic missiles and advanced aircraft because, for nearly all states, the combination of the two covers most eventualities while avoiding the great expense and high-technology challenges of long-range cruise missiles.

Piloted aircraft are sold with few restrictions, and many of them are capable of performing as delivery vehicles for WMD. Intense competition among the quite small group of major suppliers (the United States, Russia, France, Britain) has created a buyer's market. The sale of ballistic missiles is far from unknown, but much more restrictive, and only very seldom of long-range models. The Soviet Union sold versions of its short-range Scud quite widely, and there is evidence that China is eager to sell (including the transfer of several medium-range missiles to Saudi Arabia). A number of LICs, including Iraq and North Korea, have adapted the Scud technology to produce homegrown variants. Several others have attempted, with varying degrees of success, to develop their own ballistic missiles, most notably India, Taiwan, and South Korea. Those countries wealthy enough to support a space program, such as Japan, can use it to dress up missile development in civilian clothes.

Where Are We Now?

Nuclear Weapons

The end of the Cold War brought about the START agreements for a partial reversal of vertical nuclear proliferation. Under the START I treaty of July 1991, the Accord of January 1992, and the START II treaty of January 1993, the United States and the Soviet Union (and then Russia) agreed to cut their strategic warhead totals to around 3,500 each on bombers, submarines, and ICBMs from their totals in 1992 of around 8,000 for the United States and 10,000 for Russia (technically the Commonwealth of Independent States). START III is in the pipeline. U.S. and Russian tactical nuclear weapons (TNWs) are being scrapped or mothballed.

The end of the Cold War also resulted in a dramatic contraction of the world's nuclear weapon infrastructure. As required by START II, Kazakhstan, Ukraine, and Belarus had sent to Russia by December 1996 all the nuclear weapons deployed on their territory. All NATO (except some French) and former Warsaw Pact TNWs, which used to be on aircraft, surface ships, submarines, and surface missiles, are being scrapped. Between 1945 and 1990, there were 1,570 nuclear weapon test explosions, 80 percent of them by the United States or Soviet Union (IPPNW 1991). On 24 September 1996 a Comprehensive Test Ban Treaty (CTBT) was signed, so that nuclear weapons in the future will be tested through computer simulations only (Arnett 1996a). However, the vast amounts of weapons-grade uranium and plutonium in the former Soviet Union—enough to make around 100,000 nuclear weapons—is not fully under control: some is already being put on the black market by criminal groups (Arbatov 1995; de Andreis and de Calogero 1995; *Strategic Survey 1994–95* 1995: 17, 25–28).

China is continuing the qualitative improvement of a small (but possibly still expanding) nuclear force and is trying to purchase much of the necessary technology abroad (Lewis and Di 1992; van Creveld 1993: chapter 3; Gill and Taeho 1995; Johnston 1995–1996). Britain increased its SLBM warhead delivery capability through its upgrade from Polaris to Trident, but has decided not to deploy the full number of warheads its Trident SLBMs can carry (Croft 1994). Although it has scrapped its TNWs, some of the Trident SLBMs are deployed with single warheads for what it calls "substrategic" roles. France is similarly upgrading its strategic nuclear arsenal while drastically reducing its TNW capability (Ullman 1989; Karp 1991: chapter 6). France continues to deploy some tactical (it calls them "prestrategic") nuclear weapons on land-based and naval aircraft (as well as keeping some mothballed army tactical nuclear missiles). The resistance of all three to a CTBT crumbled through 1995 and 1996.

India, Pakistan, Israel, and South Africa (until the last days of apartheid in 1991) have all adopted opaque nuclear weapon policies. Israel is commonly assumed to have stockpiled around 200 nuclear weapons without admitting to their existence (Evron 1991). Of all the opaque proliferators it has been the most vigorous, and even assisted further proliferation in South Africa. Yet it has come under the least political pressure from the West due to U.S.-Israeli ties. India's nuclear weapon tests in 1998 appeared to be part of a nationalist bid for formal recognition as an (old-fashioned) great power. In addition to trying to acquire symbolic great power status, India bases its nuclear capability on strategic concerns in its relations with Pakistan and China. In the past India used the same tactic as North Korea in stoking U.S. proliferation fears in order to secure U.S. diplomatic and economic concessions as a reward for nuclear restraint. Hence India has developed, but not produced in large numbers or deployed, the short range Prithvi mobile missile and the intermediate-range nuclear-capable Agni missile. However, the fact that it has developed and displayed publicly these missiles ensures that the Indian government protects itself against charges by domestic opponents that it is weak in the face of U.S. pressure (*Strategic Survey 1994–95* 1995: 196). The Indian government has strong support from social and political elites for its nuclear policy (Cortright and Mattoo 1996). Until its nuclear tests in 1998, Pakistan did not admit officially to having nuclear weapons, although former government scientists insisted that it did (Kapur 1987; Albright 1987; Reiss 1995). These official denials were made at least partly to try to avoid being cut off from U.S. aid under the terms of the Pressler Amendment, in which Congress requires the U.S. president to certify annually that Pakistan does not have any nuclear weapons and that U.S. aid helps prevent or discourage Pakistan from acquiring them. Because President Clinton could not make this certification in 1995 and 1988 some aid was suspended. The denuclearization of South Africa is noteworthy (Spector 1992; Howlett and Simpson 1993). It had acquired its nuclear capability to a great extent through secret cooperation with Israel as part of its highly militarized strategy for the survival of white dominance. However, as this dominance crumbled, the regime decided that it did not want to leave the new, black majority with a nuclear capability, dismantled its nuclear weapons, and opened itself to inspection by the IAEA.

Among LICs, notable examples of states close to, or firmly in pursuit of, threshold or even formal nuclear weapon status are Iraq and Iran (and, in the past, North Korea, Brazil, and Argentina) (Bailey 1992; Solingen 1994; Reiss 1995). Although Libya appears to want nuclear weapons, it seems to have made very little progress toward building any, and there are occasional rumors that it has tried to buy former Soviet nuclear weapons on the black market. Iraq was well on the way to acquiring nuclear weapons until its invasion of Kuwait in August 1990 resulted in a war and a postwar UN inspection and control regime to try to eliminate its WMD programs (Dallmeyer 1995). In spite of this great setback, Iraq appears to be trying to maintain secretly as much of its WMD development capability as possible. Iran denies that it wishes to produce nuclear weapons. It is a signatory of the NPT and, as such, has the right of access to civil nuclear technology. Russia agreed in early 1995 to sell Iran at least two light-water nuclear reactors. Because Iran is an oil-rich country, many assume that it wants the reactors to develop nuclear weapons, not to produce electricity. The United States opposed the sale of Russian reactors to Iran because, it was argued, they would enhance Iran's nuclear weapon program—whereas the reactors the United States proposed to give North Korea would hinder its ability to produce nuclear weapons (Chubin 1995).

In contrast, since the early 1980s, both Argentina and Brazil have taken significant steps away from, rather than toward, threshold nuclear status in a number of diplomatic and technical agreements. As with South Africa, the domestic move toward more democratic forms of government has reversed the priority previously given to developing nuclear options. The two former rivals have now set up an open regime of nuclear cooperation between themselves and largely abandoned their resistance to integration into the nonproliferation regime (Redick 1988, 1990; Karp 1990; Reiss 1995).

North Korea may or may not have succeeded in reaching threshold nuclear status (Bracken 1993; Mazarr 1995a). Like Iraq, it seemed to be using membership in the NPT to disguise a weapons program, and on the basis of the available evidence could easily have come close to doing so. Unlike Iraq, North Korea was caught by the IAEA safeguards system that duly set off international alarm bells. Because of the collapse of its Cold War alliances the country's economic and political position is fairly desperate. Its nuclear objectives could range from desire to construct an equalizer against the rising economic and military power of South Korea to an attempt to create a bargaining counter to use in return for much needed economic aid and diplomatic recognition. Negotiations between North Korea and the United States produced an agreement in 1995, in which, if carried through, North Korea will dramatically reduce its capability to produce nuclear weapons in return for free oil and food, free nuclear reactors (albeit more proliferation-resistant ones), security assurances, and a lowering of trade and investment barriers (*Strategic Survey 1994–95* 1995: 13–14, 46–47, 180–183). Many observers have noted the contrast in U.S. treatment of Iranian nuclear ambitions (a hard line of sanctions and threats) and North Korean ones (appeasement). The message for determined would-be proliferators seems to be that the road to the threshold may be rough, but when you get there the payoff is substantial. Along the way, others will rarely be willing to attempt military intervention to destroy your program, notable exceptions being Israel's attack on Iraq's nuclear facilities in 1981 and the U.S.-led UN attack on Iraq's rebuilt and expanded WMD facilities ten years later.

The list of threshold nuclear states usually concentrates only on these supposedly more threatening LICs. However, virtually all of the advanced industrialized states—for example, Canada, Sweden, Switzerland, Taiwan, and South Korea—are in a technical position to produce nuclear weapons at short notice should their political circumstances and threat perceptions change. In fact, Sweden had a covert, extensive, and successful program between 1946 and 1972 to enable it to deploy nuclear weapons very quickly (Cole 1997). This is partly an accidental by-product of the existence of their nuclear power industries and partly a product of deliberate policy to quietly, sometimes secretly, acquire the kind of capabilities that would make weaponization easier. In 1994 Japan officially indicated that North Korea, with its potential nuclear capability and missiles capable of hitting Japanese territory, was the primary threat to its security. Japan also admitted that it itself was capable of producing nuclear weapons, although it issued assurances that there was no intention of doing so (*Strategic Survey 1994–95* 1995: 172–173). This suggests a somewhat different approach to threshold status, Deudney's "recessed deterrence," which is a form of weaponless deterrence. A state pursuing recessed deterrence may, like Japan, genuinely not want to acquire nuclear weapons, and will indicate this publicly in its treaty commitments and public statements. However, such a state conspicuously acquires all the civilian technology necessary for quick conversion to nuclear capability: a space program capable of launching satellites into orbit (thus accurate ballistic missiles, preferably, like Japan's, propelled by solid fuel) and a civil nuclear power industry covering the whole fuel cycle (thus capable of either separating plutonium or enriching uranium). For recessed deterrence no attempt to actually build nuclear weapons is necessary. The implied statement of this posture is: "Don't push me around. I don't want to have nuclear weapons, and if left alone will not acquire them. But if I am threatened, I can very quickly change policy and become a formidable nuclear weapon power." Japan is the clearest example of recessed deterrence, but elements of this policy can also be found in Germany, Brazil, India, South Korea, and Taiwan. If Sweden quietly let its potential adversaries know of its weaponization potential, then it too was pursuing recessed deterrence. However, it is possible that it kept its capabilities secret from them as well as from the public.

Chemical Weapons and Biological and Toxin Weapons

BTW proliferation is much less widespread than CW proliferation, in spite of the fact that all of the basic technologies for BTW agents are of dual use and easy to acquire. The reason for the preference for CW over BTW is that CW agents are easier to store and act much more quickly on their victims. As with nuclear weapons, there are a number of possible levels of CW and BTW capabilities, including production, weaponization, and stockpiling. Since World War II, the United States, the Soviet Union/Russia, Britain, France, China, Iraq, Syria, North Korea, and Taiwan have all conducted research into BTWs. The United States and Britain have insisted that their research was solely into developing countermeasures to attacks with BTWs. The U.S. government has claimed that the Soviet Union/Russia and Iraq appear to have led the way with a full range of BTW capabilities, but this has not been confirmed in the Iraqi case (Tucker 1993: 231). In spite of the requirement in UN resolutions for Iraq to dismantle its WMD capabilities in the wake of its military defeat in Kuwait, the UN Special Commission in charge of monitoring this process concluded in April 1995 that Iraq was concealing 250 tons of CW "precursors" (that is, the materials used to produce chemical weapons) for the nerve gas VX, and, earlier in the year, also indicated its belief that Iraq was also hiding 17 tons of "growth media" that could be used to produce biological weapons (Reuters 1990).

Both NATO and Warsaw Pact members developed enormous CW stockpiles and deployed substantial capabilities to counter CW attacks on military formations and to operate in a CW environment if they used CWs themselves. These stockpiles of warheads, bombs, and artillery shells are being reduced greatly as a response to the end of the Cold War, but some of these weapons will be retained, as will the CW countermeasures. The CW countermeasures helped increase the confidence of the U.S.-led coalition when it decided to use force to expel CW-armed Iraq from Kuwait in 1990–1991. States that may be trying to develop CWs are Argentina, Cuba, Indonesia, Saudi Arabia, South Africa (until the end of apartheid), and Thailand. States that may be trying to develop BTWs are Burma, Egypt, Iran, Syria, Israel, Libya, Ethiopia, India, Pakistan, Vietnam, North Korea, South Korea, and Taiwan. Nonstate groups willing to use terrorist tactics are dotted all over the world: they may try to use CWs or BTWs to achieve their goals. For example, the Aum Shinrikyo sect produced Sarin gas, and used it in attacks on Tokyo's subway system (Associated Press 1995a). This is the first recorded use of chemical weapons by a nonstate terrorist group.

Delivery Systems for Weapons of Mass Destruction

WMD—mostly nuclear weapons—have been deployed on such intercontinental or medium-range delivery systems as ballistic missiles based on land or submarines (ICBMs, MRBMs, and SLBMs); cruise missiles based on land, aircraft, surface ships, or submarines (GLCMs, ALCMs, and SLCMs); or aircraft with more old-fashioned nuclear bombs or stand-off missiles. The rest were similar delivery systems with shorter range or were deployed as artillery shells, depth charges, or land mines. Ballistic missiles have spread far beyond NATO and the former Warsaw Pact countries, and are becoming a standard element in the arsenals of many countries. Newly industrialized countries (NICs) and LICs with ballistic missiles with ranges over 200 kilometers at the planning, development, or deployment stages include Argentina, Brazil, Saudi Arabia, Egypt, Iran, Iraq, Israel, Libya, Yemen, India, Pakistan, Afghanistan, Indonesia, South Korea, North Korea, and Taiwan (with Algeria, Cuba, and Kuwait possessing shorter range ballistic missiles) (Fetter 1991; Harvey 1992; Potter and Jencks 1994; Scheffran 1995; Karp 1996). It is noteworthy that nearly all of these missiles have restricted range, which indicates that they have been acquired for intraregional and battlefield purposes or as the basis for developing longer range systems. Only China has acquired ballistic missiles of intercontinental range. This reflects its past experience of nuclear threats made against it by the United States and Soviet Union and its perception of itself as (and its desire to be and to be seen to be) a great power.

The only two states to invest extensively in long-range cruise missiles were the Soviet Union and the United States, with the latter being much the most enthusiastic, not least because of its anxiety to avoid casualties. The United States used many conventionally armed medium-range cruise missiles against such high-value Iraqi targets as command centers and air defense systems in 1990–1991, as well as in Bosnia in 1995, also against air defense systems. In the future, long-range or medium-range cruise missiles may become more popular as a means of circumventing antiballistic missile (ABM) systems by flying under their radar cover, although ABM systems may be modified to deal with this as part of the continuing battle between offensive and defensive force postures. As it is, short-range antiship cruise missiles (ASCMs) and/or land-attack cruise missiles (LACMs) have been bought or built by many states, including the United States, Britain, France, Russia, Yugoslavia, China, Taiwan, North Korea, India, Iran, Iraq, Syria, Libya, Israel, and South Africa (Carus 1993; *Strategic Survey 1996–97* 1997: 23–25). The dual-use nature of many of the technologies involved in cruise missiles has plenty of potential for extending their range, payload, survivability, accuracy, and reliability quickly and relatively secretly.

Conclusion: Much Proliferation and Many Remaining Antiproliferation Challenges

WMD can be traced back to premodern siege warfare and attempts to introduce disease into the encircled city. Their industrial age form was invented during World War I with the widespread use of CWs. Such weapons were subsequently held by a small number of great powers, but hardly used during World War II (except in Nazi extermination camps). It is since World War II, and especially with the addition of nuclear weapons, that proliferation of WMD and related delivery systems has taken off. This takeoff was mostly due to the Cold War. The NATO–Warsaw Pact buildup was truly staggering in scale. It brought China into the game, though largely took Japan and Germany out of it. Disposing of what are now perceived as the redundant elements of this arsenal will take decades and many billions of dollars, and even at the end of this process the capabilities for mass destruction that NATO, Russia, and China plan to retain will still be enormous. The Cold War also helped to pump WMD into selected LICs.

Proliferation of WMD has also been driven by the tripling of the number of states as a result of decolonization and by the subsequent spread of industrialization. The close linkages between civil and military technology explored above mean that as states industrialize they automatically acquire capabilities that can easily be turned to military applications. This spin-on possibility exists partly whether wanted or not, although spin-on potential can also be enhanced deliberately. In some cases (e.g., Canada's nuclear industry) the country clearly has no interest in military spin-ons. In others (notably Iraq, Argentina, Pakistan, Israel), much of the process of industrialization is or has been distorted for the purpose of generating military spin-ons. The common foundations of civil and military technology make such linkages unavoidable. They mean that proliferation occurs at two levels: explicitly (where the weapons are sought directly) and implicitly (by the spread of the capability to make them). Where states are willing, explicit proliferation can become a subject of control. But implicit proliferation cannot be controlled without restricting the spread of industrialization itself.

Across the world, a substantial minority of states is still working to acquire WMD and delivery system capabilities. Most commonly sought are ballistic missiles and CWs, with less (but still very significant) attention paid to acquiring nuclear weapons and BTWs. There are many cases where aspirations to acquire WMD and delivery capabilities have not yet been fulfilled, and thus where nonproliferation measures will be contested. Although some control measures will be possible, and some countries may change their minds (as Argentina, Brazil, South Africa, and possibly North Korea, have done), we may be faced with a situation of continual adjustment to a world in which an increasing number of actors either possesses, or has the option to possess, WMD. Nevertheless, there are some striking and positive points to note. First, possession of WMD is not seen by most states as vital to their security. Second, no non-WMD state has come under WMD attack since 1945, nor have non-WMD states been intimidated into bowing to the political wishes of states that do possess WMD (Herring 1995: especially 236–242). The worst-case scenarios of the nuclear proliferation pessimists have not been borne out, mainly because their model of nuclear security—in which failure to deploy a large, invulnerable retaliatory force invites attack or results in a dangerous "use it or lose it" policy—sees nuclear security as much more fragile than it is or, at least, has been (see Karl 1996–1997).

Antiproliferation measures that focus solely on technology can slow proliferation of WMD but cannot prevent it. However, the extent to which states pursue WMD options or convert those options into weapons is subject to negotiation, preventive action, and even reversal. Explanations for the spread of military technology—conventional as well as for WMD—and the purposes for which such military technology is sought must be understood. In other words, thinking about the proliferation of WMD must address two crucial issues: the spread of technology and the motives of decisionmakers. Those motives can be organized under the same headings as those for conventional weapons, namely domestic political motives, military security motives (capabilities to use force and threats), and symbolic motives (in terms of status and identity politics), all of which are considered in Parts 2 and 3 (see also Sagan 1996–1997). Clearly, different motives will require different antiproliferation measures, and mixed motives will complicate any antiproliferation efforts.

PART 2

EXPLAINING
THE ARMS DYNAMIC

5

ARMS RACING AND THE ARMS DYNAMIC

Controversies About the Term "Arms Racing"

Perhaps the most commonly asserted impact of military technology on world politics is "arms racing." Although arms racing is a widely used concept, opinion about it is highly divided. Some scholars advocate avoiding it as far as possible (Bellany 1975: 129; Gray 1996). The ambiguity of the term makes it applicable, at a stretch, to the whole process by which states maintain military capability, and its negative connotations therefore make it polemically useful as a broad brush with which to denigrate military policy. But the key debate is whether or not arms racing is an independent phenomenon with distinctive and significant consequences.

At the other extreme is a large body of work, both academic and lay, that sees arms racing not only as a major problem of world politics, but also as a fundamental dilemma of the whole attempt to seek security through military means (Noel-Baker 1958; Myrdal 1976; Thompson and Smith 1980; Prins 1984). Many, though not all, who take this view would identify themselves with the field of peace studies or with pacifism and peace movements. Scholars in this category often thought that the last two world wars were preceded by arms races and feared that what they regarded as the arms race between the superpowers would lead to World War III. Arms racing is from this perspective the key to the security dilemma, a dangerous phenomenon in which the effects of individual state policies for military security or military advantage are self-defeating. They argue that arms racing is not only a phenomenon in need of study, and a problem in need of remedy, but also a basis for taking a critical view of the whole strategic approach to world politics.

In between these two extremes, and to some extent blending into them, lies the strategic studies literature on arms racing. Part of this literature takes the form of attempts to construct mathematical models of arms racing (Richardson 1960; Saaty 1968; Busch 1970) or game theoretic models (Brams 1985). Another part consists of broad discussions of the phenomenon, which attempt to explain the mechanisms, motives, and definitions that underlie the concept (Huntington 1958; Gray 1971a, 1974, 1976; Gleditsch and Njøstad 1990; Hammond 1993). Some argue that arms racing much of the time is a cause of peace and stability (Hammond 1993: 263). This is an important point: it challenges a basic assumption in most of the peace studies (and much of the strategic studies) literature, which explicitly or implicitly assumes that arms races will normally end in war. One variant of this is the debate over whether the U.S.-Soviet "arms race" drained the Soviet economy, brought about Soviet efforts to get out of the arms race, and indirectly induced the end of Soviet control of Eastern Europe and the collapse of the Soviet Union itself. Whether or not one accepts this particular assessment, arms racing is seen by some not always as a fearsome trap to be avoided, but often as a useful strategic option both for states seeking to overturn the status quo in the international system and also for those seeking to reinforce it. Much of the literature focuses on what most analysts categorized as the arms race between the United States and the Soviet Union (Wohlstetter 1974a, 1974b; Nacht 1975; Thee 1986; Evangelista 1988). Some of the literature considers prenuclear age cases or a mix of prenuclear age and nuclear age cases (Wright 1942; Blainey 1973; Hammond 1993) and regional ones, especially the Middle East in the 1960s and 1970s (Rattinger 1976) and South Asia in the 1980s and 1990s (R. Thomas, 1993; Oren 1994; Arnett 1997).

In the 1990s, as the Cold War faded away, the main interest in arms racing shifted to East Asia, where superpower disengagement, the rise of China, booming local economies, and a wealth of local disputes provided fertile ground for arms acquisitions and modernizations (Ball 1993–1994; Gong and Segal 1993; Klare 1993; Gill 1994; Dibb 1995). Although some have perceived the existence of arms races in East Asia (Segal 1992; Klare 1993), what has been going on there so far does not yet warrant the label. There was a downward trend in the import and licensed production of major conventional weapons in the region between 1984 and 1993, and especially since 1988, although it has leveled out since. Between 1986 and 1994, military spending in East Asia generally remained static or declined as a share of GNP, although in most cases GNP was increasing sharply, so that overall military spending was increasing steadily but slowly in absolute terms. In one key case, namely China, there are no reliable data on military spending, but it appears to fit the pattern. The growth in military spending in East Asia between 1985 and 1995 in real terms has been over one-third, and in 1996 the expenditure continued to increase, but less quickly (Ball 1993–1994; Gill 1994; George et al. 1996: 325, 367; *Military Balance 1996–97* 1996: 174). The situation in East Asia bears some similarities to the U.S.-Soviet arms relationship during the Cold War, which some analysts (with whom we concur) regarded as insufficiently intense to categorize all or most of as an arms race (Wohlstetter 1974a, 1974b; Buzan 1987a: 114–121; Hammond 1993).

In the literature, the concept of arms racing ties into many of the main debates within strategic studies and peace studies. Arms racing connects to war through the widespread, though strongly challenged, hypothesis that arms races make war more likely (Lambelet 1975; Wallace 1982; Diehl 1983; Gray 1993a; Hammond 1993). It connects to deterrence because some argue that the maintenance of a deterrence relationship requires a form of institutionalized arms race to ensure that the appropriate military means (that is, military means that stabilize deterrence rather than create incentives to go to war) are available (Hoag 1962; Kugler, Organski, and Fox 1980; Mandelbaum 1981: chapter 5; Thee 1986: chapter 4). Much of the discussion about disarmament is based on a problem defined in terms of arms racing, and arms racing plays a major role as the referent problem for thinking about both arms control and nonprovocative forms of defense (Allison and Morris 1975; Galtung 1984a; Møller 1992; Møller and Wiberg 1994). Like the arms trade, arms racing links to subjects outside strategic studies (although those subjects are often included in peace studies), such as economic development. Inasmuch as arms racing is about the political, and not just the military, relations between states, it also has important lines of contact with work in the broader field of international relations (Waltz 1979: chapter 8).

One of the striking things about the literature on the topic is that much of the subject matter does not fit comfortably within the metaphor of a race (Wohlstetter 1974a, 1974b; Buzan 1991a: 313–319; Hammond 1993, 7; Gray 1996: 323). The idea of a race suggests two or more states strenuously engaged in a competition to accumulate military strength against each other. It also suggests that winning is the object of the exercise in terms of one party achieving a decisive change in the balance of military power. Much of the literature, however, is about the general process by which states create armed forces and keep their equipment up to date (Buzan 1991a: 313–319). These two subjects are clearly related, but they are not the same. If the meaning of arms racing is broadened to include all peacetime military relations, then it loses its ability to label abnormally intense military competition. The temptation to use the broadest meaning is strong for the polemical reasons suggested above. The broad meaning also avoids the difficult analytical problem of distinguishing between normal relations and abnormal ones. The one sound reason for adopting the broader meaning is that it draws attention to armaments as an independent global phenomenon, a perspective the validity of which was explored in Part 1.

In other words, if we assume as normal an international system in which independent states possess armed forces with which to pursue political goals, then we can also say that armaments will have their own pattern of development within that system. That pattern has distinctive effects on relations between states: it interacts with, but can be separated for analytical purposes from, the other elements that shape world politics. The metaphor of arms racing tends to be used to imply a notably intense process that contrasts with whatever passes for normality in military relations between states not at war with each other. If the term is confined to the narrower meaning, then we need both another term to identify normal military relations among states and definitional criteria to clarify the boundary between normal relations and arms racing.

There have been many attempts to define arms racing (for example, Huntington 1958: 41; Bull 1961: 5) One of the most subtle and well-thought-through attempts was that of Colin Gray (although he now rejects the concept altogether). He defined it as involving "two or more parties perceiving themselves to be in an adversary relationship, who are increasing or improving their armaments at a rapid rate and structuring their respective military postures with a general attention to the past, current, and anticipated military and political behaviour of the other parties" (1971a: 40). This definition, consonant with the general tone of the literature, suggests that arms racing is an abnormally intense condition in relations between states reflecting either or both active political rivalry and mutual fear of the other's military potential. The problem with the concept is how to distinguish this abnormal condition from normal behavior. Grant Hammond (1993: 31) tries to deal with this problem by offering a set of eight criteria for the existence of an arms race:

1. Two or more participants, though the relationship is in essence a bilateral one.
2. Specific designation of an adversary or potential adversary.
3. Military and diplomatic planning based directly on the capabilities and intent of the other.
4. A high degree of public animosity or antagonism between the parties involved.
5. Political-military linkage of state actions between or among the rival force structures and strategies.
6. An extraordinary and consistent increase in the level of defense effort in excess of 8 percent per annum.
7. The focus on a particular weapons environment or weapons system vis-à-vis the opponent with an explicit ratio goal.
8. The purpose of the effort: seeking dominance via intimidation over the rival in political-military affairs.

If defined restrictively in this way, arms races are rare: Hammond identifies only four (Japan versus Russia, 1895–1904; Germany versus United Kingdom, 1902–1912; France versus Germany, 1911–1914; Japan versus

United States versus United Kingdom, 1916–1922), but also claims to find three "military competitions" (France versus Germany, 1874–1894; United Kingdom versus France and Russia, 1884–1904; United Kingdom versus United States, 1922–1930), one "rearmament race" (United Kingdom and United States versus Germany and Japan, 1938–1939/41), one nonmilitary (and thus anomalous) space race (United States versus Soviet Union, 1957–1969), and ten short-lived, one-sided "panics." We concur with Gray's (1996: 325–328; see also 1995: 178) critique of Hammond's arms race criteria: though 1 and 2 are fine, 3, 4, and 5 are hard to measure and therefore difficult to operationalize; 6 is arbitrary (why 8 percent?); 7 is unnecessary because it occurs too commonly; and 8 is unnecessarily narrow because an arms race could also be pursued for the purpose of deterrence, improving one's ability to fight a war should one occur, or avoiding the attempt of another to achieve dominance.

These problems are compounded by the point that there is no good evidence that arms races cause war or make it more likely, in spite of all the research that has sought to establish those links. Gray (1996) takes the view that arms races are nonexistent phenomena, which, even if defined into existence artificially, have no significant consequences: hence he argues for the abandonment of the concept of arms racing completely. We think that this goes too far, not because we wish to cling to a dead concept, but because we wish to use it as part of a continuum of what we refer to as the "arms dynamic" (as opposed to a dichotomy of arms racing and non-arms racing). There would be something strange about not having a vocabulary that allows you to talk in terms of the varying pace of the arms dynamic.

The Arms Dynamic:
A Comprehensive Framework for Analysis

To capture the full range of what needs to be discussed here, some new terms need to be adopted and used systematically. There is an especially strong need to find a term for the normal condition of military relations, because it is the absence of such a term that has facilitated the overextended use of "arms racing." If we find a term for the normal condition of military relations, then we also need one to describe the whole phenomenon, including both normal behavior and arms racing. We use the term "arms dynamic," which has some currency in the literature (Thee 1986: chapter 5), to refer to the entire set of pressures that make actors (usually states) both acquire armed forces and change the quantity and quality of the armed forces they already possess. The term is used not only to refer to a general global process, but also to enquire into the circumstances of particular states or sets of states. One can ask about the arms dynamic between India and Pakistan, or one can ask how the arms dynamic affects a single state like Sweden.

The term arms racing is reserved for the most extreme manifestations of the arms dynamic, when actors are going flat out or almost flat out in major competitive investments in military capability. We accept that there is no good evidence that a shift into arms racing from a less intense version of the arms dynamic suddenly makes war more likely. However, arms racing is still a significant phenomenon because it is an expression of intensified political rivalry and because arms racing consumes more resources than less intense manifestations of the arms dynamic. Indeed, arms racing is more likely to occur when states are engaged in full mobilization for total war, and such mobilization is more likely during war, or when the expectation of war is already high, rather than during peace.

In contrast to arms racing, we use the term "maintenance of the military status quo" (or simply "maintenance") to express the normal operation of the arms dynamic. Maintenance and racing can be used to describe either the activity of a single state, the character of an overall relationship between two or more states, or the character of the relationship between two or more states with regard to a particular weapon system. Maintenance can escalate into racing, and racing can subside into maintenance.

Between the two lies a gray area in which the direction of change may be a more appropriate guide to events than any attempt to locate a given case on one side or the other of some strict but arbitrary dividing line. The U.S.-Soviet so-called arms race was something rather less than an arms race, but something rather more than the maintenance of the military status quo. This type of arms dynamic we term "arms competition" (as does Hammond, but in rather different fashion). Relations between virtually all potential adversary states fall into the gray area between maintenance and racing. Military competition accommodates the way potential adversaries (e.g., India–Pakistan, China–Taiwan) chip away at the status quo and constantly seek to improve their position, although having no confidence in gaining a decisive advantage. The outcome might be the maintenance of the military status quo, but that is not the intention of the participants— this is the familiar point that balances of power tend to form as the unintended consequence of advantage seeking. One state can be trying to get ahead of the other to gain an advantage before the other state joins, or that one state can hold an advantage and the other is trying to narrow the gap. Two famous cases of the latter, based on false perceptions, were the bomber gap and missile gap scares in the United States in the mid-1950s, and late 1950s until 1961, respectively. In both cases, the United States believed the Soviet Union had large advantages in these weapons, rushed to catch up, and then discovered that the Soviet advantages had been illusory (Kaplan 1984: chapter 10; Prados 1986: chapters 4–8). These were not proper arms races in that they were one-sided efforts and were not sufficiently intense. A near-synonym for arms competition is *buildup*. The United States responded to its missile and bomber gap perceptions with buildups. Sometimes a state may conduct a buildup without having a target and without attracting a response. An example is the buildup of the U.S. Navy during the late nineteenth century (Huntington 1958: 41–42). This unusual kind of arms buildup generally requires geographical isolation or a very low starting point. Some see the mid-1990s situation in East Asia in this light. However, if sustained, arms buildups may turn into competitions.

To complete the spectrum of the arms dynamic, we need one more concept, namely, *build-down*: as specific weapon systems are dismantled, they are replaced by a new capability that is perhaps smaller in numbers, more limited in capability, or regarded as less destabilizing. This is illustrated by Gorbachev's program of unilateral deep cuts followed by one-sided mutual reductions. These were not maintenance of the military status quo, but something less than it: the Soviet Union conceded ground on the military status quo in the belief that it would result in more mutual security. Whether or not one sees this as arms control or partial disarmament, it was part of the arms dynamic.

What Explains the Arms Dynamic? Two Models

Because build-down, maintenance, competition/buildup, and arms racing are manifestations of the same overall arms dynamic, they share many characteristics. On the basis of these concepts, what is needed to clarify the subject is not just a model of what explains arms racing, but a model of what explains the arms dynamic as a whole. Such a model would have the advantage of retaining the distinctive meaning of arms racing, while at the same time opening up the vital issue of armaments as an independent global phenomenon. It would also avoid much of the vagueness and the polemical entanglements of too broad a usage of arms racing.

The debates over what explains the arms dynamic have generally been mixed in with debates over what the arms dynamic explains. It makes sense to look at both questions, because, in choosing to study explanations of the arms dynamic, one is presuming that the arms dynamic is a significant phenomenon, that is, one with important consequences, in terms of the consumption of resources, the degree of political rivalry it marks, and the particular type or intensity of war should it occur. Most of the attempts to understand arms racing have been made in terms of models of the processes that induce states to increase their military strength, but these models can be applied to the arms dynamic as a whole. Two models dominate the literature. The first is the classical action–reaction model, which looks for the driving force of the arms dynamic in the competitive relations between states. The second can be called the domestic structure model. This seeks to locate the driving force of the arms dynamic in the internal economic, organizational, and political workings of states. It is useful to see both in the context of the technological imperative, that is, the general process of qualitative advance in technology explored in Part 1. The term "technological imperative" has been used by others, but usually in a narrower sense, more in line with what will be counted here as domestic structure (Thee 1986: 16–20).

The action–reaction and domestic structure models are complementary rather than mutually exclusive, though the process of establishing the domestic structure model in the face of action–reaction orthodoxy produced some attacks and defenses that came close to casting the two in a mutually exclusive light (Allison and Morris 1975; Nincic 1982: chapters 2–3). These models are the subject of the next two chapters. They represent a step toward explanatory theories about the arms dynamic. The historical evidence does not suggest that either of them is more correct than the other or that they can be arranged in a permanent hierarchy of explanatory power. The relevant debate is about the weight that each should be given in explaining any specific case or type of case.

6

THE ACTION–REACTION MODEL

The action–reaction model is the classical view of arms racing and provides the basis for the metaphor of a race. Most attempts to define arms racing are rooted in it. The basic proposition of the action–reaction model is that states strengthen their armaments because of the threats the states perceive from other states. The theory implicit in the model explains the arms dynamic as driven primarily by factors external to the state. An action by any potentially hostile state to increase its military strength will raise the level of threat seen by other states and cause them to react by increasing their own strength (Rathjens 1973). In theory this process also works in reverse. If states are driven to arm by external threats, then domestic economic pressures to apply resources to other items on the political agenda should lead them to build down in proportion to reductions in military capability by others. Whether action–reaction works with equal facility in both directions has important implications for disarmament.

The action–reaction model posits something like an international market in military strength. States will arm themselves either to seek security against the threats posed by others or increase their power to achieve political objectives against the interests of others. Military power can be used to achieve objectives through use of force, implicit or explicit threats, or symbolism (see Part 3). Balances (including balances in political status as well as balances of military power) will emerge at higher or lower levels of armament, depending on how willing states are to drive up the price of achieving their objectives. Counterpressure to open-ended arms competition is created both by the responses of other states to attempts by one to increase its military power and by domestic resource constraints.

The definitive illustration for the action–reaction model is the much studied naval arms race between Britain and Germany before World War I (Woodward [1935] 1964; Marder 1961: especially chapters 6–7; Steinberg 1965; Steiner 1973; Berghahn 1973; Herwig 1980; Kennedy 1980; Hammond 1993; Stevenson 1996). In this case, Germany, starting from a very low base (a small coastal navy), decided to build a major blue-water fleet. Britain reacted to preserve its position as the leading naval power. Britain was able to contain the challenge by outbuilding the German naval program, first in terms of quality by introducing a more powerful type of battleship known as the dreadnought, and later in terms of the quantity of dreadnoughts constructed. For nearly a decade before the outbreak of war this case produced clear instances of the action–reaction dynamic. Germany copied British design innovations, and Britain's annual naval construction program was linked to the rate of warship building in Germany. As with any case, the process was not entirely one of action–reaction: domestic structural factors, such as the election of a Liberal government in Britain that sought to increase social expenditure, resulted in fewer ships being laid down between 1906 and 1908 while Germany laid down more ships in the same period (Hammond 1993: 116). Ironically, although this case is popular because the action–reaction process is particularly clear, its high degree of clarity makes it unrepresentative of the arms dynamic between most states.

The action–reaction model does not depend on the process by which technological innovation causes continual improvement in military technology. However, if such innovation exists it becomes part of the action–reaction process. Even if the quality of military technology was static, and evenly distributed in the international system, the action–reaction process could still be the mechanism by which states compete militarily in purely quantitative terms. Increases in the number of battleships in one state would still create pressure for countering increases in other states. For this reason, the action–reaction model can more easily be applied than the domestic structure model to cases that occurred before the onset of the industrial revolution. Some authors nevertheless take the view that arms racing has only become a distinctive international phenomenon since the industrial revolution unleashed the forces of mass production and institutionalized innovation into the international system (Huntington 1958: 41, 43; Hammond 1993: 11).

When military competition reflects a power struggle between states, as before both world wars; during the Cold War; or between Iran and Iraq, India and Pakistan, or Israel and its Arab neighbors, it can be intense and highly focused—especially when the parties see war as a likely outcome. Even when there is no specific power struggle, or only a weak one, the action–reaction process still works at the lower levels of competition and maintenance of the military status quo. States will usually have some sense of who they consider to be possible sources of attack even when they see the probability of war as being low. This perception will ensure an element of action–reaction in military policy, albeit of a much more subdued kind than in an arms race. For build-down, maintenance, and competition as for racing, action–reaction expresses itself not only in the size of armed forces, but also in the type of forces acquired and the level of concern about modernization and readiness for combat. The action–reaction model therefore applies to the arms dynamic as a whole. One can see it working in specific cases like the British-German naval race, where political rivalry generates a power struggle and an arms race. One can also see it in the way that states arm with the actual and potential capabilities and intentions of other states in mind.

There is considerable blending of power and security motives in the behavior of states. Most military instruments can be used for offensive as well as defensive purposes. It is therefore difficult for any state to distinguish between measures other states take to defend themselves and measures they may be taking to increase their capability for aggression. Because the consequences of being wrong may be very severe, it is a commonplace dictum that prudence requires each state to adjust its own military measures in response to a worst-case view of the measures taken by others. This kind of logic has been visible not just in the Cold War, or earlier in intra-European rivalries, but also in the Middle East, between Israel and the Arabs; in South Asia, between India and Pakistan; and in East Asia, between North and South Korea.

There are problems associated with different aspects of this dictum. First, what is described as worst-case analysis is often something more moderate (worse rather than worst-case analysis) in that the real worst case is dismissed or seen as unlikely. Second, worst-case analysis is often adopted not due to prudence but as a conscious symbolic and ideological exaggeration to ensure support for military expenditure and the use of threats and force. This was the case with the important U.S. National Security Council memorandum NSC-68 of April 1950, which painted the Soviet threat and the need for a U.S. buildup in the starkest of terms. As former Secretary of State Dean Acheson (1969: 374–375) put it, the intention was to make the situation "clearer than truth" in order to "bludgeon the mass mind of 'top government'" into supporting the buildup. It was also the case with apartheid South Africa's perception of a "total onslaught" against its security. Third, worst-case analysis can be as dangerous as, and more wasteful of resources than, a more balanced threat assessment in that it can unnecessarily escalate a rivalry (Garthoff 1978, 1984). Finally, since each adjustment may be seen by some other states as a possible threat, even a system in which all states seek only their own defense can produce competitive accumulations of military strength. The set of circumstances that produces this tendency is known as the "security dilemma" (Herz 1950; Butterfield 1951; Snyder 1984; Jervis 1978, 1985; Snyder 1985; Buzan 1991a: chapter 8; Wheeler and Booth 1992). It is a dilemma because states cannot easily take measures to strengthen their own military security without making others feel less secure. If others feel less secure they may take countermeasures that may negate the measures taken by the first state. That state in turn may feel pressured to restore its preferred ratio of strength by further increases in its own armaments, and so on. The workings of the security dilemma are thus closely related to those of the action–reaction model.

Significant numbers of states in the international system do not meaningfully consider each other to be a military threat at all, do not plan in terms of possible mutual military threat, and share common institutions. This may be the case even though they have been enemies in the (possibly but not necessarily distant) past and actually have the means with which to threaten each other. These states form what is known as a "pluralistic security community" (Deutsch et al. 1957). This is true for relations between the United States and Canada, among the Scandinavian states, and among the members of the European Union. They have escaped from the military security dilemma in their relations with each other. Some states are no threat to each other simply because of their lack of capability: a security community is much more than this. It is an enormous step forward in relations between states, and the existence of this condition is one of a number of reasons to perceive limits to the utility of crude realist assumptions about the effects of anarchy in understanding international relations (Milner 1991; Buzan 1993). A somewhat lesser, but still significant, moderation of the security dilemma occurs when states form "security regimes" in which they seek to manage their disputes and avoid war (Jervis 1982, 1985).

There are vigorous debates in the literature about the reasons for the existence of these security regimes and communities, and the extent to which they are robust. Those who think they are reasonably solid tend to see them as being caused by complex interdependence (Keohane and Nye [1977] 1989) or liberal democracy. The skeptics come from a variety of perspectives. It should be noted that the security dilemma also operates within states—where the actions taken by one group to improve its security backfire due to the counteractions of another group (Posen 1993; Herring 1997a). Even members of security communities can still be faced with security dilemmas of a rather different sort in their relations with each other: they have to balance tying themselves into alliances to avoid being abandoned once they are threatened with keeping the alliance loose so that they are not dragged into wars by their allies (Snyder 1984; Christensen and Snyder 1990).

The idea of the action–reaction model is simple, but its operation in practice is complex. The model says little about motives other than that each side feels threatened by the other. Neither does it indicate whether the two actors are aware of, and are seeking to control, the process in which they are engaged. In practice, the only thing that may be clear is that their behavior is influenced in part by their sense of external threat. The specific details of the action–reaction process may be difficult to identify. This point needs to be considered in detail because the validity of the action–reaction model is widely questioned on the grounds that its supposed process is often difficult to see in practice. First the idiom of action and reaction will be examined: that is to say, the types of action that states can take within the process. Then other variables in the pattern of response will be identified, particularly magnitude, timing, and the awareness of the actors of the process in which they are engaged. Finally, it is necessary to look at the motives of the actors, which can have a considerable influence on the other variables in the action–reaction process. However, this does not mean that intentions with regard to weapons acquisition are necessarily oriented toward competition with other states: they may also be a deliberate part of domestic politics.

The Idioms of Action and Reaction

The idioms of action and reaction are numerous. The simplest is like that of the pre-1914 naval race, where two states compete in terms of a single, similar weapon system, and where the strength of the rivals can be compared directly because the weapons are designed primarily to fight each other. Action and reaction in terms of the same weapon system was also seen between the superpowers in terms of ICBMs. In this case, though, the picture is complicated by the fact that even though some ICBMs are intended to destroy each other, most are intended for bombardment of other targets. The idiom may be in terms of dissimilar weapons systems, or sets of systems, such as antisubmarine, antiaircraft, or antimissile systems versus submarines, bombers, and missiles. In such cases, the calculation of relative strengths is complicated by the large uncertainties that always surround estimates of how different, but opposed, weapons will work in combat. However, this contrast should not be overdrawn. Predicting combat outcomes between similar weapon systems is still very difficult because there are so many additional important variables such as weather, terrain, and communications or the skill, experience, and morale of the operators of those weapon systems (and the commanders of those operators). These differences have often been displayed in the wars between Israel and its neighbors. The action–reaction process may not be single weapon systems, but instead be in terms of the overall arsenals of states, with each trying to measure its relative overall capability to make war (Rattinger 1976; Baugh 1984: chapter 4). The difficulty of making such estimates is illustrated by the interminable debates that took place within NATO about what force levels were necessary to deter or defeat a Soviet invasion of Western Europe (Duffield 1995).

In competitions over military technology the distinction between quality and quantity is important (Huntington 1958: 65–89; Gray 1971a:

46–48). Potential combatants will compare not only the numbers of their weapons but also their quality. Germany had a qualitative edge in 1914 in terms of the speed with which it could mobilize its army. This edge enabled it to offset in part the larger numbers of troops possessed by its opponents, especially Russia. For a time, during the late 1940s and 1950s, the United States relied on its qualitative edge in nuclear weapons to offset the larger Soviet armies deployed in Eastern Europe (Duffield 1995). Pakistan, Israel, Taiwan, and South Korea have all sought a qualitative edge against more numerously equipped opponents. However, assessments of the quality and quantity of hardware have to be accompanied by assessments about the quality of the software and "wetware" (human beings) that accompany the weapons. Weapons per se often prove to be less important during war than other factors such as morale, strategy, logistics, or alliance politics.

Although this section is concerned primarily with what explains arms competition rather than what arms competition explains, it is worth flagging Huntington's interesting argument that qualitative arms races are less war prone than quantitative ones. His argument is that increases of quantity provide what is perceived (to a great extent falsely, considering the history of war) as a known ability to fight, whereas constant changes in quality both undermine the value of quantitative accumulation and increase the difficulty of calculating the outcome of a resort to arms (Huntington 1958: 71–79). Huntington's deductively derived hypothesis was tested to a limited degree against historical cases by Hammond, and some supporting evidence was found. The effects of this factor are seen most clearly where the arms dynamic is bilateral and focused on a single main weapon system. However, arms dynamics involve mixes of both—quality being used to offset quantity and vice versa, and quality and quantity being sought by both sides (Hammond 1993: 48, 274–275). We suspect that quantitative arms competitions or races will indicate either an intention to begin a war or an expectation of imminent war rather than being causes of wars, which appear to begin for other reasons (Blainey 1973; Lebow 1981; Gray 1993a). Competitions or races in armies, whether quantitative or qualitative, are much more a sign than competitions or races in navies or air forces that war is likely (Hammond 1993: 248–249). It is worth emphasizing that wars are rarely begun when the military balance is optimal (Lebow 1984). Instead, they are more likely to occur in response to perceived threats to interests and/or to psychological biases that lead to overestimation of the chances of military success (Lebow 1981; Herring 1995).

When the action–reaction dynamic is in terms of overall military strength, then military expenditure may become in itself an idiom of interaction. It can also play a symbolic role. This was the case with President Kennedy's announcements in May and July 1961 of increases in spending on conventional forces during the Berlin crisis. Such spending—and the increase in military spending ordered in June 1961 by Soviet leader Nikita Khrushchev—could have no practical military value in the short term for the crisis then under way: the intention was to symbolize resolve (Herring 1995: 139). A similar symbolic logic also seemed to attend the post-1991 arms-buying binge among some Middle Eastern states, though considerations of buying continued military protection from Western suppliers also counted heavily here.

When reliable data can be obtained, military expenditure is perhaps more useful to indicate the difference between arms racing and maintenance of the military status quo than it is to measure a specific action–reaction dynamic between states. For this purpose, absolute levels of military expenditure are less important than military expenditure expressed as a percentage of GNP. If military expenditure is a constant or declining percentage of GNP, then one is probably observing maintenance or build-down, especially where GNP itself tends to rise at a steady but not spectacular rate. Although absolute amounts spent will tend to rise, the increase will mostly reflect the rising costs of modern weapons compared with the older generations they replace. But if military expenditure is rising as a percentage of GNP, then the state is increasing the level of its military activity at the expense of its other activities. Such an increase cannot be sustained indefinitely. The increase's appearance indicates either a shift away from maintenance toward racing, or at least competition, or else a state caught in the squeeze of economic growth too weak to support its desired range of military commitments.

Although very useful as an indicator of the intensity of the arms dynamic, the measure of military expenditure as a percentage of GNP has to be used with caution. Different rates of growth can have a large impact on interpretation of the figures. Slow or no growth of the figure in a rapidly expanding economy may disguise a considerable military expansion, as it did in the case of Japan until recently, and as was also the case in much of East Asia during the 1990s. A rise in the figure for a static or slow-moving economy may indicate more a holding action than an expansion of military capability. Furthermore, a rise in military spending may be a necessary transitional cost in conducting a build-down. This was seen at the end of the Cold War, when the hoped for peace dividend (reduced military spending leading to tax cuts or increased social spending) turned out in some ways to be a peace tax. Dismantling weapons, reconfiguring forces, demobilizing and rehousing military personnel, redeploying military capabilities, and so on has proven to be expensive.

The idiom of action–reaction can take a variety of other forms, economic and political, as well as military. As long as the idiom remains military the process is still within the arms dynamic. Action and reaction options other than increases in military strength or expenditure are available. States can, for example, change the deployment patterns of their armed forces in ways that make them more threatening and/or less vulnerable to an opponent. Motives are usually mixed. Khrushchev claimed that in deploying nuclear missiles in Cuba, he was reacting to the invasion threat posed by the United States to Cuba. But much more than that was in play. He also wanted to react strategically to the nuclear superiority established by the United States, and symbolically to the deployment of NATO missiles on the Soviet periphery, especially in Turkey. By giving the United States a taste of its own medicine and establishing symbolic partial nuclear equality, he hoped to create the diplomatic leverage that would broaden that equality to many areas of U.S.-Soviet relations and that would let him shift resources to nonmilitary activities (Herring 1995: chapter 8, especially 154–156).

The stationing of intermediate-range nuclear forces (INFs) in the form of ground-launched cruise missiles (GLCMs) and Pershing II missiles by NATO in Western Europe was sought by some in NATO as a means of emphasizing the U.S. nuclear commitment to Western Europe in the wake of the establishment of rough U.S.-Soviet strategic nuclear parity. However, it was less a reaction to this than to the Soviet deployment of SS-20 INFs in Eastern Europe that was interpreted by NATO as a Soviet bid to achieve political leverage over Western Europe. In contrast, the Soviet Union saw itself as maintaining the military status quo by replacing old SS-4 and SS-5 missiles with SS-20s on a one-for-one basis, and was more concerned with deterring nuclear war. Hence it saw the NATO INF deployment as an attempt to overturn the military status quo and regarded NATO's portrayal of the Soviet deployment as a bid for regional nuclear superiority as a deliberate misrepresentation. What NATO perceived as a compellent capability the Soviet Union sought primarily as a deterrent and, failing that, a warfighting capability (Garthoff 1983, 1990: 71–74). Changes to more, or less, threatening deployment patterns have also been a conspicuous feature of military relations between Israel and Egypt, India and Pakistan, India and China, and the two Koreas.

States can change their operational or declaratory strategic doctrine in response to actions (including doctrinal innovations) by an opponent. Such doctrines are a key element in actual military strength, as the Germans demonstrated with their imaginative use of the rapid mechanized warfare doctrine, known as blitzkrieg, in the early years of World War II. Because they are perceived as changes in intentions, changes in doctrine (such as the U.S. shift toward a declaratory policy of warfighting strategies of nuclear deterrence starting in the 1970s) can carry just as much weight in the eyes of an opponent as increases or decreases in the size and quality of armed forces (Gray 1976: 7; MccGwire 1987, 1991; Garthoff 1990; Zisk 1993). Kimberley Zisk (1993) describes reactive doctrinal innovation between rival states as "doctrine races," although such a label will often exaggerate the pace of the innovation and the effort put into it.

When the idiom moves into the economic and political domains, the action–reaction process of the arms dynamic joins the more general one of foreign policy, and the subject shifts from strategic studies and peace studies to world politics and international political economy. The area of overlap should not be ignored. Restrictions on trade may become part of the action–reaction process, as in the long-standing attempts by NATO to prevent such dual-use technologies (militarily useful civil technologies) as computers from reaching the Soviet Union, and post–Cold War concerns regarding the spread of dual-use technologies (especially in the areas of nuclear and missile technology) to LICs.

General shifts in perception, and therefore in the character of political relations, also play an important role in the action–reaction process. Shifts toward (or away from) more negative and hostile views of an opponent can mark a major shift toward (or away from) competition or racing within the arms dynamic. Negative shifts occurred in Britain toward Germany during the late 1930s and in the United States toward the Soviet Union during the mid-1940s. Positive, or "desecuritizing" ones (Wæver 1995; Buzan, Wæver, and de Wilde 1998)—that is, ones that move issues from the security agenda and into the realm of normal politics—occurred in southern Africa with the end of apartheid. Most notably, they accompanied Gorbachev's new political thinking in international relations, which, coupled with unilateral arms reductions, triggered the end of the Cold War. A political action may also trigger a military reaction, as when states increase their military strength in response to an unleashing of revolutionary energy in a rival, as Iraq did after the revolution in Iran. Iraq saw Iran as politically more threatening but militarily weakened and therefore decided (unwisely, in view of the outcome) to attack. This kind of interplay is where the arms dynamic blends into the broader patterns of world politics.

One cannot assume that states will display consistency in the idiom of their actions and reactions: in other words, that their responses will be made in the same idiom as the actions that triggered them. The Soviet response to the large-scale deployment of ICBMs by the United States during the early 1960s was consistent: the Soviet Union deployed large numbers of ICBMs in the late 1960s and early 1970s. But the Soviet response to the earlier deployment by the United States of large numbers of bombers was not consistent, because the Soviets built antiaircraft defenses and pushed development of ICBMs (MccGwire 1987; Evangelista 1988). The U.S. response in the 1980s to the Soviet buildup of ICBMs was also not consistent. Instead of adding to its own ICBM numbers, the United States tried to open up new technology for ballistic missile defense (BMD) (Reiss 1992), although it did also modernize its ICBM and submarine-launched ballistic missile (SLBM) forces with MX and Trident missiles respectively (Spinardi 1994; Farrell 1997: 35–57). Consistent responses are more likely when the rate of technological innovation is low and when the weapons concerned are ones that can be expected to fight each other, such as tanks, battleships, and fighter aircraft. Inconsistent responses are more likely when technological innovation offers opportunities to degrade the effectiveness of existing weapons systems. Such responses are also more likely when existing defensive capability looks more attractive than a matching offensive capability or when resource constraints force one side to take unorthodox measures to stay in the competition.

Magnitude, Timing, and Awareness in the Action–Reaction Process

To the variety of idioms in which the dialogue of the arms dynamic can be pursued must be added the variables that attend the process of action–reaction itself. These variables are magnitude (what proportion the reaction bears to the triggering action), timing (speed and sequence of interaction), and awareness (the extent to which the parties involved in the process are conscious of their impact on each other, and whether they govern their own behavior in the light of that consciousness). As with idiom, these variables are almost always more complicated in reality than they are in the basic model of the action–reaction process. In addition, there is a persistent danger of falling into the assumption that one's opponent is a mirror image of oneself in terms of the perceptions, reasoning, and political structures that underlie military policy (Gray 1976: chapter 3; Jervis 1976). Such an assumption can lead to serious errors of analysis and prediction. The reverse problem—of caricaturing and demonizing the opponent and presuming that the opponent is radically different—also occurs (Herring 1995: 69).

Magnitude

The magnitude of possible reactions within the arms dynamic covers a wide range. If the dynamic progresses by mutual overreaction, then moves to outdo one's opponent can range from acquisition of greater forces to preventive war (attacking an opponent before it becomes too strong) or preemptive war (striking the first blow in the belief that an attack by the opponent was imminent). A classic example of the first of these three was Britain's announcement in 1912 that it would outbuild Germany in dreadnoughts by a ratio of 8:5, and build two equivalent ships for every extra one that the Germans added to their existing program of naval construction. However, overreaction is by no means inevitable. Of particular importance in interpreting the significance of responses are the relative starting positions of the rival states. Starting positions can be roughly equal, as they nearly were in terms of dreadnoughts between Britain and Germany in 1906, or they can be unequal, where one side starts with a lead. Examples of very unequal starting positions include the case of Britain and Germany in the older style of battleships up to 1905, and the United States and the Soviet Union in terms of long-range nuclear weapons during the 1950s and 1960s. Where the rivals are equal, the relationship between the existing level of capability and the scale of the new acquisition becomes important. Parity at low levels means that the balance can change quickly. When they are unequal, the leader may be able to tolerate some disproportion in the magnitude of the measures taken by itself and its rival.

Huntington (1958: 60) suggests that the probability of war in arms racing is at its highest when the dynamics of the race are close to resulting in a shift in the balance of power. Indeed, war may be the desired outcome for one of the parties, with arms racing as a necessary preparation for it. However, in the nuclear context, this is unlikely to be the case, because of the potential political and physical costs of using nuclear weapons. If Huntington is right, equality of military strength at low levels between nonnuclear rivals is an unstable condition because only small changes are needed to shift the balance of power.

This issue is of great importance in that much of the theory and practice of arms control and disarmament is predicated on the notion of equality as a stabilizing factor (on the grounds that neither side will have any confidence that it can start and win a war). Geoffrey Blainey (1973) argues that peace is most likely when there is a clear *im*balance of power favoring one side. Perhaps this ought to be amended to say that peace is most likely when there is a clear imbalance of power against the state that wishes to go to war. The problem with this is that motives may change so that the state that has the imbalance of power in its favor might decide to go to war. This brings us back to the idea that a broad band of equality might be the best option for preventing war. The extent to which a balance is perceived to be stable is not a technical matter. Perceptions of virtually the same balance can change radically in a short time span. In the early 1980s, both Soviet and U.S. leaders were deeply worried about what they saw as instabilities in the strategic nuclear balance unfavorable to them. Within just a few years, Gorbachev transformed perceptions of the strategic nuclear balance: the band of parity was perceived to be so broad that most existing strategic nuclear forces were regarded as redundant. To underline the point, stability rests much more on perceptions than on technology.

The idea of a sufficiency, or surplus capacity, of military capability, which becomes prominent when nuclear weapons are in play, may negate Huntington's point about the instability of parity. Past a certain point, additional destructive power offers diminishing returns in military capability, though it may still be attractive for symbolic reasons. When force levels have passed the point of surplus capacity, the incentives to match increases by one's opponent are not as strong as they are with conventional weapons, where additional numbers more obviously increase relative fighting capability. However, during the Cold War, the United States thought that having force levels beyond parity might increase the credibility of extended deterrence. In particular, the United States was concerned with bolstering its threat to use nuclear weapons should the Warsaw Pact start to win a conventional war against NATO in Western Europe.

Responses of lower magnitude may also indicate a lack of resources or political will on the part of the challenged state. Or the responses may indicate a reasoned political judgment that the arms dynamic should be allowed to generate a peaceful change in the international balance of power and status. Such a judgment reflects a decision that new realities in the international system are so basic as to be very difficult to stop, and not so adverse that they are worth opposing by war. The latter factor was an important element of the acceptance by China of India's threshold nuclear capability, and by India of Pakistan's. The willingness of the United States to accept the Soviet Union as a military equal during the SALT negotiations was influenced by both factors.

Although the idea of measured responses is clear enough in theory, in reality it is often very difficult to find reliable measures by which actions and reactions can be compared. The British-German naval race is a rare instance where comparison was easy because its idiom, dreadnoughts, was both simple and consistent: counting numbers of equivalent ships gave an accurate measure of one element of relative naval strength. Few other interactions within the arms dynamic are as accommodating as this one and, as usual, it must be emphasized that sheer numbers are often not what is decisive in the utility of weapons for the purposes of making threats, going to war, or making effective symbolic statements. Not having clear measures of military strength makes it difficult to assess the process of action and reaction with an acceptable level of accuracy. To the extent that calculation is imprecise, concepts like parity have no practical meaning. If states cannot know whether they are ahead of, behind, or equal to their rivals, then they might choose to overinsure, and thereby further fuel the process of action and reaction. Alternatively, the uncertainty could be a force for caution with regard to the decision to go to war.

Timing

The variable of timing poses even greater difficulties of measurement than that of magnitude. It is perhaps the main weakness in attempts to apply the action–reaction model to the study of the arms dynamic. The basic model assumes a clear sequence of action and reaction like that in a chess game. In theory, such a process should display a distinct pattern of move and countermove that would enable the pace of the action–reaction cycle to provide one measure of the intensity of interaction. Slow versus rapid patterns of response would give a useful insight into the character of the arms dynamic and is part of the process of distinguishing racing from maintenance. A clear sequence can sometimes be seen at the start of an arms dynamic, as when Britain reacted to the German naval program in 1904, and the Soviet Union reacted to news of the U.S. atomic bomb in 1945 (Holloway 1983: chapter 2). Similar patterns can be seen elsewhere, as in the rise of Israeli and Japanese interest in BMD systems in response to acquisitions of missiles by neighboring rivals, and in responsive acquisitions of advanced aircraft in many places. Although delayed responses may result in a more intense arms dynamic than would otherwise have been the case (Huntington 1958: 58–63), one must not generalize too readily. States may decide to catch up without believing there is a compelling need to do so as swiftly as possible.

The U.S.-Soviet rivalry did not fit the timing element of the action–reaction model. Because concern about the U.S.-Soviet case dominated thinking about arms racing and arms competition, the action–reaction model fell into some disrepute. The superpowers were not reacting so much to what the other did, as to what each estimated that the other would do in the future. This can only be called action–reaction in the very broad sense that the overall reference for the actions of each is defined by the threat from the other. The phrase "spiral model" is sometimes used to label the process of simultaneous, anticipatory interaction, the image being one of two actors locked into a smooth, continuous, and self-reinforcing pattern of mutual military stimulation (Jervis 1976: chapter 3; Russett 1983: 69; Glaser 1992). In 1908–1909, for example, Britain succumbed to fear of how many dreadnoughts Germany might build if the Germans did not stick to their prescribed naval program but instead built secretly up to the full capacity of their shipyards. Britain laid down eight dreadnoughts, so creating a concrete "reaction" to something the Germans might do but in the event did not. Modern technology creates strong pressures toward anticipatory behavior because of the long lead times required to bring a weapon system from conception to deployment—as much as ten to fifteen years for a normal weapon system like a supersonic bomber, and more (perhaps forever, the cynic might suggest) for really exotic projects like BMD (Allison and Morris 1975: 122–123; Farrell 1997: 96). Under these conditions, major decisions have to be made about future military deployments far in advance of knowledge about what the actual military and political environment will look like when the weapons become operational. One possible response to this dilemma is to build maximum flexibility and multirole potential into planned weapons systems, but this can only be done at some cost in optimal performance for a given mission.

Sometimes neither side has much incentive to race for victory, and each can be fairly certain that it can, through broad-spectrum R&D and good intelligence surveillance of the other side, prevent the other from gaining a decisive military advantage from a technological breakthrough. As in the Cold War, and in many LIC confrontations, each side may take the view that the other will be its principal rival for decades to come. Under such conditions, the timing element of action–reaction becomes almost impossible to distinguish. Mutual, anticipatory "reactions" tie the arms dynamic closely to the general process of technological innovation, which, among other things, tends to enlarge the gray area between maintenance and racing that we refer to as competition. Such competitions have taken place between Israel and the Arab states, India and Pakistan, India and China, China and Taiwan, Argentina and Chile, Argentina and Brazil, and the United States and the Soviet Union. In an institutionalized arms competition, the driving force of the arms dynamic is found increasingly within states: the external action–reaction element of rivalry is so dominated and distorted by internal factors as to be scarcely distinguishable in its own right (Allison and Morris 1975; Gray 1976: 18–22). Thinking along these lines carries us into the domestic structure model of the arms dynamic, which will be explored in the next chapter.

Awareness

How aware are the actors of the process in which they are engaged? In particular, do they understand their impact on each other, and do they try to manipulate the action–reaction dynamic either to their own or to mutual advantage (Schelling 1966: chapter 7)? The action–reaction model highlights the dangers of actors that are not aware of their impact on each other. It is a virtual truism of states that, like most individuals, they are more aware of the threats that others pose to them than they are of the threats that they pose to others (Jervis 1976). This unbalanced perception is an important element of the security dilemma in fueling an escalatory cycle of provocation and overreaction. If actors are sensitive to their impact on each other, then there is potential for managing the relationship so as to pursue balance and avoid overreaction. Such management can be approached cooperatively, in the form of negotiated agreements to restrain the arms dynamic, or unilaterally, in the form of actions by one side designed to avoid overstimulating the threat sensitivities of the other. This approach is known as reassurance (Stein 1991a, 1991b; Herring 1995: especially 51–53). Various responses to military means explored in Part 4 rest in part on the ability of states to take a more sensitive view of each other's security requirements. Among other things, the institutionalization of a long-term rivalry that cannot rationally be solved by war provides considerable incentives for joint management. However, as Gray (1971a: 56) points out, awareness also has its dangers. If one side is more keen to manage the arms dynamic than the other, it makes itself vulnerable to having its enthusiasm exploited and its relative strength weakened. Hawkish opinion in the United States saw the SALT process of the 1970s in this light, as a period of U.S. unilateral disarmament, although evidence to the contrary has been provided (Booth and Williams 1985). When suspicions arise that an attempt to manage the arms dynamic is being cynically exploited by one side, then the arms control process can itself become the mechanism that heightens the intensity of arms competition. However, U.S. doves argued that the suspicions of the hawks were driven by a desire to undermine attempts to manage the arms dynamic in order to intensify the arms competition and engage in what the doves saw as a futile attempt to reestablish U.S. nuclear superiority. Similar elements of reassurance and suspicion can be found in relations between the two Koreas (Ahn 1993) and between Israel and the Arab states (Stein 1985a, 1985b).

The Impact of Strategic Objectives on the Arms Dynamic

Strategic objectives within a rivalry have a major impact on other variables within the action–reaction process. It is, for example, reasonable to conjecture that the action–reaction dynamic between two status quo rivals each interested in maintaining its position through deterrence will be much less intense in terms of the pace and magnitude of its interactions, and much more restrained in its idiom, than a dynamic between two rivals both interested in changing their position, and both prepared to fight a war in order to do so. Eight pairs of concepts capture the most important elements of the impact upon the arms dynamic of strategic objectives. These are indicated in Table 6.1.

The first pair concerns the balance of power (economic and ideological as well as military) between the actors, and the distinction is whether their strategic objectives are to change it or to preserve their existing positions. The former is a status quo orientation and the latter a revisionist

Table 6.1 The Impact of Motives on the Arms Dynamic

Stabilizing	Destabilizing
Status quo	Revisionist
Value of peace high	Value of peace low
Secure	Insecure
Defensive military strategy	Offensive military strategy
Deterrence	Compellence
Reassurance	Reliance on threats
Risk averse	Risk acceptant
Averse to difficult tasks	Acceptant of difficult tasks

orientation. Revisionism aimed at territorial expansion has the most obvious potential for war. Status quo actors are concerned primarily with security and loss avoidance: revisionist actors are more interested in power maximization and pursuit of gain (Buzan 1991a: 298–310; Schweller 1994; Herring 1995: especially 47–49). If any major state seeks to change its international status as a high priority, then the probability arises that it will seek to increase its military strength. Its moves in this direction are likely to lead to an arms race or at least a military competition with those whose interests are challenged by its ambitions. This was certainly the case with Germany prior to both world wars and with Japan during the 1930s. It was also the case in the Arab-Israeli struggle, although ceased to be so between Egypt and Israel after the 1973 War and between Syria and Israel as of the mid-1990s, when Israel became more receptive to trading land for peace. In the 1990s, China became an object of much speculation as to whether it is developing into a revisionist challenger.

The second pair concerns the value of peace: the higher the value of peace, the more stable and less intense the arms dynamic may be, all other things being equal (Herring 1995: 42–43, 242–243). The value of peace is likely to be high when both sides have nuclear weapons. Attachment of a low value to peace can lead to arms competition or racing because warfighting preparations generate open-ended military needs. When war is considered to be a rational instrument of policy, then there is no absolute ceiling on the force requirements of either side. The needs of each are determined according to the capability of the other in a potentially endless cycle of action and reaction. The existence of exaggerated cycles of overreaction may be a signal that war is increasingly likely to occur. If the value of peace is high, then there are possibilities for avoiding open-ended competitive accumulations. From the mutually assured destruction (MAD) perspective, nuclear deterrence can in theory be achieved by possession of a guaranteed capability to devastate one's opponent. Such a capability is considerably less sensitive to increases in an opponent's strength than is the case in warfighting rivalries.

The remaining pairs can be summarized briefly. The third relates to how secure are the states involved: insecure states are more likely than secure states to be involved in an escalatory arms dynamic (Glaser 1992). The fourth concerns the military strategies of the actors: reliance on defensive military strategies is more stabilizing than reliance on the offensive. Fifth, an emphasis on deterrence is more stabilizing than an emphasis on compellence. Sixth, reassurance of the opponent as well as the use of threats is more stabilizing than reliance solely on threats. Seventh, risk aversion is more stabilizing than willingness to take risks, although risk aversion by one side and risk acceptance by the other leads to a deteriorating situation for the risk-averse side. Eighth, a state willing to take on difficult tasks is more likely to fuel action–reaction processes than one averse to such tasks.

Despite the obvious importance of strategic objectives in the action–reaction dynamic, their role in practice is difficult to assess for a number of reasons. First, strategic objectives may be attributes of situations rather than (or as well as) actors; the objectives cannot be detached completely from the constraints, dangers, and opportunities posed by the distribution of power in the international system or by the vagaries of internal politics. A state may only be wedded to status quo objectives because it has reached the limits of its power and so is incapable of creating change.

Second, states usually adopt a set of strategic objectives that incorporate elements from both columns of Table 6.1. Only in propagandist fantasies (or theoretical exercises) is one side the risk-averse, status quo oriented, defensive, deterrent, reassuring actor and the other a risk-acceptant, revisionist, offensive, compellent, threatening actor. In the late 1960s, Israel was an insecure status quo state that felt it necessary to adopt an offensive military strategy to deal with the combined military might of its Arab opponents, and carried out that strategy to great effect in the 1967 Six-Day War. Charles Glaser (1992) proposes different policies for dealing with secure expansionist states, insecure expansionist states, insecure status quo states, and secure status quo states.

Third, it can be difficult to distinguish between the pairs of strategic objectives in the two columns of Table 6.1. Is the opponent secure or insecure? How highly does the opponent value peace? How averse is the opponent to risk? These are usually tough questions. Indeed, not only do decisionmakers often find it difficult to decide how secure they feel, how much they value peace, how averse they are to risk, and so on, but they may not even address these questions. There are other facets to the problem of distinguishability. Similar objectives (such as defense of the status quo) may be served by different strategies (such as offensive or defensive military strategies), and offensive and defensive military strategies may both be served by similar military capabilities. The latter point indicates that there are important but unclear limits to what one can infer from an opponent's capabilities. Power struggles can be about well-entrenched states trying to crush opponents that, even if they do not directly challenge the status quo in the international system themselves, might threaten it symbolically should their internal system succeed and look attractive.

The efforts of the United States to undermine Communist Cuba and Nicaragua and fundamentalist Iran are examples of this. Indeed, these examples show the problems of simply labeling one state as status quo and another as revisionist (Herring 1995: 29–30, 47–49, 53–58, 233–234). In its efforts to maintain and extend its Latin American hegemony, the United States was seeking to overturn significant aspects of the status quo.

While strategic objectives appear to be important elements in the action–reaction process, they pose great difficulties for both analysis and policy because they often cannot be either isolated or identified accurately. If the response to this uncertainty is to assume the worst, then valuable opportunites for cooperation may be lost and the operation of the security dilemma may be intensified sufficiently to cause arms competition, arms racing, or even war. If assumptions about strategic objectives are too optimistic, there is a danger that one's opponent will interpret conciliation as weakness and, by seeking to exploit the situation, create the conflict that the conciliatory behavior was aimed at avoiding.

These problems, along with the others outlined above, explain why the action–reaction model has fallen out of favor despite its many attractions. Although its basic logic has force, its specific ideas are frequently difficult to apply to particular cases. In addition, there are many cases where the model does not seem to provide anything like a complete explanation for observed behavior. Frustration with the model has therefore driven inquiry away from interaction factors between states and toward domestic ones within them.

7

THE DOMESTIC STRUCTURE MODEL

The domestic structure model rests on the idea that the arms dynamic is generated by forces within the state. It functions as an alternative to the action–reaction model only in the sense that the two models compete for primacy of place in ability to explain observed behavior within the arms dynamic. In a narrow sense, the literature on the domestic structure model dates from the 1970s and the failure of the action–reaction model to explain adequately what went on between the superpowers. In a broader sense, however, it is simply an extension of the long-standing tradition that seeks to explain the behavior of states primarily in terms of their domestic structures and affairs (Waltz 1959: chapters 4–5; 1979: chapters 2, 4).

The proponents of the domestic structure model did not argue that the rivalry between the superpowers was irrelevant, but that the process of the arms dynamic had become so deeply institutionalized within each state that domestic factors largely supplanted the crude forms of action and reaction as the main engine of the arms dynamic. The external factor of rivalry still provided the necessary motivation for the arms dynamic. But when "reactions" become anticipatory, the state has, in effect, restructured itself internally on a long-term basis to deal with the arms dynamic. R&D laboratories work to push the frontiers of military technology ever forward. Arms production facilities are kept going with orders so as to maintain capacity, and over time (and along with other military facilities) they get absorbed into the budgetary and electoral processes of the state.

An almost exclusively domestically oriented arms dynamic is sometimes referred to as "autism" (Dedring 1976: 79–81). Autism exists when the military behavior of states is generated much more by internal considerations than by any rational response to external threats. If need be, external threats will be manufactured to bolster domestic unity. Military capability may be acquired more for prestige, or to reinforce the government's hold on the country, than in relation to external threats. Where autism takes hold, the consequences for vigorous interstate rivalries are serious. Excessive egocentrism in the behavior of rival states is an almost certain path to friction and paranoia in relations among them. If autism is taken to extremes, it makes the domestic structure model of the arms dynamic an alternative, rather than a complement, to the action–reaction model. If the arms dynamic is driven powerfully from within states, then it becomes much more difficult to damp down. Any state that reduces its own military strength in hope of a response from its rival will be disappointed if its rival's armaments are determined more by internal than by external factors. Autism looks rather different when it refers to the behavior of states concerned almost exclusively with internal security. Such states, if they do not produce their own arms, will suck them in from the world arms trade or as military aid from friendly states. In some cases the weapons are sold or military aid given not to the government but, if it exists, the military opposition to the government.

Extreme autism is rare, and so the interesting question about the domestic structure model is not whether it is better than the action–reaction model in some general sense, but what proportion and aspects of observed behavior each model explains for any given case. Which structures and mechanisms within the state become the main carriers of the arms dynamic?

Most of the studies supporting the domestic structure model focus on the case of the two superpowers (Allison and Morris 1975; Kaldor 1982, 1990; Holloway 1983: chapters 6–8; Burton 1984; Evangelista 1988; Farrell 1997), partly as a matter of priority because of the intrinsic importance of the superpower case, and partly by default because information from other cases was harder to come by. Since much more information was available about domestic structure variables in the United States than in the Soviet Union, the U.S. example dominated the literature, although some analysts made a great deal of headway in understanding the Soviet case (Holloway 1983; Evangelista 1988; Garthoff 1990; MccGwire 1987, 1991). The past and continuing importance of the U.S. case makes the exercise worthwhile but requires us to keep in mind questions about how applicable the whole model is to other types of case. Because the superpower case dominates the literature, one cannot help noticing how much of the existing material on the domestic structure model applies only to states that are major producers of arms. As was explained in Part 1 such states are still few in number, although their number is increasing. The relevance of the domestic structure model for the greater numbers of nonproducers and part-producers remains largely unexplored. Since significant numbers of these are, or have been, engaged in long-term military rivalries (India and Pakistan, North and South Korea, Iran and Iraq, Israel and Arab neighbors) they are in principle candidates for at least some of the internal institutionalizations that feed the domestic structure model. The growing literature on military industrialization in the LICs contains a great deal of material that supports much of the domestic structure model. There is usually no explicit testing of the model (Katz 1986; Kapstein 1992; Bitzinger 1992, 1994), although there are notable exceptions (Graham 1994).

The domestic structure model offers a whole range of factors to explain the arms dynamic. The principal ones are the institutionalization of military R&D; the institutionalization of military production; economic management; electoral politics; the military-industrial complex; organizational politics; the unifying and identity-creating roles of military threats; and internal repression and civil war. The normative question that underlies consideration of these factors is how they should be seen. Are they a reasonable response to long-term rivalries? Or are they a distortion of the national political economy, a distortion that serves powerful vested interests and, whatever the validity of its origins, becomes a self-serving mechanism that promotes and perpetuates the rivalry that justified it?

Domestic Structure Explanations of the Arms Dynamic

Institutionalization of Military Research and Development

The institutionalization of military R&D plays a major role in the domestic structure model (Gray 1976: 39–43; Thee 1986: chapters 3, 5; Adams and Kosiak 1993; Farrell 1995, 1997: chapter 3). The Soviet Union tended to follow U.S. innovations like the multiple independently targetable reentry vehicle (MIRV), ballistic missile submarines, and cruise missiles (Holloway 1983; Evangelista 1988). Occasionally, it took an independent course, as when it largely skipped heavy bombers and moved straight to ICBMs during the 1950s. By a combination of its own work and spying on the West it managed not to fall too far behind. It could draw level in areas like armored vehicles, where the technologies were relatively mature and the rate of change slow. The Soviet R&D establishment seemed to have its agenda set rather more by what happened in the West than by any general assault on the frontiers of the possible (Holloway 1983: 147–150). Although the Soviet Union was not wholly comfortable in being second, it had the advantages of making the United States carry the costs of leading the innovation process, and was relatively pleased to sustain a position not so far behind the leader that it jeopardized its military credibility or symbolic standing.

However, given that only a small number of major arms-producing states spend heavily on military R&D, the logic of this factor can only be applied in a few cases. The role of R&D relates closely to the discussions of technological revolutions and the technological imperative in Part 1. What makes R&D distinctive within the domestic structure model are the measures that arms-producing states take when the rhythm of technological development puts pressure on them to adopt a long view of military procurement. The increasing involvement of the state in military R&D is a historical trend that began to gather force in the nineteenth century and culminated in the symbiosis of state and science in the nuclear age (Pearton 1982). In the modern era, military technology is so capital intensive and takes so long to develop that any state wishing to be at the leading edge has no choice but to create or encourage a permanent R&D establishment. No state can become a major arms producer without its own R&D base, and since technological improvement is a continual process, the establishments that support it necessarily become permanent. A fully independent R&D base now appears to be beyond the reach of all states: the trend since the 1980s has been for the flattening of the top of the hierarchy of arms-producing states.

On the one hand, R&D establishments are created because the complex and expensive nature of technology requires them. On the other hand, the establishments become mechanisms that set ever higher standards of expense and complexity, increase the pace of technological advance, and work relentlessly to make their own products obsolete. In promoting their own organizational security they necessarily become promoters of technological change. Although their offerings are not always accepted for production, as witness such projects as the British Blue Streak missile, the U.S. B-70 bomber, and the 1960s and 1980s U.S. versions of BMD, they do mount a continual challenge to accepted standards of adequate military technology. Thus what starts as a response to a problem becomes part of the process by which the problem is continuously re-created and even exacerbated. These establishments reflect the technological conditions stemming from industrial society. They may also have become important in shaping the civil economy by giving preferential boosts to a variety of dual-use technologies, most notably in the aerospace, nuclear, and computer fields (Buzan and Sen 1990).

Despite its domestic roots, and its self-contained nature, the institutionalization of military R&D can in one sense be viewed as part of the action–reaction model. States competing at the leading edge of technology must have an R&D establishment to be in the game at all—and up to a point, so must states seeking to sell less sophisticated technology, though the resources involved are far smaller than in the leading-edge states. In the 1980s Brazil, for example, developed and sold a relatively simple armored personnel carrier that had the attraction of being cheaper and more reliable than the more high-technology offerings from the more industrialized countries (but see Conca 1997, on the problems facing Brazilian military production). Since the end of the Cold War, the justification for the enterprise of R&D has shifted significantly (but not entirely) toward trade rather than interstate rivalry. If the leading edge of military technology is continually moving forward, one effect of R&D is to complicate the task of differentiating arms competition from maintenance of the military status quo. The continual background of qualitative improvement means that in both cases states will tend to upgrade their military technologies.

The end of the Cold War raises interesting questions about the future role of military R&D in the arms dynamic. The collapse of superpower rivalry should have sharply reduced incentives for spending on military R&D, thus slowing down the pace of military technological innovation. Russia is indeed largely out of the top ranks of the game for economic reasons, though it is still just within the group of seven states that dominate military R&D (in rank order: United States, France, Britain, and Germany, with Russia, China, and Japan all roughly at the same level). The United States has pruned its military R&D expenditure by 25 percent, but is still spending more than eight times as much as its nearest rival (France). The major European powers are broadly holding their expenditures steady while Japan, South Korea, and India are still increasing theirs (Arnett 1996b: 381–392).

The dramatic cut in global military R&D due to the end of the Cold War ($60 billion in the mid-1990s—down 50 to 55 percent in real terms since the mid-1980s) undermines any claims of a self-sustaining, autistic process (Arnett 1996b). The United States, and perhaps the Europeans and the Japanese, may try to maintain relatively high levels of military R&D while cutting back on production and deployment. This could reflect a desire to be able to get back into the game should a new military challenger arise, or to maintain a substantial qualitative edge over the many countries around the world now equipped with modern weapons supplied by the major producers. The supplier states, and particularly the United States, want to retain a capacity to fight countries like Iraq without risking huge casualties.

Institutionalization of Military Production

The forces leading to the institutionalization of R&D are both linked to and similar to those for the institutionalization of military production, and so this factor is also limited to the small group of major arms producers. Production and R&D often share close organizational links in high-technology industries. Furthermore, for a particular weapon system, R&D and production may be concurrent rather than consecutive (Farrell 1995, 1997: chapter 3). Arms-producing states perceive the same need to maintain military production capabilities in being as they do to maintain a permanent R&D establishment (Kaldor 1982: 60–65; Adams and Kosiak 1993). Maintaining military production capabilities in turn normally involves government support for the whole range of basic industries on which military production depends, so bringing a wide range of industrial interests into the picture (Sen 1984). This constellation of capabilities is usually known as the defense industrial base, although we prefer military-industrial base, because its products are not necessarily used for defensive purposes.

The need to maintain a standing capacity for arms production is reinforced where there is a long-term rivalry. A long-term rivalry is usually
seen as requiring not only a degree of permanent mobilization in case there
is a rapid move toward war, but also the capacity to expand production
quickly to support the war effort. A policy of weaponized deterrence, as
opposed to weaponless deterrence or deterrence through strategic nonviolence, is usually also seen as requiring a substantial degree of permanent
mobilization to keep the necessary forces in being and up to date. During
the Cold War, the high level of activity in the R&D sector speeded up the
cycle of obsolescence and so required production capability to keep up
with the flow of replacement weapon systems. A factor working against
this is the way in which much civil technology can be converted to military uses, and a state can adopt a policy of preparing for rapid civil to military conversion should it be seen as necessary. In the post–Cold War
world, it will be interesting to see whether the leading producers will
maintain high levels of R&D while cutting back production capacity.

One way of squaring this circle is to encourage arms exports. Ex-
cluded from the arms trade are some nuclear weapon delivery systems, notably missile submarines, ICBMs, and heavy bombers, which are seldom
transferred to other countries. Aside from these systems, governments seek
to generate both sufficient volume and sufficient continuity of orders to
keep their military industries going. This is not just a matter of keeping
plant in being but also of maintaining skilled teams of designers and work-
ers. As the market for conventional weapons is saturated in the post–Cold
War world, so subsidies for arms exports have increased. Governments
trumpet loudly about the jobs secured through arms exports deals but keep
as quiet as possible about the subsidies used to secure those deals (World
Development Movement 1995). Military exports accounted for only 1.7
percent of British exports between 1985 and 1994 but received 33 percent
of government export credit guarantees, and between 1990 and 1994 the
Export Credit Guarantees Department had to use an average of approximately $400 million per year in taxpayers' money to recompense arms
companies when countries defaulted on their payments for weapons. The
British government looks likely to lose approximately $1.5 billion to arms
companies through such guarantees due to Iraq's refusal after its war with
the U.S.-led coalition in 1991 to pay for British weapons received
(Sweeney 1993: 31–32). Other hidden British government subsidies include the funding of two-thirds of military R&D (as opposed to one-third
of civilian R&D) and payments of approximately $600 million per year
(about 20 percent of the value of arms exports) to arms industries to allow
them to undercut the prices of their competitors. Overall, the arms trade,
like the nuclear industry, is much less lucrative than governments like to
make out. Commercial rationales for it disguise the deeper priority of
keeping the military industrial base in being for use by the state.

The other way to square the circle is to provide a volume of orders for one's own armed forces that is sufficiently large and regular to keep in being an armaments industry of the desired size and scope. In this way, the desire to maintain capacity results in the creation of an internalized push for arms production up to a level sufficient to meet the needs of the industry. That push will produce a pattern of arms production that bears no direct relation to any action–reaction dynamic with a rival power, even though the need to maintain a capacity of a given size is defined by the existence, and the character, of the external rival.

Economic Management

The interests of political leaders are served by having predictable military budgets, and this contributes to the shaping of military procurement by organizational momentum. If military budget decisions can be made routine, then less time has to be spent arguing over them. More planning stability can then be given both to organizations concerned with military affairs and to programs that compete with military requirements in the annual process of budgetary resource allocation. Domestic political interests can also impinge on the budgetary process in several ways that feed into the arms dynamic. The government may decide to use increased military spending as a means of stimulating demand within the economy—though again this only applies to the small group of significant arms producers. This technique is especially useful in a country like the United States, where Keynesian measures of economic stimulation might, in themselves, attract ideological opposition. It is easier to get taxpayers (and legislators) to consent to subsidies for high-technology industries if they are justified as necessary to the military security of the country. For example, President Truman played up fears of a possible Soviet invasion of Western Europe to secure congressional support for military spending that would prop up the U.S. aircraft industry, which had expanded massively during World War II (Kofsky 1995). Military spending tends to be less controversial than welfare measures and other public works, and governments are more in control of the variables that govern the need for military measures. The international system may oblige by providing threats that are real enough to be exaggerated if the need to do so for economic reasons arises.

Electoral Politics

Political factors can influence military spending more directly, particularly when electoral considerations come into play (Gray 1971a: 74–75). For arms-producing states, military procurement decisions can make a big impact on patterns of employment and income in specific electoral districts or constituencies. Whether in terms of new investment and new jobs, or the maintenance of existing plants and jobs, such decisions cannot avoid entanglement in the political process by which individual politicians and political parties seek to enhance their electoral appeal. Members of the U.S. Congress even play to this perception of "pork barrel" politics: Kenneth Mayer (1991) has shown that they try to make it look as if military contracts are awarded to their district because of their political sway, even when other reasons actually underlie the decision. On a larger scale electoral considerations can shape the way that parties campaign on military issues (Baugh 1984: 101–103; Gray 1976: 33–36). The U.S. presidential campaigns leading up to the Kennedy administration in 1960 and the Reagan administration in 1980 are instructive in this regard. In both cases the winning candidates raised alarms about military weakness created by their predecessors and promised to build up the armed forces. It is always difficult to separate genuine concern from calculation of electoral advantage in such cases. James Lindsay (1991) argues that members of the U.S. Congress are concerned with good policy as well as pork barrel politics for electoral purposes. What we can say is that, in many states, pointing to foreign threats is frequently an effective means of getting political support. Only when states and their societies either take up antimilitary attitudes (as in Japan and Costa Rica) or become firmly embedded in security communities (the European Union) does this ploy cease to be easily available.

The Military-Industrial Complex

There is an obvious parallel interest among the organizations concerned with R&D and production, those concerned with consuming military goods, and the politicians with their economic and electoral concerns. This parallel interest underlies the idea of a "military-industrial complex," a term coined by President Eisenhower, which generated a sometimes polemical literature during the early 1970s. The concept of a military-industrial complex had the merit of pointing to the importance of domestic structural inputs into the arms dynamic. It led to the more detailed studies of the individual components of domestic structure reviewed here. It also drew attention to the possibility that the process of arms acquisition had a momentum of its own that might not serve whatever was defined as the national interest, and that was both strong enough and independent enough to be an important part of the arms dynamic. In other words, coalitions of particular military-industrial interests sometimes deliberately cooperate to promote their own interests, even at the expense of the national interests they are meant to serve. This was the case with the U.S. B-1 bomber program, where the U.S. Air Force, aircraft manufacturer Rockwell, and a group of Congress members combined to ensure its acquisition (Kotz 1988; Brown 1992; Farrell 1995, 1997). However, military-industrial interests collectively do not form a single unit or political actor and do not dominate national policy: they are usually deeply divided and in competition with each other (Sarkesian 1972; Gray 1976; Rosen 1973; Koistinen 1980; Kaldor 1982; Graham 1994). Key questions for any weapons procurement process are whether it can be subordinated to broader security goals and whether it can be made accountable to the public (Singh 1997). The idea of a military-industrial complex obviously came out of the conditions in a major producing state, the United States. However, the concept has also been applied to the Soviet Union (Bialer 1987) and to countries such as Sweden and Japan (Ikegami-Andersson 1992) and Brazil (Conca 1997). For states without a significant arms industry the idea is more problematic, but it could perhaps still be used to identify within a state a nexus of military and political interests capable of influencing military expenditure for its own purposes. States in which the military plays a major role in government would be particular candidates for this type of nonproducer military-industrial complex.

Organizational Politics

The military-industrial complex style of analysis of the arms dynamic was preceded and arguably has been superseded by the evolution of a variety of organizational politics approaches. The excessively sweeping nature of the military-industrial complex perspective has been a key element in its downfall. Many studies of the arms acquisition process in the United States (Allison and Morris 1975; Gray 1979: chapter 2; Gray 1979; Evangelista 1988; Farrell 1995, 1997) point to a major role for the momentum that arises out of the desire to simplify and stabilize the process of government and out of the conservative character of large organizations, although Edward Rhodes (1994) has challenged this view robustly.

Armed services organizations often develop fairly fixed views of their missions and the mainstream weapons systems that they prefer. These views are shaped as much by national historical experience, by the traditions of the individual services, and by the interests of organizational survival, as by considerations of what the opponent is doing. Service views play a major role in which systems get built or bought. The U.S. Air Force, for example, has a long-standing attachment to bombers. This attachment owes at least as much to air force traditions and self-image as it does to the rather strained argument that bombers add necessary flexibility to a long-range bombardment capability that is more effectively and cheaply achieved with cruise and ballistic missiles (Kotz 1988; Brown 1992; Farrell 1997). At its mildest, the conservatism of the armed forces results in types of weapons being kept in service longer than the evolution of technology would dictate. Examples of this range from horse cavalry through battleships to heavy bombers. At worst, it results in the syndrome that Mary Kaldor (1982) labels "baroque technology," in which favored weapons are developed to such a pitch of complexity that their ability to function in combat becomes doubtful. Aircraft like the F-111 tended in this direction, and much of the criticism of the Strategic Defense Intiative was on grounds that it would be far too complex to work reliably. Theo Farrell (1995, 1997) has rightly argued that much more attention should be paid to what he calls "macro-wastage" of billions of dollars on weapon systems that are not needed or do not work than to "micro-wastage" of millions of dollars on cost overruns and overcharging by manufacturers. Even inter-service rivalry often gets channeled into a routine "fair shares" principle of budget allocation.

Because military organizations tend to be conservative, the question arises as to the source of innovation in such organizations. In a very useful review essay that tackles this issue, Farrell (1996) applies the distinctions drawn by W. Richard Scott (1992) between organizations as rational, natural, or open systems. The rational systems view is that organizations innovate to pursue clear goals more effectively and resist innovation that seems to be inefficient. According to natural systems theory, organizations seek to survive—they resist innovations that threaten their existence and back those that protect them. This is the classic bureaucratic politics approach developed by Graham Allison (1971) (cf. Rhodes 1994). Finally, open systems theory—also known as "the new institutionalism"—presents organizations as socially constructed by factors internal and external to them: they embody rules and cultures. Innovation here is a product of changes in the forces of social construction. These three approaches are summarized in Table 7.1.

The rational systems approach is rarely used in organizational analysis now. The trend in recent years has been from an emphasis on the natural systems approach to a preference for open systems theory. The natural and open systems literatures overlap significantly because both do not take organizations at face value. This literature is an important corrective to a potential pitfall of the technological imperative notion—namely, a tendency to presume that technology is developed simply as a natural response to the development of scientific knowledge. Among many others, Judith Reppy (1990) has pointed out that it is just not the case that if a piece of weapon technology can be made, it will be made: the empirical record clashes strikingly with claims of technological determinism. The sociology of technology approach inherent in natural systems theory to some degree, but especially in open systems theory, is a key that will unlock more doors than a rational systems or technologically determinist approach (Farrell 1996). It makes no difference whether it is the Trident missile program (Spinardi 1994), increases in missile accuracy in general (MacKenzie 1990), the way in which U.S. nuclear weapon damage assessments take into account blast but not thermal effects (Eden 1992, 1995), the adoption then rejection of Western military doctrine by Japan in the

Table 7.1   Organizational Politics and the Arms Dynamic

Organizations	Functions of organizations	Examples in literature	Examples of sources of innovation and relevant literature
Rational systems	Efficient pursuit of clear interests	Doubler 1994, Rhodes 1994	• Improve efficiency: Doubler 1994, Rhodes 1994
Natural systems	Survival: accommodate networks of interests (interests creating ideas)	Allison 1971, Posen 1984, Evangelista 1988, Rosen 1991, Zisk 1993, Avant 1994, Farrell 1997	• Defeat in war: Posen 1984 • Civilian intervention plus military "mavericks": Posen 1984, Farrell 1997 • Visionary officers: Rosen 1991, Farrell 1997 • Cross-organizational policy communities: Zisk 1993
Open systems	Being shaped by and shapers of socially constructed rules/ cultures/ideas (ideas also creating interests)	Bijker, Hughes & Pinch 1990, MacKenzie 1990, Powell and DiMaggio 1991, Scott 1992, Scott et al. 1994, Eden 1992, 1995, Mayer 1994, Spinardi 1994, Kier, 1995	• Changes of environment by organization: Eden 1992, 1995, Cameron 1994 • Learning from/rejection of ideas from other countries: Humphreys 1995 • Diverse, competing sub-cultures: Vennesson 1995, Kier 1995

1920s (Humphreys 1995), or variations in the ways in which LICs adopt and adapt Western military technology.

The Unifying and Identity-Creating Roles of Military Threats, Real and Unreal

The general line of the more nuanced military-industrial complex and organizational politics arguments can be expanded from mere electoral considerations and applied to the functioning of the whole state as a political organism (Gray 1976: 31–33; Burton 1984; Kaldor 1985, 1990). The basic case here is that states are relatively fragile political structures and that the task of governing them is made possible in some cases, and easier in others, by cultivating the unifying force of military threats. Such threats will thus be positively sought out and amplified by governments even where the objective basis for them is weak. Without the threats, domestic divisions and dissatisfactions would rise to higher priority on the political agenda, either threatening the status of the ruling elite or making the process of government more difficult. Such arguments have an obvious relevance to politically weak states like Pakistan, where the religious basis of the military and political rivalry with India helps to hold together a country otherwise threatened by serious ethnic and ideological splits. The threats also apply, albeit in a milder fashion, to such military postures as France's strategic nuclear forces designed to emphasize national prestige. Some writers have interpreted the superpower relationship in this light, where the unifying stimulus of rivalry helps to disguise stale ideologies and economic systems incapable of living up to the expectations of their populations (Burton 1984; Kaldor 1985). David Campbell's (1992: 8) approach shows how U.S. foreign policy can be understood "as a practice central to the constitution, production, and maintenance of American political identity," rather than only taking U.S. foreign policy solely for what it purports to be—a necessary means for dealing with the outside world.

Civil War and Internal Repression

For many weak states (Buzan 1991a: 96–107), the primary way in which domestic politics and the arms dynamic interact is that arms are acquired to have the means to fight civil wars or repress domestic populations. In these cases, unity and identity by means of external military threats may not have been attempted or may have failed. In 1995 thirty major armed conflicts were being waged, and every single one was taking place primarily within, not between, states. If the opponents of state repression are fighting back, the demand for arms and military training is likely to be higher and the involvement in the arms dynamic deeper. Where the state is weak, and internal violence is a major feature of domestic political life, then that violence may become the principal determining factor in how that state relates to the arms dynamic.

In nearly all cases of civil war and internal repression there is significant involvement by other states, often the United States and the Soviet Union (and now Russia)—Serbia and Croatia in the war in Bosnia–Herzegovina; Pakistan in Afghanistan; Israel, Syria, and Iran in Lebanon; and both South Africa and Cuba in Angola and Mozambique provide other examples, often in terms of arms supplies and military training for strategic, ideological, or economic reasons (Harkavy 1985; Neuman 1988; Pearson, Brzoska, and Crantz 1992; Herring 1997b). Liberal democracies ostensibly have values antithetical to supporting internal repression, but in practice varying combinations of perceived economic and political interests have ensured that these democracies frequently arm brutal dictatorships or states headed by leaders chosen through unfree elections. Although the member states of the Organization for Security and Cooperation in Europe passed a declaration in 1993 that opposes arms sales that might be used for internal repression or exacerbate existing conflict, the arms trade and military aid have been essentially unaffected (World Development Movement 1995). For example, in 1995 the Conservative government in Britain lifted its ban on the sales of military equipment (including counterinsurgency equipment) to Guatemala even though the Guatemalan army routinely massacres civilians as part of a repression in which it has killed around 150,000 people since 1945 (O'Shaughnessy 1995). The Labour government elected in 1997 has pledged to end British exports of weapons intended for internal repression purposes; whether or not it will act on this remains to be seen. In the 1970s, the United States dispensed tens of millions of dollars of military aid in arms and training to support regimes that routinely tortured and murdered their citizens—in Latin America: Argentina, Bolivia, Brazil, Chile, Colombia, the Dominican Republic, Guatemala, Haiti, Mexico, Nicaragua, Peru, Paraguay, Uruguay, and Venezuela; in Europe: Greece, Portugal, Spain, and Turkey; in Asia: Indonesia, the Philippines, South Korea and South Vietnam; in the Middle East: Saudi Arabia and Iran; and in Africa: Morocco and Tunisia (Klare 1977; Chomsky and Herman 1979).

Although this aspect of the arms dynamic is mostly of low technology and involves relatively small resources compared with those spent on major weapons systems, its political and human impact is large and widespread (Wolpin 1986). Furthermore, using local authoritarian regimes to repress any direct or symbolic threat to perceived U.S. interests and having them buy at subsidized rates the means to do so has assisted the United States in staying at the leading edge of the arms dynamic. In other words, the low-technology, low-pace aspect of the arms dynamic can be functional for the high-technology, high-pace aspect. For instance, the trade in small arms contributed significantly to the genocide in Rwanda in 1994 (Goose and Smyth 1994). With the end of the Cold War and the collapse of the Soviet Union, the superpower rivalry incentive for the United States to pump arms into weak states has gone. However, antileftist ideological motives remain, and commercial and criminal motives and actors are strong.

As is illustrated by the inquiries into the arming of Iraq, commercial interests willing to sell arms are quite ruthless and are often sanctioned by their nations' governments. Further examples are in postapartheid South Africa, which is unable to stop the illegal flow into its civil society of small arms left over from civil wars in Angola and Mozambique, and South Asia, which is similarly flooded with illegal small arms from Afghanistan (Smith 1995). Then there are the leftover weapons from the former Soviet Union that are seeping into Europe and many other places through organized-crime channels.

The problem is not only that small arms are being distributed for political reasons, but that they are cheap and readily available through both legal and illegal channels. In this sense, the low-technology, low-pace aspect of

the arms dynamic is a source of problems even for states generally identified with the high-technology, high-pace end of the arms business. Small-
arms proliferation is a minor part of the arms dynamic but it has major
consequences for world politics.

Variations in the Domestic Structure Model

The fact that the domestic structure literature draws so heavily on the U.S.
experience, and to some extent on the Soviet one, makes it problematic to
assume that the model can be applied to other cases and other types of case
without modification.

Differences Between the U.S. and Soviet Cases

Although there may have been useful parallels between the superpowers in
terms of military production requirements, governmental momentum, military lobbies, and autism, there were differences in terms of R&D style,
history, military tradition, economic management, and political pressures
(Jahn 1975; Holloway 1983: chapters 6–8; Evangelista 1988). The Soviet
Union was not driven by the same deeply rooted market forces that made
and continue to make technological innovation such a feature of the U.S.
political economy. It did not have the same kind of internal pluralism that
allowed nongovernmental organizations to become powerful domestic actors. Nor did it have the competitive party structure and nongovernment
press that made public opinion, within limited parameters, an important
factor in Western debates about defense policy and military procurement.
In one sense, it was argued that the Soviet Union did not have a military-
industrial complex because there was no independent set of military interests within it. In another sense, it was argued that the whole country was
a military-industrial complex because military and governmental interests
were interlocked both organizationally and in terms of shared views
(Bialer 1987).

Differences Between the United States and
Other Western Democracies

There are also important differences between the United States and the
other Western democracies, even though some of the political parallels are
more in harmony than they were between the superpowers. In many of
these countries, the electoral appeal to foreign threats is much less attractive than it is in the United States. During the Cold War, this was evi-
denced by the consistently lower level of military expenditure (as a percentage of GNP) in Japan and most of the Western European states, as

compared with the United States. With a few exceptions, the arms industry is also weaker in relation to the economy, more under state control, and under much higher pressure to export in order to both survive and to achieve economies of scale.

Differences Between Major Arms Producers and Minor or Nonproducers: Primary and Secondary Arms Dynamics

If we try to carry the domestic structure model to the arms dynamic of the part-producers and nonproducers, many of which are LICs, the content of the model needs substantial reworking. The idea of some degree of internal generation of the arms dynamic probably remains valid for most countries, but the form it takes varies widely according to the type of political economy in the state concerned. The most generally applicable elements of the domestic model are the existence of organizational pressures from the military establishment on weapons procurement and the domestic insecurity factors behind autism. Even these common factors will vary greatly from country to country. Organizational pressures from the military, for example, will take forms in states where the military runs the government quite different from those in states where the military is subordinate to civilian political leaders. In addition, as discussed above in the subsection on civil war and internal repression, quite a few LICs are so politically weak that domestic security problems define their principal requirement for armed force. This adds a strong practical dimension to the autism case, for it means that the demand for weapons is determined by the insecurity of the government in relation to its own citizens. This factor is present to some degree in all countries. It is relatively insignificant in the politically stable states in the West, more significant for states in the middle range, like India and Brazil, and dominant for weak states like Sri Lanka, Chad, Algeria, and Sudan.

In countries where the arms industry is small, or nonexistent, many of the most powerful forces evident in the U.S. case will not operate. In the absence of an arms industry there can be no R&D or production-sector push, little electoral factor in the siting of arms industries and the disposition of procurement orders, and no Keynesian demand management of the economy to drive the arms dynamic from within. In such countries, military procurement requires imports, and is therefore more clearly at odds with the economic interests of the state than in cases where procurement supports a domestic industry. Although the top end of the arms production hierarchy has flattened somewhat, there is still a clear gap between the top arms producers and all the rest: as Eric Arnett points out, "It remains difficult for any but a few producers to develop military systems embodying advanced technology" (1996b: 381). This underscores the importance of our distinction between primary and secondary arms dynamics.

The Shift in Emphasis from Primary and Toward Secondary Arms Dynamics

There is a need for a new distinction in analyses of the arms dynamic between relationships in which the participants are themselves major producers of arms and those in which they are primarily importers. This distinction applies to the arms dynamic as a whole, but is particularly important in cases of arms competition and arms racing.

There will be gray-area cases in which the participants are part-producers (the two Koreas) or in which one side is a significant part-producer and the other is a nonproducer (e.g., apartheid South Africa and the front-line states). More rarely, one might find an arms competition between a producer and a nonproducer (e.g., the United States and Cuba). We can use the term "primary" to designate the classical arms dynamic between major producers, and "secondary" to designate one involving only lesser part-producers or nonproducers. Since, as argued in Chapter 3, the diffusion of production capability is a slow, although certainly accelerating process, many countries will remain dependent on arms imports—especially in major weapons systems—for quite some time, and many will always be nonproducers. This means that secondary dynamics are not about to fade away.

The great bulk of the existing literature about arms competition and arms racing has stemmed from concern about relations among great powers and therefore assumes that races are primary. Yet decolonization, and the diffusion of modern weapons through the arms trade, has created a whole new arena in which the arms dynamic is largely secondary in character. Given the development of a security community incorporating most of the great powers (Buzan 1991b; Goldgeier and McFaul 1992), primary arms dynamics will probably be of diminishing interest in the post–Cold War era. In contrast, if the widespread assumptions about a more regionalized post–Cold War international system are true, then secondary ones will be of increasing interest. If regional security complexes (Buzan 1991a: chapter 5) become more prominent because of the withdrawal of superpower rivalry, then secondary arms dynamics could well become the main focus of concern for this subject.

Surprisingly, the few writers who have taken an interest in cases of secondary arms competitions and races have largely ignored the difference of condition with which they are dealing. Gray's (1971a: 53–54) notion of "hierarchy" gets no closer than the argument that secondary arms races are simply local proxy manifestations of races among the great powers. Kaldor's (1982: chapter 5) idea of a "world military order" goes no further than describing the process of technological diffusion and the uniformities of military technology that it is creating in the international system as a whole. These views are valid as far as they go but they do not give the full picture. They ignore, or discount, both the real independence of the arms dynamic among LICs and the very substantial difference that being dependent on imports rather than on production makes to the whole process of peacetime military interaction between states. The burgeoning literature on the arms trade has been integrated with the literature on arms competition and arms racing to only a very limited degree. What literature there is tends to focus on the impact of the arms trade and arms transfers on the intensity and outcomes of interstate and civil wars rather than on the conduct of peacetime interstate rivalries (Harkavy 1985; Neuman 1988; Pearson, Brzoska, and Crantz 1992).

If a secondary arms dynamic is to any large extent a proxy event for a great-power rivalry, then the first obvious difference is that such a dynamic cannot be considered as a strict dyad (that is, a two-party interaction). At least four states will be involved: the two local clients and their two great-power sponsors. Even if the secondary dynamic is largely a local affair one cannot remove the influence of arms suppliers. The arms dynamic between India and Pakistan is certainly more independent than proxy, but the embargo on arms supplies by the United States and Britain in 1965 had a major impact, especially on Pakistan. External suppliers affect secondary arms dynamics by determining the amount and the quality of the weapons supplied. They can inflate a secondary dynamic into an arms race, or at least arms competition, by pumping large supplies to one or both sides at low cost, as the superpowers did in the Middle East and South Asia. They can also try to restrict the quality and/or quantity of arms made available, although, except for the special case of nuclear technology, this is difficult in a buyer's market. The end of the Cold War has had the mixed effect of reducing the strategic incentive to supply or sell arms while increasing the economic incentive to sell them.

Perhaps the main point of difference between primary and secondary arms dynamics in terms of arms supply is that in a primary dynamic the rate, volume, and quality of supply are mainly constrained by the R&D, productive, and budgetary capacity of the rivals themselves, whereas in a secondary dynamic these variables are under the much looser constraint of what suppliers will agree to provide. A pace of supply set by productive capacity is more predictable than one set by markets. In a primary dynamic, states that are rivals will usually have a reasonable knowledge of the maximum production capabilities of their opponents. Major qualitative transformations in forces like MIRVs or BMD will almost always give plenty of warning and take a long time to be deployed in numbers substantial enough to change the military balance. That warning time gives the rival power an opportunity to respond in some way that will preserve the military balance. By contrast, in a secondary dynamic, where total numbers of weapons are usually, but not always, much smaller than for great powers, new weapons can be introduced rapidly, unexpectedly, and in unknown quantities.

During the Cold War, for example, the Soviet Union made massive transfers of weapons to Egypt, Syria, Somalia, and Ethiopia within short periods. Since the end of the Cold War there have been major imports of arms into the Gulf, South Asia, and East Asia. Such injections can change a local military balance very quickly. However, there are no guarantees of securing a favorable outcome even with a favorable military balance (Harkavy 1985; Neuman 1988; Pearson, Brzoska, and Crantz 1992). Since the potential for arms transfers is a constant condition of life for states dependent on arms imports, there is reason to expect that secondary arms competitions and races will be much more volatile and much more difficult to manage than primary ones. In other words, the technological imperative—the pressure to respond to frequent qualitative changes in military technology discussed in Part 1—is in one important sense easier to live with when it is internalized within states in the form of independent production capability.

Conclusion

The idea of a domestic structure input into the arms dynamic will have a nearly universal validity, but the particular form of it will be different in each country. Use of this model thus requires considerable caution against overgeneralization from the U.S. case, and sensitivity to the quite different features that will mark other cases, especially those involving LICs that do not have substantial arms industries and/or that are preoccupied not with interstate rivalry but with civil war or internal repression. Much of the primary-model literature built up during the Cold War may therefore be of only marginal relevance in the era we are now moving into, which seems much more likely to be dominated by secondary arms dynamics. Even some of the former great powers may get pulled into more secondary modes as the ability of any state to be a full-scope producer is undercut by globalization of the arms industry. Because fewer of its factors operate in a secondary arms dynamic, it seems reasonable to suppose that the domestic structure model will have proportionately less influence in secondary arms dynamics than in primary ones. At the very least, hard questions need to be asked about whether R&D, production, electoral, economic, and military-industrial complex factors work in the same way and with the same effect in part-producers as they do in the full-producer versions of the model. Organizational and weak state factors, which are not dependent on arms production, may of course also play a substantial role in secondary dynamics; but it is hard to avoid the conclusion that in the type of arms dynamic most likely to be prominent in the future, action–reaction factors may well be more dominant than domestic structure ones. It is also hard to avoid the conclusion that the literature in this area needs to be quite fundamentally reformulated and redirected if it is to retain its relevance for the post–Cold War era.

8

RELATING THE TWO MODELS

The action–reaction and domestic structure models of the arms dynamic are most usefully seen as complementary. To get a full picture of the arms dynamic it is also necessary to relate the two models to the technological imperative discussed in Chapter 3. This chapter draws out the ways in which they interact and then considers some of the problems of theorizing about the arms dynamic.

A Technological Imperative, Not Technological Determinism

One can envisage a world in which the technological imperative is absent or extremely weak. Indeed, it was relatively weak in preindustrial history and is also relatively weak for very many states in the world, namely those not engaged in or having little expectation of becoming engaged in serious interstate military rivalry. However, the technological imperative is important because it defines a condition that is deeply structured for states engaged in such rivalry. For the action–reaction model, the technological imperative sets a context in which the technological conditions influencing (but not determining) military power and security are subject to frequent change (Smith and Marx 1994). States involved in rivalries cannot be sure that their existing weapons will remain effective. They may worry that their rivals will gain a military advantage by being the first to achieve a decisive technological breakthrough, although the states may reassure themselves with the thought that such breakthroughs are rare. That said, one of the interesting features of the post–Cold War era is that states at the technological leading edge no longer see each other as military rivals, and therefore will be less driven by the possibility of being outpaced.

Where military rivalries exist, however, the instability caused by the technological imperative creates pressure on states to lead, or at least to not fall too far behind, the pace of change by continually modernizing their armed forces. Large R&D establishments or reliable suppliers may be sought to ensure the capability to respond to both anticipated and unanticipated developments in the military capability of the states' adversaries. If states in intense rivalries fail to keep up with the pace, then it is possible that the effectiveness of their armed forces will decline in relation to the states that do. If these states succeed in keeping relatively close to the leading edge, then the probability of being caught at a disadvantage is reduced, albeit at a higher cost for military provision.

The force of this technological imperative is in most cases mitigated by a number of factors. First, military technology is only one factor, and usually not the most important, in determining the ability of states to achieve political objectives through war, threats, or symbols. Second, most states most of the time do not perceive a serious prospect of war, or the need to use immediate deterrent or compellent military threats, or the need to stay at the technological leading edge to satisfy symbolic political goals. States not engaged in vigorous rivalries have much less to fear or gain from the technological imperative. Many states are more concerned about repressing potential or actual political dissent or about fighting civil wars. (The latest, fanciest model of electric shock baton may be made domestically or bought, but there is no powerful imperative to do so—old electric cattle prods will do pretty much as well for torturing prisoners.) In civil wars, leading-edge technology can be valuable but is extremely unlikely to be decisive. Stinger antiaircraft missiles supplied by the United States to Afghan rebels inflicted losses on Soviet helicopter gunships, but the ebb and flow of the Soviet-Afghan war was caused principally by political factors—for one, Gorbachev's unwillingness to keep paying the political, human material costs of the war and ever shifting patterns of factional fighting among the rebels.

If some states do try to meet the challenge of keeping up with the technological leading edge, they face other pitfalls. They may pursue expensive and futile technological fixes for political problems. In Vietnam, in the 1960s and 1970s, the United States threw every piece of technology short of its nuclear, biological, and chemical (NBC) arsenal (except for chemical defoliants) into the fray, but never did solve the crucial problem of the South Vietnamese dictators' having little political legitimacy. States trying to stay with the technological leading edge also face the costs of embarking on a process that produces an endless flow of new weapons and possibilities of new weapons. That process can provoke a response among other states. A decision to take up the challenge laid down by the technological imperative can result in states behaving in a way that looks like arms racing or arms competition, but where the principal motive is as much keeping up with the leading edge of technological standards as it is keeping up with other states. When the pace of technological innovation is high, one result is to blur the boundaries between the categories within the arms dynamic (i.e., build-down, maintenance, competition/buildup, and racing).

The shifting standard of the technologically possible can render profound changes in the character of the dominant weapons of the day. These changes sometimes result in defense being easier than offense, as with barbed wire and machine guns during World War I, and sometimes in offense being easier than defense, as with the union of nuclear weapons and missiles during the 1950s. The problem of which condition prevails, for how long, and how clearly it is perceived not only affects relations between individual rivals, but also the stability of the international system as a whole. When the defense is dominant, and perceived to be so, aggression is more difficult and less likely, and military security easier to achieve, than when technological conditions favor the offense. It follows also that if the defense is dominant, then resources invested in defense will go further than equivalent amounts invested in offense, and vice versa. The general progress of technology sometimes favors the one, and sometimes the other, and there may be relatively little that states can do to alter quickly the character of whatever technology prevails at a given time.

The main impact of the technological imperative on the domestic structure model is in the setting of technological change as a permanent problem for state military planners. Because military planners have to expect technological change, they tend to institutionalize the process of change within the state, either in terms of permanently organized R&D or in terms of regular imports of up-to-date weapons from better equipped producer states. This qualitative pressure affects all states, whether producers or nonproducers, to some degree, and is one of the most conspicuous features of the post-1945 arms dynamic. Although action–reaction and domestic structure factors do play a substantial role in it, it is important not to lose sight of the point that both sets of factors are themselves heavily conditioned by the independent process of the technological imperative. Nevertheless, it must be stressed that one can perceive the existence of a technological imperative without perceiving technological determinism. The technological imperative represents an unavoidable requirement to consider how to respond to the frequent technological advances of the contemporary world. It does not determine what that response will be or even whether there will be a response of any vigor: that will be influenced to varying degrees by political, domestic structure, and action–reaction factors.

Action–Reaction Promotes National Institutionalization of the Technological Imperative

Action–reaction processes probably serve as a general stimulant to the technological imperative. Insecurity (and, beyond that, pursuit of power) means that more resources are pushed into advancing military technology than would otherwise be the case. This is reinforced by the fragmentation and competition in the commercial world that also pushes the pace of technological innovation. Some theorists argue that these fragmenting, competitive factors of insecurity and capitalism are intertwined. The fact that the highly fragmented and competitive state system of Europe was the birthplace of the revolution of frequent technological change gives weight to this view. It can also be argued, however, that in terms of the international system as a whole, political fragmentation leads to some stifling of the technological imperative, particularly in the huge duplication of effort in national military R&D. Even this, however, is being undermined by the increasing denationalization of the leading arms industries.

It is easier to trace the impact of action–reaction on the technological imperative through the mediating effect of the domestic structure model. The action–reaction model clearly provides a strong motive for states to institutionalize military R&D, but only if the underlying expectation of frequent technological change already exists. If technology was static, then the pressure from action–reaction would impinge only on production capability as states sought to ensure that their rivals could not gain a decisive advantage by exploiting superior capacity for military production. It is thus the combination of action–reaction and technological imperative pressures that generates powerful incentives for some states to create permanent military R&D and production sectors within their economies. Once established, these sectors become both an independent input into the arms dynamic and a part of the idiom in which some states compete with each other.

Domestic Structure

Domestic structure factors in turn influence both action–reaction and the technological imperative. The institutionalization of military R&D, as described above, is part of the larger process that produces the technological imperative. Military-industrial capacity is both a response to and a part of the general condition of technological change. This self-reinforcing circular relationship helps to explain not only the strength of its position within states, but also the strength of opposition to it on the grounds that its activity reproduces the conditions that require its own existence. This latter charge is true, but it is a truth that ought not to be exaggerated. The interests that make up a state's military-industrial capacity are not wholly responsible for the process of technological change. Other forces are also at work. Nevertheless, the fact that military-industrial interests reinforce the trend toward technological change means that there is a serious problem to be addressed.

The presence of domestic structure factors disrupts the process by which the action–reaction model is supposed to work. The existence of an internally driven element of the arms dynamic dissolves the boundary between action and reaction. In so doing, it makes reaction into a continuous process rather than an episodic one and reduces the sensitivity of each side to the specific actions of the other. Increases or decreases of strength by either side may elicit little or no response from the other if armaments programs are locked into a set of domestic structures. When responses do occur, they will be influenced in form, substance, and timing by the internal machineries through which they must pass, perhaps so heavily that it is difficult to discern them as responses at all, whether in terms of idiom, magnitude, or timing.

To the extent that each side is internally driven, neither can easily manage the rivalry by making conciliatory moves. Such moves would encounter opposition from organizationally vested interests within the state making them. If the moves were made, the other state would have difficulty responding to them because of the momentum of its own internal processes. The existence of domestic structure variables thus tends to lock the action–reaction process by institutionalizing it within states. Once locked in this way, states are less able to influence either their own behavior or that of their opponents in the arms dynamic. The result is that the arms dynamic becomes less of a conscious interaction between rivals and more of an automatic process moving in parallel within the rivals. Only major moves aimed at redefining the whole political relationship can break out of this trap, as Gorbachev's revolution in Soviet foreign and security policy showed, even if he did fail in the end to reinvigorate and reconstruct the Soviet Union.

Domestic structures can also generate political consequences for the action–reaction processes (Gray 1976: 100–102). To the extent that the domestic structure model is accepted as the dominant explanation for the arms dynamic, proponents of more arms procurement can argue that higher levels of arms will have no effect on opponents because the opponents' levels of arms are determined internally. Thus hawks in both superpowers argued that implementation of their preferred arms programs would not cause responses from the other superpower because the arms dynamic within the rival was, the hawks claimed, determined by the domestic pressure of its military-industrial complex. If both sides think in this way, and the action–reaction process works to a significant degree, then the political use of this analytical idea will create pressure in favor of a steady rise in overall force levels.

A big question for the future is how these cross-linkages between the models will work in secondary arms dynamics, where the domestic structure factors will certainly be different from those in primary ones, and perhaps less influential overall.

Problems in Studying the Arms Dynamic

The use of our proposed composite for analyzing the arms dynamic, though an improvement, by no means solves all the problems attending the study of this difficult phenomenon. The problems discussed are not unique to theorizing about the arms dynamic: they are part and parcel of the problems involved with social science theorizing in general.

Problems Caused by Basic Concepts Being Sites of Political Struggle

The different models can be seen as representing different aspects of reality, but they can also be seen as political attempts to construct reality by portraying it in a certain light. As already noted, the domestic structure model can serve the interests of those wishing to argue that arms increases by their side will not stimulate reactions from a rival. The action–reaction model fits into the needs of those advocating arms control, and the idea of a technological imperative could serve the needs of those wanting to argue that nothing can be done about the whole process. The ease with which ostensibly empirical analytical devices can be used for polemical purposes is thus one of the principal difficulties impeding the debate about arms racing and the arms dynamic more generally. Even the normative status of arms racing is disputed. Despite the widespread negative connotation attached to it, there are quite a few writers prepared to discuss it and arms competition as useful substitutes for war in the management of relations between states (Huntington 1958: 83; Gray 1974: 232–233; Howard 1983: 17–20; Hammond 1993). This normative ambiguity highlights the danger of polemical use that so plagues discussion of the arms dynamic.

Problems in Generalizing from Highly Diverse Cases

The range of behavior within the arms dynamic, added to the complexity of the phenomenon detailed above, has largely defeated attempts to produce a coherent theory of arms competition or arms racing. Gray's (1971a, 1974, 1976) efforts resulted in 7 reasons why states engage in arms racing, 10 descriptive categories, 5 strategies, 5 outcomes, 11 process dynamics, and 6 patterns of interaction. Gray went on to challenge the utility of Grant T. Hammond's similarly complex taxonomies (Hammond 1993; Gray 1995, 1996). At best, the traditional approach leads toward an analytical framework, like the one elaborated here, which provides a menu of ideas and categories for application to particular cases.

Drowning by Numbers: Problems with Quantitative Methods

A rather different, but in the end no more successful, approach has been adopted by the many writers who have built on the pioneering mathematical work of Lewis Richardson (1960). Richardson tried to reduce the essentials of the action–reaction model to a small number of quantifiable variables that he could express in terms of equations. The use of formal models with highly restricted assumptions about the variables in play is often a useful way of opening up and exploring patterns of relationships that would be neither obvious nor easy to handle if one tried to trace them through the jumbled complexities of historical evidence. As a fruitful way of thinking in the abstract, the Richardson school can claim considerable success.

The difficulty of Richardson's approach has been in trying to bridge the gap between highly simplified abstract models and analysis of historical cases. Three problems have prevented this attempt from having much success. The first is that the Richardson approach is tied to the imperfections of the action–reaction model. Richardson's models assume that action–reaction is not only the major driving force of arms racing but that it is a deterministic relationship (Busch 1970: 196–197). That assumption does not fit well with the observed behavior of actual states, which seems to proceed on the basis of a considerably more complicated and diverse set of factors.

The second problem stems from the first in that the rigor of the models cannot be sustained once their highly simplifying assumptions are relaxed sufficiently to incorporate some of the basic complexities of the real world. In the models, one can assume rational actors, perfect information, uncomplicated two-party situations, and a set of actions and reactions that occur in a clear sequence of cause and effect. In the real world, actors are not always rational calculators; information is seldom perfect; states are concerned in their arms policies not only with more than one opponent, but also with allies; and reactions are not always in strict sequential relationship with the actions that are supposed to cause them (Busch 1970; Brubaker 1973: 203–204).

Reliance on simplifying assumptions is an unavoidable necessity of using quantitative methods. Assumptions do not have to reflect reality: they only have to be useful in generating theory. Indeed, it is impossible to avoid making assumptions that exclude big chunks of reality regardless of which methodology one adopts. A theory that was "realistic" in the sense of fitting all of reality would be useless because it would be impossibly complicated. For example, in assuming rationality, one can deduce important things about how rational decisionmakers might act in various circumstances. To assume rationality is to assume that decisionmakers are rational significantly often, not to assume that they are always rational. However, to the extent that the assumption does not fit reality, so the applicability of the theory will be limited. Theory can be both valid and limited in applicability. Attempts to adjust the Richardson models to the complexity of real situations run into awkward problems. How, for example, would one disentangle the arms dynamic between India and China from that between India and Pakistan on the one hand and China and Taiwan on the other? Enriching the variables to try to capture more of reality reduces the clarity that makes the models useful in the first place.

The attempt to engage the models with cases raises a third problem, which is the difficulty of obtaining reliable quantitative measures with which to link the power of the equations to conditions in the real world. Richardson's use of military expenditure as a measure of arms racing, though obviously convenient, is widely thought to be too crude (Bellany 1975: 120–124), but finding more specific measures has proved extremely difficult (Busch 1970: 230–233; Luterbacher 1975: 200–202; Gillespie et al. 1979: 256–257). Here the method runs into a problem that afflicts all quantitative approaches to the study of world politics. Reliable data are hard to get for many countries, especially regarding sensitive areas like military expenditures. Even the study of superpower relations was hampered by lack of firm, comparable data about the Soviet Union. Much of the data available are difficult to compare even within the same period. Measures of GNP, for example, are notoriously inaccurate for countries still possessing a large barter economy that does not register in calculations of monetary value. Few reliable data sets extend far back into history, and even where they do it is hazardous to assume that values have the same significance across historical periods.

The use of statistical techniques also seems prone to generating arguments about method because "apparently insignificant research choices can collectively influence results in a profound way" (Diehl 1983: 210–211). In the case that gave rise to that remark, one author found a 90 percent correlation between arms racing and war, and another found that 77 percent of major-power wars were not preceded by an arms race (Diehl 1983; Wallace 1982). The frequency of such disputes, as well as the specialized language in which they are necessarily conducted, go a long way to explaining why there is relatively little communication between those studying arms racing using the Richardson method and those whose focus is on historical case studies or more traditional analysis in the style of Huntington, Gray, and Hammond.

Conclusion

Taken together, the problems discussed above have contributed to a still relatively weak theory at the heart of the cluster of subjects that make up strategic studies and peace studies. The end of the Cold War adds to this weakness by moving to the forefront a set of secondary arms dynamics that are not well represented in the literature. Setting arms racing into the comprehensive framework of the arms dynamic is valuable but is by no means a panacea. A process has been defined that underlies and influences the whole range of military relations among states (and within states engaged in civil wars). That process is influenced by the political structure of the international system and the scientific and technological drive of what is now a global civilization. Its most extreme form is arms racing, which is widely but not universally held to be a dangerous and undesirable condition. Its regular form is maintenance of the military status quo, which some see as a necessary, and even desirable, consequence of preserving independent states, and others see as wasteful, undesirable, and potentially dangerous. Between racing and maintenance lies competition, and on some occasions the least intense option of build-down has been taken. All of these manifestations of the arms dynamic are highly controversial in analytical, normative, and policy terms. These conflicting attitudes toward the arms dynamic run through the whole strategic debate: they influence positions on force, threats, symbolism, arms control, nonoffensive defense, and disarmament, which are the subjects of Parts 3 and 4.

PART 3

USING
THE ARMS DYNAMIC

In Part 1 we traced the arms dynamic, and in Part 2 we considered explanations of it. Our intention in Part 3 is to analyze the uses to which the arms dynamic has been put. Broadly speaking, military capabilities can be used in three ways: to inflict violence, to make threats, and/or to make symbolic statements that construct how actors see themselves, each other, and the role of force in their relationships. These three functions are conceptually distinct, but we are aware that they overlap in a host of ways. The boundaries we have constructed between them are for analytical purposes. As a general rule (to which there are important exceptions), the making of threats and symbolic statements requires a credible ability to inflict violence. There is nothing fundamentally new about these three functions. All would have been as clear (although by no means precisely the same) to the military rulers of ancient Assyria, Sparta, or Rome as they were to the builders of the British and German navies before World War I or to the contemporary rulers of India and China. However, during the Cold War, the development of nuclear weapons substantially downgraded interest in the use of force and correspondingly upgraded interest in threats and symbols. Threats in particular came to dominate the literature of strategic studies and peace research in the form of expositions and critiques of deterrence theory and, especially, the issue of nuclear deterrence of nuclear attack. There were two main forces behind this shift. First was the simple fear of the consequences of using nuclear weapons in what might become an all-out war. Second was the more calculated consideration of many people (but not everyone) that the overall destructiveness of nuclear weapons had made meaningless the distinction between winning and losing, and thus had gutted the essential purpose of traditional military strategy. There was even some celebration that the shift from actual use of force to mere threats represented a moral advance in security relations.

In this part of the book we attempt a restoration of the balance in thinking about the functions of military capability. Even during the Cold War, the technological products of the arms dynamic were used not only to make deterrent threats but also to convey general symbolic messages, to make compellent threats (that is, threats intended to make someone do something), and to exercise offensive and defensive force. Concern with nuclear deterrence is certainly not dead, as can be seen in Indo-Pakistani relations, but the end of the Cold War has moved it well down the list of priorities for many states. Hence there is more need to think about the other uses to which military capability can be, and is being, put. Chapter 9 examines the use of force, Chapter 10 the use of threats, and Chapter 11 the use of symbols. We also want to consider throughout these chapters the extent to which different types of technology—especially weapons of mass destruction versus conventional weapons—influence both the use and the effectiveness of force, threats, and symbols.

9

FORCE

When it is used directly to inflict violence, military capability can be deployed with one or more purposes in mind. It can be used defensively or offensively. It can be used to repel or reverse attacks, to retaliate, to invade, to punish, or to reduce the military capability of opponents. During the Cold War, and especially in the West, it became quite commonplace to argue that the use of force, and especially its offensive uses, was in decline. In this chapter we discuss the human and material cost of the use of force; offer reasons why there is a reduced occurrence of the large-scale use of force between states; and argue that the contemporary use of force is primarily intrastate, often brutal, usually instrumental, and not fundamentally new in nature. We conclude that the utility of force, overall, is very mixed rather than simply declining.

The Nature of Force

To use force is to act intentionally and physically against an object or an unwilling person. The use of force often inflicts physical damage—but not always, as when people are shoved aside or are restrained physically. We use the term "force" synonymously with "violence." Hannah Arendt (1973b: 114) reserves the term "force" for "the energy released by physical or social movements," but this is a departure from common usage with no noticeable gains. John Keane reserves the term "violence" for "the unwanted physical interference by groups and/or individuals with the bodies of others" (1996: 66–67; see also p. 6) and sees violence against objects as different from violence against people, but without saying why. We agree that there are very significant differences, especially the fact that people feel pain and discomfort while objects do not, and this underlies our view that violence against people is worse than violence against objects. However, degree also matters—many people would prefer to be hit than have their homes and all their possessions destroyed.

The use of force against people and against objects overlaps very significantly in that violence against both is frequently used as a means of attaining or exercising power. Violence is often exercised against both simultaneously for this purpose; and such violence, as Arendt (1973b: 111, 115) argues, relies on instruments, especially technology. One can inflict damage with a fist in a face, but destruction can be magnified enormously through technology, with a finger on a trigger. A recurring theme of security discourse is the tyrant who can rely on technology to minimize the need to rely on people. A key safeguard against the tyrant is that even tyrants require people to do their bidding. Tyrants must find some means of persuading people to act with and for them so that they may be powerful. Purely coercive rule is impossible; even tyrants must have some legitimacy among at least some of their subjects. Ironically, however, this safeguard works better within states than between them. Tyrants must have some domestic supporters, but this logic need not constrain them in exercising violence outside their borders. As numerous episodes in history attest, invaders may treat the people they conquer as animals, to be enslaved, or as vermin, to be eradicated.

Although technology as a force multiplier is feared as a shortcut to achieving power by coercion, and although the effective use of force is a sign of competence at one level, at another level the use of force is often seen as an expression of political failure. As Kurt Vonnegut put it, "violence is the last refuge of the incompetent" (quoted in Wallander 1988: 1). The reasoning behind this understanding is both practical and moral. If politics is about the shaping of human behavior for the purpose of governing large groups of people, then violence is an expensive, unstable, ethically questionable, and in the longer run not competitive way to proceed. It may be cost-effective for extreme purposes such as inflicting or defending against genocide, and it may be necessary (according to those unpersuaded by strategic nonviolence) to preserve political independence. But it is generally inefficient compared with the various forms of government and international relations that depend on legitimate authority and consent. Nevertheless, some theorists have argued that force is the ultimate form of power and that the internal order and the external power of states ultimately rest on force. Such ideas underpin some realist thinking about international relations as a struggle for power, and they contrast with other views of politics, whether domestic or international, that focus on authority. The idea that force is the bottom line of politics is widespread, and underlay the efforts of radical leftists such as the Baader–Meinhof group in Germany, who believed that their terrorist actions would provoke the state into using violent repression, thus revealing its "true" nature.

It is not always clear what is meant by force being the ultimate form of power. If it means that force is the last resort, then this can be shown empirically to be wrong: force is often used before resort to other means of exerting power. If it means that where all other methods fail force can succeed, the problem is that other means can succeed where force fails. What political methods will succeed depends on the objectives, the context, the actions of other actors, skill, luck, and other factors combined. Force can never be exercised purely on its own without other political factors coming into play. Once force is used other means of exerting power also have to be used. In Bosnia, NATO had to accompany Operation Deliberate Force with political maneuvering and follow it up with the Dayton peace agreement. We see force and power as different things, rather than the former being the ultimate or essential type of the latter. Power is about the ability to influence the thoughts and actions of other people in a desired fashion: the use of force may or may not help to achieve this. Force only becomes the ultimate source of power in any sense during war, and even then it has to be used with other instruments. In the broad range of domestic and international politics short of war, force is merely one element of politics and one component of power.

What counts as violence is socially constructed and therefore open to differences of definition and opinion both within and between societies. In Western societies, more acts of force against the person such as rape, corporal punishment of children, and school bullying are being delegitimized by being labeled as violence. Only since 1991 could a man be charged under English law with raping his wife (Kennedy 1992: 130–132). The effects of extending categories are uncertain. Changes in perceptions about what counts as violence or the use of force are products of campaigns against nonstate as well as state violence. The extensiveness and diversity of these campaigns may be thought of as a positive moral sign, but they may also have problematic effects. They may, for example, frighten many people by making them feel that violence has become ubiquitous. They may also weaken the military credibility of the state in the eyes of others. Despite its impressive military technology, the United States is often considered by others to be soft because of its fear of casualties. It was notable during the Gulf War against Iraq that Western concern for the scale of Iraqi casualties was a significant factor governing the behavior of coalition forces. This attitude contrasts markedly with the desire for high enemy casualties that has attended most of the major wars of this century.

Such changes of attitude are far from universal. Countries such as China, Indonesia, and Sudan are quicker than most to use force against their citizens. Iran, Iraq, and China have all recently demonstrated low sensitivity to high casualties in wars with neighbors. According to Physicians for Human Rights, virtually everyone who is detained by the police in Turkey is tortured, whether through suspension above the ground, beatings, violence against sex organs, electric shocks, or the use of high-pressure cold-water jets. However, Turkish doctors responsible for examining detainees do not regard beatings as a form of torture (Nuttall 1996).

From the available information, it is unclear whether this represents the insensitivity of those who see beatings by police as inevitable, normal, and even acceptable, or a sensitivity that the horrors of torture can far exceed a simple physical beating. Extending a category may devalue it.

Genocide is a special and important category of violence (Cigar 1995; Prunier 1995; Horowitz 1996; O'Kane 1996; Rummel 1996; cf. Uekert 1995) Some object to calling what happened to the Bosnian Muslims in the first half of the 1990s genocide on the grounds that perhaps thirty times more Jews were murdered in Hitler's genocide. On the other hand, extending a category may allow one to deal with more. Referring to the actions against Bosnia's Muslims as genocide is a way of emphasizing that something exceptionally awful has happened that goes well beyond what is normally suffered by communities in war, partly in terms of the scale of violence, but also in terms of the intentions of the opponent to eliminate that community as far as possible within a particular territory. The contested nature of violence within and between communities underlies many of the political disagreements about human rights.

A number of efforts have been made to broaden conceptions of violence. The most famous is Johan Galtung's (1984b) development of the idea of "structural" violence (see also Jabri 1996; Burton 1997). Jamil Salmi (1993: 22–23) has proposed a related typology of direct violence ("deliberate injury to the integrity of human life"), indirect violence ("indirect violations of the right to survival" by nonassistance or making dangerous changes in the natural or social environment), repressive violence (denial of fundamental social, civil, and political rights), and alienating violence (denial of higher rights in terms of living conditions, social ostracism, or the ending of a way of life). Salmi presents a depressing catalog of human suffering, and there is much to be said for considering it in all its forms. However, to adopt his typology for our particular project would be an unhelpful widening of perspective to virtually all of politics. What can be said is that for the foreseeable future, world politics will be marked by substantial differences of opinion not only about what counts as violence, but also about the legitimacy (or not) of varying degrees of use of force for a variety of political purposes, both domestic and international.

The Costs of Using Force

The contested nature of force spills over into any attempt to calculate the costs of using it. As in any accounting exercise, it is possible to take positions along a spectrum that ranges from very narrow (or tight) views of what should be included in the account, to very broad (or loose) ones. In this respect, trying to calculate the costs of using force is similar to trying to integrate ecological factors into economic accounting. At a minimum the cost calculation of using force would have to include the following:

- The cost of building and maintaining the instruments and organizations of force
- The cost of operating armed forces during the use of force
- The cost of losses incurred to armed forces during the use of force
- The costs of destruction to civilians and nonmilitary property during the use of force (so-called collateral damage)

In a wider view one could add, inter alia, the following:

- The opportunity costs to the economy of all of the above
- The environmental costs of building, testing, and operating military forces
- The political and moral costs of emphasizing coercion in political relations
- The human and social costs of being exposed to violence

The Saferworld Foundation's True Cost of Conflict program, for example, takes into account economic damage (such as lost trade and damage to infrastructure and agriculture), starvation, disease, human rights abuses, and refugees. To take the last example alone, in 1969 there were 9.8 million refugees from 34 countries: by 1992 there were 16.6 million refugees from 36 countries (Weiner 1996). In 1994, 13 million people were displaced within states. The principal reason behind their flight has been the use of force. Others are trying to draw attention to impact on children of the use of force: in wars between 1985 and 1995, 2 million children have been killed, 4 or 5 million have been disabled, 12 million have been driven out of their homes, over 1 million have lost their parents through death or separation, and 10 million have been psychologically damaged—and the light weight of modern weapons has contributed to the use of children as soldiers (Goodwin-Gill and Cohn 1994; Brittain 1995). Klein (1994: 14–15, 28) is right to argue that strategic studies has traditionally been very squeamish about discussing the social and material costs of violence and preparation for violence. Indeed, "collateral damage" is only one of many euphemisms used in strategic studies. Many in strategic studies take death and destruction very seriously and are motivated to a significant degree by the desire to find ways of avoiding it through such strategies as deterrence. However, many also subordinate concern with the killing involved in war almost completely to the objective of working out how to defeat the opponent. In their policy recommendations for war in Southeast Asia in the late 1960s and early 1970s, many U.S. strategists combined euphemism, the extravagant use of force, and unconcern with the broader costs involved.

In addition to disputes about what to include, there are problems in trying to cost the use of force. One is the technical problem of how to count. When force is used people usually die, but how many? There are different ways of calculating not only how many armed conflicts there are, but also how many people have died in those conflicts. Such considerations are important for understanding the implications of the arms dynamic on conflict. The Stockholm International Peace Research Institute (SIPRI) counts only "battle-related" deaths, but most of those who die because of wars do so indirectly. They are not killed by bombs and bullets but by disease, starvation, exposure to the elements, and forced labor (Krippendorff 1981). In one of the more extreme examples, the native population of Mexico fell from between 9 and 25 million at the time of its conquest by Spain in 1520 to between 1 and 2 million in 1550 (Krippendorff 1981: 98). The dwarfing of battle casualties by postcombat deaths continues to the present. In the fighting in 1991 to expel Iraqi forces from Kuwait, the U.S.-led coalition suffered around 250 dead and Iraq possibly as few as 6,000 dead (half of whom were civilians), although some estimates of the latter are more than ten times higher (MacArthur 1993: 255–257; Mueller 1994: 156–158). In contrast, unknown tens of thousands died during the repression of the subsequent Kurdish and Shiite uprisings in Iraq (MacArthur 1993: 256–257; Mueller 1994: 156–158), and the economic sanctions imposed on Iraq since the war have resulted in the death of around 500,000 Iraqi children under the age of five between 1991 and 1996 (O'Kane 1996). Although the UN Security Council has agreed to permit Iraq to sell oil to raise money for food and medicine, the implementation of this deal had not yet occurred by mid-1997. Each side of this dispute blames the deaths on the intransigence of other side. The United Nations, and especially the United States, is determined that the sanctions should stay in place until it is satisfied that it has fully dismantled Iraq's NBC and associated missile capabilities, and is prepared to accept those deaths that receive minimal publicity in the outside world. For his part, Saddam Hussein has chosen to concentrate spending what little money the country has on rebuilding the armed forces and maintaining the apparatus of his rule of terror. His limited cooperation with the UN Special Commission on Disarmament in Iraq (UNSCOM) reflects his fear that the long-term imposition of economic sanctions may provoke a coup attempt or hinder his ability to exercise power in the future. It has nothing to do with the suffering of ordinary Iraqis, whom he rules to a great extent (but not solely) by terror and violence anyway. The immediate causes of the deaths of the Iraqi children have been disease, malnutrition, and inadequate medical facilities, but the sanctions that brought about these conditions would not have been imposed had Iraq not invaded Kuwait. How many of these casualties should be counted as the cost of using force? And how would one quantify the psychological and physical damage done to millions of people caught up in these events but not killed by them?

A second problem is that costs may well be very unevenly distributed between the participants. This unevenness may be a simple matter of one side bearing more and the other less. But it may be more complicated if each side bears costs of a different type and values the factors involved differently. For example, how would one calculate the relative costs of the Vietnam War to the United States and Vietnam? Vietnam paid vastly more in death and destruction, while the United States paid more in money and reputation. Calculation of cost can blur into calculations of worth. Since Vietnam won the war its costs seem more acceptable, while those of the United States seem less acceptable because it lost.

Reasons for the Reduced Frequency of Large-Scale Use of Force Between States

Large-scale use of force between states is less frequent in the late 1980s and the first half of the 1990s than at any time since 1945. There are four overlapping and mutually reinforcing factors influencing this: fear of the cost of war, interdependence, the spread of liberal democracy, and growing sensitivity to casualties. Interstate war is more likely where these factors are not present. For example, the long and very bloody Iran–Iraq War was fought between undemocratic, nonnuclear states that had leaders who were willing to have their people suffer high casualties.

Fear of the Costs of War

Fear of the costs of using force has grown, and both the price and the power of military technology promote this fear. In part, it is simply about the opportunity costs of building and maintaining armed forces and weapons systems as opposed to pursuing other social goals, but mainly it is about fear of the costs of war. Since 1945 this fear has focused principally on nuclear weapons. The argument that nuclear weapons strengthened deterrence, and so made both nuclear and conventional war between nuclear states less likely, is accepted widely (Waltz 1981; Betts 1988; Jervis 1988, 1989; van Creveld 1991, 1993; Sagan and Waltz 1995) but not unanimously (Mueller 1988, 1989; Sagan and Waltz 1995). The causal mechanism is fear of escalation, as discussed in the next chapter. However, fear of the costs of war began to operate to a significant degree before the nuclear age (Buzan 1991a: chapter 7). It was very palpable in parts of Europe after the 1914–1918 bloodletting, and it did not require nuclear weapons for Europeans (and Japanese) to have learned by 1945 that their powers of destruction had outgrown almost all of the political objectives over which they had traditionally gone to war with each other (Mueller 1989; see, more generally, Gabriel 1987; Zeldin 1994; cf. Pick 1993).

Interdependence

The arguments linking interdependence to a decline in the use of force (Keohane and Nye [1977] 1989) stem from classical liberal arguments about the benign effects of free trade. One key argument is that economic openness reduces incentives to use force for economic gain. If access to resources and markets is made the general rule, then states have no incentives to build closed territorial domains. Force is generally essential for such empire building but is largely irrelevant to complex market relations. A second key argument is that opening trading arrangements increases both specialization and (because they are more economically efficient) welfare. As states become more specialized, and more dependent on trade to sustain levels of welfare, the cost to them of using force rises. To the extent that war disrupts economic relations interdependence makes that cost higher. When levels of specialization pass beyond a certain point, the resort to force becomes difficult because of the inability of states to mobilize independently. Over the past few decades interdependence has grown markedly among the Western states, and may have contributed powerfully to the virtual elimination of war among them. With the abandonment by the Soviet Union and China of autarkic economic policies, the logic of interdependence would seem to be well placed to play an ever wider role as a constraint on interstate war in the international system.

The Spread of Liberal Democracy

Wars between liberal democracies appear to be much rarer than wars between states that are not liberal democracies or between liberal democracies and other states, and this appears to be related to the nature of liberal democracy itself (the burgeoning literature includes Doyle 1983a, 1983b; Mueller 1989; Russett 1993, 1995; Russett and Maoz 1993; Owen 1994; Ray 1995; Russett and Ray 1995; Rummel 1996; Maoz 1997, forthcoming). However, these claims have been disputed vigorously from many angles (Cohen 1994, 1995; Layne 1994; Spiro 1994; Ayoob 1995: 194–195; Farber and Gowa 1995; Oren 1995; Macmillan 1996). There are definitional problems about the necessary and sufficient conditions for a country to be counted as a democracy. Was Germany a democracy in 1914? Was Britain (whose women did not then have the right to vote)? Anyway, it appears that democracy alone is not enough: it must be liberal democracy (Owen 1994; Oneal et al. 1996). Iran is in some ways quite democratic in that voting plays a significant role in its politics, but it is certainly not liberal (Fukuyama 1992: 44). France, fearing an Islamic victory, has opposed elections in Algeria since 1991.

Illiberal democracy may make war more likely because of the tendency of elites to try to ensure electoral support through populist and extreme ethnic nationalist rhetoric and policies (Mansfield and Snyder 1995; Wolf et al. 1996; Herring 1997a, 1997b). Although wealthy liberal democracies rarely if ever go to war with each other, their relationship with the rest of the world has not been so peaceful. We emphasize this here at some length because of this relationship's almost total neglect, or its misrepresentation as defensiveness in a dangerous world, in the liberal democratic peace literature. Liberal democracies have been extremely intolerant of states that do not wish to be part of a global market economic system (Chomsky 1994; Klein 1994: chapter 4). Such occasions have not been the exception but the rule in the establishment of empires over the past few hundred years, and then in the maintenance of Western, and especially U.S., influence after decolonization.

If one accepts the claims of the "liberal democratic peace" school, and wants to reduce interstate war still further, then increasing the number of liberal democracies in the world would seem to be the way forward. Promoting liberal democracy to make war less likely is constrained by the way in which the United States, in particular, has a long history of attempting, often successfully, to bring about the overthrow of elected governments that it regards (often with exaggerated fear) as too economically protectionist or left-wing. Examples include Iran in 1953, Guatemala in 1954, Guyana between 1953 and 1964, Indonesia in 1957, Ecuador between 1960 and 1963, Costa Rica in the 1950s and 1970s, and Chile between 1970 and 1973. Currently the evidence is unclear, but the United States may also have been involved in trying to subvert elected governments in Greece in 1967, Jamaica between 1976 and 1980, and Australia in 1975 (Van Evera 1990; Pilger 1992: 185–238). It has only tolerated or promoted democracy where it expects that country to be open to U.S. economic penetration. In places such as El Salvador, it endorsed as valid elections that were conducted in an environment of antileftist state terror, but opposed elections in Vietnam and Nicaragua when it anticipated left-wing victories. Although U.S. journalists like to see themselves as speaking truth against power, the dominant form of the news coverage of the U.S. role in these cases has been to present an image of U.S. policy as essentially benign and prodemocratic, but capable of making tragic mistakes (Herman and Chomsky 1988; Pilger 1989; Cumings 1992; Pedelty 1995). The view that the United States lost the Vietnam War because of negative television coverage is a myth: it lost the war because it failed, in spite of the massive use of force at great cost to itself, but far greater cost to Vietnam, to make the Vietnamese people submit to the dictatorships it sought to impose (Pilger 1989: 254–265).

In recent years, as more and more states have opened up access to their economies, the United States has perceived less need to resort to such policies. U.S. President Bill Clinton has emphasized that he accepts liberal democratic peace theory and has stated his intention of promoting liberal democracy to promote peace. The growing number of liberal democracies in the world is an encouraging sign. From 1972 to 1994, their number more than doubled from 44 to 107, and of 187 states in 1994, 58 percent were liberal democracies, reaching all regions of the world for the first time (Huntington 1991). How much the United States helped or hindered this process is contested. The collapse of the Soviet Union took with it much of the international legitimacy of, and external support for, one-party states. It put markets and democracy into a hegemonic position. In recent years, especially in the democratic revolutions in Eastern Europe, the news media have facilitated an important demonstration effect. People could see that forces of liberal democracy were winning victories, and were encouraged to act. However, one must guard against unwise promotion of crude democratization in illiberal societies that lack the social cohesion to make democracy work. There are questions about how stable much of the new wave of democratization will be.

Democratic values have shallow roots in many states and, where multiparty democracy reinforces ethnic and/or religious divisions, may simply turn out to be a formula for the elective dictatorship of a fixed majority group. One must also guard against unwise backing of illiberal forces in societies where there is real potential for liberal democracy. Which of these two categories Western policy fell into in the case of former Yugoslavia will be disputed endlessly: what we can say is that the symbolic politics of illiberal democratization in former Yugoslavia encouraged war. More generally, whether failed democracies contribute more than non-democracies to inter- or intrastate violence remains to be seen.

Sensitivity to Casualties

There is a new sensitivity in liberal democracies to casualties being incurred (and to a much lesser extent inflicted) by their forces, especially where there appears to be little to be gained from such sacrifices of life and where there are gruesome pictures of casualties in the mass news media. This was strikingly the case in Somalia, when the death of some U.S. soldiers in 1993 contributed to a U.S. withdrawal (Ramsbotham and Woodhouse 1996: chapter 7; Shaw 1996: 170–171, 179). It also explains in part the unwillingness of the United States in 1994 to invade Haiti to remove the military dictatorship there. The main U.S. objective—stopping the flow of refugees from Haiti to Florida without bringing about a regime change that would be too far to the left—was achieved without the use of force anyway because the United States was able to intervene as part of a negotiated settlement.

In the contemporary international system, some governments (most obviously China, Iran, Iraq, and Afghanistan) remain quite insensitive to military casualties, while others have become hypersensitive (especially to their own casualties, but sometimes to those of their opponents), most obviously the United States, Germany, and Japan. The new sensitivity among Western governments to casualties among their forces became known in the United States as the "Vietnam syndrome" and in the West more broadly as "combat reluctance" or "self-deterrence." For some, such as the International Institute for Strategic Studies, this is a "problem" (*Strategic Survey 1995–96* 1996: 48–57). For others, combat reluctance on the part of the West would on balance serve their values. For yet others, the problem is that the West is combat willing when it should be combat reluctant (against Iraq in Kuwait, perhaps) and combat reluctant when it should be willing (against Serb nationalists in Bosnia, perhaps).

Whatever the explanation(s) for this trend—liberal democracy, mistrust of government, smaller families, higher value placed on human rights—it reinforces a characteristic of advanced capitalist societies to move toward ever more capital-intensive modes of destruction. This move reflects the same logic as the parallel one toward more capital-intensive modes of production. It both reduces labor costs (and power) and centralizes control. In the case of capital-intensive destruction, it also reduces the political cost to governments of resorting to force by enabling one's own casualties to be kept low. But this trend seems steadily to raise the basic costs of building and maintaining armed forces. With a single fighter aircraft now costing several tens of millions of dollars, and a major aircraft carrier several billion dollars, the financial costs of military technological modernity are increasingly formidable.

Sensitivity to casualties, and especially civilian ones, has had three other significant consequences with regard to technology.

The first is a paradoxical one. Images of suffering relayed by the technology of the news media create pressure for humanitarian action of some kind to allay that suffering, but sensitivity to casualties makes effective military intervention politically more difficult (Mandelbaum 1994; Ramsbotham and Woodhouse 1996; Shaw 1996). We explore the issue of humanitarian intervention in greater detail later in this chapter.

Sensitivity to casualties has accelerated the second effect, namely, research into and development of what are usually called "nonlethal" weapons. These may be designed to act against people or objects, and may be acoustic (to cause pain and disorientation), chemical (to incapacitate people or damage equipment, for example, by making metal brittle or surfaces slippery), immobilizing (through sticky substances), light based (to blind people or equipment), microwave (to damage electronics), or power disruptive (to prevent equipment working, for example, by biodegrading fuel) (*Strategic Survey 1995–96* 1996: 48–57; Kokoski 1994). Because "nonlethal" weapons can actually be lethal—for example, sticky foam can suffocate people, damaged vehicles can crash—we prefer to call them "low-lethality" weapons (LLWs). However, since the intention with such weapons is not to kill, the use of "nonlethal" is still reasonable. The debates surrounding low lethality are a perfect illustration of the fallacy of technological determinism, that is, that technology alone can ever determine outcomes. LLWs will result in fewer deaths if they are used as a substitute for such traditional weapons as lead bullets and high-explosive grenades. However, they will result in more deaths if they are used as a substitute for nonviolent crowd control in political conflicts within states or for nonviolent negotiations between states: they may help grease the slope from nonviolence to massacre or nonviolence to war. The impact of LLWs will depend on the objectives, values, tactics, and training of those using them and those faced with them. Although much of the technology is new, LLWs as such have been around for a long time, most notably in the form of plastic and rubber bullets, tear gas, pepper sprays, and electric belts. Much can be learned from the record of their use, including the blinding, maiming, and death of many of those against whom they have been used.

Finally, coverage of the suffering of victims of landmines in particular has helped bring about moves toward the delegitimization and banning of landmines. The places in the world most infested with literally millions of landmines include Iran, Iraq, Kuwait, Afghanistan, Cambodia, Bosnia, Croatia, Nicaragua, Sudan, Somalia, Rwanda, Angola, and Mozambique, and each week some 2,000 people are killed or maimed by landmines (Roberts and Williams 1995; Goldblat 1996b; Fairhall 1997). The indiscriminate death and injury, the way that it goes on many years after the fighting is over, the sickening sense that apparently safe places may be deadly, the campaigns of organizations such as the International Committee for the Red Cross, and news media coverage have all combined to produce this delegitimization. Many states have indicated their support for a total ban on their production: only the states that produce them on a large scale—especially China, Russia, and India—have opposed the ban. Some are trying to mitigate the worst effects of landmines by technological fixes such as "smart" landmines, which deactivate or self-destruct after a set period. As with LLWs, the implications of smart landmines are ambiguous and not technologically determined: they may be deployed in addition to, rather than instead of, "dumb" landmines. They may slow the delegitimization of antipersonnel mine warfare or (in the same way that "neutron bombs" in the 1970s increased hostility to nuclear weapons) accelerate it. Military experts cannot agree on whether states giving up antipersonnel (as opposed to large antitank or antiship) mines are putting themselves at a significant military disadvantage (the former chairman of the U.S. Joint Chiefs of Staff, General John Shalikashvili, says they are not), or whether the mines are on balance worth having when the longer-term costs are taken into account.

The new controversy over landmines is an excellent illustration of the way that evaluation of both the wider costs and benefits and even the narrower military utility of a piece of military technology cannot be assessed objectively or be assessed simply through technical performance characteristics: as ever, the process is political and value laden.

The Contemporary Use of Force: Mostly Intrastate, Often Brutal, Mostly Instrumental, and Not Fundamentally New

In spite of the positive trends just discussed, there is a growing literature which argues that in the late twentieth century the use of force is changing dramatically and mostly for the worse in a number of ways. As we see it, there are indeed dramatic changes, but some of them are for the better. Only some of them are for the worse, and there are often reasons to doubt claims that supposed deteriorations reveal much that is new.

The first theme is that intrastate war is burgeoning: hence, in spite of the costs, the use of force continues to be a major factor in world politics. There is much in this point. Where there are severe conflicts of interest between social groups and where weapons are available to those social groups, war is always possible. This is especially the case where those groups are geographically close to each other, a circumstance that occurs more frequently within states than between them. Ideally, the state should prevent such wars within its own jurisdiction by establishing both a legitimate monopoly on the use of force and an overarching political authority. But where the state is too weak to fulfill these functions, the sustained use of political violence becomes likely, with the two main objectives being the overthrow of governments or the secession or at least internal autonomy of particular tracts of territory. Since 1945 and the beginning of the process of decolonization, civil wars have heavily outnumbered interstate wars. By creating a whole new set of weak states and arbitrary international boundaries, the collapse of the Soviet Union and communism in Eastern Europe gave further impetus to the dynamics leading to civil war. In 1995 according to SIPRI, thirty major armed conflicts were being waged in twenty-five locations, and every single one was taking place primarily within a state, not between states (Sollenberg and Wallensteen 1996; see also Table 9.1).

SIPRI defines a major armed conflict as "prolonged combat between the military forces of two or more governments, or of one government and at least one organized armed group, and incurring the battle-related deaths of at least 1,000 people during the entire conflict" (Sollenberg and Wallensteen 1996: 15). The most intense of these (in terms of causing more than 1,000 battle-related deaths in 1995) were taking place in Bosnia–Herzegovina, Russia (Chechnya), Turkey, Afghanistan, Sri Lanka, Algeria, Angola, Liberia, and Sudan: only the conflict in Bosnia–Herzegovina had come to a halt by the end of 1996.

Table 9.1 SIPRI-Defined Major Armed Conflicts in 1995

Location and year force commenced/ recommenced		Opponents of government	Total deaths up to and including 1995
Europe			
Bosnia–Herzegovina	1992	[Govt. of Bosnia–Herzegovina and govt. of Croatia vs.] • Serbian Republic + Serbian irregulars + Yugoslavia	25,000–55,000
Croatia	1990	• Serbian Republic of Krajina + Yugoslavia	6,000–10,000
Russia	1994	• Republic of Chechnya	10,000–40,000
Middle East			
Iran	1991	• Mujahideen e-Khalq	• •
	1979	• Kurdish Democratic Party of Iran	• •
Iraq	1991	• Supreme Assembly for the Islamic Revolution in Iraq	• •
	1980	• Patriotic Union of Kurdistan + Democratic Party of Kurdistan	• •
Israel	1964	• Palestine Liberation Organization	>12,500
	1964	• Non-PLO groups	
Turkey	1984	• Kurdish Worker's Party	>17,000
Asia			
Afghanistan	1978	• Hezb-i-Islami	>15,000 (excludes
	1990	• Hezb-i-Wahdat	over 1 million dead
	1979	• Jumbish-i Milli-ye Islami (National Islamic Movement)	in earlier phases of this conflict)
Bangladesh	1982	• Chittagong Hill Tracts People's Co-ordination Association/Shanti Bahini (Peace Force)	3,000–3,500
Cambodia	1979	• Party of Democratic Kampuchea (Khmer Rouge)	>25,500
India	• •	• Kashmir insurgents	>37,000
	1981	• Sikh insurgents	
	1992	• Bodo Security Force	
	1988	• United Liberation Front of Assam	
Indonesia	1975	• Revolutionary Front for an Independent East Timor	15,000–16,000 (excludes around 200,000 civilian dead since the invasion of East Timor in 1975)
Myanmar (Burma)	1948	• Karen National Union	>14,000
	1993	• Mong Tai Army	

(continues)

Table 9.1   Continued

Location and year force commenced/ recommenced		Opponents of government	Total deaths up to and including 1995
The Philippines	1968	• New People's Army	21,000–25,000
Sri Lanka	1983	• Liberation Tigers of Tamil Eelam	>32,000
Tajikistan	1992	[Govt. of Tajikistan + Commonwealth of Independent States (CIS) Collective Peacekeeping Force in Tajikistan/Russia + CIS Border Troops vs.] • United Tajik Opposition	20,000–50,000
Africa			
Algeria	1992 1993	• Islamic Salvation Front • Armed Islamic Group	25,000–45,000
Angola	1975	• National Union for the Total Independence of Angola	122,000 (since restart of war in 1992). Around 1.5 million military and civilian war dead since 1975
Liberia	1989	[Govt. of Liberia + Economic Community of West Africa Monitoring Group vs.] • National Patriotic Forces of Liberia	>150,000
Sierra Leone	1991	Revolutionary United Front	20,000
Somalia	1991	[No effective central govt.] • United Somali Congress factions/Somali National Union	• •
Sudan	1983	• Sudanese People's Liberation Army (Garang faction)	37,000–40,000 (military)
Central and South America			
Colombia	1978 1978	• Revolutionary Armed Forces of Colombia • National Liberation Army	• • (Around 30,000 have died in the civil wars of the last 30 years or so)
Guatemala	1968	Guatemalan National Revolutionary Unity	<46,300 (95% civilian)
Peru	1986 1986	• Shining Path • Tupac Amaru Revolutionary Movement	>28,000

Source: Based on Sollenberg and Wallensteen 1996.
Notes: Underlined cases indicate over 1,000 battle-related deaths in 1995 alone. The symbol • • means that SIPRI found no reliable figures. The symbol ------- means that the conflicts listed are separate.

The SIPRI criteria for a major armed conflict do not capture a significant element of internal violence that feeds into the arms dynamic, namely, murder and torture by states of their own people when those people have not organized themselves to fight back militarily (i.e., when there is no civil war). These repressive states still maintain a large proportion of their armed forces to not only carry out those acts of violence, but also by an overwhelming show of capability to intimidate the people and deter them from organizing the kind of resistance that would bring the conflict within the SIPRI definition of a major armed conflict. Furthermore, SIPRI's figures also exclude armed conflict where both or all parties are not national governments. This leads to omissions, which SIPRI still notes (Sollenberg and Wallensteen 1996: 17), such as the fighting between nongovernmental actors in 1995 in Bosnia, Afghanistan, northern Iraq, the Kashmir region of India, Liberia, Myanmar, Somalia, and Sudan.

The second theme is that there has been a descent into a "new medievalism" of dispersed political authority and dispersed violence instead of the supposed past of contests between centralized states (Eco 1986; van Creveld 1991; Enzensberger 1994; Kaplan 1994; Holsti 1996). It will come as a surprise to many that there were substantially *fewer* SIPRI-defined major armed conflicts in 1995 (30 in 25 locations) than in 1989 (36 in 32 locations) when the Cold War came to an end (Sollenberg and Wallensteen 1996: 15). Hence the occurrence of civil wars in the Balkans and former Soviet Union since the end of the Cold War is not representative of the global picture—it is the reverse. Martin van Creveld emphasizes what he sees as the undermining of the Clausewitzean distinction between the government, the army, and the people. The claim made by van Creveld that recent wars have been fought by informal rather than professional armies has an important element of truth in it (see also Holsti 1996). However, conventional war in terms of large-scale combat between professional armies or by professional armies against other opposition has occurred a number of times in the 1980s and 1990s, including China–Vietnam, Iran–Iraq, the Gulf War, the Israeli invasion of Lebanon, the Falklands conflict, Eritrea, Croatia versus elements of the former Yugoslav National Army, South Africa's role in Namibia, and the war in Angola (McInnes 1993). In addition, many nonstate military formations have developed formal command structures, rank systems, training programs, and so on—for example, the Chechen rebels, the Bosnian Serb Army, and the forces of the Croatian Defense Council (HVO) in Bosnia have followed this pattern so that they have been much more than civilians bearing arms. Indeed, the HVO was run directly from Croatia by the Croatian regular army. It is true that, in addition to states fighting it out, there are also drug barons, pirates (literally, in the South China Sea), ethnic warlords, heavily armed organized criminals, and religious and political militias. However, all of these violent actors were around in the past.

No society has escaped the use of force within it, whether by the authorities, individual citizens, or groups of citizens. This is what John Keane (1996: 14) refers to as "the problem of incivility" within civil society. Its extreme form he labels "uncivil society," that is, a society dominated by such violence. To the extent that civilization is about the progressive elimination of violence (although, of course, it has been and can be defined in other ways), all societies in this world have a long way to go yet: there is much violence within societies and regression to increased levels of violence occurs. Keane (1996: 36) refers to "one of the most disturbing enigmas that any political theory of violence must face: that there are times and places when civilized manners can and do peacefully cohabit with mass murder." He gives as his examples the terror regimes of Stalin and the Nazis. Less murderous but more uncomfortable is the way the United States combined a significant degree of liberal democracy with murderous wars in Vietnam, Laos, and Cambodia. Where Keane perceives there to be hope is in what he calls a "politics of civility" aimed at delegitimizing and eradicating violence in all its forms, be it genocide, violence against children, or penal violence (Keane 1996: 19–31). Against the conceit of comparing states that have supposedly solved the problem of violence with those that have not, he writes in terms of a highly complex, global pattern of civility versus incivility within all societies. In this political struggle there is the perennial problem of whether the overall level of violence is reduced by concentrating the means to use force in the possession of the state to prevent some citizens from exploiting others, or by dispersing the means of violence to groups above and below the state so that the state is inhibited from launching internal or external campaigns of violence. This question cannot be answered a priori—the answer will vary from case to case. Keane (1996: 5) suggests this sense of growing, ubiquitous, and diverse violence at home and abroad may be due to increased reporting of that violence through the burgeoning news media, especially television. That is part of the story. One must also add that the end of the Cold War had two effects. The first was to focus much more attention on the gangsters and others who had actually been around all along. The second was in some cases to spark off new violence through power struggles in Chechnya, Nagorno-Karabakh, Tajikistan, and former Yugoslavia. In addition, while to some extent news media presentations of the use of force are a kind of sick entertainment that audiences like, or learn to like, and are in this way delivered to advertisers, there is also the effect of the delegitimization of violence for many of those viewers. People do not simply watch violence as infotainment. They feel revulsion, even shame and guilt (Keane 1996: 177–185), and this can create pressure for action, dismissed by some politicians as "the 'do something' brigade."

The third theme is that acts of violence such as systematic rape in Bosnia, the wiping out of whole villages in Liberia, or the cutting off of people's lips, ears, or arms by the Christian fundamentalist Lord's Resistance Army (LRA) in Uganda represent either a return to exceptionally medieval violence or something new. However, the torturing, terrorizing, and killing of civilians have always been with us. The all-out war conducted by the United States primarily against the civilians of Vietnam was aimed at terrorizing them into accepting U.S.-backed dictatorships, forcibly relocating them so that they could be concentrated and controlled, or killing them if they opposed U.S. wishes. The My Lai massacre of March 1968, in which the men, women, and children of the village of that name were killed by U.S. troops, was not an aberration but part of the "pacification" of Vietnam by utterly destroying its villages so that the National Liberation Front (NLF) would have no base from which to operate (Chomsky 1973: 26–32; 1993: 260–262). In one province, Quang Nam, the forces of the United States and its allies completely eradicated 307 of 555 hamlets, mainly by killing large numbers of peasants, forcing the rest to leave, and destroying their homes and possessions (Chomsky 1973: 32). The CIA's Phoenix Program involved the torture and execution of around 50,000 Vietnamese (Chomsky and Herman 1979: 9, 71, 75, 78; Pilger 1989: 240, 258), and U.S. forces indulged in the practice (captured on film) of taking people up in helicopters and throwing them to their deaths. The appalling treatment of civilians by the U.S. forces was matched in brutality but not in scale by the NLF. What is particularly shocking about U.S. behavior was how it could, as a matter of deliberate policy and for years without serious opposition, incorporate force of a type and scale that seemed on the face of it to be so at odds with U.S. professed liberal democratic values.

The fourth theme is that much of contemporary violence is irrational or self-destructive or both. For the violence that has taken place in recent civil wars, in housing estates, on public transportation, in shantytowns, and during ethnic cleansing, van Creveld uses the term "low-intensity conflict," Enzensberger "molecular civil war," and Keane a new form of "uncivil war." Keane (1996: 139–141) sees such violence as "unrestrained," "random," "mindless," "autistic," and "self-destructive," carried out by "gangsters" who are "unafraid of being shot or injured," and having the effect of causing chaos. Enzensberger's line is similar in characterizing modern civil wars in terms of "the autistic nature of the perpetrators, and their inability to distinguish between destruction and self-destruction" (1994: 20). We cannot see why skinheads bombing a refugee hostel are more mindless than Nazis smashing the windows of Jewish shopkeepers during *kristallnacht*.

To return to an example given earlier, the recent ethnic cleansing of Muslims by Serb extremists was much more restrained than Hitler's Final Solution for the Jews. Extreme, supposedly ethnic, violence is not random or unstructured but patterned (Herring 1997a, 1997b; Gagnon 1994–1995;

C. Kaufman 1996; S. J. Kaufman 1996). Gangsters of all stripes who have used brutal force have not destroyed themselves and have not recklessly put themselves at risk. The drug barons of Colombia, for example, have become rich and powerful and they have surrounded themselves with bodyguards. Enzensberger asserts that "the most idiotic Serbian president knows as well as the most idiotic Rambo that his civil war will turn his country into an economic wasteland. The only conclusion one can draw is that this collective self-mutilation is not simply a side-effect of the conflict, a risk the protagonists are prepared to run, it is what they are actually aiming to achieve" (1994: 28). This is certainly not the only conclusion to be drawn. We would argue that it is completely the wrong one. These presidents and Rambos have achieved power through their actions, and the absolute economic costs of war are less important to them than their power relative to their opponents. The idea that war is irrational when the economic costs outweigh the economic gains (as is usually the case) is an old fallacy. Enzensberger's analysis is basically a polemic that uses examples highly selectively and that presents very speculative and contentious assertions as the sole and obvious conclusions to draw. Enzensberger implies that it is something new that "the combatants in Latin America's civil wars don't think twice about slaughtering the farmers they claim to liberate" (1994: 21). How is this different from U.S. troops in Vietnam infamously destroying a village in order to save it? To write that today's civil wars are "wars *about nothing at all*" and that "there is no longer any need to legitimize your actions" (Enzensberger 1994: 30, 20) is to ignore analysis that explains their various purposes.

Keane (1996: 30–31) rejects the idea that recent uses of force are either medieval or irrational: "They are in fact quintessentially modern, not only because of their implication in the struggle for territorially bound power, but also because they are illustrations of the rational-calculating use of violence as a technique of terrorizing and demoralizing whole populations and preventing them from engaging in organized or premeditated resistance." The fact that the LRA kills people for owning white pigs because the LRA's leader, Joseph Kony, maintains that the pigs are ghosts (Drogin 1996) does add a bizarre touch, but the LRA's use of violence is still generally instrumental. The LRA kills people for riding bicycles to make it harder for the country people who do not have cars or telephones to alert the authorities. They cut off lips to emphasize that informing on the LRA will not be tolerated. The superior technology and numbers of the government forces deter significant attacks upon them by the LRA.

Civil war is usually seen as involving the use of violence to overthrow or maintain a government or secede from a state. Put this way the use of force is by definition instrumental. As Keane (1996: 35) points out, no room is left for two possibilities—that the violence is essentially substate or that the violence has become an end in itself. Although we value drawing attention to substate violence and violence as an end itself, we reject the claim that such violence is radically new. As Keane is aware, the glorification of violence has had appeal across many types of political actor, from anticolonial revolutionaries and radical leftists (Sorel [1908] 1975; Fanon 1961) to militarist states such as Nazi Germany and imperial Japan. Nevertheless, as Richard Gott has argued, there are some significant new trends among contemporary guerrilla movements, especially those in Latin America. Such movements face a decline in their chances of successfully overthrowing the state (for example, the Shining Path and Tupac Amaru guerrillas in Peru or the Zapatistas in Mexico) as the counterinsurgency technology (in terms of knowledge as well as weapons) of the state has improved and as economies are more deeply enmeshed in global capitalism. In this context, guerrillas are tending to resort to futile acts of violence, empty sloganeering, and outmoded symbolic appeals to glorious revolutionary heroes of the past.

The final theme is that the main victims of the use of force are now civilians. As Enzensberger (1994: 21) puts it: "Everywhere the aim is to dispose of the defenceless." Aside from the contradiction between his claim here that the wars have an aim and his claim mentioned earlier that these wars are about nothing, he misses the fact that the majority of fatalities in war have routinely been civilians, at least since 1939, and perhaps earlier. A big exception was World War I, where the tactics of human-wave attacks against strong defenses helped ensure that civilian casualties were only 14 percent of the total for that war. Most (around 67 percent) of the 55 million dead in World War II were civilians (Brittain 1995)—the same can be said of the Korean War, the Vietnam War, the wars in Laos and Cambodia, the Chinese civil war early this century, and many others. Furthermore, as we discussed earlier, how one calculates casualties will have a radical effect on one's conclusion about the total number of casualties and thus of the relative proportions between civilian and military ones.

Although the contemporary use of force is not fundamentally new, there are two significant developments worth noting: the emergence of a zone of peace and a zone of war and the humanitarian use of force in the zone of war.

The Emergence of a Zone of Peace and a Zone of War Within the Global Arms Dynamic

Force is undoubtedly still used extensively in world politics, but its pattern of use is highly uneven, and its utility is subject to intense argument. Since the end of the Cold War it has become commonplace to divide the world into a zone of peace and a zone of war (Goldgeier and McFaul 1992; Singer and Wildavsky 1993; and in an earlier version Keohane and Nye

[1977] 1989). In its simplest form, this analysis suggests that interstate war has largely succumbed to the influence of interdependence and liberal democracy in one part of the world (centered on the West), while the old rules of war and realpolitik continue in the rest of the international system (the LICs, now effectively including much of the former Soviet empire). This analysis also suggests that intrastate violence will be much more common in the zone of war because that is where the weak states—that is, states lacking social cohesion and left over from decolonization—are concentrated. The security dangers and opportunities after the Cold War differ in some important ways if one looks at the world from the perspective of small rather than large states (Inbar and Sheffer 1997). However, much the more consequential issue is whether a state is weak or strong, that is, relatively socially cohesive (Jackson 1990; Buzan 1991a: 96–107; Copson 1994; Ayoob 1995; Holsti 1996). Most of the states in the zone of peace are strong (as opposed to powerful) states, but some of the postcolonial states have collapsed completely, and many others face major problems of state making (Ayoob 1995).

A perspective in which there is a neat picture of two separate zones is too simple. The zones are connected in six extremely important ways. First, there is the arms trade. Second, there is the political-military threat of intervention (and from some perspectives, nonintervention) from the zone of peace into areas of the zone of conflict. Third, there are (more remotely) military threats emanating from the zone of conflict to the zone of peace (such as concerns about proliferation of missiles and WMD). Fourth, the two zones are fundamentally integrated in the sense that they are part of the same global capitalist economic system, with the zone of conflict in very much a subordinate position. Fifth, the zone of conflict has been to a great extent constituted by the zone of peace in terms of the ideas governing the rules of the game (statehood, sovereignty, and so on). Sixth, there are similarities across the two zones in terms of the areas of violent conflict that exist within many Western cities. Overall, those in the zone of peace should not be too quick to pat themselves on the back or to believe that the troubles of the zone of conflict have nothing to do with the zone of peace. It is possible to perceive two zones with distinct patterns while still arguing that there is a global arms dynamic.

The "two zones" perspective could be replaced with a more nuanced spectrum. This would start with "chaos" (Buzan 1991a: 5), in which there are no ordering ideas for the system, war is common, and high degrees of hostility are the norm. Fortunately, there are no such regions in the world. Next there would be zones of war, labeled elsewhere by Buzan (1991a) as "conflict formations," in which intrastate war and interstate war are relatively common and interlinked, but amity and order in relations occur as well. Kalevi Holsti (1996: 146–149) puts Africa, parts of the former Soviet Union, the Middle East, Central America, South Asia, and the Balkans into this category. Holsti also suggests a new category for regions such as Southeast Asia, namely, "zones of no-war," in which civil and interstate wars are not very common, but in which militarized crises and arms competitions are. Then there would be zones of peace, such as the Caribbean, South Pacific, and East-Central Europe, in which there are occasional disputes with a minor degree of militarization, but no expectation of war with others in the zone, and hence no military planning that assumes the other may be the enemy. In "pluralistic security communities" (Deutsch et al. 1957) (such as North America, Western Europe, and Australasia) there would not only be no expectation of war, but no expectation of any kind of militarized dispute, and the existence of common norms, common institutions, and economic interdependence. Beyond lies integration into a single, strong state. This more nuanced approach allows the exploration of hypotheses such as Holsti's claim that South America shows that "democracy is not a necessary condition for the development of no-war zones, and possibly even for zones of peace" (1996: 149; see also chapter 8). He also argues that South America is an anomaly because it has a significant degree of intrastate war (hence it would be a zone of war) but very little interstate war (hence it looks more like a no-war zone or a zone of peace). Although it is important to consider such arguments, it is still useful to work in terms of a substantial and important pattern of unevenness in the use of force that divides roughly into two zones.

Use of Force for Humanitarian Purposes in the Zone of War

The possibility that force might be used in the zone of war in support of humanitarian purposes has been explored recently (although some would see this use of force as a betrayal of those humanitarian purposes). Much of this is linked to dramatic changes in UN peacekeeping (Roberts 1994). Up to the end of 1987 there were thirteen UN peacekeeping operations and no new ones were initiated between 1979 and 1987. They operated on the basis of consent of host governments, nonuse of force (except in self-defense), and impartiality between the parties to the dispute. They were there to monitor and to stand between parties that did not wish to fight. Due to the end of Cold War rivalry, twenty new UN peacekeeping forces were created between May 1988 and October 1993. Additional peace-keeping missions have been undertaken outside the UN framework. For example, Russian peacekeepers are trying to maintain a fragile truce between Georgian central government forces and the forces of separatists in the Georgian region of Abkhazia. The separatists fought a war of independence between 1992 and 1994, with 10,000 dead and 150,000 refugees. Post–Cold War UN peacekeeping forces are different in that they take on a wide range of tasks (such as monitoring elections, protecting "safe areas,"

guarding weapons, and rebuilding government authority), and they sometimes have mandates in which consent of the government of the territory is
less important (Roberts 1994, 1996; Weiss 1995; Mayall 1997; Ramsbotham and Woodhouse 1997; Durch 1996). As a result, the use of force
by UN units or by national or NATO units operating within a UN mandate
has become more common.

To a great extent peacekeepers are being deployed where there is no
peace to keep, and hence peace enforcement action is constantly on the
agenda. Use of force for humanitarian purposes in peacekeeping missions
faces a host of challenges (Roberts 1994, 1996; Weiss and Minear 1994;
Barnes 1996; Findlay 1997; Pugh 1997; Jakobsen, forthcoming). UN mandates have been ambiguous about whether the force is acting under UN
Charter Chapter VI, "Pacific Settlement of Disputes," or Chapter VII, "Action with Respect to Threats to Peace, Breaches of the Peace, and Acts of
Aggression." Hence there is a basic lack of clarity over the extent of consent required, over the degree of impartiality between the parties, and over
whether the force can be used for anything more than self-defense. There
is increasing support for the notion that UN peacekeepers should be impartial in their implementation of their mandate rather than impartial between the parties on the ground. Such operations involve multinational,
collective action, which often makes the credible threat and effective use
of force that much more difficult (Weiss 1994; Palin 1995; Bennett, Lepgold, and Unger 1996; Jakobsen, forthcoming). More and more states are
providing forces for peacekeeping operations due to the end of the Cold
War, including Germany, Japan, Russia, and the United States (Findlay
1996). Any involvement of German or Japanese peacekeepers in the use of
force would be highly sensitive due to memories of German and Japanese
militarism during World War II. To make matters crucially worse, national
governments have failed to provide the United Nations with the political
will and military resources to act effectively. They have done so because
they tend to assess what to do in terms of their own interests without trying to really understand what is going on (King 1997; Wesley 1997). They
tend to assume that civil war is due to irrationality, incompatible values, or
irreconcilable ethnicities. Charles King (1997) argues that more effective
involvement is possible if actors understand that there are structural reasons
for civil wars to drag on—the personal interests of leaders, the difficulty
leaders have of ensuring that their decisions are carried out, the way fighting on can appear to be worthwhile even when it is not, strong commitment
and ability to fight on, the varying status of actors involved, and the exac-
erbation of all of these problems by the security dilemma. All this is taking
place in an environment in which nongovernmental organizations are increasingly significant (Willets 1995; Ramsbotham and Woodhouse 1996)
and in which there is sometimes a great deal of international media attention (Minear, Scott, and Weiss 1996; Shaw 1996).

Conclusion

Within the uneven pattern of a zone of peace and a zone of war the debate about the utility of force continues. "What is force used for?" is not the same question as "What is force useful for?" Use is not utility. The latter involves a cost-benefit analysis of force relative to the objectives pursued, to the strength and objectives of other actors, and to the timescale. Even if objectives can be attained through the use of force, their attainment may involve excessive cost. The unification of Vietnam, the liberation of Kuwait, and the expulsion of Soviet troops from Afghanistan were all achieved by the use of force, but whether these achievements were cost-effective remains open to argument. It is difficult to know what should count in the cost-benefit analysis and how the elements (such as civilian deaths and damage to economic infrastructure) should be weighed against each other. The perception that force is declining in utility springs partly from the growth of nonviolent international relations among the Western states. But it may also grow out of a sense that the costs of using force are rising in relation to the gains. This in turn might spring either from a real rise in costs (such as higher levels of death and destruction) or a change in the way that costs are valued (higher sensitivity to casualties or to economic disruptions).

Force is never used on its own: it is always used in conjunction with other factors such as economic and ideological power, and so it is difficult to separate out the value of force. The classic statement of the instrumental perspective on the use of force is by Carl von Clausewitz ([1832] 1984: 87, 88), who said variously that war is "an instrument of policy" and "a continuation of political intercourse, carried on with other means." Michael Howard (1983: 22) has suggested that most wars in the past 200 years have occurred because people are reasoning beings. However, as he also acknowledges, there is plenty of evidence that their reasoning often goes awry. Those who resort to force often find that things turn out very differently from what they anticipated (Lebow 1981; Blainey 1973; Maoz 1989; Herring 1995). Furthermore, some versions of militarism see the use of force as an end in itself or as a means to achieve unity, identity, glory, solidarity, belonging, heroic self-sacrifice, and even glorious defeat. This is a long way from Keane's civil violence in which the use of force is a necessary evil. John Mueller (1989) argues that large-scale use of force between the wealthier states of the world is obsolete: in particular he points out that there has been no war since 1945 between the forty-four wealthiest (per capita) states. He attributes this obsolescence to its "perceived repulsiveness and futility," with the psychic costs of war rising due to higher value being placed on human life, and the physical costs of war rising due to the fragile nature of modern economies with the increasing importance of their information and high-technology dimension. Even though we would accept that reversal is always possible, our analysis provides some support for the trend perceived by Mueller. However, the rest of the world is still the arena of large-scale use of force; some of the wealthiest states still use more limited force against each other, and especially against less wealthy states; and the use of force by states and nonstate actors still occurs within the wealthiest states. To the extent that force is being used less and that there is a decline in expectations that force will be used, so the use of threats (and the credibility of threats when they are made) must also come into question.

10

THREATS

Military threats are commitments to use force in the future if certain specified things are done or not done. They are certainly not the only type of threat in play in the international system, but because they involve the potential breakdown of nonviolent political relations, they occupy a special category (Buzan 1991a: chapter 3). Such threats can cover the whole range of offensive and defensive uses of force discussed in the previous chapter. Often the threats are quite diffuse, as when an actor fears another, simply because the other has the military capability, and may have the inclination, to use force. China, India, Iran, and Iraq are all seen as threatening by many of their neighbors on this basis, as, in a much wider circle, is the United States. But when rivalries become highly focused and yet incentives to avoid war are high, military threats can become a central instrument of strategic policy. This was what happened between East and West during the Cold War. Such threats can be used to try to *deter* other actors (stop them from doing something that they would otherwise do) or to *compel* them (make them do something that they would not otherwise do). Under the spur of war avoidance created by fear of nuclear weapons, thinking about these issues gave rise to the vast and intricate edifice of deterrence theory.

Defining Terms

One of the principal sources of confusion—and therefore of dispute—in the debates about strategic concepts arises from views about the relationship between *defense* and *deterrence*. Some authors treat the two as distinct, alternative, and in some ways incompatible approaches to policy (Snyder 1971: 56–57; Art 1980: 5–7; Waltz 1981: 4–5), while others argue, or assume, that there is a broad overlap between them (Gray 1982a: 84–92). The definitional problem is easier to understand if it is approached

157

using the distinction between *retaliation* and *denial* as military strategies. Retaliation involves the infliction of punishment on an opponent in response to an attack. The punishment need not take place within the same area as the attack that provoked it. Its principal purpose may be to inflict reciprocal cost. Retaliation was one of the motives behind Israeli airstrikes and artillery bombardments following Islamic *hisb'allah* rocket attacks from southern Lebanon into Israel in 1996. Denial involves direct resistance by force to the attempt of another to attack areas that are under one's control. The essence of denial is to block an attack by physical opposition to the forces making it, as in British attempts to shoot down German bombers during the Battle of Britain, and Iraq's defense of the city of Basra against Iranian forces during the 1980s war.

In military terms, denial and defense have virtually identical meanings. Those who treat deterrence and defense as alternatives are assuming that deterrence is likewise synonymous with retaliation. In this view, the terms defense and deterrence thus reflect the distinction between denial and retaliation. This narrow view is questionable. The essence of deterrence is the making of military threats to prevent another actor from taking particular actions. Deterrence is about stopping unwanted actions before they occur. Nothing in that definition restricts the threats to retaliation. There is no reason why the threat of a stout defense cannot fulfill the requirements of deterrence. Logically, therefore, the concept of deterrence encompasses both denial and retaliation. Its proper opposite is not defense, with which it runs partly in parallel, but what Thomas Schelling has called "compellence," which is the use of threats to make your opponent do something (Schelling [1960] 1980; 1966: 66–91; Herring 1995: chapter 1; Jakobsen forthcoming). Threats aimed at making an opponent cease doing something share characteristics of deterrence and compellence (Herring 1995: 16–17). There are two remaining distinctions with which one needs to be familiar. The first is Patrick Morgan's (1983) distinction between *immediate* and *general* deterrence. Immediate deterrence is the use of specific threats to prevent someone from doing something that is being seriously considered, and general deterrence is the use of a standing threat in order to prevent someone from seriously considering doing something. The other distinction is between *direct* (sometimes called "core") deterrence—the use of threats to prevent someone from doing something to the deterrer—and *extended* deterrence, the use of threats to prevent someone from doing something to a third party.

Retaliation and denial represent two major threads in the debates about deterrence. In some eyes these threads are complementary, and the term "deterrence" is used in a way that incorporates them both. In other eyes, they are seen as contradictory, and the term "deterrence" is used more narrowly to refer exclusively to threats of punishment by retaliation.

This is often the case in writings about nuclear deterrence of nuclear attack, where denial was thought to be ineffective or impossible: the missiles, it was thought, would always get through—and even if only a few got through, the results would still be disastrous. In this narrower view, defense is seen as a strategy that is different from, and frequently incompatible with, deterrence. The difference between these two views has profound implications for the military means and strategies by which deterrence is implemented. If nuclear deterrence is purely retaliatory, then one is led to a rejection of strategic defenses (that is, damage limitation through passive defenses such as fallout shelters or active defenses such as antiballistic missile and antisatellite [ASAT] systems) because it relies on a condition of mutual vulnerability. If it relies on denial, then it makes sense to deploy strategic defenses in order to try to limit damage while pursuing victory.

If one takes the broad view of nuclear deterrence, then the concept blends easily into traditional strategies for defense with conventional weapons. Although the term deterrence did not become important in strategic debate until the early years of the nuclear age, the idea that strong defensive forces would help to prevent opponents from attacking has always been a central element in strategic thinking. Fortifications like the Maginot Line that France maintained on its border with Germany and China's Great Wall against the barbarians exemplify deterrence by denial in traditional military strategy. Indeed, Samuel Huntington (1983–1984) objected to NATO's reliance on denial in its conventional deterrence strategy toward the Warsaw Pact in which NATO effectively signaled its preparedness to fight on Western European territory only. He argued that deterrence by denial should be augmented by the threat of "conventional retaliation," that is, a NATO invasion of Eastern Europe in response to a Warsaw Pact invasion of Western Europe. The idea that deterrence could be achieved by threats of punishment other than those associated with denial only came to fruition when nuclear weapons provided much larger, high-speed means of destruction than had hitherto been available, which could be delivered with high confidence even if the opponent's conventional armed forces were winning. Only then did the term itself become a major element in strategic thinking. The elements of a capability for deterrence by retaliation were building up during the 1920s and 1930s with the development of long-range aircraft armed with chemical and high-explosive bombs. These developments, however, were neither potent enough nor sufficiently dramatic to break the mold of traditional strategic thinking in the way that nuclear weapons did (cf. Price and Tannenwald 1996). Their combination of enormous destructive power and apparent unstoppability, and the horrendous risks associated with using them against similarly equipped opponents, made threats the centerpiece of Cold War strategic theory.

Analytical Perspectives and Unanswered Questions

The strategic concepts discussed above have been applied to the study of threats from many different perspectives. Particular aspects of threat, such as reputation, credibility, time pressure, domestic electoral factors, culture, the security dilemma, and the relationship between threats and the use of force are among those that have been examined in the literature. Threats are central to state and nonstate terrorism, whether it be ethnic cleansing in former Yugoslavia or genocide in East Timor. In both cases, much of the violence was a way of threatening those left alive, either to get them to leave particular areas (in the case of former Yugoslavia) or accept assimilation (in the case of East Timor). Threats are an important aspect of state and intergroup repression and violence more generally (Arendt 1969, 1973b; Uekert 1995; Keane 1996). Others have written about nonviolent means used by nonstate actors to foil threats of violence by states. However, the literature is dominated by work on the use of conventional and nuclear threats in interstate relations. There is an immense literature on particular cases, while comparative case study analysis has sought to discover patterns in the use of threats in interstate relations. Some of the work focuses on particular states, such as the United States (Payne 1970; George and Smoke 1974; Blechman and Kaplan 1978; George 1991; McCalla 1992; George and Simons 1994), the Soviet Union (Kaplan 1981; Adomeit 1982), and China (Whiting 1975; Segal 1985; Zhang 1985; Gurtov and Hwang 1980). Other contributions look at a much wider range of cases, including pre-, non-, and post–Cold War cases (Quester 1966; Snyder and Diesing 1977; Lebow 1981; Leng 1983; Maoz 1983, 1989; Huth and Russett 1984, 1988; Huth 1988; Brecher, Wilkenfeld, and Moser 1988; Wilkenfeld, Brecher, and Moser 1988; Brecher and Wilkenfeld 1989; Lebow and Stein 1990a, 1990b, 1994; Paul 1994; Richardson 1994; Herring 1995; Jakobsen forthcoming).

An important new literature is emerging on the use of threats, often combined with use of force to enhance the credibility of those threats by UN forces or by multinational or national forces carrying out UN mandates during civil wars. In a striking example in August 1997, Czech and British troops from the multinational Stabilization Force (S-For) surrounded police stations in the Serb-nationalist-run Bosnian town of Banja Luka. They issued an ultimatum to the Serb police to allow UN officials from the International Police Task Force to search for illegal weapons. Five minutes before the expiry of the ultimatum, the Serb police capitulated and 2,500 illegal weapons were seized (Coleman and Reuter 1997). This example is significant in that the action was taken as part of the UN policy of supporting Biljana Plavšić, president of the Serb Republic within Bosnia, against Radovan Karadžić, who has been indicted to stand trial in The Hague for war crimes and who has many supporters among the Banja Luka police. It is also significant in that it shows that threats can work, even in the kind of messy internal political struggles in which the United Nations is increasingly becoming involved.

There is a whole host of types of threat that might have slightly or greatly different dynamics: threats may be military or nonmilitary, they may be used to deter or compel, the action being deterred or compelled may be military or nonmilitary, and these elements can be combined in many different ways. There would seem to be important differences between nuclear deterrence of nuclear attack and conventional deterrence of conventional attack (Morgenthau 1976; Lebow 1987a; Betts 1988). But what about nuclear deterrence of conventional attack and conventional deterrence of nuclear attack? To what extent are threats involving chemical weapons (Moon 1984; Price 1994, 1997; Price and Tannenwald 1996) and biological weapons or even very high-yield conventional weapons (and hence all potential weapons of mass destruction) similar to threats involving nuclear weapons? And can nuclear weapons deter chemical or biological attack? The literature has yet to address these questions in sufficient depth, even though a mixed system of nuclear, chemical, and biological weapon deterrence is emerging in the Middle East. The extent to which the general-immediate and direct-extended distinctions can apply to compellence as well as deterrence has only recently been explored (Herring 1995: 19–21), and there has also been very little specific analysis of the workings of general deterrence (Morgan 1983; Freedman 1989b; Huth 1993). It is also generally assumed that deterrence is easier than compellence, but this remains to be shown (Herring 1995: 28–33).

Similarly, there is a presumption that extended deterrence is more difficult than direct deterrence. But extended deterrence may work in one case (perhaps because the beneficiary of the deterrence is clearly of vital interest to the deterrer) while direct deterrence may fail in another (perhaps because the deterrer has insufficient military capability to mount a credible defense). Other factors may also be important. U.S. extended deterrence was not simply about preventing external territorial aggression against its allies, as it is normally presented in the strategic studies literature, it was also part of the expansion of the global market system (Klein 1994: 82, 112). Much work remains to be done on these important questions, and few attempts have been made to compare the conclusions of a wide variety of studies (Levy 1988, 1989). We will focus on the central issue of when threats work and when they provoke, and then go on to consider the more specific issue of nuclear deterrence of nuclear attack.

When Do Threats Work and When Do They Provoke?

With threats, one actor prevents another from taking some action (in the case of deterrence) or makes another do something (in the case of compellence) by raising the latter's fear of the consequences that will ensue by failure to comply. The use of threats implies the existence of two parties, the threatener and the threatened. There are significant differences between deterrent and compellent threats (Schelling 1966: 66–91), but both share these and other similarities. Because threats are not the only factor in shaping behavior, it is difficult to assess their effectiveness. Has the deterree remained quiescent because the deterrer's policy has been effective? Or has inaction resulted simply from the deterree having weak motives on the issue? Is the deterree indifferent or even averse toward the actions about which the deterrer is worried, and therefore would not take them whether actively deterred or not? The question of motives is also a problem for assessing compellence: has the action taken place because the target of the compellence threats was intent on doing it anyway? The degree to which one can know the answers to these questions varies considerably, and the potential for misperception is substantial. Sometimes the calculation is easy: the United States is indifferent about taking military control of Canada, and therefore Canada does not have to mount a substantial deterrence policy against that contingency.

However, in cases with a substantial amount of military-political rivalry and hostility, the calculation is much more difficult. If one asks how strongly motivated North Korea is to invade South Korea, credible cases can be made for a range of interpretations, with no clear means of deciding reliably among them. Under such ambiguous conditions, many will see prudence as dictating the mounting of some deterrence. Once threats are made, it becomes easy to slip into the assumption that the outcome is only a result of those threats. Because they cannot be known reliably, the other incentives bearing on the target's behavior are often ignored or discounted in thinking about threats. If the worst-case assumption (that the deterree would attack if not deterred) is taken for granted, then motives are assumed to be very strong, and deterrence appears to be more difficult than it is if in reality the deteree's motives are not that strong. Deterring fanatics is more difficult than deterring opportunists, and mistaking one for the other can heavily affect whether threats are effective or not. Furthermore—and this is something inadequately appreciated in the deterrence literature—reliance on threats can be provocative in cases where the opponent is strongly motivated by the belief that compliance with the threat would result in significant losses. In such cases, an opponent may believe that attack or defiance is the only option to prevent a bad situation from becoming worse (Lebow 1989; Herring 1995: 49–59, 67–69). This appears to have been an important factor in Saddam Hussein's refusal in 1990–1991 to withdraw completely and unconditionally from Kuwait: he appears to have calculated that he had more to lose in a humiliating withdrawal than in a "glorious" military defeat. This was also a case in which the threatener, President Bush, was at the very least not terribly concerned whether his compellent threats failed because war against Iraq would allow him to achieve some short-term objectives, such as destroying much of Iraq's military capability (Herring 1995: chapter 11).

Another factor related to the effectiveness of threats is the target's tolerance for costs. If the target is "soft," that is, sensitive to costs, then it will be easier to influence even if its incentive to ignore deterrence threats or resist compellence threats is high. If the target is both soft and weakly motivated on the issue at stake (two factors that are often not independent of each other), threats are very likely to be successful. Haitian paramilitary gangs backed by the military dictatorship deterred intervention by U.S. military forces by threatening "another Somalia," a reference to the deaths of a number of U.S. service personnel in fighting with Somali domestic factions that precipitated a U.S. withdrawal. At the time, President Clinton was under pressure for supposedly being weak and indecisive on foreign policy issues, and the brutality of the Haitian dictatorship was causing many to flee in unseaworthy craft toward Florida. To end the embarrassment of returning refugees against their will or have them stay in the United States, Clinton used economic sanctions and military threats to try to oust the Haitian dictators. When this failed and he proved unwilling to carry out his military threats, he agreed to a compromise with the regime in which the power structure remained essentially the same but with a reduction in the terror tactics against the populace and the return of Jean-Bertrand Aristide who, before the coup, had been elected president with 80 percent of the vote.

If the target is "hard," and willing to accept punishment, then exercising influence through threats will be more difficult. China under Mao went out of its way to establish just such a hard image of itself. Looking at basic motivation is essentially a political approach to threats. The importance of taking these political considerations into account when assessing threats cannot be overestimated. If they are ignored or discounted, the opponent's behavior will appear to result solely from the threats made. Such a perspective leads easily to an unbalanced and excessively militarized view of world politics.

The main rational component of threats is the logic of costs and gains resulting from taking the action (deterrence) or not taking it (compellence) in defiance of specific threats. It is this component that receives the bulk of attention in deterrence theory. The target has to calculate the balance between the possible gains and the possible costs that result from taking, or not taking, given actions. In the early decades of this century, for example, many in Germany believed that the modernization of Russia would soon foreclose any possibility of German hegemony in Europe. Part of Germany's motivation for war was thus a sense of being within a window of opportunity. Inaction was expected to result in a worsening of Germany's position in the international hierarchy of power. Decisionmakers who are strongly motivated, especially when they fear losses if they do not act, can perceive the existence of a window of opportunity where none exists. This was most clearly the case when President Truman sent U.S.-led UN forces into North Korea in October 1950 without taking sufficiently seriously Chinese threats of counterintervention (Lebow 1981; Herring 1995: chapter 5; Christensen 1996). However, the mere existence of the perception of a window of military opportunity is not sufficient to produce an attack: there must also be a sufficiently strong motivation to act, whether based on fear of loss or hope of gain.

Looking at the other side of the coin, Dan Reiter (1995) has made a strong case for the position that preemptive war, in which one state attacks another because it thinks that it is about to be attacked by the other (as opposed to preventive war, which involves cutting an opponent down to size before it becomes too strong) is very rare and much less common than is generally believed. Reiter could identify only three cases out of sixty-seven interstate wars between 1816 and 1980: Germany's attack on Russia in July 1914, China's attack on U.S.-led UN forces in the Korean War in 1950, and Israel's attack on Egypt in 1967. Furthermore, in all three cases, the preemptive attacks were associated not just with beliefs that there were significant military advantages to striking first, but also with very hostile images of the enemy and other important motivating factors.

The calculation made by a rational target in relation to a threat has to weigh both the comparative value of costs and gains and the level of probability that the threat will be carried out. The target's calculations thus encompass four basic variables: the level of possible costs (perhaps in terms of lost and damaged national assets; lost or suppressed ideological values; heightened threats; and diminished power, status, and independence); the level of possible gains (perhaps in terms of expanded power, status, and/or territory; increased independence; reduced threats; and extended political influence); the probability of possible costs being inflicted (which has to do with calculations about the motivation, capability, and credibility of the threatener); and the probability of possible gains being acquired (which requires calculations about the relative capabilities of the opposing forces, including possibly shifting coalitions and alliances). These four variables yield an infinity of possible combinations of outcome regarding the effectiveness of threats. Weighing these values and probabilities is the central problem of threat analysis, for decisionmakers as well as academics. A volume edited by Alexander George and William Simons (1994) examines "coercive diplomacy," which the authors define as "efforts to persuade an opponent to stop or reverse an action": in their view this is neither deterrence nor compellence but something in between. They argue that the conditions associated with successful coercive diplomacy are clear objectives, strong motivation, asymmetry of motivation favoring the threatener, sense of urgency in the target, strong leadership, domestic support, international support, fear by the target of unacceptable escalation, and clarity of terms.

In a more general study that seeks to explain the outcomes of international crises, Herring (1995) considers the type of threat (deterrent or compellent, direct or extended, and immediate or general), the military balance (conventional and nuclear at various levels), the interests at stake (personal, intrinsic, and strategic), and psychological and strategic cultural factors. He concludes that decisionmakers are motivated by varying mixes of the exploitation of opportunities or by fear of losses. He argues that the differences between deterrence and compellence influence the tactics used during crises, but that those differences are not generally a key factor in crisis outcomes (win, loss, compromise, and peace or war). When both sides have nuclear weapons, both tend to be more cautious, and no great advantage accrues to the side with nuclear superiority, however measured. When only one side has nuclear weapons, the nonnuclear state is not at a great disadvantage because, as the nuclear taboo has taken hold, the threat of nuclear use for anything other than retaliation to nuclear attack or to stave off decisive homeland defeat has become less and less credible. By nuclear taboo we mean "a strategic cultural prohibition against the use of nuclear weapons . . . an assumption that nuclear weapons should not be used rather than a conscious cost-benefit calculation" (Herring 1995: 240; see also Price 1994, 1997; Price and Tannenwald 1996; Kier and Mercer 1996; Botti 1996).

Superiority in conventional forces (especially in the local as opposed to the overall balance) is generally much more valuable because it is much easier for the opponent to believe that you will use those forces. However, where decisionmakers are strongly motivated, they will often not be deterred or compelled by the opponent's military superiority (see also Stein 1985a, 1985b; Paul 1994; Pape 1996). This resoluteness can be irrational, but it can also be a rational response to a difficult situation in which a gamble is worth taking or in which a losing war is expected to produce a better net outcome than compliance under threat. Fear of loss, often due to domestic political pressures, is often central to producing the strength of motivation that brings about the failure of even vigorous threat making (Lebow 1981, 1989; Lebow and Stein 1990b). Strength of motivation, and its potential for producing resolute, even irrational, behavior is the most important single factor in understanding international crisis outcomes. As will become clear below, the issue of strength of motivation is also central to the workings of nuclear deterrence.

Nuclear Deterrence of Nuclear Attack in Theory and Practice

If deterrence theory raised threats to the center of strategic thinking, it did so in a very selective way. Deterrence theory was heavily shaped by the perceived practical pressures of the Cold War. It was born of the short-lived supposed opportunity for the United States to use unilateral nuclear threats to deter conventional moves by the Soviet Union, and it grew up with the use of mutual nuclear threats to stabilize relations between two nuclear armed superpowers. Although deterrence thinking centered on the effects of nuclear weapons, both theory and practice reflected the mix of nuclear and conventional forces in play between the superpowers. One part of it evolved in relation to two geographically detached states threatening each other's heartland and nuclear capabilities with nuclear strikes. The other part evolved in response to mutual threats of attack and invasion posed by the huge conjunction of conventional and nuclear forces that built up in Europe. There are many possible angles on nuclear deterrence theory and policy. In the predecessor to this book, Buzan explored the evolution of nuclear deterrence theory and policy (1987a: chapter 11) and the debates about their relationships with defense, rationality, ethics, the arms dynamic, and foreign policy (1987a: chapter 13). In this chapter we argue that nuclear deterrence theory is not just a Western artifact, but contains substantial inputs from the Soviet Union and China. After this necessary piece of groundwork, we go on to consider whether nuclear deterrence of nuclear attack is easy or difficult. This approach has the great merit of reducing an enormously complex literature and set of ideas to a question that is both simple and of tremendous policy significance.

Although we refer below to the "easy" school and the "difficult" school, we do not mean that those who theorize or make policy about nuclear deterrence are all in one school or the other, or all think exactly the same things within each school, or all accept all of the precepts of one school and none of the other. James DeNardo (1995) has shown that the views of individual U.S. nuclear novices and experts are usually more eclectic and complex than the easy-difficult divide suggests. His work also underlines our point yet again that technological determinism is a fallacy. The nuclear deterrence preferences of individuals are shaped by the interaction of their usually deeply ambivalent views about not only particular weapons but more general principles of security (especially strength versus symmetry). There is much to be said for the application of DeNardo's approach to preferences to threats more generally, including conventional deterrence, conventional compellence, nuclear compellence, and WMD other than nuclear weapons. If that approach was applied to the preferences of non-U.S. novices and experts, it might produce nuanced measurements of degrees of difference in strategic culture (cf. Cortright and Mattoo 1996). It could also be used to compare preferences of civilian and military decisionmakers. Perhaps most important, if nuclear deterrence cannot be relied on in the long run, it can help us think through the preference coalition politics of moving to a nonnuclear world. However, the down side to DeNardo's approach is that we end up with a very complicated model of preferences, options, and debates. It should be seen as a supplement to, rather than a replacement for, analysis of schools of thought.

Nuclear Deterrence Theory Is Not Just a Western Artifact

The development of nuclear deterrence theory, and thus of most of the literature on deterrence, hinges on the distinction between deterrence by denial/warfighting, and deterrence by retaliation/punishment. In the West, and particularly in the United States, thinking about deterrence developed initially out of enthusiasm for the new strategic possibilities of deterrence by nuclear retaliation. It is these origins that have resulted in literature that is supposedly about deterrence in general but is actually about nuclear deterrence of nuclear attack. In the decades since the first burst of enthusiasm for pure retaliatory strategies, deterrence theory has come under sustained pressure to incorporate more and more elements of denial. The subsequent evolution of deterrence theory in the West covers the whole range of issues arising from these two different approaches to deterrence and the interplay between them. The term deterrence is appropriate even for the stronger denial views, because the overarching threat of nuclear devastation makes war avoidance the central priority for both strands of thought.

In the non-Western declared nuclear powers, the Soviet Union and China, no comparable enthusiasm for the logic of nuclear deterrence by retaliation ever developed. Nuclear weapons made their impact on strategic thinking in these countries in a context dominated by traditional military priorities and by a political unwillingness to entertain the idea that national security could be based on mutual vulnerability with one's opponent. Both China and the Soviet Union favored deterrence by denial, but with China relying on a relatively small nuclear arsenal (Segal 1983–1984: 22–25). They did so strongly enough that the idea of deterrence did not emerge as distinct from their general preoccupations with defense and did not have the separate identity, the theoretical elaboration, or the policy importance that it did in the West. To put it differently, although in the West retaliation is generally associated with minimum deterrence, denial (otherwise known as warfighting) can also go with minimum deterrence, both logically and in the case of Chinese policy. However, both the Soviet Union and China developed ideas about denial because, unlike the United States, they were worried about being invaded. Furthermore, the differences should not be exaggerated, so the United States developed ideas about denial in case of an invasion of NATO territory.

Because of the differences of emphasis and context, Western thinking about deterrence has been much more wide-ranging than that which came out of the Communist states and that continues to come from China. Until well into the 1970s, the denial declaratory policy of the Communist powers and the retaliatory declaratory policy of the West shared little common ground. Of course, in spite of its doctrine, China may still actually have been mainly preoccupied with nuclear retaliation rather than denial, and Khrushchev sought to emphasize nuclear retaliation rather than conventional denial. Since the late 1970s, the logic of deterrence by denial has become much more prominent in Western academic thinking about nuclear weapons and in Western declaratory policy. This convergence does not mean that deterrence thinking became identical between East and West. It does mean that the overlap of the two sides' nuclear assumptions increased significantly. There was also a significant degree of movement toward retaliatory nuclear deterrence in the Soviet Union under Gorbachev. Post-Soviet Russia under Boris Yeltsin has not reversed this trend but has not positively articulated a new nuclear doctrine. Furthermore, for both sides throughout the Cold War, denial has mostly dominated nuclear weapons acquisition and operational policy.

Chinese policy continues to be dominated by deterrence by denial but with a significant element of punishment. In recent years, China has articulated a doctrine of "limited deterrence" of counterforce (that is, targeting military and especially nuclear installations) and countervalue (that is, targeting the civilian population and industrial base) across the spectrum of tactical, theater, and strategic nuclear weapons; this doctrine would require a much bigger nuclear arsenal than what it currently possesses (Johnston 1995–1996). Although China has been deliberately vague about the size of its nuclear arsenal to keep its potential opponents guessing, it appears that it increased its number of nuclear warheads steadily from the mid-1960s through to the early 1980s, since when the number has leveled off to a total of perhaps 400, but possibly anywhere between 200 and 650 (Johnston 1995–1996: 31–32). Overall, although there are very significant differences in nuclear theory and practice between the various nuclear states, they still have much in common and the strategic concepts used in this chapter can be applied to all of them (Herring 1995: 74–81).

Is Nuclear Deterrence of Nuclear Attack Easy or Difficult?

Whether one sees nuclear deterrence of nuclear attack as being easy or difficult depends partly on one's assessment of the basic motivation of one's opponent(s). It also depends on how profound a transformation one thinks nuclear weapons have made in the balance of costs and risks. Before the nuclear age, deterrence was relatively difficult in part because prevailing military technologies made it hard to raise the possible costs above the possible gains. Germany and Japan, for example, could reasonably make a military bid for power as recently as World War II. The gains to them of winning would have been large in terms of regional empire and world power. The nature of the then prevailing military technology did not suggest that the cost of losing would be either disproportionate to the stakes for which the military gamble was being played, or wholly catastrophic to the historic destiny of their nations. Nevertheless, the leaders of Germany and Japan did see war as a huge gamble and did not believe that their regimes would survive military defeat. In the event, the costs of losing, though substantial, were bearable for most ordinary Germans and Japanese. Total defeat cost some territory, casualties up to 10 percent of the population, a few years of humiliating foreign occupation, a decade or two of economic hardship, and perhaps five or six decades of political subordination in world politics (Organski and Kugler 1977). Germany was divided into three states, but one of these was still large enough to be the biggest economy in Western Europe, and East and West Germany are now unified. A similar calculation applies even within the nuclear age to nonnuclear countries and explains the willingness of countries like Iran and Iraq to engage in long and costly wars.

Since the 1950s, the deployment of large arsenals of nuclear weapons has made such military gambles between nuclear states far more hazardous. With nuclear deterrence, the possible costs are raised to the level of the obliteration of the state as a political and cultural entity. Under such conditions, possible costs are always much higher than possible gains, since within most value systems no gain could offset the complete destruction of the state and nation making it. The question is therefore whether the permanent and massive ascendancy of costs over gains makes deterrence with nuclear weapons easy. Nobody seriously disputes the cost-imposing potential of nuclear weapons, and so the grounds for debate about the ease and effectiveness of deterrence shift to the question of degrees of risk. In other words, although there is no room for doubt that massive nuclear arsenals *can* impose unacceptable costs, there is still considerable room for doubt about whether they *will* be used to achieve that end, especially when deterrence is mutual. It is differences of opinion about the probability, or degree of risk, attached to costs that underlie the debate about whether nuclear deterrence of nuclear attack is easy or difficult.

The "Easy" School

Deterrence is easy if the magnitude of the possible cost overawes considerations about the degree of risk. In other words, when potential costs become effectively infinite, as they can be with nuclear weapons in sufficient numbers, then calculations about degrees of risk become much less important. Under conditions of possibly infinite cost, the deterree's incentives to think about risks as a subject worthy of serious, practical calculation drop so drastically that even low probabilities of incurring that cost will be sufficient to deter. Furthermore, there is likely to be a substantial negative spillover from infinite costs into the level of possible gain. Costs of that magnitude may well obliterate both the deterree and the prospect of gain. Such would have been the case if the United States had destroyed both the Soviet Union and Western Europe during the course of an East–West war. The "easy" school assumes that at least moderate degrees of caution and responsibility govern the minds of decisionmakers even where basic motivation is high. They therefore think that medium or even quite low risks of total loss will be sufficient to deter.

The easy school also assumes that fanatical zeal or desperate need to use nuclear weapons even in the face of a potential nuclear response is extremely unlikely to arise. This assumption is an important element in the position of the easy school because an opponent who is not extremely strongly motivated, and who would only use nuclear weapons based on a calculation of a clear opportunity to avoid a nuclear response, is much easier to deter. Opportunists are calculating by definition and are therefore more likely to be impressed by the possibility of infinite costs than are zealots or desperate decisionmakers. For the reasons already argued, the easy school tended to view the Soviet Union as, at worst, opportunist in its motivation toward the use of nuclear weapons. The easy school is much more divided over its assessment of some states, in particular North Korea, Libya, Iraq, and Iran, but is more (yet not wholly) sanguine about the possession of nuclear weapons by India and Pakistan. For these analysts, the most plausible route to the use of nuclear weapons, even in the face of a potential nuclear response, would be the prospect of total homeland defeat to an opponent perceived to be bent on genocide. The easy school would not have confidence that, say, Israel would not use nuclear weapons if it was losing a conventional war against a nuclear armed Arab coalition with the declared aim of wiping Israel off the map. In other words, the easy school might take the position that nuclear deterrence of nuclear attack is not easy in all circumstances, although the school might argue that the Arab coalition would probably be forced to moderate its objectives.

The "Difficult" School

Those who think that nuclear deterrence of nuclear attack is difficult attach less weight to the impact of infinite costs and more weight to the possibility of highly motivated deterrees. They therefore see a significant relationship between costs and risks. They assume that actors will not just weigh possible gains against possible costs, but that they will also calculate the odds or risks involved. On these assumptions, even though possible costs (given significant numbers of nuclear weapons) will always outweigh possible gains, nuclear use might still be worthwhile if the probability that the costs will be inflicted is sufficiently low. In other words, the "difficult" school assumes that calculations of risk are not substantially discounted even when possible costs are raised to very high or infinite levels. The school assumes a mentality in which perceived good chances of a partial gain will be sought even against the risk of a total loss, provided the odds against the total loss occurring are low enough.

The Policy Implications of Easy Versus Difficult

If nuclear deterrence of nuclear attack is easy, then the essential policy requirement is possession of sufficient actual or potential nuclear capability to threaten your opponent with some form of "infinite" costs. The emphasis of this approach is on the reasoning of the deterree (Waltz 1981: 4–5). If the deterree has doubts that the attack will be anything less than 100 percent successful in preventing nuclear retaliation to assured destruction levels, then the high potential costs will be an effective deterrent. The whole position of the easy school rests on the assumption that uncertainty in the minds of the deterree's decisionmakers will stop them from acting if possible costs are very high. Nuclear weapons make it quite simple to create such uncertainty, amplifying as they do the well-established unpredictabilities of war as an instrument of policy. In the prenuclear age and in nonnuclear relations in the nuclear age, deterrence was and is usually much more difficult because potential costs often did not convincingly outweigh potential gains.

The easy school can be divided roughly into three policy preferences: mutually assured destruction (MAD), existential deterrence, and weaponless deterrence (although it should be emphasized that it is logically perfectly plausible to see nuclear deterrence as easy and prefer a nuclear warfighting strategy or see it as difficult and—less plausibly—prefer MAD, existential deterrence, or weaponless deterrence).

First, there are those who believe that, even against the largest states, a force of several hundred nuclear warheads (and perhaps something only a fraction of that size) would be able to inflict "unacceptable damage." If a state can keep such a force convincingly secure against a disarming first strike or a decapitation attack that destroys its ability to launch its weapons, then it possesses an assured destruction (AD) capability against its opponent (Jervis 1989). When both sides have this, it becomes MAD. Since the effectiveness of the deterrent derives principally from the magnitude of the threatened cost, policymakers will not have to be excessively concerned about their opponent's calculation of risks. Many writers share the view that the essence of deterrence lies in the fear of war created by the existence of a surplus capacity of destructive power (Steinbrunner 1976: 237–238; Brodie 1978: 65; Jervis, 1979–1980: 617–633; 1979: 299; 1989; Bundy 1988). Since uncertainty is easy to create when possible costs are very high, the required conditions for effective nuclear deterrence are not difficult to meet, but only as long as the opponent is not desperate, fanatical, or irrational. In this view, nuclear weapons have transformed strategic relations by making available a surplus capacity of destructive power.

Second, there are those who perceive nuclear deterrence of nuclear attack to be "existential," that is, inherent in the existence of substantial numbers of nuclear weapons, regardless of declaratory or operational doctrine (Bundy 1984, 1988: 593–594; Freedman 1988). This is similar to, and possibly slightly broader than Morgan's (1983) concept of general deterrence. Although existential deterrers should logically not care whether or not a MAD capability exists, some advocate possession of such a capability, possibly as a kind of insurance against their being wrong and the advocates of MAD being right. Existential deterrence is particularly appealing to those who worry about accidental or unauthorized use of nuclear weapons, and reciprocal fear of surprise attack, because this form of deterrence is compatible with taking most nuclear weapons off alert and putting them into storage.

Third, there are those who see weaponless deterrence (alternatively labeled "virtual" deterrence by Michael J. Mazarr) as operating or capable of operating. The basic idea is that nuclear deterrence can be present even after all nuclear weapons have been abolished as long as the capability exists to produce them (Schell 1982, 1984; Booth and Wheeler 1992; Mazarr 1995b). This amounts to a direct rejection of the technologically deterministic view that nuclear disarmament cannot be achieved because nuclear weapons cannot be disinvented and its replacement with another technologically deterministic position. India and Pakistan are "opaque proliferators," which are somewhere on the borderline between weaponless and existential nuclear deterrence. The most common assessment of the situation between them is that they have the capability to assemble nuclear weapons quite quickly, and have not deployed any or enunciated a nuclear doctrine. In traditional nuclear deterrence theory, this is a very dangerous situation in which the technical incentives to attempt an attack to eliminate the other side's nuclear capability are high. However, this is contradicted by the Indo-Pakistani crisis over Kashmir in 1990, when this borderline weaponless/existential nuclear deterrence seemed to contribute significantly to averting war between the states, and the technical difficulties of eliminating the opponent's nuclear capabilities appeared to be very high, even without weapons deliberately deployed in invulnerable modes (Hagerty 1995–1996; see also Fetter 1996; Hagerty 1996). A move by the two states toward a supposedly more stable MAD configuration with deployment of large, invulnerable second-strike forces would be unnecessary, costly, and possibly even dangerous if they misread each other's intentions. As the nuclear taboo strengthens, existential and even weaponless nuclear deterrence of nuclear attack increases in reliability and appeal, whereas MAD seems excessive. Japan, which assiduously maintains all the civil technologies necessary for nuclear weapons, but also has a strong antinuclear weapon policy, is probably the clearest example of weaponless deterrence. Its threat is to go nuclear if its foreign policy environment deteriorates (Buzan 1988, 1995a; Samuels 1994).

If nuclear deterrence is difficult, then policy requires not only sufficient capability to threaten high costs, but also measures to persuade one's opponent that the level of risk posed is as close to certainty as possible. One's opponent is assumed to be constantly searching for opportunites to attack where the risks of having costs inflicted are low enough to justify gambling for possible gains, despite the fact that possible costs are always larger than possible gains. The assumption here is that nuclear weapons have made little basic difference to the operation of traditional Clausewitzean assumptions about the utility of war as an instrument of policy. To deter such an opponent risks must be kept high. Most of the ways of raising risks are presented by the difficult school as requiring expanded conventional and nuclear arsenals to give the deterrer a range of denial and retaliatory choices between doing nothing and resorting to all-out nuclear war, although the easy perspective is also fully compatible with limited use of nuclear weapons. Flexible response is possible with an appropriately configured small nuclear arsenal, but those in the difficult school usually prefer a larger arsenal, which enables a longer list of targets to be threatened. Although the easy school may choose targets other than cities, the difficult school is more concerned with other targets, including the opponent's strategic forces, political establishment, conventional armed forces, and transportation and communication networks. If nuclear deterrence really is difficult, then increasing the range of targets may increase the effectiveness of threats. However, those of the easy persuasion see such additional threats as irrelevant, or even dangerous by being provocative to the opponent, or tempting to use if they create an illusion that nuclear war can be controlled or even won.

The Ease or Difficulty of Nuclear Deterrence is Contextual, Not Inherent

When looked at in abstract terms, as above, deterrence theory can lead to either easy or difficult conclusions about the implementation of nuclear deterrence policy in general. But deterrence theory is not applied in a vacuum: there are many conditions that affect the ease or difficulty of deterrence policy. Sometimes the impact of these conditions is clearly toward either easy or difficult. The availability of nuclear as opposed to conventional military threats, for example, is crucial to the easy case—but in other cases their impact is ambiguous. For example, one might argue that the two-party (bipolar) assumption central to most contemporary deterrence thinking marks a logical limitation of virtually the whole literature.

Alternatively, although AD force requirements could be increased by assuming that all the other nuclear states might launch a coordinated attack, this need not be the case if forces are deployed in an invulnerable fashion. Furthermore, if existential deterrence is what matters, then such worries need not even be considered. Instead, deterrence of nuclear attack would flow from the mere existence of substantial nuclear arsenals, regardless of calculations of second-strike capabilities based on combinations of forces.

Those who are very strongly persuaded by the easy perspective may still conclude that nuclear deterrence of nuclear attack is easy even if several of the conditions seem to pull toward difficult. This position requires that the impact of possibly infinite costs be seen as so compelling that it overrides all other considerations. Another view is that the easy perspective can be eroded by difficult conditions, and that the efficacy of deterrence policy thus depends significantly on the nature of the conditions within which it is applied. These conditions can be grouped under four headings: technology, the political objectives of deterrence, political relations, and strategic culture. The ramifications of these variables (as well as the implications of bipolarity and multipolarity and of geography) are explored at greater length elsewhere (Buzan 1987a: 172–190), and we consider them here only briefly. It should be noted that there is an extensive literature examining the impact on conventional deterrence of all of these factors (e.g., Lebow 1981; Huth 1988; Hopf 1991). The sets of conditions can occur in numerous combinations. In many of these, pressures toward making deterrence easier will be canceled out by others making it more difficult, and the net effect will be small. In others, however, the effects will line up, possibly in a mutually reinforcing pattern, to produce strong pressures toward making deterrence either easier or more difficult.

A combination like the following would add considerably to the difficulty of nuclear deterrence of nuclear attack:

- Counterforce technology outruns protective measures for secure second-strike forces, thereby increasing tension through fear of first strikes, and counterforce technology is pursued competitively by both sides
- One or more of the states has extended deterrence objectives
- Each side perceives the other as being strongly motivated (through fear of loss, hope of gain, fanaticism, or irrationality) to threaten its vital interests, especially through conventional war
- Most important, one side, or both, is fanatical or irrational, sees nuclear war as winnable, or sees nuclear holocaust as desirable

Conversely, a combination like the following would make deterrence considerably easier:

- Second-strike forces are not threatened by first-strike forces, and technology policy is governed by concern for stability
- All states in the deterrence relationship are pursuing only direct (rather than extended) deterrence objectives
- The states involved do not perceive their vital interests to be in jeopardy due to the actions of the opponent
- Most important, neither side is fanatical or irrational, sees nuclear war as winnable, or sees nuclear holocaust as desirable

The difference between these two scenarios defines the political latitude for action to make deterrence easier. Indeed, the biggest nuclear question of all is lurking in the background: Can nuclear deterrence of nuclear attack be relied on in the long run? Even if one thinks that nuclear deterrence is easy, it may all still go horribly wrong one of these days. If one thinks that it cannot be relied on forever, what should be done? Some advocate a shift toward combining offensive nuclear warfighting capabilities and passive and active nuclear defenses with aggressive antiproliferation measures (including force). Others argue for the retention of nuclear weapons, but only deemphasized and in the background as a last resort deterrent, in the framework of MAD or existential deterrence. However, if the advocates of these positions still accept that nuclear deterrence is unreliable in the long run (as did Colin Gray, Lawrence Freedman, and Patrick Morgan, for example, in their remarks at the British International Studies Association annual conference in 1996), then they are basically resigning themselves to the occurrence of nuclear war one of these days and are confining themselves to seeking to limit the damage caused by it. Hence others advocate a nuclear-weapons-free (NWF) world, either relying on weaponless nuclear deterrence, or finding ways of relying only on nonnuclear and not solely military deterrence (Karp 1992; Rotblat, Steinberger, and Udgaonkar 1993; MccGwire 1994; MacKenzie 1996: chapter 10; cf. Canberra Commission 1996; Freedman 1997). The question then becomes whether going for an NWF world might make nuclear use or nuclear war more likely during the disarmament process or due to nuclear rearmament after it. All three approaches—high, low, or no reliance on nuclear weapons—have risks, and there is no high confidence way of knowing which makes nuclear war or nuclear use least likely.

Conclusion

Threats are used for many purposes (deterrence, compellence, and so on), are linked to many strategies (such as offense and defense), and use a range of means (conventional weapons and WMD). Anyone making threats has to consider a whole range of factors, and must balance enhancing the credibility of the threats made with not provoking the target. Even if a threat works, it might set a precedent or violate or create a norm in a way that is counterproductive in the long run (Kier and Mercer 1996; Katzenstein 1996). As our discussion of nuclear deterrence illustrates, although threats share certain general characteristics, technology is one of the major variables that shapes their impact.

The Links Between Force, Threats, Conventional Weapons, and Nuclear Weapons

Use of conventional force for defensive or offensive purposes can enhance the effectiveness of conventional deterrence or compellence. Israel has sought to establish the credibility of its conventional deterrent and evolve toward stable relations with the Arab states, in part through repeated wars (Inbar and Sandler 1995a). The same may be said of Indo-Pakistani relations. Perhaps recent progress in Israeli-Palestinian peace negotiations suggest that this has borne fruit, but the very fact of those repeated wars shows that, if progress was made, it was made painfully. The revolutions in firepower, protection, mobility, and communications discussed in Chapter 2 have, with varying degrees of success, been brought to bear on compellence as well as deterrence with conventional forces, and the actual use of force has been an important part of that process. In contrast, whereas nuclear weapons are generally seen—with notable exceptions (Mueller 1988, 1989; cf. Jervis 1988, 1989)—to have had an important impact on deterrence, nuclear compellence appears to have been relatively (but not completely) inconsequential (Betts 1987; Bundy 1988; Herring 1995). The use of conventional force as a deliberate part of trying to make nuclear deterrence or compellence more credible is illustrated by the Sino-Soviet border clashes of 1969, in which the Soviet Union was trying to make China desist from making challenges on their border and to pressure it into settling the border issue formally (Herring 1995: chapter 9). This can also be seen in the use of force by the United Nations at various points in former Yugoslavia (Jakobsen forthcoming).

From this analysis it can be seen that there are important links between the use and threat of force. Although a shift to more use of threats might be thought progressive in terms of reducing the actual use of force, ironically some use of force occurs at least in part to make threats more credible. Much symbolic and reputational politics has taken place to try to establish the credibility of nuclear threats, for compellence as well as deterrence, in the absence of actual nuclear use since 1945. The gradual delegitimization of nuclear weapons, which seems to be part of the developing nuclear taboo, is making this process steadily more difficult. Efforts to undermine the nuclear taboo by technological means—specifically the miniaturization of nuclear weapons in terms of explosive or radiation yield combined with increasingly powerful conventional weapons—have failed because nuclear weapons, regardless of size, are widely seen to be in a separate class. The thought of any nuclear use is objected to widely not just because of calculations of potential escalation but also due to a gut feeling of horror.

Even with the existence of a nuclear taboo, the question remains as to what to do with nuclear weapons if you possess them, and the answer to this, to a great extent, flows from positions on whether nuclear deterrence of nuclear attack is difficult or easy.

"Nuclear Deterrence Is Difficult" Logic

Warfighting nuclear deterrence policy rests on the difficult logic that the effectiveness of deterrence depends on keeping both the size and the probability of the possible cost to the deterree as large as possible. Its principal emphasis is therefore on operational nuclear forces. These forces need to be capable of fighting, and in some sense winning, nuclear wars across a spectrum of contingencies ranging from warning shots and small-scale conflicts at one end to full-scale theater nuclear wars and central wars at the other (Gray 1980, 1984; Gray and Payne 1980). The force requirement is therefore large. Because its effectiveness depends on how it compares with opposing forces, it is also open ended. In addition to secure second-strike forces, a maximum deterrence posture requires a wide range of counterforce, strategic defense, and theater nuclear forces. The essential argument of warfighting deterrence policy is that "there can be no such thing as an adequate deterrent posture unrelated to probable wartime effectiveness" (Gray and Payne 1980: 19–20). China is running into precisely this problem in trying to develop its doctrine of limited deterrence. Warfighting deterrence represents an attempt to maximize self-reliance, minimize the necessity to entrust one's security to the restraint of one's opponent, avoid military and political stalemate, and allow the goal of victory to be pursued for its traditional political and military purposes.

"Nuclear Deterrence Is Easy" Logic(s)

Opponents of warfighting deterrence argue that these goals are essentially unachievable and that there is no choice but to rely on the restraint of the opponent. Warfighting nuclear deterrence policy, despite the points in its favor, cannot escape undermining not only the stability of deterrence but also the security that it is aimed at producing. Incessant arms competition maximizes the vulnerability of deterrence to technological change and constantly challenges the ability of deterrers to maintain a basic secure second strike. It breeds tension not only through arms competition and fears of first strike, but also by the fact that preparations for warfighting, even if justified in deterrence terms, can make each actor look aggressive in the eyes of those trying to deter it. Appearances of aggressiveness in the form of broad-spectrum offensive military capability are easily interpreted by opponents as evidence of high basic motivation to resort to force. That interpretation further reinforces the "difficult" logic and thus further justifies the warfighting deterrence policy. The high tensions that can result, when added to the context of intensely innovative and competitive nuclear deployments, make accidental war a major hazard of maximum deterrence. This worry about accidental war holds even for those who think that the "easy" perspective is otherwise powerful enough to prevent intentional war at all levels of deployment above assured destruction.

Advocates of MAD claim that their policy harnesses the war-preventing potential of nuclear weapons at the lowest possible level of cost and risk, defines a ceiling of sufficiency for nuclear forces, and thereby greatly reduces the pressures for arms racing; reduces the intensity of the security dilemma by confining threats based on offensive weapons to a purely reactive role; avoids the excessively complex logic of the difficult school; and requires the parties to deterrence to recognize that their securities are interdependent, and hence encourages them to think about security in holistic and cooperative terms, as well as self-centered ones. However, although a shift to exclusive reliance on MAD would represent a significant step away from nuclear warfighting deterrence for the United States and Russia, it would also represent a big escalation in the arms competition between such states as India and Pakistan. The experience of the latter two states suggests that stability can lie more in the existential-weaponless spectrum of nuclear deterrence.

Thus far, in line with strategic studies and peace studies generally, we have focused on the uses of military means in terms of force and threats. However, military means can also be used at another, much less commonly considered, level, namely that of symbols.

11

Symbols

Within mainstream strategic studies and peace studies, only rather limited attention has been paid to the use of symbols by the state and by nonstate actors in their pursuit of military security and other objectives. Although there have been notable exceptions (Sabin 1987; Jervis 1989), only critical security studies has taken seriously the insight that the use of symbols (that is, things that stand for other things) is an essential part of security politics (Krause and Williams 1997). How things are named or labeled shapes how they are seen. How they are seen shapes how they are located in the political landscape for purposes ranging from funding to the use (or abstention from the use) of force. The ability to invent and manipulate symbols in pursuit of policy goals defines much of what politicians do, and applies no less to the arms dynamic than to other aspects of politics.

The United States and Soviet Union acquired vast nuclear arsenals. Yet there were no obvious gains in terms of the ability to use force or threats beyond that offered by much smaller nuclear arsenals. The Strategic Defense Initiative (SDI) was ostensibly about protecting the United States. Yet this was a program that was very unlikely to ever be effective at actually degrading the Soviet Union's ability to destroy the United States. Modern military equipment is sought by newly independent LICs. Yet those weapons are likely to deteriorate and be unusable in the low-technology LICs. The most high-technology modern military equipment has also been sought after by oil-producing Gulf states in the wake of the invasion of Kuwait by Iraq. Yet the invasion of Kuwait and its retaking by a vast U.S.-led UN coalition showed that the small, high-technology armed forces of states such as Kuwait and Saudi Arabia are of little value in providing a denial capability against a state such as Iraq. All this apparently strange behavior indicates a large element of symbolic politics at work within the arms dynamic. Huge nuclear arsenals symbolized the United States' and Soviet Union's status as the two superpowers, and the SDI symbolized, among other things discussed below, the withdrawal of U.S.

acceptance of Soviet symbolic equality. LICs and the Gulf states have acquired modern military equipment to symbolize their sovereign statehood. Although useless in achieving the military objectives for which they are supposedly acquired, these weapons have often been highly effective at achieving their symbolic objectives. Their very lack of practicality encourages flurries of symbolic politics to compensate.

Clearly, symbolic politics as it relates to the arms dynamic needs to be examined further. In this chapter, we discuss the nature of symbolic politics in general. Then we consider the most familiar kinds of symbols regarding the arms dynamic, namely those associated with military technology and strategy. Then we consider those that condition the use of force and threats, and how this relates to construction of identity. The cases of former Yugoslavia and Rwanda show how use of ethnic symbols can structure political violence so as to legitimize ethnic separatism and reduce the possibility of military intervention to prevent it, while the case of the United States illustrates the role of symbolic threats as a foil against which to construct a national identity. The case of terrorism is explored to illustrate additional dimensions of symbolic politics. After that, our consideration of symbols as they relate to surveillance and "cyberwar" leads into a discussion of the challenge posed by "interpretivism" to more conventional modes of analysis.

The Nature of Symbolic Politics

In important ways, the currency of political and other communication (and its subset of deliberately manipulated communication, propaganda) is symbols (Lasswell, Lerner, and Speier 1979a; Baudrillard 1981; Edelman 1985; Thompson 1990; Bourdieu 1991). Symbolic analysis seeks to explain why what we believe occurs is often different from what actually occurs. It does so in terms of the ambivalent relationship between people and the state, which both protects and threatens. To a great extent politics involves the need of people for symbolic reassurance that they are being protected and not threatened by the state. The state balances both symbolic reassurance of society in general and material rewards for particular groups within society. For example, the existence of nuclear weapons and the potential for horizontal proliferation creates a fear of nuclear attack. Security policy in general, and investment in ABM systems in particular, is ostensibly about minimizing the possibility of or damage inflicted by such an attack. However, there is fundamental uncertainty about whether ABM systems will contribute to this objective, have no effect, or even make things worse. It is this very uncertainty that provides fertile ground for symbolic politics. Fear creates a desire for reassurance. Research into ABM systems can provide reassurance, if not necessarily actual protection.

Alternatively, if the symbolic politics are handled badly, the actions of the state can lead people to see the state's actions as a source of threat: the ABM research may be interpreted as an investment in a capability to start a nuclear war. Which way it goes will be a result of symbolic politics, regardless of the practical effect on the nuclear threat itself. In the meanwhile, there are very large material rewards for those involved in the research into ABM systems.

A valuable distinction, conceived initially by Edward Sapir and expanded upon by Murray Edelman (1985: 6), is between "referential" and "condensation" symbols. "Referential" symbols are "economical ways of referring to the objective elements in objects or situations: the elements identified in the same way by different people." Hence symbols indicating things such as weapons, casualties, or whatever are basic building blocks of communication and analysis. In contrast, "condensation" symbols "evoke emotions associated with the situation. . . . They condense into one symbolic event, sign, or act patriotic pride, anxieties, remembrances of past glories or humiliations, promises of future greatness." A good example of a condensation symbol is the negotiating table that literally straddles the border with one side in North Korea and the other side in South Korea. So many hopes, fears, and memories are evoked by that arrangement. The less possibility of a reality check, the more possibilities there are for the play of condensation symbols. Remoteness, which is often a feature of foreign policy and security issues, assists in the operation of symbolic politics. However, reality can never be checked directly anyway. However close to home the event, it has to be interpreted, and so there is always room for the play of condensation symbols. The same event will be interpreted by different groups of people radically differently because of differing plays of condensation symbols.

If symbols can evoke the same reaction in many people, it will help to hold them together as a group, regardless of the symbol's relationship to reality. When political actors engage in symbolic politics, they are giving people what they need and want. Hence politics needs to be analyzed both conventionally (will this ABM system have a significant ability to deter or degrade a nuclear attack?) and symbolically (is research into this ABM system reassuring the public and evoking other, diverse positive reactions at home and abroad, such as belief in the technological and other capabilities of the society?). Communication encourages others to give you what you want rather than you having to take it by force, and symbolic politics help enormously in facilitating and legitimizing that process. The essentially ritual activities associated with symbolic politics unify because people are "reaffirming their common interest, denying their doubts, and acting out the result they seek."

Symbolic activity has the effect of unifying the actor and the audience by suspension rather than promotion of critical thought—it can hardly be overstated that such activity is about satisfaction of needs, not the grasping of reality (Edelman 1985: 16–19, 114, 124). Consider this statement: "The most intensive dissemination of symbols commonly attends the enactment of legislation which is most meaningless in its effects upon resource allocation" (Edelman 1985: 26). This is the key to why attention in the U.S. weapons acquisition process focuses much more on what Theo Farrell (1995, 1996) calls "micro-wastage" (such as $500, or whatever, hammers) rather than "macro-wastage" (such as entire weapon systems costing billions of dollars that are of questionable utility, like the B-2 bomber). The public wants reassurance that its money is not being wasted, and the secretary of defense explaining at length, as he did, that he got the money back for the overpriced hammer helps to achieve that. "Noisy attacks on trivia" are functional in terms of symbolic politics (Edelman 1985: 38).

In symbolic politics, Edelman argues that "it is not uncommon to give the rhetoric to one side and the decision to the other. . . . The integral connection is apparent between symbolic satisfaction of the disorganized, on the one hand, and the [material] success of the organized, on the other" (1985: 39). For example, he claims that symbolic assertions that the weak must be protected and that disputes must be resolved nonviolently tend to be accompanied by material outcomes in which the weak are exploited by force (1985: 56–57). As he suggests, the value of this symbolic process lies in reassurance of the exploited weak and anxious onlookers that exploitation of the weak is wrong, and, if it does occur, will at least not be allowed to proceed "to the point of eliminating" the weak. The relevance of these ideas to the conflict in former Yugoslavia is vivid. The symbolism of the international community was full of declarations of the illegitimacy of ethnic cleansing, its determination to protect the civilian population, and its commitment not to accept the acquisition of territory by force. However, the symbolism's practical decisions had the material effect in most cases of rewarding and legitimizing the outcome of ethnic cleansing and territorial acquisition through the way the Dayton peace plan has been implemented. Similarly, the symbolism of the arms embargo was of minimizing bloodshed and preventing escalation even though it is at the very least plausible that the reality was increased bloodshed and escalation as those determined to carry out plans of violent ethnic separation felt emboldened.

Symbolism in Military Technology and Strategy

At its simplest, one can see symbolic politics operating in how weapons systems are named. Sometimes weapons are designated like cars, with the intention of suggesting performance capability: Tiger tanks, Sidewinder missiles, and Atlas ICBMs. This is particularly important where their performance capability is disputed. For example, there is doubt whether Stealth aircraft are particularly stealthy. The practice of naming warships after national symbols can backfire. One of Hitler's pocket battleships was named *Deutschland*, which was fine for peacetime patriotic purposes, but created the worry of what the effect would be if a ship carrying the country's name was sunk by the enemy. Sometimes weapons systems are named with the much higher symbolic ambition of defining their place in a particular conception of military security and strategic policy. Examples of this are Safeguard and Strategic Defense Initiative, both ABM systems whose names focus on self-protection (generally seen as legitimate) and mask their possible use as a shield behind which the sword could be wielded more effectively for offensive purposes. Reagan's attempt to do something similar with the Peacekeeper missile was a failure. Opposition to this name was so widespread that the missile is still referred to by most people as the MX, even though this designation is a standard one for all new missiles and means "missile experimental." Labeling technology with symbolic intent may help in getting it funded.

It may also be thought useful to construct certain capabilities or deployments in symbolic ways. NATO's characterization of its forces in Europe as a "tripwire" was a way of both presenting them as minimalist and nonaggressive to home audiences, while compensating for their relative operational weakness in the eyes of the enemy. What Robert Art (1980) calls "swaggering" might also be thought of in this way: ostentatious but not specifically threatening displays of military capability can serve both to reassure allies and increase the credibility of one's threats in the minds of opponents (see also Tunander 1989). This is as true of traditional forms, such as naval demonstrations, as it is of contemporary technological swaggering, such as encouraging belief in the ubiquity of one's surveillance capabilities or the infallible accuracy of one's precision-guided munitions. Efforts were made to manipulate (often through the media) perceptions of the role of military technology in the U.S.-led war against Iraq. During and after the war there were debates over the success of U.S. Patriot missiles in shooting down Iraqi Scud missiles, the number of Scud missile launchers destroyed, the performance of U.S. stealth aircraft, and the effectiveness of Tomahawk cruise missiles. To a limited extent these debates are the products of the ambiguity of the evidence. However, U.S. military sources initially exaggerated their effectiveness and sought to present ambiguous video evidence as unambiguous, as if the pictures spoke for themselves. These representations have had lasting influence.

Five years later, in an item reporting Margaret Thatcher's advocacy of an ABM system for "the West," BBC 1 television news stated that the threat of an Iraqi missile attack had been "real," that this was shown by the existence of the Iraqi missile program, and that the use of Patriot missiles against Scud missiles "showed that one missile could shoot down another" (*The Nine O'Clock News,* BBC 1, 9 P.M., 2 March 1996). These words were spoken over film of an explosion in a night sky and then a daylight picture of a smashed missile lying on the ground. The viewer was meant to assume that the explosion was a Patriot successfully intercepting a Scud and that the smashed missile was one such Scud. This representation has been the norm (MacArthur 1993: 162), yet there is evidence to suggest that the Patriots destroyed none of the Scuds in flight—the night-sky explosion shown on the television news was the Patriot detonating—whether that detonation was close enough to a Scud to damage or destroy it is another question. Furthermore, the debris from the Patriots and from damaged Scuds increased Israeli casualties and damage (MacArthur 1993: 162). However, the deployment of the U.S. Patriot system to Israel served a much more important symbolic function. The Scud attacks were probably intended to provoke Israeli retaliation, which Saddam Hussein hoped would make it more difficult for Arab states such as Syria and Egypt to stay in the U.S.-led coalition. The literally spectacular symbol of the Patriot deployment made it much easier for the Israeli government to avoid falling into this trap. Hence the Patriots were politically effective even if they were militarily ineffective.

Symbols not only create ways of thinking about things. They also close off other ways of thinking. For this reason Paul Chilton (1984) calls the language of nuclear strategy "nukespeak," as a deliberate echo of the "newspeak" of George Orwell's *Nineteen Eighty-Four.* Carol Cohn (1987) labels the language of nuclear strategy as being "techno-strategic." By this she means that it is derived from and focused on weapons, not people. She argues that it legitimizes and obscures rather than articulates the values associated with nuclear strategy. The emphasis is on euphemism, such as "collateral damage" rather than "dead civilians," or nuclear weapons with more blast and less radiation being described as "clean bombs" in spite of the enormous destruction they would wreak if used. Nuclear symbolism also tends to be religious (right from the outset with the Trinity nuclear test in 1945) and sexual (with phrases like "penetration aids," "erector launcher"). Its sexual and especially phallic symbolism have been a gold mine for some lines of feminist antimilitarist writing. Helen Caldicott (1984), for example, played on Freud by writing of the East–West nuclear rivalry in terms of "missile envy." For these writers, nuclear strategy also involved self-deception in confusing competence in manipulating nuclear symbols and language with competence to fight a nuclear war. They argued that it helped to make the unthinkable thinkable and to insulate the nuclear thinker from the horrors of real nuclear war (see also Scheer 1982; Kull 1988; Lifton and Markusen 1990).

While there are some insights worth considering in this literature, it also contains a streak of technological determinism. The technology did not produce a single way of thinking about the implications of that technology, and even within the language of nuclear strategy it is possible to envision weaponless nuclear deterrence. Furthermore, many of those involved in thinking about nuclear strategy were not sucked into self-deception but felt themselves to be grappling with a terrible paradox—that in order to prevent nuclear war, it was necessary to contemplate fighting one. These people worried that to admit or to act as if nuclear war would be utterly disastrous would be to leave oneself open to nuclear attack or nuclear compellence.

Symbolism in the Identity–Security Nexus

Symbolic politics influences how, under what conditions, and against whom, force and threats are used. Labeling territory as "sacred" for some reason, such as being the birthplace of the nation, can be used to legitimize and make possible the use of force and threat. This has been the case with Kosovo for Serbia even though 90 percent of the population are Albanian Muslims. Even where the use of force is unlikely, defining territory as somehow sacred or essential to the national sense of being can still be seen in action, for example in Chinese posturing in territorial disputes. Reagan's designation of the Soviet Union as "the evil empire" is also a good example of the use of symbols to shape the use of threats. It was almost a declaration of symbolic war. It signaled a sharp change from the Nixon–Kissinger and Carter policy of at least formally accepting the Soviet Union as an equal and a potential partner, replacing it with a symbol that legitimized a much more suspicious and hostile policy. Against an evil empire, one was justified in increasing defense spending and raising the profile of threats in attempts to manage its behavior. On this level, symbols are about how actors construct themselves and others in reciprocal and often mutually reinforcing patterns. The symbols they use define and support the whole range of political relations, including military security. The importance of these patterns is revealed in the processes of securitization and desecuritization, when things are set up or torn down as threats to, or referent objects for, security (Wæver 1995; Buzan and Wæver 1997; Buzan, Wæver, and de Wilde 1998; cf. McSweeney 1996). What is or is not constructed as a threat or a referent object is most obvious when it changes. Striking cases of this are the unraveling of the Cold War, starting in the mid-1980s, and the transformation in South Africa during the early 1990s. In the latter case, symbolic politics shifted from race war reinforced by images of "total onslaught," and justifying extreme security measures, to images of toleration, accommodation, and the need to reconceptualize South Africanness. One can imagine a similar transformation of symbolic politics should the two Koreas ever reunite.

False Discourses of Ancient Ethnic Hatreds:
Former Yugoslavia and Rwanda

One of the most important ways in which the symbolic politics of identity interacts with military security is when subhuman designations of others are used to facilitate mass killing. In this process, the mass communications media are dual-use technology with a vengeance. Because they can be used to create war or sustain peace they are vital instruments in symbolic politics. Control of communications technology provides a means of influencing how events are framed and how the fundamental assumptions underlying interpretations of events are established. The point is well understood in that there is a constant struggle to influence how events are covered in news media. In the 1990s, a concern with the issue of "ethnic conflict" developed. Ethnic conflict is a strategic myth in the sense that it is not ethnic groups that are fighting each other, but sections of ethnic groups led by those who claim to speak on behalf of the supposed whole. These ethnic groups are not actually totally fixed, completely separate groups of people—their separateness is created and molded through representational practices.

The myth came about due to a confluence of interests in the post–Cold War era between advocates of ethnic separatism who want to avoid being intervened against, the news media that generally latch onto and amplify simple stereotypes, and onlookers who in most cases prefer humanitarian aid to other forms of action (be it military intervention, arms supplies, or political support for those opposed to the exaggeration of ethnic differences and opposed to the promotion of ethnic separation). All these interests were served by portrayal of some recent conflicts as wars of ancient ethnic hatreds, springing naturally and inevitably out of their deep differences and bloody histories, and hence suddenly exploding given half a chance. This depoliticized discourse drew attention away (deliberately on the part of some of the extremists) from the political objectives served by the violence. The victims of the violence were not supported much beyond humanitarian aid because an underlying theme of the discourse—sometimes explicit but usually implicit—is that the victims would have been the victimizers if they had the upper hand, as they supposedly have in the past.

This perspective crystallized as a major interpretation of the conflicts in former Yugoslavia. It sidelined the evidence that these conflicts did not erupt simply because the collapse of communism had ended the authoritarian rule necessary to keep these people from each others' throats. Instead, Yugoslavia was held together by a delicate political balance among different groups within a centrally planned economy. The balance was destroyed in part by the stresses of a shift to a market economy, but mainly by Slobodan Milošević's pursuit of power through the revival and exploitation of intolerant Serb nationalism (Gagnon 1994–1995; Woodward

1995; Silber and Little 1996; Campbell 1998a, 1998b). This then was echoed in the political strategy of Franjo Tudjman in his bid for power in Croatia, among some Croats within Bosnia itself, and to a limited extent among some Muslim politicians. In this process, control of the news media was central (Thompson 1994). In the news media within and outside former Yugoslavia, the fighting was widely (but not exclusively) portrayed as wars of Muslims versus Croats versus Serbs with only a tiny amount of coverage given to the continuing political struggles within each group between advocates of multicultural tolerance and advocates of ethnic purity (Herring 1997b). It is striking that this discourse was adopted by many journalists who were in favor of military intervention to stop ethnic cleansing. In other words, the very words they found themselves using undermined the objective they were trying to achieve. Many people were in favor of military intervention and believed there was a duty to act if possible. However, the symbolism of it as an essentially ethnic war in which opponents would be extremely resistant to threats or force made military intervention seem very much less feasible. Opponents of the "ancient ethnic hatreds" thesis were pushing against an open door as far as academic research is concerned, but not among many of the public and politicians.

The ancient ethnic hatreds symbolic template adopted by many in the international news media and the international community to explain and respond to events in former Yugoslavia was transplanted with virtually no modification, and even some exaggeration, to the horrendous violence in Rwanda in 1994. The massacres were part of a deliberate strategy by some Hutu ethnic separatists to eliminate all political opponents, both Tutsi and Hutu who were willing to share power with Tutsi. This was centrally orchestrated political violence by ambitious and utterly unscrupulous people. Their control of Radio Télévision Libre des Mille Collines was central to portraying Tutsi as subhumans and cockroaches who should be exterminated and to convincing many Hutu that Tutsi were about to massacre them and could only be prevented from doing so by being killed first (African Rights 1995; Prunier 1995). Many Hutu, as with many Serbs and Croats and some Muslims in former Yugoslavia, were forced to kill in order to implicate themselves. And many Hutu—again, as with many in former Yugoslavia—were killed for refusing to become killers. The Hutu ethnic separatists presented the slaughter to the world as an uncontrolled and uncontrollable spontaneous interethnic conflict. With few exceptions, the international news media and international community uncritically accepted this portrayal. This case also underlines the point that enormous human suffering can be inflicted with only a tiny input from the arms dynamic: the murder of around 1 million people was carried out primarily with clubs and machetes, and to a lesser extent with bullets (Goose and Smyth 1994).

We do think that ethnicity played a role in the outbreak of war in former Yugoslavia and Rwanda. Ethnic separatists had some ethnic differences, fears, and hostilities with which to work. Our main point is that any analysis that does not take into account the role of political factors misses a crucial factor (Kacowicz 1994; Hardin 1995; Human Rights Watch 1995b; Roberts 1995; King 1997). In the event, the dominant "ethnic clash" interpretation enabled the advocates of ethnic separatism to legitimize their views among many potential supporters, the media to get a simple and recurrent explanation for its stories, and the international community to justify its limited engagement (because not much can be done about such intractable and irrational conflicts). Although in both Rwanda and Yugoslavia a very significant amount of deliberate deception did take place, we are not arguing that people are generally mere dupes of the media. Furthermore, conflicts with an ethnic dimension are not necessarily primarily elite led. Stuart J. Kaufman (1996) argues that the post–Cold War fighting over the Nagorno-Karabakh region of Azerbaijan was primarily mass led on both the Armenian and Azerbaijani sides. In contrast, he argues that the fighting in the Russian-speaking region of Trans-Dniester in Moldova was elite led on the Russian side and mass led on the Moldovan side.

The United States Has Identity Politics Too

It might be thought that identity politics is something that only happens "out there," in those places where "ethnic conflict" and "nationalism" are a problem—that identity politics has nothing to do with strong states (that is, those that are relatively cohesive in sociopolitical terms). However, even strong states such as the United States are faced with permanent problems of identity politics. As Campbell (1992: 105; see also 251) argues: "If all states are 'imagined communities,' [see Anderson 1983] devoid of ontological being apart from the many and varied practices which constitute their reality, then America is the imagined community *par excellence*. For there has never been a country called 'America,' nor a people known as 'Americans' from whom a national identity is drawn." Hence in the United States symbolic politics over identity has been central, and the symbolic politics of the arms dynamic has played a major role in that politics (Franklin 1988; Campbell 1992; Sherry 1995; Ruggie 1997).

At one level, the U.S. role in the Cold War was a historically unique response to the Soviet Union, but it was also only one of a whole range of processes through which U.S. political identity was established and reinvented (Campbell 1992: chapter 6). The same could have been said about the Soviet Union. The challenge posed by the Soviet Union was one of the existence of a challenge to capitalism in general and U.S. dominance of the capitalist world in particular. The Soviet Union did indeed pose a military threat. But the main Soviet challenge was to U.S. identity in the sense that the Soviet Union's potential for success as a society based on collectivism and state ownership was a threat to the idea that a society based on individualism and private ownership was the best, right, and in the long run the only, viable, or attractive type of society. As such, the Soviet Union had to be made to fail in case its appeal broadened. Struggles within U.S. society for economic and social justice were represented as alien to the U.S. way of life and as the work of foreign Communist agitators. A recurrent image in the (re)construction of U.S. identity is the frontier, which provides opportunity for expansion and profit but which is also a place inhabited by the kind of lawless savage who "only understands force and cannot be reasoned with" (Campbell 1992: 164–166). Other characteristics include the widespread use of oaths of loyalty in government and private corporations, the actual internment or drawing up of internment plans for tens of thousands of U.S. citizens, and the keeping of files on hundreds of thousands of supposedly potentially deviant individuals (defined extremely broadly). The purpose "was not the rooting out of an objective threat, but the reproduction of a standard, an optimal mean around which those modes of being considered normal could be organized" (Campbell 1992: 173). At the same time, civil liberties and welfare provisions for "normal" U.S. citizens in general improved significantly.

Thus, as has often been pointed out, anticommunism became a kind of defining ideology for the United States during the Cold War, and its removal has in some ways left the country casting about for a new antagonist against which to define itself.

International Terrorism: Small Cloud, Big Symbolic Shadow

A striking example of symbolic politics relating to force and threats is international terrorism. In its annual report *Patterns of Global Terrorism 1996* (1997), the U.S. State Department defines terrorism as "premeditated, politically motivated violence perpetrated against noncombatant [including off-duty unarmed military personnel] targets by subnational groups or clandestine agents, usually intended to influence an audience" and international terrorism as "terrorism involving citizens or the territory of more than one country." According to this report in 1996 there were 296 incidents of international terrorism, which resulted in 311 deaths and 2,652 woundings. This was the lowest annual total of incidents for twenty-five years, but the totals for dead and wounded were among the highest. One-third of the deaths and half of the woundings are accounted for by a single truck-bomb attack in Sri Lanka by the separatist group Liberation Tigers of Tamil Eelam. Among the year's total, 24 of the dead and 250 of the wounded were U.S. citizens: most of these resulted from another truck bomb in Saudi Arabia. No international terrorist attacks occurred in the United States. The State Department has designated seven states as sponsors of international terrorism (Cuba, Iran, Iraq, Libya, North Korea, Sudan, and Syria).

It is striking that, in comparison with other causes of death and injury, international terrorism is a very minor threat. Furthermore, if you are a U.S. citizen, the risk of being killed or injured by an act of international terrorism is almost vanishingly small: it is much more dangerous to stay at home in the United States, where you are at dramatically greater risk from violent crime. Yet, according to *Patterns of Global Terrorism 1996*, the Department of Defense alone spends $5 billion a year protecting its personnel from international terrorism. *Patterns of Global Terrorism 1996* tries to square the circle by saying that the small number of casualties shows the success of those efforts at prevention. However, this does get around the point that what is defined as a threat and what are seen as the appropriate responses are not simply based on body counts. There is an intense degree of what we referred to earlier as condensation symbolism surrounding the idea of terrorism. It has the unifying value of something virtually everyone can label as "wrong." The symbol "terrorist" is a standard element of efforts to delegitimize the force and threats used by an opponent. What gets labeled as terrorism and what does not are important sites of symbolic political struggle, and this labeling provides an important gauge of the symbolic correlation of forces.

Focusing primarily on nonstate terrorism reflects in part a Weberian-style culture in which states seek the monopoly of legitimate force. *Patterns of Global Terrorism 1996* accepts that domestic terrorism causes many more casualties than international terrorism. It might also add that domestic terrorism by states, with exceptions such as Algeria, generally causes many more casualties than domestic terrorism by nonstate actors (Human Rights Watch 1995a). *Patterns of Global Terrorism 1996* says that terrorism is difficult to distinguish from politically inspired violence in general. This is crucial because this is the space that allows for the play of symbolic politics. Although Iran, Iraq, and Libya continue to support terrorist groups in the Middle East, the report notes that as far as we know, Cuba and Sudan did not sponsor any acts of international terrorism in 1996, and Syria has not sponsored any since 1986 nor North Korea since 1987. Nevertheless, they remain on the official U.S. list of state sponsors of international terrorism. The official reason is that they continue to allow terrorist groups to base themselves within their territory. The claim is that terrorism is being used as a referential symbol, but this is secondary to the condensation symbolism involved. Application of the State Department's own definition consistently could result in many of the actions of the United States and its allies, such as Israel, to be counted as acts of international terrorism (Chomsky 1986, 1989), although this would be challenged by those who would argue that they generally do not target noncombatants *directly*. To a great extent, people look for, and are given, reassurances that their state consistently opposes terrorism.

Symbolism in Surveillance and Cyberwar

The increased emphasis in recent years on the threat of nonstate terrorism, the increased speed of war and diplomacy, and the dramatically increased use of intelligence-gathering and surveillance technology are seen by Der Derian (1992) to have had important effects. Following from the work of Paul Virilio (Virilio and Lotringer 1983; Virilio 1986, 1989), he argues that they have produced a situation in which the representation of difference as otherness has increased and in which realities are even further removed from their origins. Hence, according to Der Derian, reality, always mediated, is now hypermediated, and the traditional study of world politics fails to take this into account. There is evidence to support the view that the factors identified by Der Derian and others are operating. There are obvious contrasts, such as the slow speed of World War I technology, to the high speed of modern technology. Nuclear weapons plus modern delivery systems have produced the potential for staggeringly quick large-scale destruction, and have compressed decisionmaking time to unmanageably small levels. ICBMs take only thirty minutes to hit anywhere in the world, and the Pershing II missiles deployed by NATO in West Germany could have hit Moscow in nine minutes. In addition, information and capital flows have accelerated and become globalized, state control of those flows has increased in absolute terms but failed to keep pace with the overall increase, representation and surveillance are global and instantaneous, face-to-face combat has been augmented by long-range combat in which surveillance is needed to see and confirm the destruction caused, political gains are to be made increasingly from representations of war rather than actual events on the battlefield, and historical events (such as the collapse of communism in Eastern Europe) seem to happen more quickly (Der Derian 1992: 130, 133).

From such effects Der Derian concludes that "international relations is shifting from a realm defined by sovereign places, impermeable borders and rigid geopolitics, to a site of accelerating flows, contested borders, and fluid chronopolitics. In short, pace displacing space" (Der Derian 1992: 129–130). Yet he argues that the concept of speed has little place in the study of military security and world politics, and suggests that is probably because their discourses are so geocentric and state-centric. The argument is not simply that scholars are failing to keep up and to integrate this new factor, but that traditional approaches are incapable of coping with it (Der Derian 1992: 135–136). Der Derian's analysis is helpful in underlining the need to consider speed, but it is overstated. We would argue that we seem to be moving not from geopolitics to chronopolitics, but from a complex situation in which there are both kinds of politics into an even more complex situation in which there is more of both. Furthermore, in both mainstream world politics studies of interdependence and mainstream strategic studies, analysis of the security implications of information age technology, concepts such as dynamic density, interaction capacity, and transaction speed are central (Buzan, Jones, and Little 1993: chapter 4).

Der Derian (1992: 175) portrays the 1990–1991 Gulf War as the first "cyberwar," by which he means "a technologically generated, televisually linked, and strategically gamed form of violence that dominated the formulation as well as the representation of U.S. policy in the Gulf." He argues that "the combination of surgical video strikes and information carpet bombing worked" in maintaining support for the war and that in the Gulf, as with cyberwar more generally, war and simulation became "irrevocably blurred" (1992: 185, 181; see also Baudrillard 1995). Computer simulations were used intensively and extensively in training, targets were located by satellites and radar and locked onto by lasers or night sights, and evidence of destruction was gathered through video cameras and satellite photography. This is not new, but it was more the case than usual in this conflict. He asserts that in cyberwar, "The construction and destruction of the enemy other would be: measured in time not territory; prosecuted in the field of perception not politics; authenticated by technical reproduction not material referents; played out in the method and metaphor of gaming, not the history and horror of warring" (1992: 182; see also C. H. Gray, 1997). This is overdrawn dichotomy: both happened. Imagine the political furor if the coalition forces had left half of Kuwait under Iraqi control. It is also strange to separate perception from politics, because politics is very much a battle of perceptions. Furthermore, observers were sent in to see for themselves and did not simply rely on technological surveillance of the destruction caused by the war or of Iraq's acceptance of disarmament provisions. A significant amount of the horror of war was communicated in reporting of the bombing of a bunker in Baghdad, in which television cameras were able to show that dozens of Iraqi civilians died, and what became known as the Highway of Death, where large numbers of Iraqi soldiers were killed as they attempted to retreat from Kuwait.

The attempts to control perceptions of the war through technological representations (especially television and video) of technology (e.g., smart weapons, Patriot missiles) were unusually extensive (Cumings 1992; Kellner 1992; Taylor 1992; MacArthur 1993) but still have a long history (Knightly 1975). For Jean Baudrillard (1995: 46–47), the conventional view of television in the West is that the camera should tell the truth, whereas he argues that the camera cannot tell the truth. As a result, he sees those who deliberately use television to lie as being more in tune with the nature of the medium. We accept that the camera cannot tell the truth directly, but it can be more truthful or less truthful, and the more sophisticated mainstream critics of the television coverage of the Gulf conflict are arguing for it to be more truthful (for example, in showing casualties as well as high-technology weapon systems). When Baudrillard (1995) wrote his essay, "The Gulf War Did Not Happen," what he meant was that war in the usual sense of sustained combat between two sides did not happen: instead, it was a totally one-sided slaughter. As Paul Patton (Baudrillard 1995: 17–19) points out in his introduction to Baudrillard's piece, Chomsky makes the same argument from a mainstream position.

Conclusion: Interpretive Versus Explanatory Approaches

We have presented various ways in which symbols matter in the relationship between the arms dynamic and world politics. Some of it draws on the work of those such as Edelman and Jervis, which, like most of the rest of this book, is fairly traditional and positivist in its cause–effect explanatory approach. However, some of it draws on the works of writers such as Campbell, Der Derian, and Baudrillard, which are rooted in different approaches that can broadly be labeled as "interpretivist." For analysts in this tradition, words are actions. If the study of symbols is to be taken seriously as part of the arms dynamic, then it is important to understand what the interpretivist approach is about, and how it differs from the explanatory one. We attempt a summary and elaboration of Campbell's dichotomy between the explanatory and interpretive approaches in Table 11.1.

Interpretivism "acknowledges the improbability of cataloging, calculating, and specifying the real causes, and concerns itself instead with considering the manifest political consequences of adopting one mode of representation over another" (Campbell 1992: 4; see also 246–249 and 1993: 8). For the interpretivist, discourse and the "real world" are not separate—the discursive/nondiscursive distinction is rejected. What results is an exploration of cultural economies, that is, systems in which valorized symbols (i.e., symbols to which constantly renegotiated values are attached) flow and are exchanged (Der Derian 1992: 78). Decisionmakers do not simply seek to achieve security against objective threats: "Security . . . is first and foremost a performative discourse constitutive of political order" because, in discussions of security, there must be a definition of what is under threat and of the origin of the threat (Der Derian 1992: 253; see also Dillon 1996). In this sense, decisionmakers create as well as respond to threats. Security is never achieved or achievable, and the permanent production of threat provides a rationale for the existence of the decisionmakers. This produces a change in how foreign policy is conceived:

> Foreign policy shifts from a concern of relations between states which takes place across ahistorical, frozen and pregiven boundaries, to a

Table 11.1   Our Summary of Campbell's Explanatory-Interpretive Dichotomy

Explanatory approach	Interpretive approach
Ontology, epistemology, methodology	
Objective and subjective, observer and observed, and fact and value are separable	Objective and subjective, observer and observed, and fact and value are inseparable
Discourse is about language	Everything is a text/discourse: drop the discursive/nondiscursive distinction
One has a dichotomized view of the world	One sees oneself in the other
More facts get us closer to reality	Surveillance mediates reality and creates more intertextuality
Rationalization of existing interpretations is taken at face value	There is denaturalization of existing narratives
The purpose of analysis is to determine the correct interpretation by testing theories against facts	The purpose of analysis is to disturb dominant narratives by offering counter-narratives: this shows the political origins of those dominant narratives. There are no noninterpreted, nontheorized facts
Study causes: find the truth	Study effects: examine the political effects of truth claims
States, people, and violence	
The people create the state	The state and the people are mutually constitutive
States seek to eliminate insecurity	Insecurity is necessary for the existence of the state
Protection of state sovereignty is necessary for international order	State sovereignty is always unattainable and its pursuit is costly
The identity of the state is fixed and unproblematic (except for weak states [those lacking sociopolitical cohesion], especially LICs)	The identity of all states is fragile and a site for permanent political struggle, especially so for the United States
Violence is regulative	Violence is constitutive
Interdependence is a product of the interaction of previously sovereign states	Interdependence is an unavoidable part of the existence of states
Ethics	
Actors are autonomous and free: agency is presumed	Agency and identity are political: agency is problematized
Choice exists between engagement and nonengagement: there is no ethical imperative for the analyst	Engagement is unavoidable: the ethical imperative of deconstruction is fostering difference and contesting those who would suppress difference
The ethical disposition of states is grounded internally and based on rules	Ethical dispositions are located in the nature of our relationship toward difference and otherness
Ethics should produce rules for behavior	Ethics should promote acceptance of difference rather than treatment of difference as negative otherness

concern with the establishment of the boundaries that constitute, at one and the same time, the "state" and "the international system." Conceptualized in this way, foreign policy comes to be seen as a political practice that makes "foreign" certain events and actors (Campbell 1992: 69).

This approach is presented by interpretivists as being different from discussing the impact of domestic factors on international politics or international political factors on domestic politics on the grounds that the interpretivist approach does not treat them as separate. Der Derian (1992: viii) uses the label "antidiplomacy" to describe the "late modern condition of international relations," which he sees as representing "a challenge to traditional diplomatic practices, a new discursive formation of statehood based on a techno-strategic triad of surveillance, terror, and speed, and paradoxically, the possibility for a radical transformation of the states system." Like Campbell, he is interested in challenging the assumptions underlying the conventions of world politics, in events in world politics that challenge those conventions, and in those intellectual challenges as events in world politics and vice versa.

Interpretivists argue that in politics differences are often portrayed not as debates over identity (differences within) but as products of external threat (differences between) (Ashley 1988: 257; Campbell 1992: 71, 236). As Klein (1994: 7) puts it, "Strategic Studies empowers the displacement of difference." To the extent that differences within appear to exist, they are often portrayed as being of external origin. For example, in the debate over nuclear weapons, interpretivists point out that the "natural" choice is portrayed in mainstream analyses and politics as far as possible as being about types of deterrence: the discourse excludes the option of nonnuclear versus nuclear security. When a significant antinuclear opposition developed, as in Britain during the early 1980s, the opposition was frequently represented as dupes of Soviet propaganda and as security threats rather than as genuine dissenters with a different and legitimate perspective. Internal differences get presented not as legitimate parts of a diverse society responding to an inherently ambiguous and uncertain world, but as "really" external and to be eliminated as fundamental threats (Campbell 1992: 75; Klein 1994: 6–7). Opposition to the presence of nuclear weapons, especially in Denmark, Japan, and New Zealand in the 1980s, was labeled as a "nuclear allergy," as if to imply those who held such views were ill, reacting inappropriately to something that is actually good for them (Campbell 1992: 96; Hook 1984). The same also occurred on the antinuclear side: Caldicott (1984: 13) characterized the earth as being "infected with lethal macrobes (nuclear weapons) that are metastisizing rapidly, the way a cancer spreads in a body" and examined the U.S.-Soviet nuclear arms competition in terms of prognosis, case history, germs of conflict, physical examination, pathogenesis, and missile envy, and "other psychopathology." Acceptance by nuclear weapons advocates that there was room for fundamental doubt about reliance on nuclear weapons and acceptance by nuclear disarmers that nuclear disarmament had its own risks would have produced a very different debate and possibly a different outcome from the one that occurred. A clash of certainties is a very different matter from a dialogue of uncertainties.

Interpretivists emphasize the distinction between difference (the acceptance of which is potentially benign) and the framing of difference as otherness (in which the others are lesser). The former does not have to lead to the latter, although it often does. The temptation to label difference in terms of a negative otherness is powerful: otherness is based on a series of dichotomies with one implicitly or explicitly superior to the other: subject/object, inside/outside, superior/inferior, self/other, rational/irrational, true/false, order/disorder, strong/weak, sane/insane, normal/pathological, health/illness, reason/emotion, private/public, free enterprise/government intervention, individual/group, stability/anarchy, masculine/feminine (Campbell 1992: 72, 74, 85, 94, 96, 234, 235; 1993: 26; Der Derian 1992: 149; Klein 1994: 5–6, 34). Interpretivists define violence as the attempted suppression or denial of difference: indeed, the whole explanatory mode of analysis is described as being violent due to what is portrayed as its attempts to find the truth. As the alternative, interpretivists propose that we accept and accommodate difference.

There is a whole universe of argument about the methodology, politics, and coherence of interpretivism that need not concern us here. There is also a difficulty about whether and to what degree interpretivist understandings can be blended into the traditional ways of strategic thinking. The point is that interpretivism is an important approach to understanding symbols, and, as we hope we have demonstrated, symbols are an important element in understanding the arms dynamic. And if interpretivism has problems, so too does the explanatory mode when it come to dealing with the social universe. We accept that in the social world nothing is self-evident, everything must be interpreted, and, in principle everything can be changed. One does not need simply to accommodate oneself to necessity. We do think that some explanations are better grounded theoretically and empirically than others, without thinking that there is a radical theoretical-empirical divide, and while accepting that further work may supersede those explanations. We accept that subjectivity is unavoidable because the world is not perceived directly but is apprehended selectively and indirectly through thoughts and words, with the result that important things are left unsaid—silent and even silenced.

Although in academic analysis as well as political debate, ambiguous evidence is presented as unambiguous (sometimes deliberately, sometimes unwittingly) in order to serve interests, that does not mean that there are no grounds for choice between interpretations. These grounds are not absolute and devoid of subjectivity, but neither are they purely relative and subjective. Klein (1994: 101) makes an important point when he states that "the Clausewitzean legacy, of analyzing armed force as an instrument of political purpose has . . . limited the vision of strategic analysis in seeing war in terms of its 'use value' rather than as a critical element in the general discursive economy of a country's overall development and state-building." In our view, the instrumental approach to the study of military security can usefully be supplemented by an interpretive approach: there is no need to throw out the Clausewitzean baby with the explanatory bath water. The interpretive approach provides us with important additional ways of perceiving the most basic issues surrounding military security, technology, and world politics, and encourages us to approach analysis in terms of a dialogue of uncertainties rather than a clash of certainties.

Awareness of the uses of symbols helps "denaturalize" the ways in which people talk about the arms dynamic, helps us think about how we ended up seeing it and using it in one way rather than another, and helps to consider alternative ways of seeing and using it. One of the more obvious examples of this would be SDI, which Reagan stated would make nuclear weapons "impotent and obsolete." This view of the potential for SDI met with widespread, but by no means total, skepticism, and so Reagan's view did not seem natural: it appeared to be one of a number of disputed interpretations. However, views on many issues to do with military technology and security are routinely presented as natural, obvious, and commonsensical, such as, "If others have nuclear weapons, we [whoever "we" might be] have to have them," "If we don't sell weapons, someone else will," or the assumption that military threats can only be countered by military means (as opposed to, say, strategic nonviolence). Alternative views often do exist—that is accepted by interpretivists—but those views are usually marginalized and effectively silenced. Some of those in the mainstream point to the existence of those marginal voices as proof that the whole range of views has been considered (or as being so obviously wrong-headed as to be unworthy of more than the most superficial consideration), and explain their marginalization as a product of the weakness and unpopularity of those views in the marketplace of ideas. Nevertheless, the mere existence of alternative views is a challenge to established views and shows that they are not actually natural or obvious but contestable and contested. The occasions when transformations of the symbolic universe take place, such as in South Africa and at the end of the Cold War, reveal the drama with which the "natural" and "unnatural" or "right" and "wrong" can change places or alter.

Decisionmakers pursue some technologies and strategies but not others, or pursue them with differing intensities at different times. The traditional, objectivist approach of seeing these variations as flowing naturally from changes in the threats and opportunities posed objectively by the military security environment can be challenged from the interpretivist perspective. This challenge is perhaps at its most stark in the case of national identity, where threats may be seen as a political necessity rather than as an episodic problem. Political leaderships act upon a never ending need for the creation, maintenance, and rearticulation of identity. One might ask, "If there is no 'them,' then how do we—or even can we—define 'us'?" The interpretivist response is that "difference" does exist, but that its construction as "otherness"—as an absolute "us" versus "them" in which we are good and they are bad—has negative human consequences. Interpretivists argue for seeing oneself in the supposed other (for example, one's common humanity as well as one's cultural differences) as part of the basis of ethical judgment. The construction of "them" is widely thought to make the political management of "us" easier, and explains the otherwise curious observation that some people seem to be searching for a new enemy now that the Cold War has deprived them of the Communist threat. There is danger that a "clash of civilizations" mentality will enable the politically constructed "Western" and "Islamic" worlds to enter a mutually reinforcing cycle in which each constructs itself as us to the other's them (Wæver et al. 1993: chapter 7).

PART 4

CONTROLLING
THE ARMS DYNAMIC

12

MILITARY MEANS AS A SOURCE OF SECURITY PROBLEMS

Military means create as well as solve security problems. The first major manifestations of the view that military means are a problem in themselves occurred after World War I and took two forms. One was a worry about what was called arms racing. This started by looking backward, reflecting on the escalating, competitive military expansions that were perceived by some to have been a major cause of the war, although this causal connection is disputed. With the spread of industrialization, the arms dynamic looked like it was becoming an autonomous process in which states forced each other to grind out ever more numerous, costly, powerful, and sophisticated weapons. The concern was that they would have to do so whether they wanted to or not, and industrialization therefore seemed to add a new factor to the traditional sources of friction and dispute among states. In particular, it seemed to exacerbate the security dilemma—the process by which even defensive preparations of one state can create insecurity in others and that may lead to a spiral of competitive arming. The security dilemma had been a long-standing feature of international relations. The fear was that the institutionalized technological innovation and mass production that had come into being with the nineteenth-century industrial revolution would so intensify the process that arms rather than politics would be the driving force of insecurity.

The second worry looked forward, and was that the aircraft and chemical weapons developed during World War I would quickly evolve into WMD capable of threatening civilization itself. Interwar images of waves of bombers destroying cities with a combination of chemical and explosive weapons have the same apocalyptic quality that later came to be associated with nuclear weapons. The idea that "the bomber would always get through" carried the same message of fear for interwar generations as unstoppable ICBMs did for the nuclear age. Fear of war began to outweigh fear of defeat (Buzan labels this the defense dilemma—see Buzan 1991a: chapter 7). Like the security dilemma, this fear of war was also influenced

by the much enhanced role of technological innovation in military relations. However, the fear of war was focused on the rising speed and scale
of destructive potential and the decreasing ability of societies to defend
themselves against such attacks.

Against this background, seeking national security through military
strength seemed independently to increase not only the probability that
war would occur, but also the scale of violence that any war would unleash. The development of deterrence theory (especially nuclear deterrence
theory) in the 1950s at first appeared to offer a way of resolving the problem of the arms dynamic and war that had haunted the interwar period. By
tying the fear of war to the goal of war prevention, deterrence neatly short-
circuited, at least theoretically, the link between the arms dynamic and
war. Under deterrence, acquiring arms was not simply to be a naked preparation for war but a means of serving peace. To many, but not all, deterrence theorists, the surplus capacity for nuclear destruction even seemed to
offer a way of avoiding the previously open-ended arms accumulation of
traditional arms dynamics. This apparent solution turned out to be short-
lived. Deterrence became a doctrine that not only justified huge accumulations of nuclear weapons, but, by spawning theories of nuclear warfighting, made the arms dynamic look (falsely, according to the advocates of
those theories) once more like a harbinger of war. With the late Cold War
fusion of nuclear deterrence and the arms dynamic, military means seemed
to have outrun political ends. Human survival hung on a theory that com-
manded no agreement among its adherents, and on less than perfect command and control over the forces of Armageddon. The view that nuclear
deterrence itself had become a major independent security problem posed
obvious difficulties for strategic studies as a field. If nuclear deterrence is
defined as a problem, then the main body of nuclear strategic thinking,
which is about how to use or threaten to use the instruments of force most
effectively for political ends, cannot escape being seen as part of that problem (MccGwire 1984, 1985–1986).

Since the end of the Cold War, these worries about deterrence have
been substantially reduced in priority, though not eliminated, by the large-
scale reductions of nuclear arsenals, the moves to much lower levels of
readiness for nuclear conflict, and the disappearance of some of the political issues that were used to justify readiness for war. However, concern
about military means as a cause of security problems has revived in the
post–Cold War world in terms of a whole range of other issues, including
the arms trade, landmines left after war, psychological trauma, ecological
and economic damage, profusion of criminality and corruption, and politicians hiding behind national emergency to suspend civil liberties and due
process (Keane 1996: 153–163). Trying to understand and deal with these
problems is complicated by global and regional economic forces and the

growth of mass-communications media (Keane 1996: 167–177). Action to deal with them is made less likely by the fact that unlike nuclear war, they are less obviously a challenge to the power of those who control states, and for some may even work to increase their power.

For strategic studies, the most worrying aspect of military means being seen as a cause of security problems is that it makes the field part of the problem. Strategic studies helps to legitimize the role of military means in human affairs by perpetuating and institutionalizing the intellectual position that those means can be used effectively to tackle political problems. Traditional strategic thinking has tended to present the arms dynamic and the international anarchy as conditions of existence that require a response. The emphasis of that thinking is on the problem of military means in the hands of others and on questions of military means in relation to the security ends of states. By concentrating on the traditional view that the problem is military means in the hands of others, strategic thinking helps to sustain the attitude that one's own military means are more a solution than a problem in themselves. The weakness of deterrence theory, as it is often constructed, is that it accepts technological and political conditions as given and seeks to come up with a military solution to the military and political problems posed by those conditions. In the nuclear context, that solution itself generates risks of a sufficient order to raise doubts in some minds about the logic, the morality, and even the sanity of the whole exercise. Given its traditions and priorities, the field of strategic studies cannot reasonably be expected to take the lead in promoting this radical view of military means as a problem. That role falls naturally to the fields of peace studies and critical security studies. However, strategic studies does contain a considerable amount of the knowledge necessary for thinking about the problems caused by military means, and the debates about arms control, nonoffensive defense, and disarmament do penetrate it quite deeply.

Disagreements About the Seriousness and Tractability of the Problems

Major disagreements exist about both the extent and the character of the problems posed by military means. These disagreements can be described along two dimensions. The first is how serious the problems are. The second is how tractable the problems are in the sense of whether anything can be done about them. On both dimensions, opinion ranges along a continuum from high to low, but the interactions between them can be understood by looking at the extreme ends, simply represented in a 2 x 2 matrix in Table 12.1.

Table 12.1   Opinion on Military Means as a Cause of Security Problems

Very serious + intractable	Very serious + tractable
Not very serious + intractable	Not very serious + tractable

Very Serious

Those who see the problems as very serious are mostly worried about war. For some, the issue is moral: war is a bad thing, a blot on the record of human behavior. For others (and the two groups are not mutually exclusive) the worry is more instrumental, and has both security dilemma and fear of the costs of war components. The former is that the arms dynamic will increase the probability that war will occur. From this perspective, arms competition and arms racing increase tensions, and deterrence (conventional or nuclear) creates risks of accidental war and uncontrolled escalation. The latter is that if conventional war between the major powers or nuclear war between any states does occur, the consequences will be cataclysmic. Even conventional war between lesser powers can be devastating for the societies involved, as demonstrated by Iran and Iraq during the 1980s.

Deterrence creates a paradox between these two worries. Measures to reduce the destructiveness of war may increase the probability that it will occur, and measures to reduce its probability may require increasing the threat of destruction if war does occur. In the nuclear context, the worry about the consequences of war has assumed a special status that is almost independent of concerns about degrees of probability. Given the probably terminal consequences of all-out nuclear war, any chance, even one close to zero, that it will occur is sufficient grounds for many people to see the problem as extremely serious. It is because of this fear of consequences that any apparent increase in the probability of nuclear war—such as that produced by talk of warfighting strategies for deterrence in the early 1980s—arouses strong opposition. Since, for most people (but not all), the costs of fighting an all-out nuclear war outweigh almost any conceivable consequences of surrender and defeat, the view that military means are a very serious problem rests for many people primarily on fear of nuclear war. Those who take this view usually express themselves in terms that give primacy to the concept of peace. More recently, concern about the potential costs of conventional war has manifested itself in terms of high sensitivity to casualties, especially when incurred for goals that are peripheral to the core concerns of national security.

Not Very Serious

The view that military means do not pose very serious problems in terms of the possibility of war between the major powers has been much reinforced by the winding down of the superpower nuclear confrontation. In the post–Cold War world, the possibility of war among the major powers has almost disappeared from the political agenda. But even during the Cold War it was entirely possible to take this view by drawing on the idea of existential deterrence. The very dangers that drove some to see military (especially nuclear) means as the prime problem, struck others as a major creative force against nuclear war. By this reasoning, the balance of terror was profoundly stable for political reasons. The deep and widespread fear of nuclear holocaust prevented war not only at the technical level of rationally calculated costs and risks within specific situations, but also by changing the whole framework within which the major powers related to each other politically. The balance of terror was therefore to be welcomed rather than rejected. From this perspective, conventional as well as nuclear war between the major powers was very improbable. The arms dynamic, both conventional and nuclear, maintained deterrence in the face of technological change and so worked to prevent war and to support state objectives of national security through strength. This view carries through into the post–Cold War era, though more in the background. The belief in stability through deterrence is often reinforced by the belief that liberal democratic states are extremely unlikely to go to war with each other. In the post–Cold War world, the problem of war is increasingly seen as being confined to the non-Western world, the West having become a zone of peace. The possibility that modern weapons are problematic in themselves does not cancel out the traditional problems caused by their being in the hands of others.

Intractable

The view that the problems are intractable stems for some from the belief that conflict is a more pervasive feature of human relations than cooperation, perhaps because of a negative view of human nature, and/or because of the durability of the fragmentation of political life into states with their own military capabilities. This way of thinking is particularly associated with classical realism (Buzan 1984b), which draws a sharp distinction between international order (which lacks overall government) and the internal politics of strong states. Classical realists argue that the structure of anarchy shows every sign of continuing its self-reinforcing existence as the defining feature of the international political system; that interdependence has not radically undermined state sovereignty; that states and nationalism are almost universally accepted values; and that there is no sign of the ideological consensus, or the political harmony, or the accumulation of power, that would be necessary to shift from anarchy to some form of world government. From this perspective, states will find it extremely difficult to conduct their relations without the basic security of national armed forces.

The technological conditions that underlie the problems created by military means also look highly durable to realists, who point to the ways in which the base of knowledge and industrial capacity for military production are entangled with the general process of economic life in advanced societies. From this they conclude that military options are inherent in scientific and industrial societies and that the options unavoidably impinge on political relations under conditions of anarchy. On this reasoning, there is no obvious escape from the problems posed by military means: the problems are a product of deeply rooted political, economic, and technological structures. The realists might conclude that there are not sufficient political resources at hand to change these structures and that it is not even obvious how one might set about creating such resources in anything but the very long term. As with views on the seriousness of the problem, these extreme views on tractability are connected by a spectrum of mixed opinion. It is quite possible to think that there is some room for movement within the existing structures of politics and technology even if one accepts that the basic structures cannot themselves be changed for the foreseeable future (Buzan 1984b).

Tractable

The view that the problems posed by military means are tractable is often related to faith in the potential for change and greater harmony in human affairs. This faith is essentially that if people's attitudes, norms, or values can be changed, then their behavior will change, and that increased harmony is an achievable social condition. Much of history can be read as confirming the malleability of human values and relations, whether it be the decline of monarchy, the partial triumph of antislavery, or the twentieth-century shift in attitudes toward more equality for women. Since the problem of military means is self-made, it lies within the area of potential human change. The instruments of force are concrete objects, and one might conclude that it is within the power of the human species to alter or cease the activities that lead to their production, and that it is possible to change the attitudes of fear, mistrust, and ambition that motivate the accumulation of weapons. In the early and mid-1980s, much appeal was made to the common value of survival as a positive foundation for changing attitudes toward military means (Report of the Independent Commission 1982; Report of the Secretary General 1985). This was taken up by the Soviet Union under Gorbachev's leadership, and helped bring about the end of the Cold War and huge reductions in conventional and nuclear forces. Since then, appeal has been made mainly to the value of liberal democracy as the basis for the demilitarization (or at least reduced militarization) of politics between and within states.

Combinations of Positions

There is no necessary correlation between views on the seriousness of the problems and assessments of their tractability. By looking at the combinations in Table 12.1 one can therefore gain some useful insights into the way people respond to the problems posed by the existence of military means. The combination of "very serious" and "tractable" means that the incentives for change are seen as high and the barriers to it as low. Such a view can lead to enthusiasm for radical and transformative measures like disarmament or NOD. The combination of "very serious" and "intractable" could possibly radicalize opinion against the political structures that underlie intractability. Or it could be one route to arms control, where the emphasis is on reducing dangers by managing what cannot be changed radically. The combination of "not very serious" and "tractable" points in contradictory directions: toward inaction on the grounds that the problems are not very serious but toward action on the grounds that something can be done. The combination of "not very serious" and "intractable" represents orthodox strategic opinion about the efficacy of deterrence and the durability of international political conflict. It can point either to more relaxed support for arms control than those who come to it from the "very serious" opinion or to the harder position of the nuclear warfighting theorists, who see the problems mainly in terms of military means in the hands of others and who favor deterrence through competitive strength. A myriad of more subtle combinations is of course possible as one moves up and down the spectrums of opinion separating the two sets of extremes in Table 12.1: it would be a very worthwhile area for further research (cf. DeNardo 1995). This diversity of opinion on basic issues explains why the debates about the problems caused by military means are so complicated. Some may take a particular position on the nature and seriousness of the problem as a whole, but people more usually adopt a position according to the specific context (regional, historical, technological, and especially nuclear versus conventional).

Tackling the Problems Caused by Military Means: Arms First, Politics First, and Both Together

These different perspectives, and their combinations, shape the debate about military means as a problem in themselves. In theory, remedial measures can seek to change the military means themselves, seek to change the political relations that result in actors in world politics arming against each other, or do both.

The arms first approach argues that military means cause problems for essentially military reasons. It argues that the existence of weapons exacerbates the threats that states and other actors feel from each other, and looks for evidence for this in arms competition and arms racing. It represents arms as constituting an independent factor contributing to the overall insecurity of the system. It suggests that lower levels of weapons might reduce these perceptions of threat without changing relative strengths, and might enable trust to develop that would help resolve political disputes.

The politics first approach sees military means as causing problems for fundamentally political reasons. The fragmented nature of relations in the international system may be presented as forcing political actors into the security dilemma. In addition, a host of specific political disputes about territory, ideology, and power can be seen as obliging the actors to look after their interests by arming themselves. Those actors will therefore remain armed until either the anarchy is transformed into a more orderly and hierarchical world state or until interdependence matures sufficiently so that they settle their disputes peacefully. From this perspective arms simply reflect genuine political insecurities, and until those are removed the problems caused by military means will remain. To begin solving the military problems one has therefore to set about reforming political relations.

A third perspective is that arms reductions cannot begin until political relations improve, and political relations cannot improve until arms reductions have lowered tensions. One approach alone is seen as being unable to break into the closed circle because the logic of each is undone by its connection to the other. Furthermore, any successes are seen as vulnerable to twin pressures: arms agreements are vulnerable to shifts in political relations, and political relations are sensitive to arms developments. The difficulty of dealing with both together may produce stalemate. However, addressing both issues together may result in dramatic and sustainable arms reductions and reduced political tensions.

On one level, arms control, NOD, and disarmament are all arms first approaches in that they focus on controlling arms, reshaping their deployment and use, or getting rid of them. However, there is nothing inherent in them that is antipathetic to addressing politics first or combining concerns with politics and arms. Indeed, knowing when to emphasize arms first, politics first, or both together would seem to be a vital factor in maximizing the chances for success.

In principle, these three positions are always present in the debate about military means. In practice, however, their relative strength and political salience and influence wax and wane according to the political conditions of the day. During the Cold War, the nuclear confrontation generated high salience and strong polarizations of opinion. The apparent fixity of superpower rivalry weighed against politics first and focused most attention on the weapons themselves. For some parts of the international system, the end of the Cold War has almost inverted this picture, restoring primacy to politics, and pushing weapons more into the background. In Southeast Asia and Southern Africa political changes made for big reductions in the intensity of the security dilemma. However, the security dilemma continued to operate more or less unabated in some regions such as South Asia and the Middle East, and also in the former Soviet Union and former Yugoslavia. Western concerns tended to be fixed on fears of spillover from places where the old rules of international relations are still believed to be operating. One element of this concern was the way in which the security dilemma in places such as the Middle East was mediated very little by the fear of war, despite the impact of modern weapons.

The Security Dilemma, The Two Zones, and the Arms Dynamic

In terms of the security dilemma at least, the post–Cold War world seemed to have become two worlds: a zone of peace in which the traditional military-political forms of the security dilemma were much muted, and a zone of war in which they continued to operate largely unabated. Among the member states of the zone of peace, the action–reaction component of the arms dynamic has almost disappeared, meaning that a substantial chunk of humankind now lives within an apparently stable security community. But since this part of the planet contains nearly all of the most technologically advanced societies, the domestic structure side of the arms dynamic is still alive and well within it. Ironically, the zone of peace contains most of the world's high-technology arms production, generates nearly all of its military R&D, and accounts for the bulk of world military expenditure. This world is still at the heart of the technological imperative, but given its evolution toward more mature forms of anarchy, the independence of the military variable is increasingly under question. It is easy, for example, to imagine that within the zone of peace the dual-use issue between civil and military technology might cease to generate any security dilemma, because no military threats are perceived and no military applications envisaged. Military potential would be there, as in nearly all technological developments, but the nature of political relations would unlink this fact from any sense of military threat.

In the zone of war most things proceed according to the old rules, with the action–reaction component of the arms dynamic remaining strong, and the security dilemma active. The domestic structure side of the arms dynamic was always weaker (or at least much more narrowly based) for these states because of their relatively small, backward, and import-dependent arms industries. For some, the domestic structure side is strengthening a bit with industrialization, but it is still nowhere as strong as it was among the traditional full-spectrum producers. Many states in this zone will never have substantial arms industries, and only a handful are ever likely to join the dwindling ranks of full-spectrum producers.

Nevertheless, in the post–Cold War world, politics first and both together would seem to be operating with a vengeance in some big and significant parts of the international system. Among a large, powerful, and perhaps growing group of states, political developments have either weakened or eliminated the security dilemma in terms of relationships between potential enemies (as opposed to the security dilemmas that operate in relations between allies—see Snyder 1984). Since this group contains most of the world's great powers, it does not seem an exaggeration to say that we are witnessing a substantial, if still partial, revolution that may go a long way toward solving (or simply removing) many of the classical problems of the interplay between military means and security dilemmas.

Thus when considering debates over the value of various forms of arms control, NOD, and disarmament in tackling problems associated with the existence of military means, two sets of things need to be borne in mind. First is the framework of alternative perspectives and understandings sketched out above. Second is the political revolution in military security partly created by, and partly simply revealed by, the ending of the Cold War. This revolution has not just changed the balance of arguments about the problem of military means. It has also created a new geostrategic framework that undermines assumptions of universality in the application of these debates. There are now two (admittedly deeply interrelated) zones with quite different profiles in significant respects, and a big set of questions about how these two zones should and will relate to each other in terms of military security. This radical change in the nature of the problem has created major disjunctures for long-standing traditions of arms control, NOD, and disarmament as ways of thinking about the problem of military means. In the post–Cold War world, assumptions of a universal problematique have become more questionable. The pressing need is to think about how ideas for controlling the arms dynamic can be applied to a more diverse set of political and military conditions.

13

ARMS CONTROL

In comparison with NOD and general and complete disarmament (GCD), arms control is a less ambitious response to the problems caused by military means. This is not to say that arms control is necessarily easy to achieve. NOD requires major restructuring of the military instrument, and GCD seeks to replace the military instrument with nonmilitary means. Arms control is an attempt to manage the arms dynamic, whether unilaterally or by negotiation, in such a way as to restrain arms competition and tendencies toward arms racing and to reduce instabilities in relations between rivals. At times, arms control may incorporate partial (as opposed to general and complete) disarmament, usually under the label "arms reduction," as has happened in Iraq and former Yugoslavia recently. Arms control, NOD, and partial disarmament all seek to make the military instrument more effective (by reducing its self-defeating side effects) and less costly. Arms controllers are less worried than disarmers about weapons as problems in themselves. For the most part, those who advocate arms control see the problems caused by military means as less serious and less tractable than do disarmers. Arms controllers see military means more as things that may enhance security if properly managed, but that may generate serious risks of unwanted conflict and expense if left untended (Freedman 1984b: 35–37). The problem in arms control terms is the military and political instability that results from each side's fear that the other will achieve military superiority. The basic principle of arms control is that states—or other actors, such as the two "entities" that make up Bosnia–Herzegovina or the factions that have tried on and off in recent years to cooperate in ruling Cambodia—should find ways of reassuring each other that they are not seeking military superiority (Freedman, 1989a: chapter 5). Such superiority is defined not necessarily as more weapons but as an effective offensive war-winning capability. Arms racing is therefore a problem because it suggests a desire for offensive superiority. Arms control assumes that the parties involved, even though rivals, want to avoid war. The objectives are to reduce or deny nuclear first-strike capabilities, to sideline deployment of destabilizing new technologies, and to maintain the military status quo at the lowest level compatible with stable military relations.

Arms control is often presented as realistic management of political conflict rather than achieving some grander vision of peace and security (Blechman 1980: 118–119). It is about strengthening the operation of the balance of military power against the disruptive effects of the arms dynamic, especially arms competition, arms racing, and technological developments that tend to make nuclear and nonnuclear deterrence more difficult (Bull 1961: 62–64). On the grounds that it provides a way of making small first steps that might, if successful, pave the way for disarmament later, arms control is able to attract some of those who support disarmament (Blechman 1980: 112–118). Like NOD, arms control may sometimes encourage deployment of preferred (because stabilizing) weapons systems like air defense systems or short-range rather than long-range bombers. Its key word is restraint, rather than reduction (Bull 1961: ix–xi). Its repertoire includes such measures as preferred types of weapons and modes of deployment; communications arrangements and codes of conduct between rivals; and the setting of levels for new weapons systems, which may involve either ceilings on deployment or banning deployment altogether. This is much broader than the approach of disarmament through simply disarming but much narrower than disarmament through strategic nonviolence (SNV) (both of which are explained in Chapter 15). Its basic principles are appropriate for nonnuclear as well as nuclear military relationships (Posen 1992; McCausland 1996).

Historical Overview

In this chapter we concentrate on formal arms control, that is, diplomatic negotiations leading to treaties regarding arms, although arms are also controlled informally in terms of unilateral actions to bring about reciprocation, and unilateral R&D, procurement, reconfiguration, and nondeployment decisions (Ramberg 1993). The history of formal arms control is quite short (Carter 1989; Thompson 1991; Adler 1992; Goldblat 1996a; *Arms Control Reporter* monthly; *Military Balance* annual; *SIPRI Yearbook; Strategic Survey* annual).

Although concern over particular weapons (such as crossbows) goes back a long way, organized efforts at control date back to the Hague Peace Conference of 1899. This considered a range of measures, such as banning dumdum bullets, chemical weapons, and the dropping of bombs or firing of weapons from balloons, but in the end its output was restricted to an elaboration of some of the laws of war. The 1921 Washington Naval

Conference limited the number of capital ships for the United States, Britain, France, Italy, Japan, China, Belgium, the Netherlands, and Portugal. All nine agreed not to build capital ships for ten years and the conference agreed on ratios of capital ships among the United States, Britain, Japan, France, and Italy. However, this agreement disintegrated in the pressures leading up to World War II.

The full development of the concept of arms control was a by-product of nuclear deterrence theory in the late 1950s. Its role was to make nuclear deterrence into a means for turning arms competition and tendencies toward arms racing between the superpowers and their allies into a mechanism for encouraging the maintenance of the military status quo, or even arms reductions at levels sufficient for mutual deterrence. Avoidance of arms racing was perceived to be necessary if nuclear deterrence was to be protected from the disturbing pressures of competitive technological change. Arms control maintained continuity with the older disarmament tradition by picking up its goals of reducing defense costs and lowering the probability of war. At least until the end of the Cold War and the collapse of the Soviet Union, the promotion of arms control was partly a reaction against the failure of ambitious disarmament schemes to have any impact (Freedman 1984b: 35–37). Disarmament suffered because, when proposed without a commitment to SNV, its own principle was seen as inevitably undermining deterrence. Arms control, by contrast, was widely perceived as reinforcing deterrence. However, those who saw deterrence, nuclear or conventional, as resting on a manifest capability to fight and win any war that might occur thought that arms control undermined deterrence by distorting military strategy and in particular by sacrificing superiority and allowing opponents equality (Williams 1983: 77–78; Gray 1992).

The peak of Cold War interest in arms control was during the two decades from the late 1950s to the late 1970s, when it was closely associated with détente between the superpowers. The main arms control agreements were the following:

- The Partial Test Ban Treaty (PTBT) of 1963 that banned (for signatory states only) nuclear weapon test explosions in the atmosphere, under water, and in space (but not underground)
- The Hotline Agreement (1963) to install a U.S.-Soviet direct telex link between the leaders to help improve crisis management
- The Agreement on the Peaceful Uses of Outer Space (1967) banning emplacement of nuclear weapons there
- The Nonproliferation Treaty (1968), in which many nonnuclear states promised not to acquire nuclear weapons in return for access to civil nuclear energy and a promise by the nuclear weapon states to negotiate partial then complete nuclear disarmament in good faith

- The Seabed Treaty (1971) banning emplacement of nuclear weapons and other WMD beyond a 12-mile limit
- The Strategic Arms Limitation Talks (SALT I and II), running from 1969 to 1979, to limit strategic nuclear forces. The climate induced by SALT produced several agreements setting limits on deployments of nuclear weapons; extending the 1963 PTBT arrangements; limiting the deployment of ABM systems in the ABM Treaty of 1972; controlling the provocative behavior of naval forces; and formally (but not in actuality) banning biological weapons in the Biological and Toxic Weapons Convention (BTWC).

Nevertheless, by the late 1970s, arms control was in deep trouble (Blechman 1980). Political relations between the superpowers were deteriorating over competition in the LICs (particularly Angola and Afghanistan); over NATO insistence in the Mutual and Balanced Force Reductions (MBFR) talks that the Warsaw Pact make larger cuts than NATO in order to eliminate what NATO presented as Warsaw Pact conventional superiority; and over the ascendancy in U.S. domestic politics of the "difficult" school of nuclear deterrence, which was both unsympathetic to arms control and hostile to the Soviet Union. Arms control had failed to stem the growth of nuclear arsenals, had not led to a reduction of rivalry between the superpowers, and had not produced adequate measures to control problematic new technologies such as MIRVs and cruise missiles. From the perspective of the politically dominant hard-liners in the United States, arms control had led the United States to weaken itself. In their view, U.S. security was in jeopardy because an aggressive Soviet Union was in command of significant military superiority. They believed that a vigorous round of arms buildup, arms competition, and even arms racing was therefore required to restore the credibility and effectiveness of U.S. military power.

Under these conditions, political support in the United States for arms control was undermined. Those whose real interest was disarmament were disillusioned by the continued increases in military arsenals under the arms control regime. Many of those who favored nuclear deterrence were drawn into the difficult school on the basis of the belief that the Soviet Union had exploited U.S. interest in arms control to advance its own military and political interests (Freedman 1982: 42). By the early 1980s, the Reagan administration was promoting SDI as an alternative to the whole nuclear deterrence system by proclaiming that the objective was to make nuclear weapons, as Reagan put it, "impotent and obsolete." Arms control was largely reduced to a sustained propaganda duel between the superpowers over proposals for negotiations on intermediate-range and long-range nuclear forces. There was little evidence of will on either side to engage in serious substantive negotiations. Advocates of disarmament campaigned against NATO's deployment of cruise and Pershing II missiles in Europe. In the United States, arms controllers mainly devoted themselves to campaigning for a freeze on strategic nuclear forces in an attempt to stop both the escalation of the military budget and the move toward arms racing with the Soviet Union.

At the time, some drew the conclusion that "the essence of arms control theory, that potential enemies can co-operate in the military sphere, has been discredited" (Freedman 1982: 52; see also Gray 1992). This conclusion was predicated on the dependence of arms control on political conditions, a characteristic illustrated both by the intensification of superpower rivalry in the late 1970s and early 1980s and the revival of arms control from the mid-1980s as superpower rivalry began to wind down. Despite the hopes of some of its promoters, arms control during the Cold War proved incapable of moderating the superpower rivalry in any deep or permanent way. However, it was successfully revived a few years later by the political changes following Gorbachev's revolution in the Soviet Union. Despite perceptions of its bankruptcy, arms control remained the dominant concept for thinking about the problems caused by military means. Furthermore, no popular new idea surfaced to provide fresh impetus in the way that arms control did in the late 1950s. Some of those who remained committed to arms control adopted a position of existential nuclear deterrence. Others argued for what they presented as a return to a purely technical arms control, unencumbered by the political baggage of détente (Blechman 1980: 112–125; Freedman 1982: 53–54; Windsor 1982).

The Gorbachev revolution brought about a dramatic shift from propagandistic arms control talks to serious arms reductions, formal and informal, nuclear and nonnuclear. The collapse of the Soviet empire in Eastern Europe, and then of the Soviet Union itself, accelerated the already wide-ranging process of partial disarmament and demobilization between NATO and the Warsaw Pact states. During the Cold War arms control was very much dominated by the superpowers and their alliances: hence this chapter gives those arms control efforts much coverage. Since the end of the Cold War, arms control has been driven primarily by the United States and its NATO allies and has focused mainly on issues relating to WMD and the delivery systems associated with them. There is also growing interest in regional arms control (Inbar and Sandler 1995b).

The centerpiece of nuclear reductions has been the START process between the United States and the (now former) Soviet Union. START I (signed in 1991 and ratified in 1994) was quickly followed by START II, which aims to bring U.S. and Russian strategic nuclear warhead totals to 3,500 or under by 2003 and to restrict ICBMs to one warhead per missile. START II (signed in 1993) was ratified by the United States in 1996, but in mid-1997 still awaited ratification by Russia. Still, both sides are way ahead of their reduction timetables, and all relevant warheads have been removed from Belarus, Ukraine, and Kazakhstan. Although technical questions are part of the problem, Russia's slowness to ratify is also a sign of hostility to the expansion of NATO to include some former Warsaw Pact states, to U.S. interest in BMD which may jeopardize the ABM Treaty, and to the fact that under START II, Russia will have to make bigger cuts than the United States. Nevertheless, in March 1997 U.S. President Bill Clinton and Russian President Boris Yeltsin agreed that under START III, they would cut their warhead totals to between 2,000 and 2,500 by 2007. Discussions have been under way for a number of years because the United States wishes Russia to allow a clarification of the ABM Treaty to make it permissible to deploy ABM systems against theater ballistic missiles but not faster moving ICBMs. Russia is concerned that such a "clarification" would actually put a treaty-violating strategic ABM system within easy reach.

When the Conventional Forces in Europe (CFE) Treaty was agreed upon in 1991, the totals of tanks, armored combat vehicles, and artillery pieces allocated to each state were predicated on balancing NATO and Warsaw Pact nations. Now that some former Warsaw Pact states have joined NATO and others are by no means Russian allies, the balance is swinging heavily against Russia. The May 1996 review conference took these developments into account. Russia sought (with some success) only a marginal increase in its total due to its military commitments in Chechnya and Armenia. By mid-1997, the revisions had not been ratified by all thirty states party to the treaty. The review conference agreed that further talks should take place to replace bloc limits with national limits, to let other states in the Organization for Security and Cooperation in Europe become party to the treaty, to expand the treaty to take into account transport and airborne warning and control system (AWACS) aircraft, and to reduce force levels further. To reassure Russia about NATO expansion, NATO has proposed that combined foreign and domestic weapon numbers deployed in a country could not exceed its national ceiling.

The United States and Russia cooperated by presenting progress in START as reason for nonnuclear states to accept an indefinite extension of the NPT. In 1995, a review conference of all signatories did agree to extend the NPT indefinitely, and only thirteen states (including India, Pakistan, Israel, Brazil, and Cuba) remained outside the treaty. The nonnuclear weapons states attached a set of nonbinding principles to the extension: that a Comprehensive Test Ban Treaty (CTBT) be agreed during 1996, that production of fissile material for nuclear weapons be banned, that progress toward total nuclear disarmament be made, and that nonnuclear weapon states be given preferential access to civil nuclear power facilities. Due to the failure of International Atomic Energy Agency safeguards to detect

Iraq's clandestine nuclear weapons program, those safeguards are being tightened. Opposition among the declared and opaque nuclear weapon states to a CTBT gradually crumbled, and the treaty was signed in September 1996. India has declared that it will not sign the treaty, and Pakistan stated that it will join only if India does and there are no inspection provisions. However, the CTBT will contribute further to the delegitimization of nuclear testing. Negotiations over a ban on production of fissile material for nuclear weapons became bogged down with the insistence by some states with stockpiles that existing stockpiles be omitted from the talks and some of those without stockpiles demanding that existing stockpiles be included. The most notable success of recent years for the nuclear nonproliferation regime was North Korea's tacit promise in 1995 to abandon its nuclear weapon program in return for greater and subsidized access to civil nuclear technology, although this arrangement remains fragile.

Nonnuclear states have been making progress in another related area, namely, nuclear-weapon-free zones (NWFZs). All geographically relevant states have signed the 1974 Treaty of Tlatelolco for a Latin American NWFZ, the 1985 Treaty of Rarotonga proclaiming a South Pacific NWFZ, and the 1995 Pelindaba Treaty for an African NWFZ. All five declared nuclear states have signed the relevant protocols to say that they will respect them. Protocol signatures from the declared nuclear states for the 1995 Southeast Asian NWFZ treaty have been delayed due to problems over legal issues, the existence of nuclear-related military bases, and transit rights for nuclear-powered and/or nuclear-armed ships and submarines. Proposals have been aired for NWFZs for both Eastern Europe (plus former Soviet states Belarus, Ukraine, Lithuania, Latvia, and Estonia), and the Middle East (including all WMD, not just nuclear ones).

As part of a comprehensive agenda on WMD, talks have also been taking place regarding delivery systems and nonnuclear WMD. A fundamental problem for those trying to negotiate a verification protocol to be added to the BTWC is the difficulty of preventing cheating. In the wake of Iraq's expulsion from Kuwait in 1991, extremely intrusive inspection was imposed on it by the U.N. Special Commission on Iraq of a type and extent inconceivable for any BTWC protocol. Nevertheless, Iraq appears to have been able to conceal the vast bulk of its biological weapons program, as well as much of its chemical weapon and ballistic missile capability. Modern civil biotechnology may be just too small, low-profile, and mobile to monitor effectively. Efforts to improve verification should continue, but in the end the international community must rely on states' being deterred by the political costs of being found to have cheated and the calculation that cheating will not give them a decisive military advantage. The Chemical Weapons Convention (CWC) of 1992 banning chemical weapons had in October 1996 the required sixty-five ratifying states for it to come into force in April 1997. States that failed to ratify before the treaty came into force are not entitled to seats on the executive council of the Organization for the Prohibition of Chemical Weapons or to provide staff members.

The Missile Technology Control Regime (MTCR) of 1987 had expanded its membership to twenty-eight states in 1996 and expanded its aims to preventing the spread of technology related to ballistic missiles capable of delivering NBC warheads, with some additional attention also being paid to cruise missile technology and civil space programs. However, some states with ballistic missile programs (Ukraine, India, North Korea, Iran, Iraq, and Egypt) have not joined the MTCR or agreed to work within its guidelines. Some nonsignatories (China, Israel, and Romania) have agreed to the guidelines, but China's position is viewed with skepticism due to its record of selling ballistic missile technology. Even if the MTCR were to be effective in its own terms, missile technology is still spreading in that more and more states (including India, Indonesia, Malaysia, Mexico, Singapore, South Korea, and Taiwan) are developing the ability to build their own missiles.

Although the main focus of arms control has been on missiles and WMD, there have been some conventional arms control (and disarmament) efforts beyond CFE. The 1992 UN Register of Conventional Arms asks suppliers and recipients of major conventional weapons (e.g., tanks, missiles, warships) to report transfers in what is intended, at least initially, as a measure designed for confidence building through transparency. It shares the transparency concept with other measures such as the 1992 Treaty on Open Skies agreed between NATO and the former Warsaw Pact states. Because suppliers often notify the United Nations of transfers even when recipients do not, the register records around 90 percent of transactions. Some states hope to expand the register to include existing holdings and national procurement, but this move has been blocked by China, India, and Israel, among others. The register may one day be a springboard for greater controls on the arms trade.

In the meantime, the Coordinating Committee for Multilateral Export Controls (COCOM), which was established in 1949 and wound up in 1994, was succeeded by the Wassenaar Arrangement approved in 1996. COCOM's aim was to prevent weapons or militarily useful civil technologies from the advanced industrial countries reaching the Communist states. Wassenaar adds Russia and most of the former Warsaw Pact members to the Western states. It is aimed at producing voluntary restraint to prevent the transfer of weapons and dual-use technologies to states considered by its thirty-three (originally twenty-eight) members to be particularly threatening (currently Iran, Iraq, Libya, and North Korea). Some weapons of concern, such as landmines, do not fall within the UN register's definition of major weapons. The Convention on Certain Conventional Weapons of 1982 (generally known as the Inhumane Weapons Convention) seeks to ban or at least limit the use of what are regarded as particularly nasty weapons, such as landmines, booby traps, incendiaries, and explosive devices that have fragments difficult to detect. The convention's 1995 conference agreed to ban the use and transfer (but not production) of lasers that have the explicit purpose of blinding. In 1996 the conference agreed that mines outside mapped, guarded zones must automatically self-neutralize within 120 days, all landmines with eight grams or less metal content must be detectable, and stocks of landmines must conform to these standards within nine years. Some states (such as Belgium and Britain) have voluntarily banned production, transfer, import, and export of anti-personnel mines, while others have banned export of nondetectable ones. Clearly, the legitimacy of landmines is in decline, and a ban may be reached among the fifty states engaged in the Ottawa talks or possibly through the Geneva Conference on Disarmament. Although perfect verification of a landmines ban would be impossible due to their ease of production, transportation, and concealment, anyone who actually used them under conditions of a ban could come under heavy pressure.

It can be seen from this brief survey that arms control efforts have covered the whole range of weapon technologies and civil technologies with potential military uses. It can also be seen that arms control goes in and out of fashion: from the high point of détente, to the low of the second Cold War, to a substantial revival as part of the transition into the post–Cold War era. Arms control can be analyzed in terms of military, economic, and political issues, and it is to those issues that we now turn.

Military Issues

Arms Control for War Avoidance

Arms control proposals usually rest on the assumption that even enemies can share a common interest in war avoidance. There is thus no reason why arms control cannot be applied to nonnuclear as well as nuclear rivalries. Nuclear weapons do, however, make the common interest in survival between rivals much more compelling than the common interests that might be generated by desire to avoid a conventional arms competition or arms race. Rivals might also develop a secondary interest in reducing the costs of military expenditure, though autism might well override such a development.

Some advocates of strategic nuclear arms control based their proposals on the further assumption that sharing the condition of mutually assured destruction (MAD) (i.e., being vulnerable, whether one wanted to be or not) would force a convergence in superpower nuclear policies toward a doctrine of MAD (i.e., preferring to be vulnerable as a matter of strategic choice). This distinction between condition and doctrine is vital to understanding the significance of MAD. The expected convergence on MAD doctrine did not occur. Instead, both sides emphasized nuclear warfighting, and their negotiating positions in the SALT and then START talks tended toward protecting or enhancing their nuclear warfighting capabilities. It is noteworthy that arms control and partial disarmament are still continuing in this context: in other words, an unambiguous commitment to MAD is not a prerequisite for them.

Whether or not arms control has actually had any effect on making war less likely is highly debatable. Those in favor of arms control usually assume that it makes war less likely, although it is also plausible that it makes war more likely (by increasing political friction or by interfering with the operation of the balance of power), or is simply irrelevant. However, the common interest in preventing war, conventional or nuclear, points to two areas for cooperation that flow from the possibility that arms control can contribute to war avoidance: the avoidance and/or management of crises, and management of the arms dynamic in such a way that maintenance of the military status quo does not deteriorate into arms competition or arms racing.

Crisis Avoidance and Crisis Management

Avoiding or managing crises made sense because it is in crisis conditions that deterrence is most likely to come unstuck (Lebow 1981; Jervis, Lebow, and Stein 1985; Lebow 1987b; George 1991; Sagan 1993; Herring 1995). Both superpowers had experienced the dangers of crisis in their 1962 confrontation over the Soviet deployment of missiles in Cuba and U.S. unwillingness to tolerate it. That experience provided an important basis for the decade and a half of détente and arms control that followed it. In a crisis, acute pressure of time and uncertainty of information make rationally calculated behavior at best difficult, and at worst impossible. The probability of misinformation and misunderstanding rises sharply, and the problem of reliable communication becomes severe. Poorly understood standard operating procedures in military bureaucracies make precise central control over military moves difficult. In a crisis, mistakes or accidents can have disproportionate effects on the decisions of both sides. The desire to avoid war comes under intense counterpressure from the compulsion not to lose. In a crisis, the need to preserve face and credibility thus works directly against the overall constraint of the fear of triggering war.

The compressed timescale and high intensity of crisis might make behavior extremely difficult to control. The particular problem in crisis management is to ensure that the use of military means does not generate an action–reaction momentum of its own that would outrun the ability of political leaders to maintain the primacy of politics (George 1984). To reduce the probability of finding themselves in this situation, the superpowers devised several measures. They improved their ability to communicate with each other quickly; devised codes of conduct to lower the probability of unwanted clashes resulting from contact between their armed forces; discouraged the spread of nuclear weapons to minor powers; and agreed on confidence-building measures, such as notification of major military movements, as a method of reducing uncertainties about each other's behavior (Landi et al. 1984; Desjardins 1996). The NATO–Warsaw Pact crisis avoidance and crisis management measures have not been widely copied by other states. One exception was the telephone "hotline" link between the Soviet Union and China, but this proved ineffective in their severe border crisis of 1969 (Nixon 1978: 568). Another is the hotline between the Georgian Parliament and the Supreme Council of South Ossetia. In a really intense crisis, it is possible to imagine decisionmakers deciding to go to war in a preemptive attack because they thought (possibly inaccurately) that they were about to be attacked. Whatever the merits of the action–reaction dynamic in describing the arms dynamic, it can operate with a vengeance during crises. However, Dan Reiter (1995) has shown that preemptive wars are very rare. He found only three cases out of the 67 interstate wars between 1816 and 1980, namely Germany's attack on Russia in 1914, Chinese intervention into the Korean War in 1950, and Israel's attack on Egypt in 1967, and even in those cases preemption was not unambiguously the primary motive. Key elements in explaining this are that preemption is politically costly (you look like the aggressor and thus may alienate potential allies) and is often a self-denying prophecy (awareness that you may provoke a preemptive attack often results in measures to reduce the opponent's incentives to do so).

Managing the Arms Dynamic

The second main area for arms control is management of the arms dynamic to minimize its pace. This objective is less urgent in war prevention terms than crisis avoidance because the hypothesis that arms races can cause war is highly disputed, whereas the hypothesis that mismanagement of a crisis can cause war is widely accepted. The objectives are to reduce the negative impact that destabilizing weapons will have on crisis dynamics and to reduce economic costs. During the Cold War, the superpowers' record of restraint in the face of technological opportunities for nuclear counterforce and strategic defense was not good, although they did manage to avoid unrestrained arms racing. Where the technology was reliable, as it was for counterforce capability such as MIRV, the tendency was to develop and deploy it. The 1972 ABM Treaty restraints were as much an admission of impracticability as a statement of preference. This partly explains why that treaty is now in danger, the other factor being the political judgment that ABM systems are desirable.

Arms control may simply divert resources from one area of military activity to another (Gray 1974: 209; Brooks 1975: 75). This is the same problem as the one that arises for partial disarmament. If restrictions are placed on specified types of weapon, such as the banning of orbital weapons, the low ceilings on ABM systems, or even the high SALT ceilings on long-range ballistic missiles, then the resources that would have gone into those weapons might simply flow to unimpeded lines of development, such as cruise missiles and the R&D for ABM systems. On this basis, arms control may shape the arms dynamic but do little or nothing to diminish its size or pace. At worst, arms control may complicate its own future by releasing resources toward developments like cruise missiles that will themselves be difficult to restrict once they reach production.

Military Balance Measurements and Verification

Where there is a firm political will to reach an arms control agreement, disputes and fears over how to measure a fair military balance or how to verify compliance with the agreements will usually be overcome. Where the political will backing arms control is outweighed by the dynamics of rivalry and insecurity, these issues will feature prominently, and may well dominate the whole arms control process. At worst, arms control negotiations, like disarmament ones before them, can become a purely propaganda exercise, with each side mainly concerned with pinning responsibility for failure on the other. Arms control efforts can sour political relations (Desjardins 1996). Like disarmament, arms control is easiest when it is least necessary (as in end-of-war conditions) and most difficult when it is most necessary (during the peak period of rivalry). Where there is a political will, there is usually an acceptable way to measure and verify (an important exception being biological weapon programs, which are easily concealed). In this sense, disputes over these questions are of secondary importance, even though they are a necessary part of reaching agreement, and can make agreement harder to reach.

The arms control literature and Cold War practice have been distorted by an obsession with the technicalities of measurement and verification. Arms control initiatives that introduce ever more concepts and techniques tend to ignore or discount the crucial political context, and too easily take the diplomatic posturing at face value. The key is not the technical difficulties themselves, but the interplay between them and the political policies of the rival powers. The almost metaphysical and yet supposedly technical debates surrounding ways of measuring parity for the purposes of East–West arms control have been demystified ably by Warner Schilling (1981) and Richard K. Betts (1987: chapter 5). Underlying the mumbo jumbo of "parity," "essential equivalence," and so on was the basic political question of whether or not the West should accept rough Soviet military equality or whether it should try to regain military superiority. Western decisionmakers generally felt in the 1970s that regaining military superiority was not possible, but did not want to say so publicly. They pursued militarily insignificant "advantages" wherever possible in the arms control process and adopted obscure language to hide this from the public and to an extent from themselves (Kull 1988).

Economic Issues

The rationales for arms control are primarily military and political. One seldom sees the linking between arms control and development that one sees between disarmament and development. The reason for the relatively low profile of economic factors in arms control is clear: since no major assault on the arms dynamic is envisaged, no major release of resources from military to other uses is likely to result. The source of savings from disarmament is obvious, because a shrinkage in the size of the military establishment must quite quickly result in annual expenditure savings even if scrapping weapons does not in itself generate surplus revenue. If any savings result from arms control, they are much less visible because they tend to be reductions in hypothetical future expenditures rather than cuts in present ones.

Managing the arms dynamic by such arms control means as deployment ceilings and restrictions on types of weapons may result in savings on what would have been spent in the absence of such restraints. In other words, by defining terms agreed to for maintenance of the military status quo, arms control can keep military expenditures from rising to the higher levels necessary to sustain open-ended arms racing. These savings are by no means unattractive, and are part of the propaganda of arms control. Yet they are marginal compared to what disarmers offer, and they do not make much impact on the day-to-day reality of large expenditures for military purposes. To the extent that arms control means favoring one kind of weapon over another, it offers little economic incentive. Managing the arms dynamic releases states neither from the pressure of the technological imperative nor from what is widely perceived as the associated security need not to fall too far behind the leading edge of qualitative advance in comparison with their rivals.

Political Issues

Arms control contrasts with what we call "disarmament by simply disarming" (see Chapter 15) by taking the political structure of the international system as a given and seeking to work within its constraints. It claims to offer a way of opening up clear grounds for joint gain between rivals. Unlike GCD, with arms control, rival states could pursue some security interests jointly without having to give up either their own armed forces or their political-military rivalry. Advocates of arms control hope that what they see as the low sacrifices and significant security gains offered by arms control might serve as a way of beginning to build habits of trust and cooperation between rivals. Arms control could start with incremental agreements. It might build steadily into an increasingly broad range of cooperation that would eventually begin to mute the political rivalry, and perhaps even lead to disarmament. In this way, arms controllers offer an "arms and politics together" approach rather than an "arms first" or "politics first" approach.

During the period of East–West arms control between 1963 and 1979, however, the linkage of arms control to expectations of improved political relations proved to be a greater burden than the arms control process could bear. The process became deeply entangled with political détente, and the state of arms control talks was seen as a key barometer of East–West relations. Any positive political influence exerted by the arms control process was easily overwhelmed by the intensifying U.S.-Soviet rivalry in the LICs, growing U.S. resentment at what it felt to be its loss of nuclear superiority, and growing Soviet resentment at what it felt to be a U.S. attempt to reestablish nuclear superiority. Arms control was not able to insulate détente from East–West rivalry. Many analysts responded to these developments by arguing that U.S. linking of arms control and détente was a mistake (Blechman 1980: 106–112; Luttwak 1980a; 1980b: 137–139). Calls for a return to a more strictly technical arms control are based on this analysis.

The mistake was the classically U.S. one of seeking technological solutions to political problems. The Soviet leadership gave primacy to politics as part of their ideology. Soviet leaders were in no doubt that arms control depended on détente rather than the other way around (Blechman 1980: 106–112). This equally overstated position was an important factor in the failure of pre-Gorbachev Soviet leaders to understand that actions with regard to particular weapons (such as the deployment of SS-20 missiles in Eastern Europe to replace SS-4s and SS-5s) could have very important political effects (such as further imperiling détente). However, it was Gorbachev's more sophisticated grasp of the interaction of the political and military spheres that enabled him to break the arms control logjam through weapons initiatives (large conventional and nuclear unilateral reductions to induce reciprocation) and political initiatives (the new political thinking that sought to undermine the U.S. image of the Soviet Union as the enemy). The more far-reaching the arms control proposals, the more important changes in political relations will be for those proposals to be implemented. However, the attraction of arms control for some is that it does not necessarily require states to give up either their military strength or their political rivalries. Indeed, arms control talks may even intensify arms competition.

How Arms Control Can Generate More Arms than Control

Arms control can generate more arms than control in two ways.

First, it can create demand for weapons when parity is being pursued in terms of detailed similarity of forces. That pursuit leads to each side assessing its strength against that of the other on the basis of comparisons in each separate category of weapons—ICBMs, SLBMs, intermediate-range nuclear forces, tanks, aircraft, troop numbers, and so forth. Equal numbers in particular weapon categories matter not because of their military utility but because they symbolize equality. This process can be reinforced by the perception that third parties will also assess in this way the relative symbolic political status as well as military prowess of the actors involved. Such calculations lead to perceptions of weakness on the basis of an imbalance within any significant category, rather than to comparisons in terms of overall military capability. Pressure to correct specific imbalances strengthens the domestic bargaining position of those who want to acquire the weapons in question, but whose case might otherwise not be strong enough to prevail in the fierce competition for a share of the military budget. Thus the domestic pressures in the United States favoring large, multiwarhead ICBMs, an antisatellite system, and chemical weapons became stronger simply because the Soviet Union had them. The Soviet Union seems to have experienced a parallel process in relation to cruise missiles and enhanced-radiation warheads (generally known as neutron bombs). Sometimes there are good strategic reasons for acquiring parallel weapons systems (such as those situations in which the best antitank weapon is another tank). The danger is that arms control will lead to some acquisitions for the sake of symbolic rather than military equality.

A second, related point is that pressure can build up for the acquisition of weapons as "bargaining chips," which are not in the end cashed in for an arms control agreement. Because arms control is about the management of conflict rather than its resolution, the process of arms control easily gets absorbed into the overall framework of rivalry. Negotiations can become a forum in which the rivals display their supposed "strengths," both to each other and to their audience in the rest of the world. Because of this competitive element, and also because the outcomes of negotiations affect national policy, arms control can become an important element in domestic political debate. Great play can be made of the need to negotiate from a position of strength and to avoid sending one's diplomats naked into the bargaining chamber. By this process, arms control becomes a means for justifying new weapons programs to put the country in a strong position to bargain. Much is made of the claim that unless one's negotiators have plenty of chips with which to play, there is a danger that they will be forced into a weaker position by a rival who has more to give away. This kind of thinking played a conspicuous role in U.S. policymaking, notably in the long debates about the MX missile. The notion of the bargaining chip is an all-purpose legitimizing device for almost any weapon system in such a competitive context. Once initiated, major weapons projects acquire domestic momentum and become difficult, though not impossible, to stop (Farrell 1996). In the end arms control can make management of the arms dynamic harder rather than easier.

The Ambiguous Impact of Technological Innovation

Unlike GCD, arms control makes no attempt to stop the arms dynamic. This position is taken on what is presented as the pragmatic grounds that however desirable such a solution might be, it is impossible to achieve within the existing political framework of international anarchy, which is itself portrayed as durable. Arms control therefore makes no pretense of being a permanent single solution to the problem of military means. What it offers is a continuous process of management as a way of responding to political and technological change. This essentially piecemeal and reactive stance means that arms control always confronts a menu of issues that changes continuously in response to advances in technology. Sometimes the changes will favor arms control, such as the vast improvement in surveillance and information-gathering technology that enables actors to monitor each other's activities. Other changes make arms control more difficult by increasing the ease with which weapons can be concealed (by making them smaller, more mobile, or more self-contained) or by increasing the uncertainties about the actual capability of a given weapon (such as dual-capability systems that can and do carry either mass-destruction or conventional warheads). If there is ever a complete ban on landmines, the potential for leakage is very substantial for these small, easily produced and transported weapons. Even so, the possibility of cheating could be regarded as tolerable because it would be unlikely to give the cheat a decisive military advantage, and even a leaky ban would save tens of thousands of people from death and maiming.

Because arms control cannot stop the processes of innovation and the politics of weapons acquisition, it is particularly vulnerable to adverse technological and political developments. This means that its achievements can be fragile. The most striking recent illustration of this vulnerability is the conflict between increasing enthusiasm in many countries for BMD and the 1972 ABM Treaty. New technological opportunities threaten to bring down what is arguably the most significant arms control achievement of the pre-Gorbachev period (Drell et al. 1984). Of course, for advocates of BMD this is a good thing: the undermining of a treaty that is either out of date or should never have been agreed to in the first place.

Several factors prevent arms control from reaching into the R&D process to anticipate such developments. First, the process of R&D does not lend itself to clear predictions of future military technology. Even where a development can be anticipated, its implications will be ambiguous because they depend as much on politics and strategy as on technology. This is very much the case for attempts to think through the implications of information age technology (*Strategic Survey 1995–96* 1996: 29–40). This is also the case with the CTBT on nuclear weapons. Even pro-arms control opinion is divided on whether such a measure is desirable. Is it useful as a restraint on further development of warheads by the nuclear powers and on proliferation by nonnuclear powers? Or is it mistaken because it would block desirable improvements in nuclear forces (such as reduction in explosive yields) and erode confidence in existing stockpiles (Edmonds 1984; Howard 1985: 10; Hussain 1981; Fetter 1987–1988)? Second, secrecy about the R&D process is generally regarded as a matter of national security. Third, the West, in general, and the United States, in particular, are committed to technological innovation as a key element in their military strength, in the past against the Soviet Union and now against potential threats from LICs. They would therefore be reluctant to restrict their R&D options. The momentum of technology also creates problems for freeze proposals (in which the sides involved in the agreement simply stick to whatever levels they currently have in terms of particular weapons). A freeze would ban desirable developments in military technology as well as undesirable ones, and fix military imbalances as well as balances. In addition, under a freeze, a known and growing military potential in the civil economy would create the possibility of breakout from the agreement by whichever side decided to exploit it first.

Conclusion

Opinion on the value of formal arms control is divided radically between strategic opponents of arms control (who see it as a threat to the proper management of the balance of power), cynics (who see it as a diplomatic arena in which to soothe the public and pillory the adversary as uncooperative), confidence builders (who think it can help improve diplomatic relations), true believers (who think it can make war much less likely), and disarmers (who believe that it is a diversion from the real business of getting rid of weapons) (Williams 1983; see also Croft 1996). Arms control accepts the arms dynamic and tries to manage it. Management, however, can easily become complicity (Howard 1985: 6). As outlined above, there are many ways—bargaining chips, resource diversions, the pursuit of force symmetry, status instability—in which the process of arms control can actually stimulate hostility and the competitive accumulation of armaments. Until the mid-1980s, the record of arms control provided grounds for suspicion that the concept was more useful for putting a polite face on arms competition, and for manipulating public opinion, than it was for achieving restraint (Freedman 1982: 41). This was especially true because both sides were committed to nuclear warfighting strategies and to potential worldwide conventional war with each other. As a result, the scope for arms control was small and the perceived need for weapons large.

The experiences of the late 1980s and the first half of the 1990s show that arms control processes can be kept in place through such unfavorable times, can be combined very successfully with partial disarmament, and can be broadened into many other areas as an expression of concern and as preparation for times in which political will for serious action might emerge for those areas also. However, as Betts (1992) argues, if one sees arms control as solely being about stabilizing balances between potential adversaries, there is no point in having formal arms control where it is unclear who the potential adversaries will be. Hence, whereas CFE made sense in the context of potential East–West war, for Betts it makes no sense now in terms of military balance stabilization, especially since NATO's former adversaries are either becoming allies or are cutting their forces unilaterally anyway. If a state has to violate a formal arms control treaty to acquire the forces it thinks necessary to ensure its security (as Russia may do eventually), this may be more politically destabilizing than if there was no treaty in the first place. None of this is to deny the possibility that the CFE Treaty system is building confidence and easing tensions through the involvement of the post-Communist states in implementing the treaty's disclosure, verification, and enforcement provisions (Falkenrath 1995; see also Croft 1996). The CFE Treaty system also symbolizes and helps underpin a broadening of the Western European security community into Eastern Europe. The point is that there may be real trade-offs, and one should not assume that formal arms control is necessarily or always a good thing.

As a child of the Cold War, arms control was born with strong assumptions about political rivalry built into it. Gorbachev's revolution and its subsequent political fallout undercut that assumption for East–West relations, though some elements of it remain in relations between NATO and Russia. In the heartland of arms control, the moderating of political relations for political reasons largely sidelined its attempt to build détente with "arms first" initiatives. Instead, arms control (and partial disarmament) became more followers of political developments rather than would-be leaders of them. In the zone of conflict, arms control's assumption of rivalry remained valid across a whole range of states. But the overwhelming focus of arms controllers on the superpower rivalry meant that there was not much expertise available to connect their ideas to this diverse set of still active security dilemmas. Nor had much thought been given to the nature of the security dilemma between the zone of peace and the zone of conflict. Such arms control measures as the NPT bridged the two zones, and though many of the problems arising reflected conditions in the zone of conflict, at least some of them arose from interzonal insecurities. It remains to be seen whether arms control will retain its vitality by shifting to the remaining areas of political-military rivalry or whether it will drift into marginality within the much diminished sphere of East–West relations. If it does make the shift, then it will carry with it many of the still unresolved problems exposed by the attempts to apply it during the Cold War.

14

NONOFFENSIVE DEFENSE

The idea of nonoffensive defense (NOD) developed mostly in Germany during the 1980s (Bahr and Lutz 1988; Studiengruppe Alternative Sicherheitspolitik 1989; Møller 1991). Its original conception was as a way of defending Germany without threatening offensive strikes against the Warsaw Pact states. It emerged into the strategic debate during the dying years of the Cold War, most conspicuously during 1986–1988, when Gorbachev publicly adopted some of its key principles. It is based on a distinction between offensive and defensive strategies and the military force postures with which to implement them, and tries to build on the classical military assumption that defense is usually easier than offense. It broadly rejects the distinction between offensive and defensive weapons that preoccupied the arms control and disarmament conferences of the prenuclear era (Møller 1995c: 5). Instead, it identifies offensive force postures, military strategies, and political objectives, and the fear of being attacked that they stimulate, as the core of the problems caused by military means (Møller 1991, 1992, 1995a; Møller and Wiberg 1994).

Interest in NOD has developed in an area of overlap between the fields of strategic studies and peace studies. The concept thus offers an important opportunity to combine the intellectual forces of two fields that traditionally have not normally seen their activities as being particularly harmonious. From the peace studies side the idea was originally discussed under the label of "transarmament" (Fischer 1984; Galtung 1984a, 1984b; Sharp 1985). Transarmament refers to the process of shifting away from mutually threatening forms of military security and toward something variously termed NOD, nonprovocative defense, or defensive defense. Some interpret transarmament as a shift to strategic nonviolence (SNV), also known as civilian defense (Roberts 1967; Sharp 1985: 67): hence, for some, GCD becomes synonymous with the end product of transarmament and is a form of NOD. However, mainstream NOD advocates usually offer a military approach.

From the strategic studies side, interest in NOD has built on what was previously a peripheral theoretical interest pioneered by Adam Roberts ([1976] 1986) in strategies for territorial military defense. The more widespread interest in the 1980s among strategists grew out of Western European discomfort with extended nuclear deterrence and desire to push back the use of nuclear threats by increasing capabilities for conventional denial. Much of the debate about improving conventional defense was firmly within the mainstream strategic tradition of conventional warfighting. Some of it, however, reflected a wish to exploit a perceived shift of technological advantage to the defense in order to reorient Western European military strategy toward nonprovocative conventional defense (Windass 1985; Pierre 1986; Dean 1987; Booth and Baylis 1988; Borg and Smit 1989; Boserup and Neild 1990; UNIDIR 1990; Brauch and Kennedy 1990, 1992; Gates 1991). Here the aim was to operate within what was perceived as security interdependence and to pursue common security in terms of the mutual "right not to be overwhelmed by the military forces of the other" (Windass 1985: 120). With the end of the Cold War, and the virtual disappearance of military tensions in most of Europe, NOD thinking has shifted toward applications in the wider world (Singh and Vekaric 1989; Møller and Wiberg 1994; Caceres and Scheetz 1995; Møller 1995b, 1995c, 1995d, 1996a, 1996b, 1996c).

NOD thus ranges across a spectrum where the focus is on SNV at one end, through the many-layered strategy of territorial defense and transarmament, to a concentration on nonprovocative conventional denial options within alliances at the other end. SNV may be relied on solely but it can also be seen as augmenting rather than replacing military deterrence, while the debates about conventional denial options blend more easily into the arms control perspective. NOD is more radical than arms control because it rejects the idea that security can be achieved using offensive military capabilities, but it is less radical than disarmament because it does not reject the utility of military means in the pursuit of security. It can be seen as a reaction to the failure of disarmament and arms control to make much impact on the arms dynamic. It represents a refusal to accept nuclear deterrence as a safe and reasonable way of assuring national security, but it does share with strategic studies a belief that there is a significant role for military means in achieving security.

The distinction between offensive and defensive military capability has been debated for much of this century (Quester 1977; Jervis 1978, 1985; Gilpin 1981: 59–66; Levy 1984; Snyder 1984; Van Evera 1984; Agrell 1987; Hopf 1991; Gray 1993a; Lynne-Jones 1995; Kier 1997). Rather than review this debate we suggest the following definitions that broadly reflect common usage. *Offense* is about trying to make gains, and *defense* is about trying to avoid losses (Herring 1995: 45–49, 64, 68–69, 157). *Tactical offense* is military action to make local gains, whereas *tactical defense* is military action to avoid local losses. Of course, tactical operations can have strategic implications. Strategic offense is often seen as military action to harm the vital interests of an adversary and strategic defense as military action to protect one's own vital interests (on the politics of how things become defined as vital interests, see Brodie 1973: chapter 8; cf. Campbell 1992). This is logical and reasonable: it means that strategic offense can include attacking interests of an adversary located outside its home territory, and strategic defense can be about protecting one's own vital interests (such as allies or sea lanes) outside home territory. The problem is that if the interests to be defended are distant, and close to the home territory or vital interests of the adversary, it can be very difficult to distinguish between strategic offensive and defensive capabilities. President Nixon, for example, tried (in the end unsuccessfully) to talk up South Vietnam as a vital U.S. interest, arguing that he was defending San Francisco in the Mekong Delta.

The difference between strategic offense and defense is much easier to see if the interests to be defended are close to home territory and distant from the home territory and other vital interests of the adversary. For NOD to make a difference, strategic offense and defense must be fairly clearly distinguishable. Hence, for the purpose of our assessment of NOD, *strategic offense* is military action to harm an adversary's vital interests on its home territory, and *strategic defense* is military action to defend one's own vital interests on home territory. Even then, strategic offense and defense may still be difficult to tell apart if, for example, the vital interests of the actors are adjacent. This has been the case in relations between Iran and Iraq and especially characteristic of the most common type of military conflict in world politics, namely civil war, in which vital interests of actors—such as home territory and the civilian population—are often not merely adjacent but intermingled. In civil wars, the security dilemma is often exceptionally severe and NOD particularly difficult to apply (Posen 1993; Kaufmann 1996; Herring 1997a). For Chaim Kaufmann (1996), the option that will minimize the frequency and brutality of civil wars is population and territory exchanges to provide units to which (to put it in our terms rather than his) NOD could then be (cf. Kacowicz 1994) applicable (although whether or not such a policy will actually achieve its objectives is very much open to challenge).

Looked at in this way, it makes little sense to categorize any particular weapon as purely offensive or defensive, although efforts are often made to do so (these days mostly by critics of NOD). Mobile weapons like tanks are just as suitable for offense as for defense, and even apparently defensive capabilities like fixed fortifications, mines, fighter aircraft, and antiaircraft missiles can be used to support offensive actions. During World War II, British Prime Minister Winston Churchill commissioned a feasibility study into the offensive use of barrage balloons after reading reports of how, due to bombing raids, the heavy cables securing some of these balloons snapped, with the result that the balloons drifted along and their mooring cables damaged chimneys, telephone lines, and so on. However, the feasibility study concluded that German retaliation with the same technique would result in even more damage than Britain could inflict on German assets on the continent and the idea was dropped. The most striking contemporary manifestation of this problem is ballistic missile defense (BMD). Taken by itself BMD fits into NOD. The objective of escaping from nuclear vulnerability by putting up a defense against missiles, and of replacing mutual paralysis of threats of retaliation with the mutual paralysis of impenetrable defensive screens, is a high-technology version of NOD. The problem is that if an effective strategic nuclear defense is at any point combined with offensive capability, then defense becomes a powerful complement to offense. Strategic nuclear defense would increase incentives for first strikes by offering the attacker the possibility of blocking the target's threat of retaliatory response. The analogy here is the combination of offensive and defensive capability represented by the sword and the shield.

One of the fundamental challenges for any advocate of NOD is how to configure armed forces so that they are—and for the purposes of reassurance, mitigation of the security dilemma, and dampening of the arms dynamic, appear to be—more suited to tactical counteroffense (to expel an attacker or regain control of vital interests) and less to strategic offense. A debate raged over this in Soviet (and Western) military and political circles in response to Gorbachev's objective of shifting the Warsaw Pact nations to NOD but was not resolved before the Soviet Union collapsed. Another fundamental problem is that decisionmakers can believe not simply that the best defense is a good offense, but that the only defense is a good offense. This was true for Germany before World War I: it adopted the Schlieffen Plan, which was predicated on the assumption that Germany could only ensure strategic defense (that is, defense of the homeland) by going on the strategic offense against France and then Russia. It was also true for Soviet strategists before the Gorbachev era, who believed that, in a world war against the West, Warsaw Pact armies would have to defeat NATO in Western Europe to prevent it from being used as a springboard for an invasion of the Soviet Union (MccGwire 1987). Hence even defensive political objectives can be seen as requiring adoption of strategic offense: this is especially the case for countries that lack strategic depth and face militarily superior adversaries (such as Israel, Pakistan, Chile, and Singapore). In contrast, NATO was geared primarily to a form of what could be seen as strategic defense in the sense that it was geared mainly to fighting on NATO territory in what was known as "forward defense" along the NATO–Warsaw Pact central front. However, there was some commitment to using nuclear weapons (and then new and existing conventional technologies) to make strikes against "follow-on forces" and other military targets quite deep inside the territory of the Warsaw Pact. NATO strategy thus had some NOD-like qualities, but its force profile remained offensive enough to feed the security dilemma with the Soviet Union significantly. NATO may have thought of itself as defensive, but was not perceived as such by its opponent.

The way to deal with these ambiguities is to think not just in terms of particular weapons but in terms of the whole package of political objectives, foreign policy, interests, allies, military doctrine, weapons, logistics, and training. In general terms, NOD is about making a piece of territory hard to attack, expensive to invade, and difficult to occupy. It means preparing defenses in depth and having strong denial forces that are not suitable for long-range strategic offensive action. It also means taking measures to destroy assets of value to invaders, like transportation routes, before they can use them (although this scorched-earth strategy is unattractive to some). NOD means that one's military capability should be confined as much as possible to one's own territory. In terms of the discussion about deterrence and defense in Chapter 10, the principles of NOD make it incompatible with deterrence by retaliation, but very much seek to build on deterrence by denial (Galtung 1984a: 132–135).

During the Cold War, different versions of this overall package could be seen in the NOD practices of Sweden, Switzerland, Austria, Yugoslavia (Johnson 1973; Roberts [1976] 1986; Fischer 1982), and Japan (Momoi 1981; Satoh 1982; Berger 1993; Katzenstein and Okawara 1993; Buzan 1995a). Sweden and Switzerland both had long-standing policies of neutrality in which the principle of NOD played an important role. Both pursued self-reliant military strategies based on making the country difficult and unrewarding to occupy. Both had long-term success in staying out of the major hostilities that have raged around them, and both spent amounts very similar to those of their NATO neighbors on defense in terms of percentage of GDP during and after the Cold War (*Military Balance 1996–97* 1996: 306–307). The record of Austria was much shorter. It had neutrality imposed upon it in 1955 by World War II victors Britain, France, the United States, and the Soviet Union, and its policy of NOD suited its Cold War national security requirements. Yugoslavia's policy of NOD was well suited to making it unattractive as a target of invasion by the Soviet Union in spite of its political defiance of Stalin. With the end of the Cold War, Sweden and Austria are no longer on the front line of a confrontation and have begun to question fundamentally the relevance of neutrality. Switzerland's position and policy so far remain largely unchanged. Yugoslavia has undergone a violent disintegration, in the process raising questions about some drawbacks of NOD policy for weak states (Buzan 1994: 13). As these traditional European cases lose current relevance, there are prospects that developments in places such as southern Africa might replace them as living examples.

The Japanese case is particularly distinctive, though like that of Austria it resulted from defeat in World War II. Japan is not neutral, but a major ally of the United States. Its commitment to NOD arose from the postwar disarmament imposed on it by the United States and enshrined in article 9 of the U.S.-inspired "peace" constitution. Article 9 theoretically forbids Japan from maintaining war potential or using force in its foreign relations, but over the years this absolute prohibition has been steadily reinterpreted as allowing military self-defense. Because Japan is an island state, it has much less of a problem distinguishing between offensive and defensive strategic military capabilities than would be the case for countries with neighbors adjacent on land. Japan has only to deny itself long-range air, missile, and naval (other than antisubmarine warfare) capabilities to sustain a credible NOD posture. Its military spending was much less per capita during and after the Cold War than that of the other large industrialized states (*Military Balance 1996–97* 1996: 306–308). The significance of the Japanese case is considerably muddied by the fact of its open reliance on the United States to provide not only nuclear deterrence but also a major reinforcement component for its conventional denial capability. Although it can also be argued that the European neutrals got a substantial free ride on the military capabilities of NATO during the Cold War (and to some extent still do), Japan's reliance is so marked and so direct that its utility as a model for self-reliant NOD must be doubted. It is, however, a very interesting example of some of the problems of combining local NOD with alliance. Furthermore, as Japan takes on longer range air and surface defense of its sea lanes, it acquires some of the weaponry (but not the political desire or will, doctrine, training, or allied support) for military power projection onto the East Asian mainland (on the distinction between offensive sea control and defense of sea lines of communication, see Mearsheimer 1986, and Møller 1992: 187–194).

Military Issues

The Military Characteristics of NOD

Like arms control, NOD is quite clear about the direction that military policy should take. One can easily envisage a considerable range of end conditions that might qualify as NOD. Ongoing change in technological variables would require such end states to be continuously reassessed. It is not obvious where the boundaries around the idea should be located, especially toward the arms control end of the spectrum, where there is some area of overlap. In the narrowest interpretation, a state pursuing NOD should offer virtually no military threat outside its boundaries, while nonetheless maintaining stiff powers of resistance within them. As Johan Galtung (1984a: 127–132) and Dietrich Fischer (1984: chapters 9, 10, 12,

13) argue, such a policy could be based on a range of strategies. Some of these could be political, to do with raising the costs and lowering the incentives for other states to attack. Some could be nonmilitary, along the lines of SNV to offer civilian resistance to occupation (Roberts 1967; Sharp 1985). Some could be paramilitary, in the form of broadly based militia organizations. And some could be regular military, in terms of professional armed forces designed to undertake such specific skilled tasks as coastal, border, and air defense; demolition; and training. Conventional military resistance to attack would begin at the border with static defenses such as mines, tank traps, fixed fortifications, and professional armed forces (Windass 1985: chapter 3). Specialist armed forces would be required to take advantage of advanced technology for defense, such as the many varieties of short-range PGM that can be used against attacking aircraft, ships, armored vehicles, and even missiles. The purist image of NOD is therefore one with a high level of mass participation in defense policy, creating a defense that extends not only throughout the whole territory of the state but also throughout its society.

Within this range of possibilities, NOD is designed to have its main impact on the action–reaction part of the arms dynamic. NOD is aimed primarily at muting the security dilemma by reducing the fear of actors that they will be attacked. It does so by reducing the offensive potential of military capabilities that are designed for defense. NOD requires complete rejection of the traditional military axiom mentioned above that the best defense is a good offense. A state fully committed to NOD should pose virtually no military threat to any state that has no military designs against its home territory. Not only does it deny itself the military means for strategic offense, but in taking the trouble to design its military forces with such care, it makes a clear political statement that it has no aggressive intentions. In a system where all states pursue and are perceived clearly to be pursuing NOD, the military security dilemma would virtually cease to operate, at least at the interstate level. The objective of making all states militarily secure without threatening others would be fulfilled. Such a system would be well on the way to achieving extensive partial disarmament, since states would have low military requirements for their own external security (as opposed to internal security—the key problem for weak states). However, these positive effects hinge crucially on whether unilateral NOD moves are reciprocated by opponents, and on whether or not offense and defense can be distinguished clearly from each other.

Military Vulnerabilities of NOD
in the Face of Actors with Offensive Options

In military terms, the main difficulties with NOD policies arise in mixed systems where some states have adopted it, but others still retain traditionally structured armed forces. One of the great advantages of NOD is that it can be implemented unilaterally. Willing states can take the lead and bypass the ponderous multilateral negotiations that have so often made little progress toward disarmament and arms control. Unilateral implementation means that states with NOD must coexist with offensively armed neighbors. That condition opens up four problems for states that define NOD narrowly in terms of a capability only for defending their home territory. First, such states are vulnerable to bombardment. Second, although they can form alliances, they will lack power projection capabilities to send help to each other (Galtung 1984a: 135–138). Third, they will have little or no capability to defend security interests like shipping routes that may be remote from their national territory. Fourth, they cannot use strategic offensive options either to deter attack or as part of a strategy for expelling an invader. Of course, in practice, it is a matter of degree: states could build down their offensive capabilities depending on their perception of the circumstances and whether any reciprocation occurs. However, examining the purest form of NOD gives a clearer idea of the policy problems that can arise.

Even a state thoroughly equipped for NOD will not have the means to retaliate to a nuclear bombardment on itself, though it could mute the effects by extensive civil defense and antiaircraft and antimissile measures. In a purist interpretation, such a state might even have difficulty dealing with a conventional cross-border bombardment. By definition, a state pursuing home territory NOD has to accept that if the policy fails as a deterrent, nearly all of the collateral damage of war would occur on its own territory. Acquisition of means for either retaliation or preventive attacks on the bombarding forces would violate the basic principles of NOD and reopen the security dilemma. Vulnerability to bombardment without the means to retaliate may be seen as unacceptable or it may be seen as an acceptable alternative to the chances of war that exist anyway between offensively armed states, especially if they are nuclear armed. The state adopting NOD might calculate that it gains more security from lowering its threat to others (by reducing their incentive to attack) than it loses from the possibility of action by others.

A strict policy of NOD makes alliances difficult for two reasons: first, the principle of self-reliance is inherently contradictory to alliances, and, second, a military capability confined to national territory greatly reduces the scope for mutual military support. Some advocates of NOD tend to take the view that the policy is incompatible with alliances (Fischer 1984: chapter 11; Galtung 1984a: 135–138). Those who discussed Cold War NOD options in the context of NATO, however, had no difficulty envisaging coordinated alliance strategies along NOD lines (Windass 1985). A principle of collective self-reliance could be applied to a group of adjacent NOD states, the combination of which would produce an enlarged and possibly more coherent area of denial to confront offensive action. Forgoing alliance requires fuller mobilization of one's own resources for defense. It runs the risk of presenting an adversary on the offensive with a series of small, if hard, targets that can be picked off one at a time. As with the threat of bombardment, the weakening of alliance options suggests a military vulnerability of NOD if the problem is an offensively oriented opponent. More recent NOD thinking proposes a pragmatic compromise solution to this problem (Møller 1995d: 17–19; 1996b: 14–16). Where alliances require some tactical counteroffensive capability to expel invaders, this can be provided collectively, with each member providing a specialized component. Individual members would not possess offensive capability, but the alliance as a whole would, though only at a tactical level.

The problem of geographically remote interests arises most obviously in the case of states that are dependent on trade for economic welfare, in general, or on specific resources like oil or food, in particular. Japan, for example, has a keen interest in keeping open the straits through and around Indonesia, without which its energy supplies and trade routes would be put at risk. Russia needs to ensure that its trade can pass through the Turkish straits and the exits from the Baltic and Mediterranean seas and the Sea of Japan. A state pursuing strict NOD would be hard put to deploy military capability relevant to these tasks without violating the principle that its military capability should not be able to threaten other states on their own territory. One possible NOD solution to this dilemma is to provide naval convoying capabilities that do not have significant capability to project force against the land (Møller 1995d: 15–17).

The loss of strategic offensive capabilities in support of defensive political goals has to be weighed against the expected reduction in military threats, and the general damping down of the security dilemma, that would follow the adoption of a NOD policy. Put differently, consider the difficult choice facing someone for whom the defense of human rights was a priority. General renunciation of strategic offensive capabilities would make it much harder for oppressive actors to expand their sphere of influence, but would also make it much harder to use force to intervene against an oppressor. Based on the claim that intervention is much more often oppressive than for the purpose of protecting human rights, Caroline Thomas (1993) argues for a clear commitment to nonintervention and state sovereignty: this would be served by a general shift to NOD. This position could be augmented by a commitment to popularization of and education in SNV so that those being oppressed could challenge their oppressors themselves rather than relying on external military intervention. Encouragement of even nonviolent opposition to rulers (oppressive or not) will be seen by and represented by those rulers as subversion, as an attack on their vital interests and hence as a strategic (even if nonmilitary) offensive threat. As it is, actors often end up in the competitive situation of attempting to retain offensive options for themselves and undermine the offensive options available to actual or potential adversaries. If intervention capability with its necessarily offensive qualities is nonetheless desired within a

NOD framework, then the solution is the same as that for NOD alliances: to embed offensive capability collectively while denying it to individual states (Møller 1996b: 16–18). This solution poses a host of (not necessarily insurmountable) problems about command, interoperability of forces, and the political difficulties of achieving coherent and quick consensus on the mission objectives.

Economic Issues

Like arms control, the economic attractiveness of NOD is very limited. NOD policies offer a major shift in the character of military strength, but not savings from either the medium-term reductions of disarmament or the longer term lower levels of arms control. For reasons similar to the adverse economic effects of nuclear disarmament accompanied by increases in conventional forces, fully fledged NOD policies may cost as much as, or even more than, the policies they replace, especially if carried out in the face of opponents who do not reciprocate. NOD is aimed at restructuring, but not eliminating, the domestic component of the arms dynamic. Although the cost of major offensive systems would no longer weigh on the economy, much that would replace them would be expensive. Extensive civil defense measures, coastal and border fortifications, and high-technology defensive weapons (although some NOD schemes are of low-technology) all require large resource commitments. Costs also depend on the pace of implementation: the faster the change, the more expensive it will be. NOD does not offer escape from the technological imperative: instead, like arms control, but much more thoroughly, it would try to steer and exploit the technological imperative in pursuit of defensive strength. This, plus the possible commitment to self-reliance, requires the maintenance of an arms industry with its own R&D component.

NOD's attractiveness is primarily military and political. Its concern is to achieve a form of military security that is not self-defeating because of its security dilemma effects. Its priority is toward these goals rather than toward resource savings for alternative social purposes. However, it is possible that gradual dissolution of the security dilemma may allow for NOD at lower and lower levels so that it can achieve the sort of savings associated with partial but still substantial disarmament. Advocates of NOD do not generally feature economic incentives as part of their case, though they may do so in specific cases (Møller 1995b: 2).

Political Issues

NOD advocates believe that their approach offers the possibility of reducing tensions without either making oneself excessively vulnerable, or requiring agreement with other states. If it damps down the security dilemma, it can create promising military conditions for the resolution of political tensions. NOD requires less of a political transformation than disarmament and it avoids the dependence of arms control on the prior existence of détente. Because NOD can be pursued unilaterally it is politically flexible. It allows any state to take a lead, and so bypasses the problem of adjusting to the pace of the slowest that confronts approaches dependent on multilateral implementation. Although NOD can be implemented unilaterally even where military relations are tense, there is good reason to hope that a unilateral move would put pressure on rivals to moderate their policy. Where offensive force postures confront each other (and regardless of whether they are accompanied by defensive rationales), each side can plausibly justify its own policy in terms of the other. But if one side shifts conspicuously to NOD, the other can no longer use this argument. Indeed, the other's failure to reciprocate risks exposing it as the "real" aggressor. Some states might well be able to sustain such exposure, but NOD does at least make political life much more difficult for them. If the security dilemma represents a confusion of defensive and offensive motives, then NOD will expose this and put the process into reverse. There was a fleeting, and by no means fully worked through, case of this process at work in the final years of the Cold War, when Gorbachev initiated NOD rhetoric and some first small moves toward a more NOD-like force posture.

NOD Requires Political Cohesion

Despite the political strengths outlined above, NOD also poses some serious political problems. The most obvious of these is that, like SNV, the policy presupposes politically cohesive states in which the government rules primarily by consent rather than by force and in which domestic security concerns are not a major component of national security (hereafter "strong," as opposed to "powerful," states) (Buzan 1987a: chapter 1; 1991a: chapter 2). Without that precondition, it would be almost impossible to implement the nonmilitary and paramilitary elements of territorial defense (these are central to some NOD schemes but are not inherent to the idea of NOD). Where the state is weak in the sense that the government depends substantially on the use or threat of force to maintain control over a large proportion of its own citizens, a strategy of dispersing weapons and militia training throughout the population would be an invitation to civil war. This danger was all too clearly demonstrated by the disintegration of Yugoslavia. A population that is bitterly divided politically cannot be expected to offer united social and political resistance to an outside power unless that external threat is seen as even more dangerous. In a strong state, the dispersal of military power might be seen as an advantageous bulwark against excessive military or other elite control of politics, but many weak states can only maintain themselves as political entities by holding central control over military power. It is no accident that the idea of NOD originated in the strong states of northern Europe.

Adoption of NOD by Great Powers
Would Have Far-Reaching Implications

NOD also poses political problems, though of a wholly different character, for the great powers in the international system. The history of NOD policies is mostly that of small states. The requirement for high levels of domestic political cohesion also favors the smaller societies where such cohesion is easier to achieve (though scale may be a secondary determinant of social cohesion). NOD for great powers raises basic questions about the foundations of order in the international system (and this is true whether one sees that order as benign, oppressive, or mixed). By definition, a defensively armed state possesses little military reach. If seriously pursued by a great power, such a policy would amount to military isolationism, that is, the abandonment of any unilateral attempt to shape the international order through the external use of military power. The adoption of NOD by the United States during the Cold War, for example, would have pulled the props from under the whole security system that rested on U.S. military power. Whether one views such a development as politically desirable or not, there can be no doubt that it would have unleashed major forces of change, some of them violent and some not. Even in the post–Cold War environment, where the United States places less emphasis on military power, the adoption of NOD by the United States would have major consequences for international order in Europe, the Middle East, and East Asia.

This does not mean that NOD is applicable only to minor powers: Gorbachev adopted it as declaratory policy and began looking for ways to implement it, and China, India, Germany, and Japan have all leaned toward it in various significant ways. It does mean that the pursuit of NOD policies by great powers has broad political consequences that need to be thought through. Among other things, adoption of NOD by the great powers might require much better developed capabilities for collective action to preserve order or human rights. A system in which all the great powers had adopted NOD policies might begin to look like a "mature anarchy" and may be highly desirable (Buzan 1991a: 175–181, 261–265). As with disarmament and arms control, however, where contending great powers pursue different military doctrines, change produces dangers of instability as well as opportunities for a new, different, and possibly stronger stability.

Conclusion

Abandoning offense in favor of defense will be difficult when the boundary between offensive and defensive strategic postures is (in circumstances indicated above) hard to make clear. It is also potentially costly if loss of offensive options for political defense imposes some serious limitations and vulnerabilities on security policy. The crux of the military debate about NOD is whether strategic offense and defense can be differentiated clearly, and, if so, whether these costs are offset by the gain of mitigation of the military security dilemma. NOD offers no major economic savings (although they might occur in the long term due to demilitarization as the military security dilemma dissipates), and requires continued engagement with the arms dynamic. It will appeal to some disarmament advocates due to its rejection of nuclear weapons but cannot easily appeal to antimilitarist sentiments because of its requirement for mass participation in national defense. The political impact of this requirement for mass participation cuts both ways. On the one hand, it might be seen as militarizing all of society (Galtung 1984a: 135–138). Even though the form of militarization is likely to be decentralized, democratic, and demonstrably defensive, it would still not appeal to advocates of SNV. On the other hand, the idea of national service taps some of the moral and emotional forces—though of course not the same ones—that give political strength to both disarmament and militant nationalism. Under the right circumstances, NOD might well generate a firm political consensus: this has already occurred in a few states. It offers a synthesis of trying to escape from the security dilemma without abandoning military means of doing so. However, it requires any state that adopts it to largely set aside external military needs, ambitions, and responsibilities. An alternative to such isolationism is the creation of collective intervention capabilities either with allies or through the United Nations. This option may be possible, but its political and military requirements for trust, cooperation, and timely decisionmaking are exceptionally demanding. It is hard to imagine that it could produce robust policy under conditions such as those that now dominate the international system.

The end of the Cold War has in many ways left NOD in the same position as arms control. As another child of the Cold War, NOD shared arms control's assumptions of an operating environment largely shaped by embedded rivalries and active security dilemmas: hence narrowly "arms first" perspectives on NOD were in some ways even more dislocated by the ending of the superpower rivalry than was arms control (Wiseman 1997). Although NOD ideas were not irrelevant to restructuring military relations in Europe, they seemed much less salient in conditions where the fear of interstate war had largely evaporated. Like arms control, NOD constituted a powerful set of ideas relevant to remaining rivalries in the rest of the world but ill-equipped (at least initially) with the expertise to transfer its focus to other regions. Its problem with weak states loomed larger if its future lay mainly in the zone of conflict, and its apparent incompatibilities with intervention also needed to be addressed. Arguably, the end of the Cold War somewhat reduced its problems of application to great powers. With the great powers turning "lite" (Buzan and Segal 1996), in the sense of being less willing to use force and threats, the restrictions of NOD weigh less heavily. Again, like arms control, NOD must adapt to largely unfamiliar, though not new, cases and contexts.

15

DISARMAMENT

Advocates of disarmament believe that weapons create more political, military, and economic problems than they solve, and that the solution is to get rid of them. This view can be applied to all weapons—general and complete disarmament (GCD)—or just to specific categories of weapons deemed to be particularly dangerous, pointless, or costly, such as landmines, chemical weapons, nuclear bombs, and biological warfare agents. It can be applied unilaterally or multilaterally, can be formal (in the sense of being codified in a treaty) or informal, and can involve partial or complete elimination of the specified type(s) of weapon. The concept refers both to the process by which military capabilities are reduced and to the end condition of being disarmed.

Obviously, GCD has so far never been achieved. Substantial partial disarmament has been most easily and frequently achieved at the end of wars. At such times, it is usually unproblematic to form a consensus that wartime levels of armament are too high for peacetime purposes. It may also be easy for the winners to impose a higher degree of disarmament on the losers than they accept for themselves, as after World Wars I and II. Disarmament during peacetime as a program for managing or redefining the way in which states and peoples relate to each other has so far been much more controversial, and much less frequently or seriously tried or practiced. The end of the Cold War falls rather between these two schools, involving both some "end-of-war" type disarmament and some widespread sense that many states, particularly the advanced industrial democracies, have abandoned war as a means of relating to each other. Probably the most common motive for advocating disarmament is the desire to escape from the fear of war. This fear is powerfully conditioned by circumstances. It was very strong after the horrors of World War I. Support for nuclear disarmament peaked as a reaction against the warfighting forms of nuclear deterrence that dominated superpower declaratory policy between the late 1970s and mid-1980s (Krass 1985: 107–128). Other enduring motives for

245

it include moral disapproval of the use (and therefore of the instruments) of force, opposition to the militarization of society required by the maintenance of armed forces, and the desire to use the huge resources devoted to weapons for other social purposes.

In the historical record there has been quite a lot of disarmament if one looks at it in terms of voluntary demobilizations after wars and imposed disarmament of states defeated in war (most recently the UN commission that has been attempting to oversee reductions in Iraqi armed forces since 1991). Progress has mostly been very recent if it is defined in terms of reductions of peacetime arsenals formalized in international treaties: the START, INF, and CFE treaties codified dramatic reductions in long-range nuclear forces, medium-range European nuclear forces, and European conventional forces respectively. These have been accompanied by further large unilateral nuclear and conventional force reductions, mothballing of weapons and lowering of alert statuses by all the NATO and former Warsaw Pact states. Before the late 1980s, the history of peacetime multilateral disarmament was mostly one of failed negotiations: "failed" in the sense that disarmament did not take place. However, some argue and many believe that such negotiations were only undertaken for propaganda reasons, and that "failure" (hopefully blamed on someone else) was the real objective of the participating governments (Myrdal 1976). The few achievements like the demilitarization of the U.S.-Canadian border in 1817, the Washington Naval Agreements in the 1920s, and the Biological Warfare Convention of 1972, were separated by long periods of proposal making, campaigning, and negotiation leading nowhere.

Early multilateral moves at the Hague Conferences of 1899 and 1907 succumbed to the growing momentum of the pre–World War I arms competitions and arms races. Widespread enthusiasm for disarmament after World War I peaked with the fruitless League of Nations Disarmament Conference in 1932, and was overwhelmed by the rising political conflicts of the 1930s. The enforced disarmament of the losers after both world wars was only partly reciprocated by the winners, which demobilized down from wartime to peacetime military establishments. It did not stick for much more than a decade in either instance, and in the interwar period played a part in precipitating the rearmament of the 1930s. Ironically, soon after World War II, the United States encouraged the rearmament of Germany and Japan as counterweights to the Soviet Union. After World War II disarmament negotiations in the United Nations were mostly propaganda exercises between the superpowers. By the 1960s, arms control had largely replaced disarmament as the organizing concept for negotiations. Disarmament became largely an aspect of arms control, as in the START proposals of the early 1980s for reductions in the size of strategic nuclear arsenals.

This ineffectual record was reflected in a pessimistic and critical literature (Bull 1970; Galtung 1984b: chapter 4; Gray 1992). Despite the record disarmament, especially nuclear disarmament, still generated an optimistic literature and widespread, if episodic, popular enthusiasm (Falk and Barnet 1965; Noel-Baker 1958; Report of the Independent Commission 1982; Report of the Secretary General 1985; Weston 1991). The Geneva Conference on Disarmament has actually focused its attention on producing the Comprehensive Test Ban Treaty. Efforts to help force total nuclear disarmament by having the International Court of Justice (ICJ) declare nuclear arms illegal brought about an ambiguous advisory opinion in 1996. The ICJ stated that use or threatened use of nuclear weapons may be generally contrary to international law, that national survival may be an exception, and that all are obliged to pursue negotiations in good faith for complete nuclear disarmament. The most noteworthy advocacy of complete nuclear disarmament in recent years has been that of some of the members of the Canberra Commission, which was made up of a number of prominent retired military and political figures: this commission's report only proposed more modest measures of reductions and reduced alert statuses (Canberra Commission 1996; cf. Freedman 1997).

In the post–Cold War world, there is growing interest in partial disarmament (as well as arms control) as part of demobilization and demilitarization in the wake of what are generally deemed to be civil wars (although they often have had important international dimensions), such as in former Yugoslavia, Angola, Somalia, and Cambodia (Berdal 1996). These attempts have so far been rather problematic. In Somalia the United Nations attempted, but in the end failed, to achieve a significant degree of disarmament among the competing factions. In contrast, the Dayton Peace Agreement for former Yugoslavia aims at managing the arms dynamic between rump Yugoslavia (Serbia and Montenegro), Croatia, and the two "entities" that make up Bosnia–Herzegovina (the Serb Republic and the Bosniak–Croat Federation). Dayton fixed the military ratios of tanks, armored carrier vehicles, artillery, combat aircraft, and armed helicopters among the Serb Republic, the Bosniak–Croat Federation, Croatia, and Yugoslavia. The ratios are as follows: 1:2:3:7.5. Hence, for every one tank or other treaty-limited piece of equipment possessed by the Serb Republic, the Bosniak-Croat Federation is entitled to two, and so on. There is also provision for related confidence- and security-building measures in the form of restrictions on military deployments (with special provisions also for heavy weapons) and exercises, information exchanges, monitoring of arms production, and verification and inspection arrangements.

There are a number of striking features of this agreement. First, it is a mix of buildup, arms control, and partial disarmament. Establishing this balance is in part involving significant deliveries of weapons to the Bosniak–Croat Federation by the United States as well as reductions in the forces of the Serb Republic. Second, it is partly negotiated but also partly imposed by NATO led by the United States and acting on a UN mandate.

Third, it implicitly assumes that the Bosniak–Croat Federation will not use its in-built numerical military superiority (two to one) to make war against the Serb Republic. Fourth, it is not simply an agreement between states, but also between elements within a state. Fifth, it is of little relevance to a crucial element of Dayton, which is the protection of refugees exercising the right to return to their homes.

Military Issues

Within the military domain, disarmament confronts directly and simply both the fear of war and many of the problematic elements of the arms dynamic. Looked at crudely, disarmament merely offers the simple "arms first" formula of responding to those concerns by removing the weapons with which they are associated. However, a more sophisticated advocate of disarmament will argue for partial disarmament to be accompanied by political reassurance, confidence building, conflict resolution, and perhaps also a capacity for SNV in a "politics and arms together" approach. Partial disarmament may weaken military deterrence, but possibly not enough to bring about deterrence failure, especially under conditions of surplus capacity of nuclear weapons. Calculations about "how much is enough" are of course one of the central difficulties of deterrence policy and depend heavily on judgments about the nature of one's opponents and their incentives to attack. However, if deterrence is judged to be easy (because opponents are soft or have low motivation to attack), then partial disarmament may make war less likely by reducing the threat and provocation that one's own armed forces offer to others.

Even total disarmament need not involve the complete abandonment of deterrence. Under some circumstances a country may be able to rely on nonmilitary means to deter military attack. Among these means would be measures to ensure that the aims of the attack cannot be achieved if nonmilitary deterrence fails. During the Cold War, for example, both Sweden and Switzerland made preparations to destroy the transit routes across their countries by mining tunnels and bridges. Since access to such routes was a prime reason for anyone to attack them, such preparations added to deterrence. If the attacker's objective was to annex the society and economy, then civilian defense would be another SNV option (Roberts 1967). Arguments about weaponless deterrence are also relevant here. They turn on its head the criticism of disarmament that it cannot either get rid of the knowledge and technology that would enable states to rearm, or remove the many civil technologies that would enable disarmed states to inflict massive damage on each other. The military potential of advanced civilian economies can provide a firm basis for weaponless deterrence even where particular types and numbers of weapons (in the case of partial disarmament), or all weapons (in the case of GCD), have been dismantled. Japan is a good example of partial disarmament plus the particular form of weaponless deterrence known as recessed deterrence. The underlying points are that too much overt military deterrence can be dangerous and that weaponless or even nonviolent deterrence may be possible.

Inasmuch as wars are stimulated by the existence of competing armed forces, disarmament offers a means for attacking some of the basic mechanisms of the arms dynamic. The case can be made that disarmament can force the action–reaction dynamic to operate in reverse: hence Gorbachev's promotion of the idea of a disarmament race in which the United States and Soviet Union would compete to see who could offer the most radical nuclear and conventional reductions. If states arm themselves primarily in response to arms in the hands of others, then reductions of arms should stimulate a reverse cycle. Yet even if the action–reaction assumption is sound in relation to the arms dynamic, it does not follow that it works smoothly, or at all, in reverse. Many processes can be worked in both directions, like water to ice and ice to water, but many cannot. A device with a ratchet can be moved easily in one direction but encounters a lock when reverse pressure is applied.

During the dying years of the Cold War, the Soviet Union led an attempt to put the arms dynamic into reverse, and in so doing succeeded in bringing the United States with it for much of the way. Following from some initial Soviet concessions, the U.S. side proposed the elimination of all ballistic missiles within ten years. Gorbachev agreed, and proposed the elimination of all strategic nuclear weapons within ten years. Reagan also agreed, and proposed trying to secure the elimination of all nuclear weapons within ten years. Once again, Gorbachev agreed, conditional upon the scrapping of SDI. Because Reagan saw SDI, shared with the Soviet Union, as a vital part of total nuclear disarmament, the negotiations reverted to a much less ambitious agenda—much to the relief of some (Garthoff 1994: 285–291). Overall, the Soviet Union made much the greater concessions and ended up collapsing as a state. Nevertheless, the former Soviet states have continued (with some blips and threats) to adhere to the START, INF, CFE, and related disarmament commitments they inherited. The technological imperative, the anarchic international system, and domestic factors can all act as ratchets against attempts to reverse the arms dynamic. Changes in strategic concepts (such as adoption of ideas about NOD or SNV) or economic pressures (such as the weakness of the Soviet economy) can break the ratchet lock. So also can perceptions of a shift from wartime to peacetime conditions or of a fundamental change in the nature of world politics (such as the emergence of what some see as a liberal democratic peace), both of which did much to shape the disarmament moves of the late 1980s and early 1990s.

Even within the disarmament process there are two factors that might well sustain the action–reaction dynamic. The most obvious of these is fear of cheating by other actors. Verification procedures can never be perfect, so cheating is always a risk in mutual disarmament. It is often asserted that with the assumption that states remain hostile, or even just suspicious of each other, moves toward GCD will depend more and more on the almost impossible requirement of verification measures being made foolproof. This is not the case: instead, the stability of mutual disarmament depends on whether cheating is seen as likely to be uncovered in time to allow for effective counteraction, whether that perception is accurate, and whether it is shared by the potential cheat and potential victim. Willingness to act is at least as important as warning time. The argument that as disarmament moves toward GCD, the same amount of cheating becomes proportionately more significant is true, all other things being equal. However, other factors may well be more important: military outcomes are rarely a product of simple numerical advantages, and the political environment could easily be very hostile to cheating as GCD approaches. Worries about cheating become less important if GCD is being driven by a perception that world politics has undergone a fundamental change, with war no longer being seen as a legitimate instrument of policy. Some argue that such conditions already exist among a substantial group of states (the liberal democratic peace), but that the effect of this on the prospects for disarmament is constrained by the continued existence of the potential for war with other (nondemocratic) states in the international system.

The second factor that might sustain the action–reaction dynamic is complexity. The MBFR talks in Europe between NATO and Warsaw Pact states were often taken as evidence of the extreme difficulty of finding acceptable terms of equivalence for a large number of states, each of which perceives its security problems in relation to more than one other. Differences of size, power, geography, and internal and external security needs made for negotiations of unbelievable complexity among states still locked into serious political and military rivalry. However, as with cheating, complexity is a conditional problem rather than an inevitable one. If political conditions change toward less threatening relations, then complexity becomes less of a problem. The complexity of the negotiations was a consequence, not a cause, of political stalemate. Gorbachev cut through all these problems with astonishing decisiveness, and the result was the CFE treaty. There was no MBFR treaty because the Soviet Union before Gorbachev wanted equal cuts in forces, whereas NATO wanted the Warsaw Pact to give up more forces. There was a CFE treaty because the Soviet Union's interpretation of threat had changed, enabling Gorbachev to accept NATO's demand. The CFE treaty can be interpreted as evidence against the saying that when disarmament is necessary it is not possible, and when it is possible it is not necessary. Significant degrees of nuclear and conventional disarmament in Europe were both possible (due to the existence of political will based on changed ideas and economic pressures) and necessary (due to the risks and costs associated with two extremely heavily armed alliances poised nose to nose). However, one could argue that the end of the Cold War made the treaty unnecessary because the reductions would have happened anyway.

Disarmament is not just about getting rid of weapons: it is also about breaking up the domestic structures that institutionalize the arms dynamic. The military aspect of disarmament requires both the superficial measure of destroying weapons already in being and the deeper structural measure of excising the means for, and the interests behind, further military production. The arms dynamic cannot be unlocked, and the action–reaction cycle cannot be stopped, until the institutionalization of the arms dynamic within the state is heavily reduced. How is disarmament to be defined in terms of the domestic armed forces that states need for internal purposes? Repressive states like Burma need much higher levels of domestic coercive force than do politically open and stable states like Denmark, Sweden, and Japan. Indeed, the idea of negotiating force levels for internal repression as part of an international treaty sounds like a sick joke. Furthermore, since the vast majority of contemporary wars are civil wars, GCD would have to involve not only the weapons of states but the weapons of nonstate groups that want to take over the state, break away to form new states, or establish mafiocracy in particular regions or even entire states (such as Colombia). Even quite stable and open states like the United Kingdom are extremely unlikely to disarm completely while leaving loyalist and republican terrorist groups or criminal organizations with their armories. The issue of domestic force levels is a crucial and unavoidable factor feeding into the broader problem of how to determine what residual armament levels would be allowed to states under disarmament. What this points to is that GCD seems unattainable until the potential for significant amounts of internal violence, political or criminal, has been eliminated. Only by demilitarizing society can disarmament hope to ensure that the removal of arms would be durable and that it would create the basis for transforming international political relations. However, the requirement for demilitarization itself raises profound political questions about the nature of the state and the role of force in the process of government. These have been addressed in the SNV literature (Sharp 1980) and elsewhere (Melman 1988; Shaw 1991).

For disarmament plans, especially GCD, to be comprehensive, they must consider the extent to which every industrial society has military potential lying just beneath the surface of its civil economy. In a disarmed world, that latent potential would become a much more conspicuous feature of the power relations between actors than it is in a world where military power is manifest, especially if those actors still see a significant possibility of war between themselves. The technological imperative links progress in the civil economy to military strength because the civil and military sectors are united by the common bonds of knowledge and technology (Buzan and Sen 1990). The knowledge and technology for miniature high-power lasers or for sophisticated autonomous robots could be developed for civil uses (e.g., fusion power, mining), yet both could quickly be turned to formidable military applications, such as defense against air or missile attack and precision-guided delivery vehicles for weapons. Possession of such options might give leverage to those states at the technological leading edge, although only in situations where such technology is relevant to the context and to the objectives being pursued. In a disarmed but still anarchic world, states (and actors within states) that perceived their relations to have significant potential for war may take their relative mobilization potential into account in their relations.

As before the two world wars, the military dimension of power would be calculated not only on the extent of resources available for mobilization, but also on the speed with which civil capacity could be geared to military use and on the quality of technology available for conversion to military purposes. Fear of war might still haunt people's minds because latent military potential would be obvious, even in the prompt terms of such civil technologies as aircraft, poisons, and explosives immediately usable for military purposes. The arms dynamic would not threaten as a daily reality, but that gain would have to be balanced against the prospect of a rearmament at greater or lesser speed should the disarmament regime break down. Such rearmament might be chaotic and flat-out, or well regulated and slow-paced, depending on the political circumstances. GCD and partial disarmament could perhaps be shored up not by a balance of military potential, but by a commitment to a response based wholly on SNV in the case of GCD or partly on SNV in the case of partial disarmament. One problem here, of course, is that applying SNV in this way requires a level of sociopolitical cohesion not available in many states. But since there is almost certainly no technical way of eliminating latent military potential, the military logic of disarmament ultimately points to the conclusion that the main security measure must be to ensure that military power is delegitimized, and its utility undermined, through nonmilitary countermeasures.

Economic Issues

The main economic case for disarmament rests on the idea that resources not consumed for military purposes would be available to meet a variety of pressing human needs. The secondary case is that it would simply allow people to have more of their income to dispose of as they wish. For LICs struggling to keep up with the global arms dynamic, these other needs are usually seen in terms of development and the meeting of basic human needs in food, shelter, health, and education. Disarmament and development are often linked (Jolly 1978; Report of the Independent Commission 1982: chapter 7; Harris, Kelly, and Pranowo 1988; Ball 1989; Grobar and Porter 1989; Fontanel 1990; Chowdhury 1991), with the former seen as a way of releasing resources for the latter. GCD would not only relieve LICs of the direct strain that the maintenance of large military establishments puts on their political economies, but could also increase the levels of development aid from the more industrialized countries. In the industrialized countries, disarmament could release resources for a variety of welfare objectives, so easing the annual allocation battles in which education, health, industrial investment, and other highly valued activities have to fight with military demands for their share of the budget. It would also undo the military domination of scientific and technological R&D, so enabling the intellectual resources of humankind to be turned away from improving the instruments of violence and toward improving the human condition. Since annual global military expenditures consume close to $1 trillion each year ($814 billion in 1995—see *Military Balance 1996–97* 1996: 311), the apparent economic prize from disarmament is very large both in individual countries and for the international system as a whole. The size of the resources, the strong appeal of the alternative uses for them, and the apparent simplicity of the economic case all contribute to the political attractiveness of disarmament. The economic case for disarmament applies not only to unilateral and multilateral arms reductions but also to GCD.

Leaving aside the broader question of whether a demilitarized state is a contradiction in terms, challenging the domestic dimensions of the arms dynamic is a formidable task. It involves shrinking the armed forces and the whole R&D and production infrastructure. These are large, powerful, and often long-established components of state and society. To make social and political changes on such a scale in anything but a very slow and incremental fashion would require political resources of great magnitude. It would also require extensive economic and social redeployment of the skills and resources currently dedicated to the arms industry and the armed forces. The end of the Cold War showed that the motives behind disarmament can be strong enough to make changes on such a scale possible. Some thinking has been done about the conversion of the arms industry to civil uses and about the larger question of how the reconstruction of the domestic political economy is to be achieved (Kaldor 1980; Kennedy 1983; Cronberg and Hansen 1992; Cooper 1993–1994; Gansler 1993–1994; Gonchar 1994; Cronberg, Anders, and Seem 1995; Møller and Voronkov 1997; *Conversion Survey* annual). The contours of what would constitute a "postmilitary" (Shaw 1991) or "demilitarized" (Melman 1988) society have also been explored. It also raises difficult secondary questions about how the political economy should be recreated. Should a large, high-technology

industrial sector be preserved for civil purposes like space development
and centralized power generation, or should a disarming society take a
"greener" path, moving away from massive, centralized, high-technology
ventures altogether?

The economic gains from disarmament are nevertheless often not
straightforward. Both partial and complete disarmament raise economic
counterpressures from those parts of the economy that depend on the military for employment and prosperity. Coping with such interests would be
part of the larger political problem discussed above of handling the demilitarization of society. Partial disarmament raises the problem that the resources saved might be transferred to other military uses unless strong
pressures to use disarmament savings for other purposes existed. Very limited agreements, such as the scrapping of all chemical weapons, would not
affect the overall position of the military interest in society, and are therefore more likely to result in the resources going to other sectors of the military than to the civil sector.

If one believes that nuclear weapons have no plausible military functions but that they have to be replaced by conventional military means,
then an important dimension of the economic case for nuclear disarmament is reduced. One of the persistent attractions of nuclear weapons is
their relative cheapness for many strategic missions, especially those associated with deterrence by retaliation. This attractiveness, if anything, increased between World War II and the 1980s. The cost of ever more sophisticated conventional weapons rose steeply, and high attrition rates
attended their use in war. The logic behind the 1950s slogan of "a bigger
bang for the buck" (or "more rubble per ruble") was stronger in the 1980s
than when it was first coined. By the 1980s, cities could still be threatened
with destruction by conventional weapons, as in World War II, but the financial cost of achieving such missions had increased dramatically. What
can be achieved by a handful of nuclear weapons and delivery vehicles
would require hundreds or thousands of delivery vehicles and tens or hundreds of thousands of conventional warheads. Against strong defenses, attrition rates would be high. However, the use of force by the U.S.-led
coalition against Iraq in 1991 made a significant new trend clear. Extremely accurate weapons such as cruise missiles could inflict enormous
disruption and casualties on a society by destroying such key facilities as
water treatment plants, even if old-fashioned dumb bombs created the
most obvious and immediate destruction. Vulnerability to such carefully
targeted weapons is increasing as the infrastructure of society becomes both
more complex and more dependent on electronic information networks.

The issue of the cost-effectiveness of nuclear weapons also applies to
deterrence by denial. Discussions within NATO throughout the Cold War
about decreasing reliance on nuclear weapons almost all pointed to a perceived need for increased expenditure on conventional forces to achieve

deterrence by denial (Duffield 1995). From this perspective, the savings seem likely to be less than the additional costs, and therefore the strictly economic case for it is unattractive. However, if one believes that scrapping nuclear weapons does not require an increase in conventional forces, or if the scrapping of nuclear weapons is part of an overall shift toward SNV, then the long-run savings could be substantial. With extensive multilateral arms reductions or GCD, there is the cost of the disarmament process itself to consider. In the short term, as demonstrated by the shrinkage of nuclear arsenals at the end of the Cold War, there are substantial decommissioning costs. Some weapons are easily scrapped, but many nuclear and chemical warheads require elaborate and expensive procedures.

The claim that unless it is associated with a very widespread democratic peace, large-scale disarmament also requires at least a substantial international inspection regime, and possibly some form of world government, is plausible but arguable. Instead of regulation, countries could rely either on the development of serious capabilities for SNV or on the tendency of balances of power to form even without regulation. The risks and costs of any or all of these would not be trivial. The costs could be especially high if the thorny problem of giving the world government adequate enforcement and dispute-settlement powers was solved by creating an international armed force. Although many supporters of disarmament would be happy to use the released resources for world government, it is not clear how much, if anything, would be left over for other purposes. Anyway, world government raises a host of political problems of its own that might easily outweigh any economic case for radical amounts of disarmament.

Political Issues

Advocates of disarmament envisage four possible routes to the requisite political change: (1) the process of disarmament by simply disarming making the international anarchy and the internal politics of states less violent, (2) disarmament being linked to reform of the state system, (3) disarmament being linked to antistatism, and (4) disarmament being achieved through the adoption of SNV.

Disarmament Through Simply Disarming

One interpretation of the first route—the case that disarmament would make politics more peaceful—is that it rests on the assumption that arms are the principal source of tension in the international system and within states. In this view, most violent conflict results from factors like arms racing, militarist influences within states, misperception of intentions, and crises arising from opposed potentials for violence. If this view is true, then disarmament would indeed eliminate most sources of tension and could be expected to make international and domestic politics more secure and peaceful.

A close look at day-to-day politics raises grave doubts about whether other sources of conflict can be discounted to the extent required to sustain this view. It requires that territorial and political disputes, and power rivalries, be relatively minor sources of tension and conflict in the disarmed system or that they be major but resolvable. If they are more than minor, then disarmament will unleash its own forms of insecurity and instability (Bull 1961: chapter 2; 1970). Without a full commitment to SNV (and, most people assume, even with it), armaments are essential to the internal and external security of states. They are vital to the military dimension of the balance of power that is regarded by realists as the principal ordering mechanism in anarchic systems. This claim is open to dispute from several angles. Interpretivists, who emphasize the primary importance of attempts to create apparently natural but actually constructed views of the world, see realism as a self-fulfilling, self-validating prophecy. Those who see aspects of world politics as governed by complex interdependence or by a liberal democratic peace have quite different views on the security consequences of anarchy.

Armaments can be both an instrument of order and a threat to order (Osgood and Tucker 1967: 32). The "disarmament through simply disarming" perspective addresses only the problem side of the equation and ignores the positive functions that arms can fulfill. It begs the question of whether more security would be lost than gained if arms were removed from the system. This criticism is especially applicable to proposals for unilateral disarmament. If political disputes remain unresolved, then a major self-weakening move by one side risks raising the probability of war. It offers an aggressive state the opportunity to exploit weakness. It is an interesting and important conjecture whether war would have been less likely in the late 1930s if Britain, France, and the United States had followed a more vigorous rearmament policy than they did. It is hard to argue that unilateral disarmament by any of them would have reduced the probability of war, except in terms of peaceful conquest by Nazi Germany.

The difficulties posed by the first route of disarmament within anarchy push enquiry toward the logically more coherent second route. If it is the politics of international anarchy that make disarmament unworkable, then can the disarmament process be used to transform the political structure of the international system?

Disarmament Through International Political Reform

There are two main routes to disarmament through international political reform. Either the military security dilemma must be taken out of anarchy, or the fragmentation of anarchy must be replaced by the unity of world government. Anarchy without the military security dilemma, as under complex interdependence or democratic peace, would make arms much less necessary. This is clearly a politics first approach. The central idea is that for advanced industrial societies a liberal form of international political economy develops in such a way that reduces, or even eliminates, the prospect of war between states. There are two interconnected elements in this view. The first is that economic interdependence reduces both the incentives and the capabilities of states to use force. That in turn reduces their incentives to possess large armed forces, a process reinforced by the demands of the market to allocate resources to more productive investments. The second is the claim that democratic states rarely go to war with each other. Following this logic, a set of liberal democracies should naturally evolve into a pluralistic security community—a group of states whose members have stable expectations that they will not use force against each other and hence make no such preparations. The link to disarmament is obvious, the only problem being that such states retain armed strength against the remaining nonliberal democracies in the international system, for defensive and offensive purposes. If the zone of peace spreads to incorporate more of the system, then the possibilities for disarmament expand as the number of powers outside the security community shrinks.

For some advocates of disarmament, especially those who are in favor of GCD, there are necessary links between disarmament and world government (Singer 1962: 232–237; Harvard Nuclear Study Group 1983: 188–191). Simply disarming brings about world government, or world government brings about disarmament, or progress on both proceeds simultaneously and symbiotically. As discussed above, one of the core challenges associated with disarmament is the problem of cheating that arises as security comes to depend more on the assumed military impotence of others than on an actor's own military strength. Is GCD to be accompanied by an international enforcement machinery, or are actors to be kept faithful to their disarmament undertakings by the threat of rearmament if cheating is discovered? To ensure the stability of GCD, some propose strong inspection and enforcement machinery and potent dispute settlement provisions. To administer and control such a politically powerful and central organization would require political arrangements indistinguishable from world government. World government would have to resolve political disputes and replace the positive security function that armaments currently play in ordering the balance of power.

Linking disarmament to world government escapes the dilemma of arms first or politics first by tackling both simultaneously. However, the challenge then becomes finding a way of activating the momentous shift from a system of legally sovereign states to one of world government. Establishment of a world state involves radical political, economic, ideological, and constitutional change. It would require either a preponderance of power sufficient to overawe the many deep divisions in the world polity or an ideological consensus strong enough to make available agreed organizing principles for a global confederation of some sort. Neither of these is anywhere in sight, and global trends do not seem to favor their emergence. Only democratic capitalism is a serious contender for a world ideology, but it is a long way from overcoming the immense barriers that stand in the way of world government. Political, military, and economic power are becoming more concentrated in some ways but more dispersed in other ways in the post–Cold War, post-Soviet world.

Disarmament Through Antistatism

Other advocates of disarmament go in the opposite direction by advocating radically antistate positions: they may be green, anarchist, libertarian socialist, or some other overlapping variant (Marshall 1992). Since the state is not only at the root of military and political problems, but also blocks the path to the disarmament solution, they argue that the only logical route to peace that remains is over the corpse of the state. According to this perspective, the macro-approach of subordinating the state to world government is undesirable, unachievable, or both, and therefore only the approach of undermining the state by organizing alternatives to it remains. Immediate opportunities present themselves in local politics, where these approaches are manifested in things like withholding the proportion of taxes spent on weapons, or towns, boroughs, or even houses declaring themselves nuclear-free zones. Transnational counterstate organizations such as Greenpeace and Amnesty International also provide vehicles for these positions. Yet, even though antistatism has generated effective local action and organization for campaigns on specific issues, it has yet to popularize a political vision of a peaceful world order without states. Moreover, it has not so far escaped the dilemma that political success at the local level creates strong pressure either to build state-like political structures or else to compete for the levers of power within the existing state.

Disarmament Through Strategic Nonviolence

For advocates of SNV, disarmament is made possible by people power (that is, those who wish to rule must have the cooperation and at least the tacit consent of the people), thus providing security while dispensing with the need to resort to weapons, global capitalism, world government, or the abolition of states (Roberts 1967; Sharp 1973, 1985, 1990; Boserup and Mack 1975; Ackerman and Kruegler 1994; Randle 1994; Wehr, Burgess, and Burgess 1994). The transition could be a gradual one, with increasing confidence in SNV as success follows success, or as the reasons for failures are identified and remedied, or as strategic cultures change. The long-barren ground for formal adoption of SNV by states is perhaps now becoming more fertile as the human and economic costs of war are perceived to be less acceptable.

Very little interest has been shown in SNV within the field of strategic studies. There are a number of reasons for this. First, strategic studies is preoccupied with finding military responses to military threats, and so the strategic culture does not lend itself to exploration of SNV. Second, there is a presumption within strategic studies that SNV is a last-ditch strategy usable mainly after military defeat, and not much use for either deterrence or denial. In other words, it is presumed to have little strategic value. However, under the right conditions, SNV can be adopted to deter an attack from happening in the first place. There is nothing inherent in SNV that makes it ineffective for deterring or frustrating some types of attack, and SNV can include fomenting opposition within the attacking state. There tends to be an analytical double standard at work, with the costs and failures of nonviolence emphasized without comparing them to the often high costs and many failures of violence. Historically, strategic studies has systematically understated the costs of using force. Third, it tends to be lumped in with the pacifist's absolute moral rejection of violence rather than as a strategy that can in some circumstances be more effective in achieving political objectives than violence against an opponent that is threatening or using violence. Fourth, strategic studies is a field that has grown up primarily in the service of states, and no state has yet to adopt SNV as its principal or even secondary means of achieving its security. Fifth, strategic studies is often about assisting states in dealing with internal security challenges, whereas SNV is often a means adopted by those standing up to states.

Advocates of SNV tend to be antistatist in outlook, but are not necessarily so. They are mainly concerned with ensuring security, whether the threat emanates from states, a world government, or other actors such as criminal organizations, nonstate terrorist groups, or companies employing heavy-handed "security" personnel to break strikes or seize land. The result of all this is a huge imbalance in terms of resources plowed into exploring the utility of meeting violence with violence and threats of violence with threats of violence.

Those whose primary objective is destruction as the end in itself are the most difficult to influence through nonviolence because they cannot be restrained from acting by the knowledge that their resort to force will not make them powerful—that is, in the sense that it will not, in Arendt's formulation, make people act in concert with them. However, it is a fallacy that SNV is useless against any ruthless opponent: what matters is that the opponent understand that the use of violence will be ineffective in achieving its objectives. Indeed, brutal repression can be turned to the oppressor's disadvantage because it can be used to alienate domestic and international opinion. This alienation is more likely if the opposition remains nonviolent because it will retain the moral high ground. Utterly brutal, ruthless opponents can be and have been resisted, and furthermore they are rare. The phenomenon of bloodless revolution as in Eastern Europe in 1989 and the collapse of the Soviet Union two years later show that mere formal command of the instruments of violence is no substitute for power. As Arendt (1973b: 117) wrote some years earlier: "Where commands are no longer obeyed, the means of violence are of no use; and the question of this obedience is not decided by the command–obedience relation but by opinion, and, of course, by the number of those who share it. Everything depends on the power behind the violence."

The key to the Chinese government's successful use of force against the students in Tiananmen Square was that it retained its legitimate authority over the army. This contrasts with the case in the Soviet Union, where a dying empire no longer held authority over either its army or its people. If struggles were essentially about force versus force, the big battalions most skilled at using the best military technology would always win. The recognition that power resides in persuading people to act with you (as opposed to merely standing aside and watching force versus force) underlies the whole approach. This political struggle to nullify the state's instruments of force is at the heart of the prodemocracy protests in Serbia that began late in 1996 and the pro-labor rights protests in South Korea that were resurgent in 1997. The point to bear in mind here is that one alternative to acquiring the instruments of force to fight back violently is to render the opponent's instruments of force useless by undermining the legitimacy of the opponent's political authority. Easier said than done, of course, and those with large amounts of military technology at their disposal and, crucially, people willing to operate that technology can often successfully impose their will, although not necessarily in the long term.

The use of nonviolent tactics against those threatening or using violence is commonplace. What tends to be lacking is the strategic harnessing of those tactics to political objectives. The prospects for success will increase dramatically if nonviolence is planned rather than improvised. Progress is being made in analyzing systematically through a strategic lens the use of nonviolence. Options are being explored that stress the importance of outcome-specific, achievable, and shared objectives. These include finding ways of being able to communicate decisions among potential SNV actors that will ensure that they are most likely to be acted upon; developing operational plans that explain how success is to be achieved (such as how the tactics chosen are appropriate); ensuring flexibility so that policy, strategy, and tactics are adapted in the light of experience; acting consistently so that the opponent believes that every action will be countered with nonviolent punishment or denial; and ensuring that gains are protected and consolidated (Ackerman and Kruegler 1994). Too often proponents of nonviolence are reinventing the wheel. They tend to be unaware that others have been where they are or, if they know it, they do not learn from it. In principle, SNV offers one possible route to GCD, but there are many strategic and cultural barriers to its full exploration and adoption.

Conclusion

Military means create security problems: hence disarmament proposes the abolition of military means. The ideas that peace requires the abandonment of violence in human affairs, that the weapons and threats of mass destruction are immoral and uncivilized, that armaments represent a huge waste of resources urgently needed for human development, and that militarism is culturally retrograde have an undeniable political force. However, the perceived need for high levels of verification, the fears of cheating and of rearmament races, the worries about parity and about the military uses of civil technology, the possible continuation of the balance of power through mobilization potential, and the domestic issues of state repression, civil war, and criminal violence all reflect the basically political problems of insecurity between and within states. Humanity cannot escape from the problem of military means merely by stripping away its accumulations of weapons and its specifically dedicated military production capabilities. As long as the instruments of violence are seen to have great value for the purposes of force, threats, and symbolic politics, simply getting rid of weapons is unlikely to proceed very far and will have only limited value in creating security. Significant degrees of disarmament thus require major political changes as well as major military ones. Removing arms without removing the military security dilemma remains chronically difficult.

Dependence on political conditions used to be the main weakness of disarmament proposals. But with the changes in world politics ushered in, and revealed by, the ending of the Cold War, it becomes a kind of strength. Unlike arms control and NOD, disarmament predates the Cold War, and was more a victim than a child of it. With political conditions becoming more congenial, many of the obstacles to pursuing disarmament fade into the background. As the security dilemma evaporates, disarmament follows almost automatically, and disarmament, albeit only of the partial kind, has not done badly in the post–Cold War world. Although some countries (most notably in Asia) are building up their military strength, most of the former participants in the Cold War rivalry are making significant, though by no means drastic, cuts. Indeed, the situation with disarmament is almost the mirror image of that with arms control and NOD. Although arms control and NOD had their heyday during the Cold War, disarmament (except as a minor element of arms control) was marginalized by the intensity of superpower political rivalry. With the end of the Cold War, arms control continues to be pursued in more congenial conditions, new forms of NOD are being explored by its advocates, and partial disarmament has experienced a minor boom. While partial disarmament may find a congenial home inside the zone of peace, its prospects seem less promising than those of arms control and NOD in the zone of conflict, where all of the familiar political obstacles to it still apply.

PART 5

CONCLUSION

16

THE ARMS DYNAMIC IN
WORLD POLITICS

In this book we traced the development of the arms dynamic. Then we considered explanations for the arms dynamic that resulted from this and examined the application of military technology to the use of force, threats, and symbols. After that, we explored the military, economic, and political issues relating to the principal regulatory responses (arms control, nonoffensive defense, and disarmament) to the problems caused by military means. Although force, threats, and symbols are aimed at regulating behavior, we are referring to regulation (or not) of military means themselves. Two tasks remain. The first is to examine the extent to which regulatory approaches can be combined in order to make them more effective. The second is to explore various implications of the laissez-faire approaches (the use of force, threats, and symbols) to military security that predominate in world politics.

Can Arms Control, NOD, and Disarmament Be Combined?

Combining different regulatory approaches might allow success, by taking advantage of the best elements of each or allowing the advantages of one to compensate for the disadvantages of another, where application of a single approach would fail. A state could combine elements of partial disarmament (disbanding offensive conventional forces and counterforce nuclear ones), NOD (unilateral action, preparing defensive defense in depth), and arms control (embracing MAD as doctrine, seeking agreements to restrain force levels and types). Such a strategy could be presented as involving a contradiction of basic principles: MAD clashes with the renunciation of offensive capability central to NOD. This clash could be ameliorated by emphasizing the retaliatory, reactive nature of MAD forces. NOD plus MAD would address the difficulties posed for MAD by "salami" tactics. A strategy along these lines might be adopted by NATO, especially if the United States reduced its military presence in Europe dramatically due to a perceived lack of serious medium-term external military threat. Its more general adoption would raise questions not only about encouragement of nuclear proliferation, but also about radical changes in the role of great powers in shaping the world order for better or worse in the absence of strategic offensive conventional capabilities.

Alternatively, combining different approaches might make failure more likely (perhaps due to their incompatibility) than the consistent and vigorous application of a single approach. Can strategic nonviolence (SNV) be combined with a conditional and/or actual commitment to the use of force? A simple yes or no is not possible. There are significant problems with trying to combine violence and nonviolence. Groups that employ SNV will draw a great deal of their legitimacy simply from the fact that they are nonviolent. Furthermore, the use of violence often allows potentially violent opponents (usually states) to play to their strength, namely their vastly superior firepower. States often use *agents provocateurs* or stage violent incidents in order to give them an excuse to use force. The opposition to President Milošević in Serbia after he refused to recognize their municipal electoral gains in November 1996 and the opposition led by Aung San Suu Kyi against the Burmese military dictatorship have almost completely shied away from the use of force for these reasons.

There are many examples of nonviolence unaccompanied by use of any violence: such campaigns are often labeled as civil disobedience. However, struggles that combine elements of violence and rather ad hoc SNV are also common. The most spectacular of these has been the Palestinian *intifada* in the occupied territories. There has been far more to the *intifada* than indicated by television images of stone-throwing Palestinian youths. An enormous effort has also gone into noncooperation with the Israeli authorities and the establishment of shadow Palestinian authorities that were until recently unrecognized by the Israeli state. The agreements negotiated between Israel and the Palestine Liberation Organization have produced limited autonomy in the occupied territories, and have been seen variously as a first step toward a Palestinian state or as a sellout to the Israeli state. Either way, it is clear that the new Palestinian authorities are often at least as violent and dictatorial as the Israeli authorities they replaced. Arendt has asserted that "the practice of violence, like all action, changes the world, but the most probable change is to a more violent world" (1973b: 141). Like all one-liners (including this one), it can contain no more than a half-truth: sometimes violence can have a net effect of making the world a less violent place. At this stage, we can offer a tentative overall answer to the question of when SNV can be combined effectively with violence. They should not be combined when doing so gives the opponent an opportunity to carry out an effective massacre. They can be combined if a massacre will bring about more recruits to the opposition or if the opponent believes that a massacre will not be effective and will not carry one out.

How and whether combinations of approaches will work is strongly influenced by context. In some places, mostly in LICs, there is no serious central government authority, and the technological imperative is very much a secondary factor for the military security of many. In other places, traditional interstate rivalries dominate military security, as in much of Asia. Much of the Middle East combines the worst of these two conditions. Elsewhere, most notably among the Western states, many of the traditional international political effects of anarchy are mitigated by interdependence, a strong international society, and liberal democracy. The problems caused by military means are thus influenced by the political structure of the international system in various ways. Some problems are more affected than others by the relentless expansion of human knowledge that drives the technological imperative.

Some versions of GCD seek to escape the international anarchy through world government or through making anarchist politics ubiquitous. GCD need not try to avoid responding to the technological imperative; instead, it could use leading-edge technology to improve the credibility and effectiveness of SNV. NOD and arms control both assume the existence of traditional international anarchy: NOD makes more of a vigorous effort to lessen the effects of the security dilemma but is also more demanding politically, especially in the radical reformulation of the role of great powers that would follow from their abandonment of strategic offensive options. Arms control and NOD operate within conventional definitions of strategy and sink or swim according to their degree of success within it. GCD can involve a radical rejection of strategic discourse, but SNV attempts a radical reformulation of strategy. All three responses to the problems caused by military means require particular political conditions that the responses cannot themselves create, but that they can make more likely. Unilateral and partial arms control, NOD, and disarmament can help break political logjams, but the broader political will must be there.

In every major approach, there is always a point at which political issues begin to dominate the analysis. This occurs whether the problem is military means in the hands of others, as in the arms dynamic and the use of force, threats, and symbols; or military means in themselves, as in arms control, NOD, and disarmament. Collectively, those points are where military security and world politics blend into and influence each other. One of the difficulties in thinking about the problems caused by military means is the need to work across the academic boundary between strategic studies or peace studies on the one hand and world politics on the other. The search for solutions, whether within or outside the strategic framework, cannot confine itself to the relatively tidy domain of military factors. It must inevitably engage itself with the much broader, more complex, and messier domain of world politics. The broader view gives a more complete picture of the problem, but it also exposes the impediments that make quick solutions improbable. One needs to consider the relative merits of regulation versus laissez-faire in the pursuit of military security, and to do so in the context of a broader analysis of world politics.

Implications of the Predominance of Laissez-Faire

In the absence of comprehensive solutions through arms control, NOD, disarmament, or some combination thereof, we are left living in the laissez-faire "market" of military security in world politics. However, the nature and implications of that market are the subject of fundamental and irresolvable intellectual disputes. We now consider three perspectives: a traditional realist one, one that suggests that WMD may have transformed military security relations, and one that argues that parts of the international system to a great extent no longer operate in traditional realist terms for political reasons.

Traditional Realist Laissez-Faire

In traditional realist terms, in a laissez-faire system actors bid the price of military security up or down according to the intensity with which they compete or cooperate with each other. The market metaphor for the balance of military power is appropriate. Many independent and incremental decisions interact to determine the level of military power relevant to security, just as they determine the market value of goods in the economy. Both systems have built-in regulators, or "invisible hands," that work to prevent open-ended escalations, but these mechanisms are not always reliable, and both systems also harbor disruptive forces strong enough to overcome them. Unregulated markets of both types are therefore subject to periods of disorder: war in the one case and depression in the other.

The pure markets just described are only theoretical. In practice, markets are managed or regulated to a greater or lesser degree. However, in both cases, regulatory intervention in the market is a difficult strategy to play. This difficulty is increased when no single center of controlling political authority is large enough to encompass the market, and regulation must therefore be pursued within the fragmented political structure of international anarchy. The free play of market forces limits the extent to which any single actor can take unilateral actions without placing its security or welfare at risk. Unilateral disarmament or arms control measures, if unreciprocated, may weaken an actor's ability to resist aggressive pressures. Alternatively, even unreciprocated unilateral actions may increase military security if the main threat is not opportunistic aggression but provocation of a fearful opponent. NOD and SNV, which attempt to maximize the scope for constructive unilateral action, can be enhanced by reciprocation or cooperation.

Because large numbers of interacting factors drive the dynamic of the market, regulation requires control over a complex, flexible, and unpredictable set of conditions. If regulation is too static, then the market may adapt to nullify its effect. This happened to OPEC in the mid-1980s in terms of the supply and price of oil. Intervention creates distortion in the market. Maintaining the desired effect of an intervention usually leads to the need for more intervention in order to cope with market responses to the distortion. In the housing market, for example, rent controls can be used as an intervention intended to give security and fair prices to renters. In practice, however, their use often leads to a drying up of properties for rent, and so to the demand for the larger intervention of public housing. Likewise, disarmament can lead to increasing requirements for world government, and arms control can lead to the pursuit of broader and more elusive goals like parity and détente. The choice is not either/or between the market and regulation: the key is finding the right balance of market forces and regulation to produce the optimal trade-off in the costs and benefits. Exercising judgment on this is an imprecise art and is shaped strongly by the values of those doing so.

Neither regulation nor laissez-faire are foolproof ways to avoid costs and risks. Indeed, there is no such thing as a cost-free or risk-free strategy. Laissez-faire is by definition easier to implement, and may win on that basis alone. Yet there is still an important question of choice that hinges on the balance of costs and risks between various mixes of the two alternatives. Regulation risks not only failure, which is a return to laissez-faire, but also backlash and counterproductive effects. Public housing can achieve fair (defined as low and predictable) rents, but sometimes at the cost of creating large public slums, inflicting architectural nightmares on residents, and influencing electoral politics by creating a pool of voters directly dependent on local government. Private housing has its own costs—negative equity traps that saddle people who try to move with huge debts, housing shortages for low-income families, and occasional inflationary spirals driven by property speculation.

The same problems can be seen in the international security "market." The collapse of arms control in the late 1970s not only returned the situation to laissez-faire, but added fuel to the deterioration of relations that caused it. Even though arms control in that period did not achieve more than marginal effects on the arms dynamic, its breakdown exacerbated a period of arms competition and political hostility. The costs, benefits, and risks of that reaction in terms of the danger of war need to be weighed against those of the period of arms control and détente, when the risk of war was perceived to be lower. There are no fully objective measures for variations in the probability of war that result from the rise and fall of arms control; there are no fully objective ways of measuring any social phenomenon. There are irresolvable differences of opinion on whether or not the overall balance tipped in favor of the regulatory effort. Similar problems of evaluation affect the nonproliferation regime, where despite some recent broadening and deepening, a number of significant states still remain outside the regime. The case of GCD is more hypothetical. If an extensive disarmament regime broke down because of inadequate verification and suspicions of cheating, the resultant period of rearmament racing could be extremely dangerous. Even if GCD was accompanied by world government, there would be new dangers of global tyranny, global civil war, and global mismanagement. NOD or SNV would seem to offer the least costly outcome should GCD begin to break down, because people would be more able to resist violence in a relatively nondestructive fashion.

Whereas regulation involves risks of failure, backlash, and unanticipated negative side effects, laissez-faire is a surrender to market dynamics that have a long record of periodic collapse. The attempt to regulate at least acknowledges that military means creates real, shared dangers. The narrow pursuit of unilateral security ignores security interdependence and can open the way to dangerous and self-defeating escalations of the arms dynamic. Although a laissez-faire system does not, on past record, offer long-term hope for stability, laissez-faire dominates. The idea of national security through armed strength is simple and direct and taps the emotional sentiments of nationalism. It can still command a political majority in most countries. The domestic political appeal of national military power is one reason why an unregulated system pushes constantly against the restraints of resource limitations and fear that sometimes work to inhibit the slide to war. The unilateral security perspective can even turn resource limitations and fear into reasons to go to war.

The Transformative Effects of WMD?

The discussion of laissez-faire versus regulation so far largely rests on the political assumptions of realism. In other words, it assumes that relations between states are basically driven by power rivalries and security dilemmas. Under such conditions, laissez-faire is essentially about states looking after themselves in pursuit of national security, and regulation is mostly about interstate agreements aimed at moderating unwanted aspects of the security dilemma by manipulating the balance of military means. The same realist assumptions underlie a view that it is those military means themselves that offer the prime reason for rejecting the view that the past is a guide to its future. By placing the issue of human survival at the center of military affairs, the destructive power of modern military means has made security interdependence more obvious and more compelling than ever before. Has this development transformed the pattern of relations under a laissez-faire balance of power, or does the balance still operate in the old way but with a vastly higher risk of catastrophe attached to its periodic breakdowns? There is virtually no disagreement that WMD have greatly increased the dangers attendant on any war fought among the great powers, but there is considerable difference on the significance of this. Note that the point is not merely about nuclear weapons, but about large numbers of nuclear weapons combined with large numbers of reliable long-range delivery systems.

Some see the impact of the potential for reliable, high-speed mass destruction on the international system as transformational. The essence of the transformational view rests on the impact that greatly amplified fear of war supposedly has on the behavior of decisionmakers (see Jervis 1988, 1989). This has obvious connections with existential or even weaponless nuclear deterrence, but can also be seen as the product of specific nuclear deterrent postures. The strongest form of this view is that the very high fear of war constitutes virtually an absolute block on the resort to war among the great powers. There is a weaker version that sees fear as injecting into world politics a common interest in survival, but does not see it as sufficient to make war between the great powers impossible. That common interest is seen as providing a new political basis for more cooperative behavior within the framework of anarchy. Some agree that nuclear weapons have injected a significant element of fear into world politics, but do not see this element as transformational (Bull 1961: 8–12, 46; Mueller 1988, 1989). Others see the war-preventing aspect of nuclear weapons as offset by the dangers of war that nuclear weapons themselves introduce, and so conclude against the transformation thesis (Gilpin 1972; 1981: 213–219).

Two Zones Within a Global Arms Dynamic

The particular approach to transformation discussed above is rooted in realist assumptions about the nature of international politics. It supposes that *realpolitik* remains the basic rule of relations between states and that WMD simply impose restraints on that behavior. There is an alternative view of transformation that questions the durability of realist assumptions about international relations. In this book we rejected the realist assumption that the political-military world divides into two distinct spheres: a domestic one where order and some sort of peace prevail, and an international one marked by constant instability and threat of war. Instead, we discussed the ways in which parts of the international system show features of stability and nonexpectation of war that mitigate the pressures for military self-help, and the ways in which the rest of it suffers from a relatively high degree of domestic repression, civil war, and, occasionally, interstate war. However, we also argued that the zone of peace and zone of war are in some significant ways integrated with each other into a single global arms dynamic.

Our point is that thinking about military security is a part, and only a part, of the necessary response to the arms dynamic. The other part of the response lies in the broader study of the political and economic dynamics of world politics. Political developments such as the end of the Cold War and the collapse of the Soviet Union have dramatically reconfigured the strategic environment. As shown by the ending of the Cold War, some political developments mute the strategic problem by damping down its political causes, while others exacerbate it. Nothing could reveal the impact of political relations on military factors more clearly than the end of the Cold War, when in the space of a few years a deeply institutionalized security dilemma largely evaporated. Most of the armaments were still there, but were no longer perceived as very threatening. Likewise, the development of a world economy that makes the welfare, or lack of it, of each more dependent on that of others also has significant implications for the strategic environment. As economic interdependence grows, it not only adds to the cost of war but also provides instruments of leverage other than force with which states can try to influence each other's behavior. If the world economy became less integrated and more competitive in a mercantilist sense (i.e., with regional blocs engaged in power rivalries), then economic causes of conflict would factor into the strategic equation in a different way (Buzan 1984a).

The structural pressures of international anarchy strongly influence the arms dynamic and the military significance of the technological imperative, and the impediments to fundamental reform of the international political structure are immense. Nevertheless, the basic condition of anarchy encompasses a huge range of political possibilities (Buzan 1984b; 1991a: 174–181, 261–265; 1995d; Milner 1991; Wendt 1992). Although anarchies may be primitive and conflictual, they may also be well developed, mature, and stable (and, of course, the same can be said of politics within states). There is consequently as much scope in the political economy side of world politics as there is in its military strategic side for addressing the problems of war and peace. These larger problems cannot be addressed adequately within the confines of a single field. It is for this reason that strategic studies, peace studies, and critical security studies on the one hand and world politics on the other must not allow their debates to become detached from each other.

At present there are some signs, though not yet systemwide, that the problem of achieving military security is being eased by developments in the international political economy. There are some stunning regional developments, such as the unfolding of a security community in the European Union and the construction of security regimes in Southeast Asia,

Southern Africa, and maybe South America. On top of that is the fact that several of the main centers of power and wealth in the system (and the biggest and most dominant ones at that) have become a security community among themselves. These developments might be taken as strong signs that the threat of great-power world wars has dropped away sharply, and perhaps permanently. They might also be taken as heralding a general shift in Western thinking about war and peace away from such ideas as arms control, NOD, and disarmament and toward ideas such as democratization and liberalization. Doing so has more than just the current fashion of liberal triumphalism to recommend it.

As argued above, transferring the concepts of arms control, NOD, and disarmament to the unfamiliar complexities of the zone of war is no easy task. Putting politics first could easily be more attractive. In addition, shifting the emphasis to political solutions takes the spotlight off weapons on the grounds that if political relations can be settled, weapons do not matter much. Once states begin to feel secure in each other's company, then the fact that they possess military means and/or mobilizing potential no longer triggers the action–reaction processes of the security dilemma. If the focus is on political relations, then much of the moral heat is taken away from military means. For the West, which is still the fountainhead of military R&D and arms production and export, such a development could certainly find political support.

These changes underline the continuities of traditional anarchic international politics in other parts of the international system. Until such developments encompass the whole of the international system—which is likely to take a long time—the political pressures of immature anarchy and the fruitfulness of technological innovation will create a demand for strategic thinking, not just about relations within the zone of war, but also about relations between the zone of peace and the zone of war, and the gray areas between them. Some of the main threads of that thinking will be extensions of the trends reviewed here. Others will be new, as developments in politics and technology reshape the strategic potential of the system. As we have seen, there is room within strategic debate for diverse and contending points of view. Strategic thinking lends itself just as easily to analysis of mutual security as it does to analysis of national security. The emergence of interest in NOD and even SNV demonstrates the existence of analysts willing to begin moving down unorthodox, but important, paths.

Thinking about the impact of technology on military security needs to be informed by an understanding of world politics and of the grounds and consequences of adopting one analytical approach rather than another. The principal danger of analyzing the technological dimension of military security is that one can start treating broad strategic concepts as if they were narrow military or even merely technical ones. To lose sight of the broader political context is to lose sight not only of the purpose but also the limits of acquiring technology and pursuing military security. Finally, understanding the arms dynamic is not the same as being able to control it. Attempts at regulation through arms control, NOD, and disarmament have operated mainly at the margins, but have sometimes had important effects (many of them unintentional and some of them malign). Some people have more power than others, but all are subject to forces that are extremely difficult to control. With these caveats in mind, one can still conclude that there is plenty of thinking about the arms dynamic left to do, and plenty of good reasons for doing it.

Acronyms and Abbreviations

ABM	antiballistic missile
AD	assured destruction
ALCM	air-launched cruise missile
ASAT	antisatellite
ASCM	antiship cruise missile
ASW	antisubmarine weapon(s)/warfare
AWACS	airborne warning and control system
BMD	ballistic missile defense
BTW	biological and toxin weapon(s)/warfare
BTWC	Biological and Toxic Weapons Convention
CBM	confidence-building measure
CBW	chemical and biological weapon(s)/warfare
CCP	Chinese Communist Party
CFE	Conventional Forces in Europe
CIA	Central Intelligence Agency
COCOM	Coordinating Committee for Multilateral Export Controls
CTB	comprehensive test ban
CTBT	Comprehensive Test Ban Treaty
C3I	command, control, communications, and intelligence
C4I	command, control, communications, computers, and intelligence
CW	chemical weapon(s)/warfare
CWC	Chemical Weapons Convention
DMZ	demilitarized zone
ECM	electronic countermeasure(s)
ED	extended deterrence
EU	European Union
FAE	fuel–air explosive(s)
GCD	general and complete disarmament
GLCM	ground-launched cruise missile

GDP	gross domestic product
GNP	gross national product
GPS	global positioning system
IAEA	International Atomic Energy Agency
ICBM	intercontinental ballistic missile
ICJ	International Court of Justice
IISS	International Institute for Strategic Studies
INF	intermediate-range nuclear forces
LACM	land-attack cruise missile
LIC	less industrialized country
LLW	low-lethality weapon(s)
LNO	limited nuclear option
LOW	launch on warning
LRA	Lord's Resistance Army
LTTE	Liberation Tigers of Tamil Eelam
LUA	launch under attack
MAD	mutually assured destruction
MBFR	Mutual and Balanced Force Reductions
MIC	military-industrial complex
MIRV	multiple, independently targetable reentry vehicle
MNC	multinational corporation(s)
MRBM	medium-range ballistic missile
MTCR	Missile Technology Control Regime
MX	missile experimental
NATO	North Atlantic Treaty Organization
NBC	nuclear, biological, and chemical
NIC	newly industrialized country
NLF	National Liberation Front
NMD	national missile defense
NOD	nonoffensive defense
NPT	Nonproliferation Treaty
NSC	National Security Council
NTM	national technical means
NWF	nuclear-weapons-free
NWFZ	nuclear-weapon-free zone
PGM	precision-guided munition(s)
PK	probability of kill
PNE	peaceful nuclear explosive
PTBT	Partial Test Ban Treaty
Pu239	plutonium 239
R&D	research and development
RIMA	revolution in military affairs
RPV	remotely piloted vehicle
SALT	Strategic Arms Limitation Talks

SAM	surface-to-air missile
SDI	Strategic Defense Initiative
SIPRI	Stockholm International Peace Research Institute
SLBM	submarine-launched ballistic missile
SLCM	sea-launched cruise missile
SNV	strategic nonviolence
START	Strategic Arms Reduction Talks
TMD	theater missile defense
TNW	tactical nuclear weapon(s)/warfare
USAF	United States Air Force
U235	uranium 235
U238	uranium 238
UN	United Nations
UNSCOM	United Nations Special Commission on Iraq
WMD	weapon(s) of mass destruction

REFERENCES

Acheson, Dean (1969) *Present at the Creation. My Years in the State Department* (New York: Norton).

Ackerman, Peter and Christopher Kruegler (1994) *Strategic Nonviolent Conflict. The Dynamics of People Power in the Twentieth Century* (Westport, CT: Praeger).

Adams, Gordon and Steven M. Kosiak (1993) "The United States: Trends in Defence Procurement and Research and Development Programmes," in Herbert Wulf (ed.) *Arms Industry Limited* (Oxford: Oxford University Press for the Stockholm International Peace Research Institute), 29–49.

Adler, Emanuel (ed.) (1992) *The International Practice of Arms Control* (Baltimore: The Johns Hopkins University Press).

Adomeit, Hannes (1982) *Soviet Risk-Taking and Crisis-Behaviour: A Theoretical and Empirical Analysis* (London: Allen & Unwin).

African Rights (1995) *Rwanda: Death, Despair and Defiance* (London: African Rights).

Agrell, Wilhelm, (1987) "Offensive vs. Defensive: Military Strategy and Alternative Defence," *Journal of Peace Research,* 24:1, 75–85.

Ahn, Byung-joon (1993) "Managing Reunification in the Korean Peninsula," in *Asia's International Role in the Post–Cold War Era,* Adelphi Paper 275 (London: International Institute for Strategic Studies), 83–93.

Albrecht, U., D. Ernst, P. Lock, and H. Wulf (1975) "Militarization, Arms Transfer and Arms Production in Peripheral Countries," *Journal of Peace Research,* 22, 195–212.

Albright, David (1987) "Pakistan's Bomb-Making Capacity," *Bulletin of the Atomic Scientists,* 43:5.

Allison, Graham (1971) *Essence of Decision: Explaining the Cuban Missile Crisis* (Boston: Little, Brown & Co.).

Allison, Graham and Frederic Morris (1975) "Armaments and Arms Control: Exploring the Determinants of Military Weapons," *Daedalus,* 104, 99–129.

Amin, Ash (ed.) (1995) *Post-Fordism: A Reader* (Oxford: Blackwell).

Anderson, Benedict (1983) *Imagined Communities* (London: Verso).

Anthony, Ian (ed.) (1992) *Arms Trade and the Medium Powers* (Brighton: Harvester Wheatsheaf).

Anthony, Ian (ed.) (1997) *Russia and the Arms Trade* (Oxford: Oxford University Press for the Stockholm International Peace Research Institute).

Anthony, Ian, Pieter D. Wezeman, and Simeon T. Wezeman (1996) "The Trade in Major Conventional Weapons," *SIPRI Yearbook: Armaments, Disarmament and International Security* (Oxford: Oxford University Press for the Stockholm International Peace Research Institute), 463–533.

Arbatov, Georgi (1995) "Controlling Nuclear Weapons in the CIS," in David Carlton, Elena Mirco, and Paul Ingram (eds.) *Controlling the International Transfer of Weaponry and Related Technology* (Aldershot: Dartmouth), 101–113.

Arendt, Hannah (1969) *On Violence* (New York: Harcourt Brace Jovanovich).

Arendt, Hannah (1973a) "Lying in Politics: Reflections on the Pentagon Papers," in *Crises of the Republic* (Harmondsworth: Penguin), 8–42.

Arendt, Hannah (1973b) "On Violence," in *Crises of the Republic* (Harmondsworth: Penguin), 83–146.

Arkin, William and Richard W. Fieldhouse (1985) *Nuclear Battlefields. Global Links in the Arms Race* (Cambridge, MA: Ballinger).

Arms Control Reporter: A Chronicle of Treaties, Negotiations, Proposals (approx. monthly from January 1982) Institute for Defense and Disarmament Studies (Boston: IDDS).

Arnett, Eric (ed.) (1996a) *Nuclear Weapons After the Comprehensive Test Ban. Implications for Modernization and Proliferation* (Oxford: Oxford University Press for the Stockholm International Peace Research Institute).

Arnett, Eric (1996b) "Military Research and Development," in *SIPRI Yearbook: Armaments, Disarmament and International Security* (Oxford: Oxford University Press for the Stockholm International Peace Research Institute), 381–409.

Arnett, Eric (1997) *Military Capacity and the Risk of War. China, India, Pakistan and Iran* (Oxford: Oxford University Press for the Stockholm International Peace Research Institute).

Art, Robert J. (1980) "To What Ends Military Power?" *International Security*, 4, 3–35.

Ashley, Richard K. (1988) "Untying the Sovereign State: A Double Reading of the Anarchy Problematique," *Millennium: Journal of International Studies*, 17:2, 227–262.

Associated Press (1995a) "Sect Scientist Made Sarin," *The Guardian*, 12 May.

Associated Press (1995b) "Racist Orders Plague by Post," *The Guardian*, 17 May.

Avant, Deborah D. (1994) *Political Institutions and Military Change: Lessons From Peripheral Wars* (Ithaca: Cornell University Press).

Ayoob, Mohammed (1980) *Conflict and Intervention in the Third World* (London: Croom Helm).

Ayoob, Mohammed (1995) *The Third World Security Predicament: State Making, Regional Conflict, and the International System* (Boulder, CO: Lynne Rienner Publishers).

Ayton, Andrew and Leslie Price (1995) *The Medieval Military Revolution* (London: I.B. Tauris).

Bahr, Egon and Dieter S. Lutz (eds.) (1988) *Gemeinsame Sicherheit. Konventionelle Stabilität. Bd. 3: Zu den militärischen Aspekten Struktureller Nichtangriffsfähigkeit im Rahmen Gemeinsamer Sicherheit* (Baden-Baden: Nomos Verlagsgesellschaft).

Bailey, Kathleen C. (1992) *Doomsday Weapons in the Hands of Many. The Arms Control Challenge for the 1990s* (Urbana-Champaign: University of Illinois Press).

Ball, Desmond (1993–1994) "Arms and Affluence: Military Acquisitions in the Asia–Pacific Region," *International Security*, 18:3, 78–112.

Ball, Desmond and Robert C. Toth (1990) "Revising the SIOP: Taking War-Fighting to Dangerous Extremes," *International Security*, 14:4, 65–92.

Ball, Nicole (1989) *Security and Economy in the Third World* (London: Adamantine Press).

Barnes Jr., Rudolph C. (1996) *Military Legitimacy. Might and Right in the New Millennium* (London: Frank Cass).

Baudrillard, Jean (1981) *For a Critique of the Political Economy of the Sign* (St. Louis: Telos).

Baudrillard, Jean (1995) *The Gulf War Did Not Take Place* (Bloomington and Indianapolis: Indiana University Press). Translated and with an introduction by Paul Patton.

Baugh, William H. (1984) *The Politics of the Nuclear Balance* (New York: Longman).

Baylis, John, Ken Booth, John C. Garnett, and Phil Williams (1975) *Contemporary Strategy: Theories and Policies* (London: Croom Helm).

Beaufre, André (1965) *An Introduction to Strategy* (London: Faber & Faber).

Bell, Daniel (1974) *The Coming of Post-Industrial Society: A Venture in Social Forecasting* (London: Heinemann Educational).

Bellany, Ian (1975) "The Richardson Theory of 'Arms Races'—Themes and Variations," *British Journal of International Studies*, 1, 119–130.

Bennett, Andrew, Joseph Lepgold, and Danny Unger (eds.) (1996) *Friends in Need: Burden-Sharing in the Gulf War* (London: Macmillan).

Benoit, Emile (1973) *Defence and Economic Growth in Developing Countries* (Lexington, MA: Lexington Books).

Berdal, Mats R. (1996) *Disarmament and Demobilisation After Civil Wars*, Adelphi Paper 303 (Oxford: Oxford University Press for the International Institute for Strategic Studies).

Berger, Thomas U. (1993) "From Sword to Chrysanthemum: Japan's Culture of Anti-Militarism," *International Security*, 17:4, 119–150.

Berghahn, Volker (1973) *Germany and the Approach of War in 1914* (London: Macmillan).

Betts, Richard K. (1979) "A Diplomatic Bomb for South Africa," *International Security*, 4, 91–115.

Betts, Richard K. (1987) *Nuclear Blackmail and Nuclear Balance* (Washington, DC: The Brookings Institution).

Betts, Richard K. (1988) "Nuclear Peace and Conventional War," *Journal of Strategic Studies*, 11:1, 79–85.

Betts, Richard K. (1992) "Systems for Peace or Causes of War? Collective Security, Arms Control and the New Europe," *International Security*, 17: 1, 5–43.

Bialer, Seweryn (1987) *The Soviet Paradox. External Expansion, Internal Decline* (New York: Vintage).

Biddle, Stephen (1996) "Victory Misunderstood: What the Gulf War Tells Us About the Future of Conflict," *International Security*, 12:2, 139–179.

Bijker, Wiebe E., Thomas P. Hughes, and Trevor J. Pinch (eds.) (1990) *The Social Construction of Technological Systems: New Directions in the Sociology and History of Technology* (Cambridge, MA: Massachusetts Institute of Technology Press).

Bittleston, Martyn (1990) *Co-operation or Competition? Defence Procurement Options for the 1990s*, Adelphi Paper 250 (London: Brassey's for the International Institute for Strategic Studies).

Bitzinger, Richard A. (1992) "Arms To Go: Chinese Arms Sales to the Third World," *International Security*, 17:2, 84–111.

Bitzinger, Richard A. (1994) "The Globalization of the Arms Industry: The Next Proliferation Challenge," *International Security*, 19:2, 170–198.

Blainey, Geoffrey (1973) *The Causes of War* (New York: The Free Press).

Blair, Bruce G. (1993) *The Logic of Accidental Nuclear War* (Washington, DC: The Brookings Institution).

Blechman, Barry (1980) "Do Negotiated Arms Limitations Have a Future?" *Foreign Affairs*, 59, 102–125.

Blechman, Barry M., Stephen S. Kaplan, et al. (1978) *Force Without War: U.S. Armed Forces as a Political Instrument* (Washington, DC: The Brookings Institution).

Blomley, Peter (1984) "The Arms Trade and Arms Conversion," in J. O'Connor Howe (ed.) *Armed Peace* (London: Macmillan), 123–144.

Booth, Ken and John Baylis (1988) *Britain, NATO and Nuclear Weapons. Alternative Defence versus Alliance Reform* (London: Macmillan).

Booth, Ken and Eric Herring (1994) *Keyguide to Information Sources in Strategic Studies* (London: Mansell).

Booth, Ken and Nicholas J. Wheeler (1992) "Beyond Nuclearism," in Regina Cowen Karp (ed.) *Security Without Nuclear Weapons?* (Oxford: Oxford University Press for the Stockholm International Peace Research Institute), 1–36.

Booth, Ken and Phil Williams (1985) "Fact and Fiction in U.S. Foreign Policy: Reagan's Myths About Detente," *World Policy Journal*, 2:3, 501–532.

Borg, Marlies ter and Wim Smit (eds.) (1989) *Non-provocative Defence as a Principle of Arms Control and Its Implications for Assessing Defence Technologies* (Amsterdam: Free University Press).

Boserup, Anders and Andrew Mack (1975) *War Without Weapons: Non-Violence in National Defense* (New York: Schocken Books).

Boserup, Anders and Robert Neild (eds.) (1990) *The Foundations of Defensive Defence* (London: Macmillan).

Botti, Timothy J. (1996) *Ace in the Hole. Why the United States Did Not Use Nuclear Weapons in the Cold War, 1945 to 1965* (New York: Greenwood Press).

Bourdieu, Pierre (1991) *Language and Symbolic Power* (Cambridge: Polity in association with Basil Blackwell). Edited and introduced by John B. Thompson. Translated by Gino Raymond and Matthew Adamson.

Boutwell, Jeffrey, Michael Klare, and Laura Reed (eds.) (1994) *Lethal Commerce: The Global Trade in Small Arms and Light Weapons* (Cambridge, MA: American Academy of Arts and Sciences).

Bracken, Paul (1993) "Nuclear Weapons and State Survival in North Korea," *Survival*, 35:3, 137–153.

Brams, Steven J. (1985) *Superpower Games: Applying Game Theory to Superpower Conflict* (New Haven: Yale University Press).

Brauch, Hans Gunter and Robert Kennedy (eds.) (1990) *Alternative Conventional Defence Postures for the European Theater.* Vol. 1: *The Military Balance and Domestic Constraint* (New York: Taylor & Francis).

Brauch, Hans Gunter and Robert Kennedy (eds.) (1992) *Alternative Conventional Defense Postures in the European Theatre.* Vol. 2: *The Impact of Political Change on Strategy, Technology, and Arms Control* (New York: Taylor & Francis).

Brecher, Michael, Jonathan Wilkenfeld, and Sheila Moser (1988) *Crises in the Twentieth Century.* Vol. 1: *Handbook of International Crises* (Oxford: Pergamon).

Brecher, Michael and Jonathan Wilkenfeld (1989) *Crisis, Conflict and Instability* (Oxford: Pergamon), with contributions by Patrick James, Hemda Ben Yehuda, Mark A. Boyer, and Stephen R. Hill.

Brittain, Victoria (1995) "Children Sucked Into Global Strife," *The Guardian*, 12 December.

Brodie, Bernard (1973) *War and Politics* (London: Macmillan).

Brodie, Bernard (1978) "The Development of Nuclear Strategy," *International Security*, 2, 65–83.

Brömmelhörster, Jörn and John Frankenstein (eds.) (1996) *Mixed Motives, Uncertain Outcomes: Defense Conversion in China* (Boulder, CO: Lynne Rienner Publishers).

Brooks, Harvey (1975) "The Military Innovation System and the Qualitative Arms Race," *Daedalus*, 104, 75–98.

Brown, Michael E. (1992) *Flying Blind: The Politics of the U.S. Strategic Bomber Program* (Ithaca: Cornell University Press).

Brown, Neville (1977) *The Future Global Challenge: A Predictive Study of World Security, 1977–1990* (London: Royal United Services Institute).

Brubaker, E.R. (1973) "Economic Models of Arms Races," *Journal of Conflict Resolution*, 17, 187–205.

Brzoska, Michael and Peter Lock (eds.) (1992) *Restructuring of Arms Production in Western Europe* (Oxford: Oxford University Press for the Stockholm International Peace Research Institute).

Brzoska, Michael and Thomas Ohlson (1986) *Arms Production in the Third World* (London: Taylor & Francis for the Stockholm International Peace Research Institute).

Brzoska, Michael and Frederic S. Pearson (1994) *Arms and Warfare: Escalation, De-escalation, and Negotiation* (Columbia: University of South Carolina Press).

Budiardjo, Carmel (1991) "Indonesia: Mass Extermination and the Consolidation of Authoritarian Power," in Alexander George (ed.) *Western State Terrorism* (Cambridge: Polity Press), 180–211.

Bull, Hedley (1961) *The Control of the Arms Race* (London: Weidenfeld & Nicolson).

Bull, Hedley (1968) "Strategic Studies and Its Critics," *World Politics*, 2, 593–605.

Bull, Hedley (1970) "Disarmament and the International System," in John C. Garnett (ed.) *Theories of Peace and Security* (London: Macmillan).

Bundy, McGeorge (1984) "Existential Deterrence and its Consequences," in Douglas Maclean (ed.) *The Security Gamble: Deterrence Dilemmas in the Nuclear Age* (Totowa, NJ: Rowman and Allenheld), 3–13.

Bundy, McGeorge (1988) *Danger and Survival: Choices About the Bomb in the First Fifty Years* (New York: Random House).

Burn, Duncan (1978) *Nuclear Power and the Energy Crisis* (London: Macmillan).

Burton, John W. (1984) *Global Conflict: The Domestic Sources of International Crisis* (Brighton: Harvester Wheatsheaf).

Burton, John W. (1997) *Violence Explained* (Manchester: Manchester University Press).

Busch, P.A. (1970) "Mathematical Models of Arms Races," in Bruce Russett (ed.) *What Price Vigilance?* (New Haven: Yale University Press), 376–397.

Bush, Clive (1977) *The Dream of Reason. American Consciousness and Cultural Achievement From Independence to the Civil War* (London: Edward Arnold).

Butterfield, Herbert (1951) *History and Human Relations* (London: Collins).

Buzan, Barry (1984a) "Economic Structure and International Security: The Limits of the Liberal Case," *International Organization*, 38:4, 597–624.

Buzan, Barry (1984b) "Peace, Power, and Security: Contending Concepts in the Study of International Relations," *Journal of Peace Research*, 21, 109–125.

Buzan, Barry (1987a) *Introduction to Strategic Studies. Military Technology and International Relations* (London: Macmillan).

Buzan, Barry (1987b) "People, States and Fear: The National Security Problem in the Third World," in Edward Azar and Chung Moon (eds.) *Third World National Security: Concepts, Issues and Implications* (Lexington: University of Kentucky Press), 14–43.

Buzan, Barry (1988) "Japan's Future: Old History versus New Roles," *International Affairs*, 64:4, 557–573.

Buzan, Barry (1991a) *People, States, and Fear: An Agenda for International Security Studies in the Post-Cold War Era* (Hemel Hempstead: Wheatsheaf; and Boulder, CO: Lynne Rienner Publishers), second edition.

Buzan, Barry (1991b) "New Patterns of Global Security in the Twenty-First Century," *International Affairs*, 67:3, 431–451.

Buzan, Barry (1993) "From International System to International Society: Structural Realism and Regime Theory Meet the English School," *International Organization*, 47:3, 327–352.

Buzan, Barry (1994) "Does NOD Have a Future in the Post-Cold War World?" in Bjørn Møller & Håkan Wiberg (eds.) *Non-Offensive Defence for the Twenty-First Century* (Boulder, CO: Westview Press), 11–24.

Buzan, Barry (1995a) "Japan's Defence Problematique," *The Pacific Review*, 8:1, 25–43.

Buzan, Barry (1995b) "The Level of Analysis Problem in International Relations Reconsidered," in Ken Booth and Steve Smith (eds.) *International Relations Theory Today* (Cambridge: Polity Press), 198–216.

Buzan, Barry (1995c) "Focus On: The Present as a Historic Turning Point?" *Journal of Peace Research*, 30:4, 385–398.

Buzan, Barry (1995d) "Security, the State, the 'New World Order,' and Beyond," in Ronnie D. Lipschutz (ed.) *On Security* (New York: Columbia University Press), 187–211.

Buzan, Barry, Charles Jones, and Richard Little (1993) *The Logic of Anarchy* (New York: Columbia University Press).

Buzan, Barry and Gerald Segal (1996) "The Rise of 'Lite' Powers: A Strategy for the Postmodern State," *World Policy Journal*, 13:3, 1–10.

Buzan, Barry and Gerald Segal (1998) *Anticipating the Future* (London: Simon and Schuster).

Buzan, Barry and Gautam Sen (1990) "The Impact of Military Research and Development Priorities on the Development of the Civil Economy in Capitalist States," *Review of International Studies*, 16:4, 321–339.

Buzan, Barry and Ole Wæver (1997) "Correspondence: Slippery? Contradictory? Sociologically Untenable? The Copenhagen School Replies," *Review of International Studies*, 23:2, 241–250.

Buzan, Barry, Ole Wæver, and Jaap de Wilde (1998) *Security: A New Framework for Analysis* (Boulder, CO: Lynne Rienner Publishers).

Caceres, Gustavo and Thomas Scheetz (eds.) (1995) *Defensa no Provocativa. Una propuesta de reforma militar para la Argentina* (Buenos Aires: Editora Buenos Aires).

Caldicott, Helen (1984). *Missile Envy. The Arms Race and Nuclear War* (New York: Bantam).

Cameron, Craig (1994) *American Samurai: Myth, Imagination and the Conduct of the First Marine Division, 1941–51* (Cambridge: Cambridge University Press).

Campbell, David (1992) *Writing Security. United States Foreign Policy and the Politics of Identity* (Manchester: Manchester University Press).

Campbell, David (1998a) "MetaBosnia: A Review of the Narratives of the Bosnian War," *Review of International Studies*, 24:2.

Campbell, David (1998b) *National Deconstruction: Violence, Identity and Justice in Bosnia* (Minneapolis: University of Minnesota).

Campden, Alan D. (ed.) (1992) *The First Information War* (Fairfax, VA: AFCEA International Press).

Canberra Commission (1996) *Report of the Canberra Commission on the Elimi-nation of Nuclear Weapons* (Canberra: Australian Department of Foreign Affairs and Trade).

Cannizzo, Cindy (1980) *The Gun Merchants: Politics and Policies of the Major Arms Suppliers* (Oxford: Pergamon).

Carter, April (1989) *Success and Failure in Arms Control Negotiations* (Oxford: Oxford University Press for the Stockholm International Peace Research Institute).

Carus, W. Seth (1993) *Cruise Missile Proliferation in the 1990s,* The Washington Papers 159 (New York: Praeger).

Chatterji, Manas and Linda Rennie Forcey (eds.) (1992) *Disarmament, Economic Conversion, and the Management of Peace* (New York: Praeger).

Chellaney, Brahma (1991) "South Asia's Passage to Nuclear Power," *International Security,* 16:1, 43–72.

Chilton, Paul (ed.) (1984) *Language and the Nuclear Arms Debate: Nukespeak Today* (London: Pinter).

Chinworth, Michael W. (1993) *Inside Japan's Defense: Technology, Economics and Strategy* (McLean, VA: Brassey's U.S.).

Chomsky, Noam (1973) *For Reasons of State* (London: Fontana).

Chomsky, Noam (1986) *Pirates and Emperors: International Terrorism in the Real World* (New York: Claremont).

Chomsky, Noam (1989) *The Culture of Terrorism* (London: Pluto Press).

Chomsky, Noam (1994) *World Orders, Old and New* (London: Pluto Press).

Chomsky, Noam and Edward S. Herman (1979a) *The Political Economy of Human Rights: The Washington Connection and Third World Fascism* (Boston, MA: South End Press).

Chomsky, Noam and Edward S. Herman (1979b) *The Political Economy of Human Rights: After the Cataclysm: Postwar Indochina and the Reconstruction of Imperial Ideology* (Boston, MA: South End Press).

Chowdhury, A.R. (1991) "Defence Spending and Economic Growth," *Journal of Conflict Resolution,* 35:1.

Christensen, Thomas J. (1996) *Useful Adversaries: Grand Strategy, Domestic Militarization, and Sino-American Conflict, 1947–1958* (Princeton: Princeton University Press).

Christensen, Thomas J. and Jack L. Snyder (1990) "Chain Gangs and Passed Bucks: Predicting Alliance Patterns in Multipolarity," *International Organization,* 44:2, 137–168.

Chubin, Shahram (1995) "Does Iran Want Nuclear Weapons?" *Survival,* 37:1, 86–104.

Cigar, Norman (1995) *Genocide in Bosnia: The Policy of Ethnic Cleansing* (London: Texas A&M University/Trevor Brain).

Cohen, Raymond (1994) "Pacific Unions: A Reappraisal of the Theory that 'Democracies Do Not Go to War With Each Other,'" *Review of International Studies,* 20:3, 207–223.

Cohen, Raymond (1995) "Raymond Cohen on Pacific Unions: A Response and a Reply. Needed: A Disaggregate Approach to Democratic-Peace Theory," *Review of International Studies,* 21:3, 323–325.

Cohn, Carol (1987) "Sex and Death in the Rational World of Defense Intellectuals," *Signs: Journal of Women in Culture and Society,* 12:4, 687–718.

Cole, Paul M. (1997) "Atomic Bombast: Nuclear Decision-Making in Sweden, 1946–72," *The Washington Quarterly,* 20:2, 233–251.

Coleman, Karen and Reuter (1997) "UN Raid Reveals Arsenal Held by Karadzic Police," *The Guardian,* 21 August.

Conca, Ken (1997) *Manufacturing Insecurity: The Rise and Fall of Brazil's Military-Industrial Complex* (Boulder, CO: Lynne Rienner Publishers).

Conversion Survey [annual] (Oxford: Oxford University Press for the Bonn International Center for Conversion).

Cooper, Julian (1993–1994) "Transforming Russia's Defence Industrial Base," *Survival*, 35:4, 147–162.

Copson, Raymond W. (1994) *Africa's Wars and the Prospects for Peace* (London: M.E. Sharpe).

Cornish, Paul (1995) *The Arms Trade and Europe,* Chatham House Paper (London: Pinter/Cassell for the Royal Institute of International Affairs).

Cortright, David and Amitabh Mattoo (1996) *India and the Bomb: Public Opinion and Nuclear Options* (Notre Dame, IN: University of Notre Dame Press).

Croft, Stuart (1994) "Continuity and Change in British Thinking About Nuclear Weapons," *Political Studies*, 42:2.

Croft, Stuart (1996) *Strategies of Arms Control. A History and Typology* (Manchester: Manchester University Press).

Cronberg, Tarja and Kim Hansen (1992) "From Military to Civil Production: A Review of Recent Literature on Conversion," *Technology Assessment Texts No. 5* (Lyngby: Technological University of Denmark, Unit of Technology Assessment).

Cronberg, Tarja, Ærøe Anders, and E. Seem (1995) *Technological Powers in Transition: Innovation and Industrial Restructuring in Post Cold War Russia and the United States* (Copenhagen: Academic Publishers).

Cumings, Bruce (1992) *War and Television* (London: Verso).

Dallmeyer, Dorinda (1995) "The Iraq Experience," in David Carlton, Eleana Mirco, and Paul Ingram (eds.) *Controlling the International Transfer of Weaponry and Related Technology* (Aldershot: Dartmouth).

Daugherty, William, Barbara Levi, and Frank von Hippel (1986) "The Consequences of 'Limited' Nuclear Attacks on the United States," *International Security*, 10:4, 3–45.

De Andreis, Marco and Francesco de Calogero (1995) *The Soviet Nuclear Weapon Legacy* (Oxford: Oxford University Press for the Stockholm International Peace Research Institute).

Dean, Jonathan, (1987) *Watershed in Europe. Dismantling the East–West Military Confrontation* (Lexington, MA: Lexington Books).

Dedring, J. (1976) *Recent Advances in Peace and Conflict Research* (Beverly Hills, CA: Sage).

Deger, Sadet and Robert West (eds.) (1987) *Defense, Security and Development* (London: Pinter).

De Landa, Manuel (1991) *War in the Age of Intelligent Machines* (Cambridge, MA: Zone Books).

DeNardo, James (1995) *The Amateur Strategist. Intuitive Deterrence Theories and the Politics of the Nuclear Arms Race* (Cambridge: Cambridge University Press).

Der Derian, James (1992) *Antidiplomacy. Spies, Terror, Speed, and War* (Oxford: Blackwell).

Desjardins, Marie-France (1996) *Rethinking Confidence-Building Measures,* Adelphi Paper 307 (Oxford: Oxford University Press for the International Institute for Strategic Studies).

Deutsch, Karl W. et al (1957) *Political Community and the North Atlantic Area. International Organization in the Light of Historical Experience* (New York: Greenwood Press).

Dibb, Paul (1995) *Towards a New Balance of Power in Asia*, Adelphi Paper 295 (Oxford: Oxford University Press for the International Institute for Strategic Studies).

Diehl, Paul F. (1983) "Arms Races and Escalation: A Closer Look," *Journal of Peace Research*, 20, 205–212.

Dillon, Michael (1996) *Politics of Security. Towards a Political Philosophy of Continental Thought* (London: Routledge).

Doubler, Michael D. (1994) *Closing With the Enemy: How GIs Fought the War in Europe, 1944–45* (Lawrence: Kansas University Press).

Doyle, Michael W. (1983a) "Kant, Liberal Legacies and Foreign Affairs," Part 1, *Philosophy and Public Affairs*, 12:3, 205–235.

Doyle, Michael W. (1983b) "Kant, Liberal Legacies and Foreign Affairs," Part 2, *Philosophy and Public Affairs*, 12:4, 323–353.

Drell, Sidney, P.J. Farley, and David Holloway (1984) "Preserving the ABM Treaty: A Critique of the Reagan Defence Initiative," *International Security*, 9, 51–91.

Drexler, K. Eric (1990) *Engines of Creation* (London: Fourth Estate).

Drifte, Reinhard (1986) *Arms Production in Japan: The Military Application of Civilian Technology* (Boulder, CO: Westview Press).

Drogin, Bob (1996) "Cult Army Shatters Uganda's Peace," *The Guardian*, 2 April.

Duffield, John S. (1995) *Power Rules. The Evolution of NATO's Conventional Force Posture* (Stanford: Stanford University Press).

Durch, William J. (ed.) (1997) *UN Peacekeeping, American Policy and the Uncivil Wars of the 1990s* (London: Macmillan).

Eco, Umberto (1986) "Living in the New Middle Ages," in *Faith in Fakes: Travels in Hyperreality* (London: Minerva), 73–85. Translated by William Weaver.

Edelman, Murray (1985) *The Symbolic Uses of Politics* (Urbana: University of Illinois Press), second edition.

Eden, Lynn (1992), "Learning and Forgetting: The Development of Organizational Knowledge About U.S. Weapons Effects," American Political Science Association annual meeting, Chicago, unpublished ms.

Eden, Lynn (1995), "Constructing Destruction: The Making of Organizational Knowledge About U.S. Nuclear Weapon Effects," Triangle Universities Security Seminar, University of North Carolina at Chapel Hill, unpublished ms.

Edmonds, John (1984) "Proliferation and Test Bans," in J. O'Connor Howe (ed.) *Armed Peace* (London: Macmillan).

Ekeus, Rolf (1993) "The UN Special Commission on Iraq: Activities in 1992," *SIPRI Yearbook 1993* (Oxford: Oxford University Press for the Stockholm International Peace Research Institute).

Eltis, David (1995) *The Military Revolution in Sixteenth-Century Europe* (London: I.B. Tauris).

Enzensberger, Hans Magnus (1994) *Civil War* (London: Granta). Translated by Piers Spence and Martin Chalmers.

Evangelista, Matthew (1988) *Innovation and the Arms Race: How the United States and the Soviet Union Develop New Military Technologies* (Ithaca: Cornell University Press).

Evron, Yair (1991) "Israel," in Regina Cowen Karp (ed.) *Security With Nuclear Weapons?* (Oxford: Oxford University Press for the Stockholm International Peace Research Institute).

Fairhall, David (1997), "Armed Forces Prepare for Battle Over Mines," *The Guardian*, 17 January.

Falk, Richard and Richard Barnet (1965) *Security in Disarmament* (Princeton: Princeton University Press).

Falkenrath, Richard A. (1995) *Shaping Europe's Military Order—The Origins and Consequences of the CFE Treaty* (Cambridge MA: Massachusetts Institute of Technology Press).

Fanon, Frantz (1961) *The Wretched of the Earth* (London: MacGibbon and Kee).

Farber, Henry S. and Joanne Gowa (1995) "Politics and Peace," *International Security*, 20:2, 123–146.

Farrell, Theo (1995) "Waste in Weapons Acquisition: How the Americans Do It All Wrong," *Contemporary Security Policy*, 16:2, 192–218.

Farrell, Theo (1996) "Figuring Out Fighting Organisations: The New Organisational Analysis in Strategic Studies," *Journal of Strategic Studies*, 19:1, 128–142.

Farrell, Theo (1997) *Weapons Without A Cause: The Politics of Weapons Acquisition in the United States* (London: Macmillan).

Fetter, Steve (1987–1988) "Stockpile Confidence Under a Nuclear Test Ban," *International Security*, 12:3, 132–167.

Fetter, Steve (1991) "Ballistic Missiles and Weapons of Mass Destruction: What Is the Threat? What Should be Done?" *International Security*, 16:1, 5–42.

Fetter, Steve (1996) "Correspondence: Nuclear Deterrence and the 1990 Indo-Pakistani Crisis," *International Security*, 21:1, 176–181.

Findlay, Trevor (ed.) (1996) *Challenges for the New Peacekeepers* (Oxford: Oxford University Press for the Stockholm International Peace Research Institute).

Findlay, Trevor (1997) *Fighting for Peace. The Use of Force in Peace Operations* (Oxford: Oxford University Press for the Stockholm International Peace Research Institute).

Fischer, Dietrich (1982) "Invulnerability Without Threat: The Swiss Concept of General Defence," *Journal of Peace Research*, 29, 205–225.

Fischer, Dietrich (1984) *Preventing War: Towards a Realistic Strategy for Peace in the Nuclear Age* (London: Croom Helm).

Fitch, J. Samuel (1979) "The Political Impact of U.S. Military Aid to Latin America," *Armed Forces and Society*, 5, 360–386.

Fontanel, Jacques (1990) "The Economic Effect of Military Expenditure in Third World Countries," *Journal of Peace Research*, 27:4. 461–466.

Forsberg, Randall (ed.) (1996) *Arms Control in the New Era: Linked Restraint on Arms Deployment, Production and Trade* (Cambridge, MA: Massachusetts Institute of Technology Press).

Fortmann, Michel (1992–1993) "Opaque Proliferation Revisited," *International Journal*, 48:1.

Frankel, Benjamin (1991) *Opaque Nuclear Proliferation. Methodological and Policy Implications* (London: Frank Cass).

Franklin, H. Bruce (1988) *War Stars. The Superweapon and the American Imagination* (Oxford: Oxford University Press).

Freedman, Lawrence (1982) "Arms Control: The Possibility of a Second Coming," in Lawrence Hagen (ed.) *The Crisis in Western Security* (London: Croom Helm).

Freedman, Lawrence (1984a) "Indignation, Influence and Strategic Studies," *International Affairs*, 60, 207–219.

Freedman, Lawrence (1984b) "Strategic Arms Control," in J. O'Connor Howe (ed.) *Armed Peace* (London: Macmillan), 31–47.

Freedman, Lawrence (1988) "I Exist; Therefore I Deter," *International Security*, 13:1, 177–195.

Freedman, Lawrence (1989a) *The Evolution of Nuclear Strategy* (New York: St. Martin's Press), second edition.

Freedman, Lawrence (1989b) "General Deterrence and the Balance of Power," *Review of International Studies*, 15:2, 199–210.

Freedman, Lawrence (1997) "Review Essay. Nuclear Weapons: From Marginalisation to Elimination?" *Survival*, 39:1, 184–189.

Fukuyama, Francis (1992) *The End of History and the Last Man* (London: Penguin).

Gabriel, Richard A. (1987) *No More Heroes. Madness and Psychiatry in War* (New York: Hill and Wang).

Gaddy, Clifford G. (1996) *Price of the Past: Russia's Struggle with the Legacy of a Militarized Economy* (Washington, DC: The Brookings Institution).

Gagnon Jr, V.P. (1994–1995) "Ethnic Nationalism and International Conflict: The Case of Serbia," *International Security*, 19:3, 130–166.

Gall, N. (1976) "Atoms for Brazil, Dangers for All," *Foreign Policy*, 23, 155–201.

Galtung, Johan (1981) "A Structural Theory of Aggression," *Journal of Peace Research*, 1, 95–119.

Galtung, Johan (1984a) "Transarmament: From Offensive to Defensive Defense," *Journal of Peace Research*, 21, 127–139.

Galtung, Johan (1984b) *There Are Alternatives! Four Roads to Peace and Security* (Nottingham: Spokesman).

Gansler, Jacques (1993–1994) "Transforming the U.S. Defence Industrial Base," *Survival*, 35:4, 130–146.

Gardner, Gary (1994) *Nuclear Nonproliferation: A Primer* (Boulder, CO: Lynne Rienner Publishers).

Garthoff, Raymond L. (ed.) (1966) *Sino-Soviet Military Relations* (New York: Praeger).

Garthoff, Raymond L. (1978) "On Estimating and Imputing Intentions," *International Security*, 3:2, 22–32.

Garthoff, Raymond L. (1983) "The Soviet SS-20 Decision," *Survival*, 25, 110–119.

Garthoff, Raymond L. (1984) "Worst-Case Assumptions: Uses, Abuses and Consequences," in Gwyn Prins (ed.) *The Choice: Nuclear Weapons Versus Security* (London: Chatto & Windus), 98–108.

Garthoff, Raymond L. (1990) *Deterrence and the Revolution in Soviet Military Doctrine* (Washington, DC: The Brookings Institution).

Garthoff, Raymond L. (1994) *The Great Transition. American-Soviet Relations and the End of the Cold War* (Washington, DC: The Brookings Institution).

Gates, David (1991) *Non-Offensive Defence. An Alternative Strategy for NATO?* (London: Macmillan).

Geissler, Erhard and John P. Woodall (eds.) (1994) *Control of Dual-Threat Agents. The Vaccines for Peace Programme* (Oxford: Oxford University Press for the Stockholm International Peace Research Institute).

Gellner, Ernest (1988) *Plough, Sword and Book: The Structure of Human History* (London: Paladin).

George, Alexander (ed.) (1991) *Western State Terrorism* (Cambridge: Polity Press).

George, Alexander L. (1984) "Crisis Management: The Interaction of Political and Military Considerations," *Survival*, 26, 22–34.

George, Alexander L. (ed.) (1991) *Avoiding War. Problems of Crisis Management* (Boulder, CO: Westview Press).

George, Alexander L. and William E. Simons (1994) *The Limits of Coercive Diplomacy* (Boulder, CO: Westview Press), second edition.

George, Alexander L. and Richard Smoke (1974) *Deterrence in American Foreign Policy: Theory and Practice* (New York: Columbia University Press).

George, Paul, Bengt-Göran Bergstrand, Susan Clark, and Evamaria Loose-Weintraub (1996) "Military Expenditure," in *SIPRI Yearbook: Armaments, Disarmament and International Security* (Oxford: Oxford University Press for the Stockholm International Peace Research Institute), 325–390.

Gilks, Anne and Gerald Segal (1985) *China and the Arms Trade* (London: Croom Helm).

Gill, Bates, (1992) *Chinese Arms Transfers. Purposes, Patterns and Prospects for the New World Order* (New York: Praeger).

Gill, Bates (1994) "Arms Acquisition in East Asia," in *SIPRI Yearbook 1994* (Oxford: Oxford University Press for the Stockholm International Peace Research Institute), 551–562.

Gill, Bates and Kim Taeho (1995) *Chinese Acquisitions of Weapons and Technologies From Abroad* (Oxford: Oxford University Press for the Stockholm International Peace Research Institute).

Gillespie, J. V. et al. (1979) "Deterrence and Arms Races: An Optimal Control Systems Model," *Behavioural Science,* 24, 250–262.

Gilpin, Robert (1972) "Has Modern Technology Changed International Politics?" in J.N. Rosenau, V. Davis, and M.A. East (eds.) *The Analysis of International Politics* (New York: Free Press).

Gilpin, Robert (1981) *War and Change in World Politics* (Cambridge: Cambridge University Press).

Girling, John L.S. (1980) *America and the Third World: Revolution and Intervention* (London: Routledge & Kegan Paul).

Glaser, Charles L. (1992) "Political Consequences of Military Strategy. Expanding and Refining the Spiral and Deterrence Models," *World Politics,* 44:4, 497–538.

Gleditsch, Nils Petter and Olav Njøstad (1990) *Arms Races. Technological and Political Dynamics* (London: Sage).

Goldblat, Jozef (1996a) *Arms Control. A Guide to Negotiations and Agreements* (London: Sage).

Goldblat, Jozef (1996b) "Land-mines and Blinding Laser Weapons: The Inhumane Weapons Convention Review Conference," *SIPRI Yearbook: Armaments, Disarmament and International Security* (Oxford: Oxford University Press for the Stockholm International Peace Research Institute), 753–764.

Goldgeier, James and Michael McFaul (1992) "A Tale of Two Worlds: Core and Periphery in the Post–Cold War Era," *International Organization,* 46:2, 467–491.

Golding, Sue (ed.) (1997) *The Eight Technologies of Otherness* (London: Routledge).

Gonchar, Ksenia (1994) "Civil Reconstructions of Military Technology: The U.S. and Russia," *Journal of Peace Research,* 31:2.

Gong, Ro-myung and Gerald Segal (1993) "The Consequences of Arms Proliferation in Asia," in *Asia's International Role in the Post–Cold War Era,* Adelphi Paper 276 (London: International Institute for Strategic Studies).

Goodwin-Gill, Guy S. and Ilene Cohn (1994) *Child Soldiers* (Oxford: Oxford University Press).

Goose, Stephen D. and Frank Smyth (1994) "Arming Genocide in Rwanda: The High Cost of Small Arms Transfers," *Foreign Affairs,* 86–96.

Graham, Norman A. (ed.) (1994) *Seeking Security and Development: The Impact of Military Spending and Arms Transfers* (Boulder, CO: Lynne Rienner Publishers).

Gray, Chris Hables (1997) *Postmodern War. The New Politics of Conflict* (London: Routledge).

Gray, Colin S. (1971a) "The Arms Race Phenomenon," *World Politics*, 24:1, 39–79.

Gray, Colin S. (1971b) "Strategists: Some Critical Views of the Profession," *International Journal*, 26, 771–790.

Gray, Colin S. (1974) "The Urge to Compete: Rationales for Arms Racing," *World Politics*, 26, 207–233.

Gray, Colin S. (1976) *The Soviet-American Arms Race* (Westmead: Saxon House).

Gray, Colin S. (1980) "Strategic Stability Reconsidered," *Daedalus*, 109, 135–154.

Gray, Colin S. (1982a) *Strategic Studies: A Critical Assessment* (London: Aldwych Press).

Gray, Colin S. (1982b) *Strategic Studies and Public Policy: The American Experience* (Lexington: University of Kentucky Press).

Gray, Colin S. (1984) *Nuclear Strategy and Strategic Planning* (Philadelphia: Foreign Policy Research Institute).

Gray, Colin S. (1992) *House of Cards: Why Arms Control Must Fail* (Ithaca: Cornell University Press).

Gray, Colin S. (1993a) *Weapons Don't Make War: Policy, Strategy and Military Technology* (Lawrence: University of Kansas Press).

Gray, Colin S. (1993b), "Through a Missile Tube Darkly: 'New Thinking' About Nuclear Strategy," *Political Studies*, 61:4, 661–671.

Gray, Colin S. (1995) "Book Review: Grant T. Hammond, *Plowshares Into Swords*," *Survival*, 37:1, 177–179.

Gray, Colin S. (1996) "Book Review: Grant T. Hammond, *Plowshares Into Swords*. Arms Races and Other Pathetic Fallacies: A Case for Deconstruction," *Review of International Studies*, 22:3, 323–335.

Gray, Colin S. (1997) *The American Revolution in Military Affairs: An Interim Assessment,* Occasional Paper 28 (Camberley: The Strategic and Combat Studies Institute).

Gray, Colin S. and Keith B. Payne (1980) "Victory is Possible," *Foreign Policy*, 39, 14–28.

Gray, Robert C. (1979) "Learning from History: Case Studies of the Weapons Acquisition Process," *World Politics*, 31, 457–470.

Grobar, L.M. and R.C. Porter (1989) "Benoit Revisited: Defence Spending and Economic Growth in LDCs," *Journal of Conflict Resolution*, 33:2.

Groom, A.J.R. (1988) "Paradigms in Conflict: The Strategist, the Conflict Researcher and the Peace Researcher," *Review of International Studies*, 14:2, 97–116.

Gurtov, Melvin and Byon-Moo Hwang (1980) *China Under Threat* (Baltimore: The Johns Hopkins University Press).

Hagerty, Devin T. (1995–1996) "Nuclear Deterrence in South Asia: The 1990 Indo-Pakistani Crisis," *International Security*, 20:3, 79–114.

Hagerty, Devin T. (1996) "Correspondence: Nuclear Deterrence and the 1990 Indo-Pakistani Crisis," *International Security*, 21:1, 181–185.

Halloran, Richard (1994) "Is Japan a Military Threat to Asia?" *Arms Control Today*, 24:9, 12–17.

Hammond, Grant T. (1993) *Plowshares into Swords: Arms Races in International Politics* (Columbia: University of South Carolina Press).

Handel, Michael (1982) "Does the Dog Wag the Tail or Vice-Versa? Patron–Client Relations," *Jerusalem Journal of International Relations*, 6.

Hardin, Russell (1995) *One for All: The Logic of Group Conflict* (Princeton: Princeton University Press).

Harkavy, R. (1985) "Arms Resupply During Conflict: A Framework for Analysis," *Jerusalem Journal of International Relations*, 7:3, 5–41.

Harris, G., M. Kelly, and Pranowo (1988) "Trade-offs Between Defence and Education and Health Expenditures in Developing Countries," *Journal of Peace Research*, 25:2.

Hartung, William D. (1994) *And Weapons For All. How America's Multibillion-Dollar Arms Trade Warps Our Foreign Policy and Subverts Democracy At Home* (New York: HarperCollins).

Harvard Nuclear Study Group (1983) *Living With Nuclear Weapons* (Cambridge, MA: Harvard University Press).

Harvey, John R. (1992) "Regional Ballistic Missiles and Advanced Strike Aircraft: Comparing Military Effectiveness," *International Security*, 17:2, 41–83.

Herman, Edward S. and Noam Chomsky (1988) *Manufacturing Consent. The Political Economy of the Mass Media* (New York: Pantheon Books).

Herring, Eric (1992) "The Collapse of the Soviet Union: The Implications for World Politics," in John Baylis and N.J. Rengger (eds.) *Dilemmas of World Politics. International Issues in a Changing World* (Oxford: Clarendon Press), 354–383.

Herring, Eric (1995) *Danger and Opportunity. Explaining International Crisis Outcomes* (Manchester: Manchester University Press).

Herring, Eric (1997a) "International Security and Democratisation in Eastern Europe," in Geoffrey Pridham, Eric Herring, and George Sanford (eds.) *Building Democracy? The International Dimension of Democratisation in Eastern Europe* (Leicester: Leicester University Press), revised edition, 81–109.

Herring, Eric (1997b) "The Uneven Killing Field: The Manufacture of Consent for the Arms Embargo on Bosnia–Hercegovina," in Malcolm Evans (ed.) *Aspects of Statehood and Institutionalism in Contemporary Europe* (Dartmouth: Dartmouth Press), 159–182.

Herwig, Holger H. (1980) *Luxury Fleet: The Imperial German Navy 1888–1918* (London: Allen & Unwin).

Herz, John H. (1950) "Idealist Internationalism and the Security Dilemma," *World Politics*, 2, 157–180.

Herz, John H. (1957) "The Rise and Demise of the Territorial State," *World Politics*, 9, 473–493.

Hoag, Malcolm W. (1962) "On Stability in Deterrent Races," in Morton A. Kaplan (ed.) *The Revolution in World Politics* (New York: John Wiley).

Holloway, David (1983) *The Soviet Union and the Arms Race* (New Haven: Yale University Press).

Holsti, Kalevi J. (1996) *The State, War, and the State of War* (Cambridge: Cambridge University Press).

Hook, Glenn (1984) "The Nuclearization of Language: Nuclear Allergy as Political Metaphor," *The Journal of Peace Research*, 21, 259–275.

Hopf, Ted (1991) "Polarity, the Offense–Defense Balance, and War," *American Political Science Review*, 85:2, 475–493.

Horowitz, Irving Louis (1996) *Taking Lives. Genocide and State Power* (New York: Transaction).

Howard, Michael (1976a) "The Strategic Approach to International Relations," *British Journal of International Studies*, 2, 67–75.

Howard, Michael (1976b) *War in European History* (Oxford: Oxford University Press).

Howard, Michael (1983) *The Causes of Wars* (London: Counterpoint).

Howard, Michael (1985) *Is Arms Control Really Necessary?* (London: Council for Arms Control).

Howlett, Darryl and John Simpson (1993) "Nuclearisation and Denuclearisation in South Africa," *Survival*, 35:3, 154–173.

Human Rights Watch (1995a) *Human Rights Watch World Report 1996. Events of 1995* (New York: Human Rights Watch).

Human Rights Watch (1995b) *Slaughter Among Neighbors. The Political Origins of Communal Violence* (New Haven: Yale University Press).

Humphreys, Leonard A. (1995) *The Way of the Heavenly Sword: The Japanese Army in the 1920s* (Stanford, CA: Stanford University Press).

Huntington, Samuel P. (1958) "Arms Races: Prerequisites and Results," *Public Policy*, 8, 1–87.

Huntington, Samuel P. (1983–1984) "Conventional Deterrence and Conventional Retaliation in Europe," *International Security*, 8:3, 32–56.

Huntington, Samuel P. (1991) *The Third Wave. Democratization in the Late Twentieth Century* (Norman: University of Oklahoma Press).

Hussain, Farooq (1981) *The Future of Arms Control. Part IV: The Impact of Weapons Test Restrictions*, Adelphi Paper 165 (London: International Institute for Strategic Studies).

Huth, Paul (1988) *Extended Deterrence and the Prevention of War* (New Haven: Yale University Press).

Huth, Paul (1993) "General Deterrence Between Enduring Rivals: Testing Three Competing Models," *American Political Science Review*, 87:1, 61–73.

Huth, Paul and Bruce Russett (1984) "What Makes Deterrence Work? Cases From 1900 to 1980," *World Politics*, 36:4, 496–526.

Ikegami-Andersson, Masako (1992) *The Military-Industrial Complex. The Cases of Sweden and Japan* (Dartmouth: Dartmouth Press).

Inbar, Efraim and Shmuel Sandler (eds.) (1995a) "The Changing Israeli Security Equation: Toward a Security Regime," *Review of International Studies*, 21:1, 41–59.

Inbar, Efraim and Shmuel Sandler (eds.) (1995b) *Middle East Security: Prospects for an Arms Control Regime* (London: Frank Cass).

Inbar, Efraim and Gabriel Sheffer (eds.) (1997) *The National Security of Small States in a Changing World* (London: Frank Cass).

IPPNW (1991). (International Physicians for the Prevention of Nuclear War) *Radioactive Heaven and Earth* (London: Zed).

Jabri, Vivienne (1996) *Discourses on Violence: Conflict Analysis Reconsidered* (Manchester: Manchester University Press).

Jackson, Robert H. (1990) *Quasi-States: Sovereignty, International Relations, and the Third World* (Cambridge: Cambridge University Press).

Jahn, Egbert (1975) "The Role of the Armaments Complex in Soviet Society," *Journal of Peace Research*, 12, 179–194.

Jakobsen, Peter Viggo (forthcoming) *Western Use of Coercive Diplomacy After the Cold War: A Challenge for Theory and Practice* (London: Macmillan).

Jasani, Bhupendra and Frank Barnaby (1984) *Verification Technologies: The Case for Surveillance by Consent* (Leamington Spa: Berg).

Jervis, Robert (1976) *Perception and Misperception in International Politics* (Princeton: Princeton University Press).

Jervis, Robert (1978) "Cooperation Under the Security Dilemma," *World Politics*, 30:2, 167–214.

Jervis, Robert (1979–1980) "Why Nuclear Superiority Doesn't Matter," *Political Science Quarterly*, 94, 617–633.

Jervis, Robert (1982) "Security Regimes," *International Organization*, 36:2, 357–378.

Jervis, Robert (1985) "From Balance to Concert: A Study of International Security Cooperation," *World Politics*, 38:1, 58–79.

Jervis, Robert (1988) "The Political Effects of Nuclear Weapons: A Comment," *International Security*, 13:2, 80–90.

Jervis, Robert (1989) *The Meaning of the Nuclear Revolution: Statecraft and the Prospect of Armaggedon* (Ithaca: Cornell University Press).

Jervis, Robert, Richard Ned Lebow, and Janice Gross Stein (1985) *Psychology and Deterrence* (Baltimore: The Johns Hopkins University Press). With contributions by Patrick M. Morgan and Jack L. Snyder.

Johnson, A.R. (1973) "Yugoslavia's Total National Defence," *Survival*, 15, 54–58.

Johnston, Alastair Iain (1995–1996) "China's New 'Old Thinking': The Concept of Limited Deterrence," *International Security*, 20:3, 5–42.

Jolly, Richard (ed.) (1978) *Disarmament and World Development* (Oxford: Pergamon).

Jones, Ian and G. Wyn Rees (1994) "Britain and Post–Cold War Arms Transfers," *Contemporary Security Policy*, 15:1, 109–126.

Kacowicz, Arie Marcelo (1994) *Peaceful Territorial Change* (Columbia: University of South Carolina Press).

Kaldor, Mary (1980) "Disarmament: The Armament Process in Reverse," in E.P. Thompson and Dan Smith (eds.) *Protest and Survive* (Harmondsworth: Penguin).

Kaldor, Mary (1982) *The Baroque Arsenal* (London: André Deutsch).

Kaldor, Mary (1985) "The Concept of Common Security," in *Policies for Common Security* (London: Taylor & Francis for the Stockholm International Peace Research Institute).

Kaldor, Mary (1990) *The Imaginary War: Understanding the East–West Conflict* (Oxford: Blackwell).

Kaldor, Mary and Asbjørn Eide (eds.) (1979) *The World Military Order* (London: Macmillan).

Kaplan, Fred (1983) *The Wizards of Armageddon* (New York: Touchstone).

Kaplan, Robert S. (1994) "The Coming Anarchy," *Atlantic Monthly*, 273:2, 44–76.

Kaplan, Stephen S. (1981) *Diplomacy of Power. Soviet Armed Forces as a Political Instrument* (Washington, DC: The Brookings Institution).

Kapstein, Ethan B. (1991–1992) "International Collaboration in Arms Production," *Political Science Quarterly*, 106:4.

Kapstein, Ethan (ed.) (1992) *Global Arms Production: Policy Dilemmas for the 1990s* (Lanham, MD: University Press of America).

Kapur, Ashok (1987) *Pakistan's Nuclear Development* (London: Croom Helm).

Karl, David J. (1996–1997) "Proliferation Pessimism and Emerging Nuclear Powers," *International Security*, 21:3, 87–119.

Karp, Aaron (1990) "Controlling Ballistic Missile Proliferation," *Survival*, 33:6, 517–530.

Karp, Aaron (1996) *Ballistic Missile Proliferation. The Politics and Technics* (Oxford: Oxford University Press for the Stockholm International Peace Research Institute).

Karp, Regina Cowen (ed.) (1991) *Security With Nuclear Weapons? Different Perspectives on National Security* (Oxford: Oxford University Press for the Stockholm International Peace Research Institute).

Karp, Regina Cowen (ed.) (1992) *Security Without Nuclear Weapons? Different Perspectives on Non-Nuclear Security* (Oxford: Oxford University Press for the Stockholm International Peace Research Institute).

Katz, James Everett (ed.) (1986) *The Implications of Third World Military Industrialization. Sowing the Serpents Teeth* (Lexington, MA: Lexington Books).

Katzenstein, Peter (ed.) (1996) *The Culture of National Security: Norms and Identity in World Politics* (New York: Columbia University Press).

Katzenstein, Peter J. and Nobuo Okawara (1993) "Japan's National Security: Structures, Norms, Policies," *International Security,* 17:4, 84–118.

Kaufman, Stuart J. (1996) "Spiraling to Ethnic War: Elites, Masses and Moscow in Moldova's Civil War," *International Security*, 21:2, 108–138.

Kaufmann, Chaim (1996) "Possible and Impossible Solutions to Ethnic Civil Wars," *International Security*, 20:4, 136–175.

Keane, John (1996) *Reflections on Violence* (London: Verso).

Keeley, Lawrence H. (1996) *War Before Civilization* (Oxford: Oxford University Press).

Kellner, Douglas (1992) *The Persian Gulf TV War* (Boulder, CO: Westview Press).

Kennedy, Gavin (1974) *The Military in the Third World* (London: Duckworth).

Kennedy, Gavin (1983) *Defence Economics* (London: Duckworth).

Kennedy, Helena (1992) *Eve Was Framed: Women and British Law* (London: Vintage).

Kennedy, Paul (1980) *The Rise of the Anglo-German Antagonism 1860–1914* (London: Allen & Unwin).

Keohane, Robert and J.S. Nye ([1977] 1989) *Power and Interdependence: World Politics in Transition* (Boston: Little, Brown), second edition.

Kier, Elizabeth (1997) *Imagining War. French and British Military Doctrine Between the Wars* (Princeton: Princeton University Press).

Kier, Elizabeth and Jonathan Mercer (1996) "Setting Precedents in Anarchy: Military Intervention and Weapons of Mass Destruction," *International Security*, 20:4, 77–106.

Kiernan, V.G. (1995) *Imperialism and Its Contradictions* (London: Routledge). Edited and introduced by Harvey J. Kaye.

King, Charles (1997) *Ending Civil Wars*, Adelphi Paper 308 (Oxford: Oxford University Press for the International Institute for Strategic Studies).

Kiss, Judit (1996) *The Defence Industry in East-Central Europe. Restructuring and Conversion* (Oxford: Oxford University Press for the Stockholm International Peace Research Institute).

Klare, Michael T. (1977) *Supplying Repression* (New York: Field Foundation).

Klare, Michael T. (1983) "The Unnoticed Arms Trade: Exports of Convention Arms-Making Technology," *International Security*, 8, 68–90.

Klare, Michael T. (1993) "The Next Great Arms Race," *Foreign Affairs*.

Klare, Michael T. and Cynthia Arnson (1979) "Exporting Repression: U.S. Support for Authoritarianism in Latin America," in Richard Fagen (ed.) *Capitalism and the State in U.S. Latin-American Relations*. (Stanford: Stanford University Press).

Klein, Bradley S. (1994) *Strategic Studies and World Order: The Global Politics of Deterrence* (Cambridge: Cambridge University Press).

Knightly, Philip (1975) *The First Casualty* (New York: Harcourt Brace Jovanovich).

Kofsky, Frank (1995) *Harry S. Truman and the War Scare of 1948: A Successful Campaign to Deceive the Nation* (New York: St. Martin's Press).

Koistinen, Paul A.C. (1980) *The Military-Industrial Complex: An Historical Perspective* (New York: Praeger).

Kokoski, Richard (1994) "Non-Lethal Weapons: A Case Study of New Technology Developments," in *SIPRI Yearbook 1994* (Oxford: Oxford University Press for the Stockholm International Peace Research Institute), 367–386.

Kokoski, Richard (1996) *Technology and the Proliferation of Nuclear Weapons* (Oxford: Oxford University Press for the Stockholm International Peace Research Institute).

Kolodziej, Edward A. (1987) *Making and Marketing Arms: The French Experience and its Implications for the International System* (Princeton: Princeton University Press).

Kotz, Nick (1988) *Wild Blue Yonder: Money, Politics and the B-1 Bomber* (Princeton: Princeton University Press).

Kramer, Mark (1992) "The Global Arms Trade After the Persian Gulf War," *Security Studies*, 2:2.

Krass, A. (1985) "The Death of Deterrence," in *Policies for Common Security* (London: Taylor & Francis for the Stockholm International Peace Research Institute).

Krause, Keith (1992) *Arms and the State. Patterns of Military Production and Trade* (Cambridge: Cambridge University Press).

Krause, Keith and Michael C. Williams (eds.) (1997) *Critical Security Studies. Concepts and Cases* (London: UCL Press).

Krippendorff, Ekkehart (1981) "The Victims—A Research Failure," *Journal of Peace Research*, 18:1, 97–101.

Kugler, Jacek, A.F.K. Organski, and Daniel Fox (1980) "Deterrence and the Arms Race: The Impotence of Power," *International Security*, 4, 105–138.

Kull, Steven (1988) *Minds at War: Nuclear Reality and the Inner Conflicts of Defense Policy-makers* (New York: Basic Books).

Lambelet, J.C. (1975) "Do Arms Races Lead to War?" *Journal of Peace Research*, 12, 123–128.

Landes, David S. (1969) *The Unbound Prometheus* (Cambridge: Cambridge University Press).

Landi, Dale H., Bruno W. Augenstein, Collen M. Crain, William R. Harris, and Brian M. Jenkins (1984) "Improving the Means for Intergovernmental Communications in Crisis," *Survival*, 26, 200–214.

Langford, David (1979) *War in 2080: The Future of Military Technology* (Newton Abbott: Westbridge Books).

Lasswell, Daniel Lerner and Hans Speier (eds.) (1979) *Propaganda and Communication in World History* (Honolulu: University Press of Hawaii for the East–West Center), three vols.

Layne, Christopher (1994) "Kant or Cant: The Myth of the Democratic Peace," *International Security*, 19:2, 5–49.

Lebow, Richard Ned (1981) *Between Peace and War. The Nature of International Crisis* (Baltimore: The Johns Hopkins University Press).

Lebow, Richard Ned (1984) "Windows of Opportunity: Do States Jump Through Them?" *International Security*, 98:3, 431–458.

Lebow, Richard Ned (1987a) "Conventional and Nuclear Deterrence: Are the Lessons Transferable?" *Journal of Social Issues*, 43:4, 171–191.

Lebow, Richard Ned (1987b) "Deterrence Failure Revisited," *International Security*, 12:1, 197–213.

Lebow, Richard Ned (1989) "Deterrence: A Political and Psychological Critique," in Paul Stern, Robert Axelrod, Robert Jervis, and Roy Radner (eds.) *Perspectives on Deterrence* (New York: Oxford University Press), 25–51.

Lebow, Richard Ned and Janice Gross Stein (1990a) "Deterrence: The Elusive Dependent Variable," *World Politics*, 42:3, 336–369.

Lebow, Richard Ned and Janice Gross Stein (1990b) *When Does Deterrence Succeed and How Do We Know?* (Ottawa: Canadian Institute for International Peace and Security).

Lebow, Richard Ned and Janice Gross Stein (1994) *We All Lost the Cold War* (Princeton: Princeton University Press).

Leitner, Peter M. (1995) *Decontrolling Strategic Technology, 1990–92. Creating the Military Threats of the 21st Century* (Lanham, MD: University Press of America).

Leng, Russell J. (1983) "When Will They Ever Learn: Coercive Bargaining in Recurrent Crises," *Journal of Conflict Resolution*, 27:3, 379–419.

Levi, Barbara, Frank N. von Hippel, and William H. Daugherty (1987–1988) "Civilian Casualties from 'Limited' Nuclear Attacks on the Soviet Union," *International Security*, 17:3, 168–189.

Levy, Jack S. (1984) "The Offensive/Defensive Balance of Military Technology: A Theoretical and Historical Analysis," *International Studies Quarterly*, 28:2, 219–238.

Levy, Jack S. (1985) "Theories of General War," *World Politics*, 17, 344–374.

Levy, Jack S. (1988) "Review Article: When do Deterrent Threats Work?" *British Journal of Political Science*, 18:4, 485–512.

Levy, Jack S. (1989) "Quantitative Studies of Deterrence Success and Failure," in Paul Stern, Robert Axelrod, Robert Jervis, and Roy Radner (eds.) *Perspectives on Deterrence* (New York: Oxford University Press), 98–133.

Lewis, John Wilson and Hua Di (1992) "China's Ballistic Missile Programs: Technologies, Strategies, Goals," *International Security*, 17:2, 5–40.

Liddell Hart, Basil Henry. (1967) *Decisive Wars of History* (New York: Praeger), second edition.

Lifton, Robert Jay and Eric Markusen (1990) *The Genocidal Mentality. Nazi Holocaust and Nuclear Threat* (New York: Basic Books).

Lindsay, James M. (1991) *Congress and Nuclear Weapons* (Baltimore: The Johns Hopkins University Press).

Looney, Robert (1995) *Third World Military Expenditure and Arms Production* (Basingstoke: Macmillan).

Lucas, Michael (1985) "West Germany: Can Arms Save the Export Giant?" *ADIU Report*, 7, 1–5.

Luckham, Robin (1977a) "Militarism: Arms and the Internationalization of Capital," *IDS Bulletin*, 8, 38–50.

Luckham, Robin (1977b) "Militarism: Force, Class and International Conflict," *IDS Bulletin*, 9, 19–29.

Lumpe, Lora (1995) "Clinton's Conventional Arms Export Policy: So Little Change," *Arms Control Today*, 25: 4, 9–14.

Lundin, S.J. (ed.) (1991) *Verification of Dual-Use Chemicals Under the Chemical Weapons Convention. The Case of Thiodiglycol* (Oxford: Oxford University Press for the Stockholm International Peace Research Institute).

Luterbacher, U. (1975) "Arms Race Models: Where Do We Stand?" *European Journal of Political Research*, 3, 199–217.

Luttwak, Edward (1980a) "The Problem of Extending Deterrence," in *The Future of Strategic Deterrence: Part 1*, Adelphi Paper 160 (London: International Institute for Strategic Studies).

Luttwak, Edward (1980b) *Strategy and Politics* (New Brunswick, NJ: Transaction Books).

Lynne-Jones, Sean M. (1995) "Offense–Defense Theory and Its Critics," *Security Studies*, 4:4, 660–691.

MacArthur, John R. (1993) *Second Front. Censorship and Propaganda in the Gulf War* (Berkeley: University of California Press).

MacKenzie, Donald (1990) *Inventing Accuracy: A Historical Sociology of Nuclear Missile Guidance* (Cambridge, MA: The Massachusetts Institute of Technology Press).

MacKenzie, Donald (1996) *Knowing Machines. Essays on Technical Change* (Cambridge, MA: The Massachusetts Institute of Technology Press).

Macmillan, John (1996) "Democracies Don't Fight: A Case of the Wrong Research Agenda?" *Review of International Studies*, 22:3, 275–299.

Mandelbaum, Michael (1981) *The Nuclear Revolution: International Politics Before and After Hiroshima* (Cambridge: Cambridge University Press).

Mandelbaum, Michael (1994) "The Reluctance to Intervene," *Foreign Policy*, 3–18.

Mann, Michael (1986) *The Sources of Social Power.* Vol. 1: *A History of Power from the Beginning to AD 1760* (Cambridge: Cambridge University Press).

Mansfield, Edward D. and Jack Snyder (1995) "Democratization and the Danger of War," *International Security*, 20:1, 5–38.

Maoz, Zeev (1983) "Resolve, Capabilities, and the Outcomes of International Disputes, 1816–1976," *Journal of Conflict Resolution*, 27:2, 195–228.

Maoz, Zeev (1989) *Paradoxes of War: On the Art of National Self-Entrapment* (Boston: Unwin Hyman).

Maoz, Zeev (1997) "The Controversy over the Democratic Peace: Rearguard Action or Cracks in the Wall?" *International Security*, 22:1, 162–198.

Maoz, Zeev (forthcoming) "Realist and Cultural Critiques of the Democratic Peace: A Theoretical and Empirical Re-Assessment," *International Interactions*.

Marder, A.J. (1961) *From the Dreadnought to Scapa Flow*, 1 (Oxford: Oxford University Press).

Marshall, Peter M. (1992) *Demanding the Impossible: A History of Anarchism* (London: HarperCollins).

Martin, Luther, Huck Gutman, and Patrick H. Hutton (eds.) (1988) *Technologies of the Self* (London: Tavistock).

Marwah, Onkar (1977) "India's Nuclear and Space Programme," *International Security*, 2, 96–121.

Matthews, Ron and Keisuke Matsuyama (eds.) (1993) *Japan's Military Renaissance?* (London: Macmillan).

Mayall, James (ed.) (1997) *The New Interventionism 1991–1994. United Nations Experience in Cambodia, Former Yugoslavia and Somalia* (Cambridge: Cambridge University Press).

Mayer, Kenneth R. (1991) *The Political Economy of Defense Contracting* (New Haven: Yale University Press).

Mazarr, Michael J. (1995a) *North Korea and the Bomb: A Case Study in Nonproliferation* (New York: St. Martin's Press).

Mazarr, Michael J. (1995b) "Virtual Nuclear Arsenals," *Survival*, 37:3, 7–26.

Mazrui, Ali (1977) "Soldiers as Traditionalizers: Military Rule and the Re-Africanization of Africa," in Ali Mazrui (ed.) *The Warrior Tradition in Modern Africa* (Leiden: E.J. Brill), 236–258.

McCalla, Robert B. (1992) *Uncertain Perceptions. U.S. Cold War Crisis Decision Making* (Ann Arbor: The University of Michigan Press).

McCausland, Jeffrey D. (1996) *Conventional Arms Control and European Security*, Adelphi Paper 301 (Oxford: Oxford University Press for the International Institute for Strategic Studies).

MccGwire, Michael (1984) "The Dilemmas and Delusions of Deterrence," in Gwyn Prins (ed.) *The Choice: Nuclear Weapons Versus Security* (London: Chatto & Windus, Hogarth), 75–97.

MccGwire, Michael (1987) *Military Objectives in Soviet Foreign Policy* (Washington, DC: The Brookings Institution).

MccGwire, Michael (1991) *Perestroika and Soviet National Security* (Washington, DC: The Brookings Institution).

MccGwire, Michael (1994) "Is There a Future for Nuclear Weapons?" *International Affairs*, 70:2, 211–228.

McInnes, Colin (1993) "Has War a Future?" (review article)," *Arms Control*, 14:3, 450–458.

McKinlay, R.D. and A.S. Cohan (1975) "A Comparative Analysis of the Political and Economic Performance of Military and Civil Regimes," *Comparative Politics*, 8, 1–30.

McKinlay, R.D. and A. Mughan (1984) *Aid and Arms to the Third World* (London: Frances Pinter).

McNeill, William H. (1982) *The Pursuit of Power* (Chicago: University of Chicago Press).

McSweeney, Bill (1996) "Identity and Security: Buzan and the Copenhagen School," *Review of International Studies*, 22:1, 81–93

Mearsheimer, John J. (1986) "A Strategic Misstep: The Maritime Strategy and Deterrence in Europe," *International Security*, 11:2, 3–57.

Melman, Seymour (1985) *The Permanent War Economy: American Capitalism in Decline* (New York: Simon & Schuster), revised and updated edition.

Melman, Seymour (1988) *The Demilitarized Society: Disarmament and Conversion* (Montreal: Harvest House Ltd.).

Military Balance (London: International Institute for Strategic Studies, annually since 1958).

Milner, Helen V. (1991) "The Assumption of Anarchy in International Relations Theory: A Critique," *Review of International Studies*, 17:1, 67–85.

Minear, Larry, Colin Scott, and Thomas G. Weiss (1996) *The News Media, Civil War, and Humanitarian Action* (Boulder, CO: Lynne Rienner Publishers).

Mintz, Alex and Steve Chan (eds.) (1992) *Defence, Welfare and Growth* (London: Routledge).

Møller, Bjørn (1991) *Resolving the Security Dilemma in Europe: The German Debate on Non-Offensive Defence* (London: Brassey's).

Møller, Bjørn (1992) *Common Security and Non-Offensive Defence: A Neorealist Perspective* (Boulder, CO: Lynne Rienner Publishers).

Møller, Bjørn (1995a) *Dictionary of Alternative Defense* (Boulder, CO: Lynne Rienner Publishers).

Møller, Bjørn (1995b) "Non-Offensive Defence and the Korean Peninsula," *Working Papers 4* (Copenhagen: Centre for Peace and Conflict Research).

Møller, Bjørn (1995c) "Common Security and Non-Offensive Defence: Are They Relevant for the Korean Peninsula?" *Working Papers 7* (Copenhagen: Centre for Peace and Conflict Research).

Møller, Bjørn (1995d) "A Common Security and NOD Regime for the Asia-Pacific?" *Working Papers 8* (Copenhagen: Centre for Peace and Conflict Research).

Møller, Bjørn (1996a) "A Common Security and NOD Regime for South Asia," *Working Papers 4* (Copenhagen: Centre for Peace and Conflict Research).

Møller, Bjørn (1996b) "UN Military Demands and Non-Offensive Defence," *Working Papers 7* (Copenhagen: Centre for Peace and Conflict Research).

Møller, Bjørn (1996c) "The Unification of Divided States and Defensive Restructuring: China–Taiwan in a Comparative Perspective," *Working Papers 9* (Copenhagen: Centre for Peace and Conflict Research).

Møller, Bjørn and Lev Voronkov (1997) *Defence Doctrines and Conversion* (Dartmouth: Dartmouth Press).

Møller, Bjørn and Håkan Wiberg (1994) *Non-Offensive Defence for the Twenty-First Century* (Boulder, CO: Westview Press).

Momoi, Makato (1981) "Strategic Thinking in Japan in the 1970s and 1980s," in Robert O'Neill and D.M. Horner (eds.) *New Directions in Strategic Thinking* (London: Allen & Unwin).

Moon, John Ellis van Courtland (1984) "Chemical Weapons and Deterrence: The World War II Experience," *International Security*, 8:4, 3–35.

Moran, Theodore H. (1990) "The Globalization of America's Defense Industries: Managing the Threat of Foreign Dependence," *International Security*, 15:1, 57–99.

Morgan, Patrick M. (1983) *Deterrence. A Conceptual Analysis* (London: Sage), second edition.

Morgenthau, Hans J. (1976) "The Fallacy of Thinking Conventionally About Nuclear Weapons," in David Carlton and Carlo Schaerf (eds.) *Arms Control and Technological Innovation* (New York: Wiley and Sons), 255–264.

Mueller, John (1988) "The Essential Irrelevance of Nuclear Weapons," *International Security*, 13:2, 55–79.

Mueller, John (1989) *Retreat from Doomsday: The Obsolescence of Major War* (New York: Basic Books).

Mueller, John (1994) *Policy and Opinion in the Gulf War* (Chicago: The University of Chicago Press).

Mullin, Jr., A.F. (1987) *Born Arming. Development and Military Power in New States* (Stanford: Stanford University Press).

Mussington, David (1994) *Understanding Contemporary International Arms Transfers*, Adelphi Paper 291 (Oxford: Oxford University Press for the International Institute for Strategic Studies).

Myrdal, Alma (1976) *The Game of Disarmament: How the United States and Russia Run the Arms Race* (New York: Random House).

Nachmias, Nitza (1988) *Transfer of Arms, Leverage, and Peace in the Middle East* (New York: Greenwood Press).

Nacht, Michael (1975) "The Delicate Balance of Error," *Foreign Policy*, 22, 163–177.

Neuman, Stephanie G. (1984) "International Stratification and Third World Military Industries," *International Organization*, 38, 167–197.

Neuman, Stephanie G. (1988) "Arms, Aid and the Superpowers," *Foreign Affairs*, 66:5.

Neuman, Stephanie G. and Robert E. Harkavy (1980) *Arms Transfers in the Modern World* (New York: Praeger).

Neuman, Stephanie G. and Robert E. Harkavy (eds.) (1985). *The Lessons of Recent Wars in the Third World*. Vol. II: *Comparative Dimensions* (Lexington, MA: D.C. Heath), 53–72.

Nincic, Miroslav (1982) *The Arms Race: The Political Economy of Military Growth* (New York: Praeger).

Nixon, Richard (1978) *The Memoirs of Richard Nixon* (London: Arrow).

Noel-Baker, Philip (1936) *The Private Manufacture of Armaments* (London: Gollancz).

Noel-Baker, Philip (1958) *The Arms Race: A Programme for World Disarmament* (London: John Calder).

Nuttall, Chris (1996) "Inmates Tortured, Say Jail Doctors," *The Guardian*, 7 August.

O'Kane, Maggie (1996) "The Wake of War," *The Guardian Weekend*, 18 May.

O'Kane, Rosemary H.T. (1996) *Terror, Force and States. The Path From Modernity* (Cheltenham: Edward Elgar).

Oneal, John, Frances Oneal, Zeev Maoz, and Bruce Russett (1996) "The Liberal Peace: Interdependence, Democracy and International Conflict," *Journal of Peace Research*, 33:1, 11–28.

Oren, Ido (1994) "The Indo-Pakistani Arms Competition: A Deductive and Statistical Analysis," *Journal of Conflict Resolution*, 38:2.

Oren, Ido (1995) "The Subjectivity of the 'Democratic Peace': Changing U.S. Perceptions of Imperial Germany," *International Security*, 20:2, 147–184.

Organski, A.F.K. and Jacek Kugler (1977) "The Costs of Major Wars: The Phoenix Factor," *American Political Science Review*, 71, 1347–1366.

Osgood, Robert E. and Robert W. Tucker (1967) *Force, Order, and Justice* (Baltimore: The Johns Hopkins University Press).

O'Shaughnessy, Hugh (1995) "UK To Arm Guatemala Regime of Terror," *The Guardian*, 13 October.

Owen, John M. (1994) "How Liberalism Produces Democratic Peace," *International Security*, 19:2, 87–125.

Palin, Roger H. (1995) *Multinational Military Forces: Problems and Prospects*, Adelphi Paper 294 (Oxford: Oxford University Press for the International Institute for Strategic Studies).

Pape, Robert A. (1996) *Bombing to Win. Air Power and Coercion in War* (Ithaca: Cornell University Press).

Patterns of Global Terrorism 1996 (1997) (Washington, DC: U.S. Department of State) http://www.state.gov/www/global/terrorism/1996report/

Paul, T.V. (1994) *Asymmetric Conflicts: War Initiation by Weaker Powers* (Cambridge: Cambridge University Press).

Payne, James L. (1970), *The American Threat: The Fear of War as an Instrument of Foreign Policy* (Chicago: Markham).

Pearson, Frederic (1994) *The Global Spread of Arms* (Boulder, CO: Westview).

Pearson, Frederic S., Michael Brzoska, and Christer Crantz (1992) "The Effects of Arms Transfers on Wars and Peace Negotiations," in *SIPRI Yearbook 1992: World Armaments and Disarmament* (Oxford: Oxford University Press for SIPRI), 399–415.

Pearton, Maurice (1982) *The Knowledgeable State: Diplomacy, War and Technology Since 1830* (London: Burnett Books).

Pedelty, Mark (1995) *War Stories. The Culture of Foreign Correspondents* (London: Routledge).

Perrin, Noel (1979) *Giving Up the Gun: Japan's Reversion to the Sword, 1543–1879* (Boston: D.R. Godine).

Pick, Daniel (1993) *War Machine. The Rationalisation of Slaughter in the Modern Age* (New Haven: Yale University Press).

Pierre, Andrew J. (1982) *The Global Politics of Arms Sales* (Princeton: Princeton University Press).

Pierre, Andrew J. (ed.) (1986) *The Conventional Defense of Europe: New Technologies and New Strategies* (New York: Council on Foreign Relations).

Pilger, John (1989) *Heroes* (London: Pan Books), revised edition.

Pilger, John (1992) *A Secret Country* (London: Vintage), updated edition.

Posen, Barry R. (1992) "Crisis Stability and Conventional Arms Control," in Emanuel Adler (ed.) *The International Practice of Arms Control* (Baltimore: The Johns Hopkins University Press), 231–246.

Posen, Barry R. (1993) "The Security Dilemma and Ethnic Conflict," *Survival*, 35:1, 27–47.

Potter, William C. and Harlan W. Jencks (1994) *The International Missile Bazaar: The New Suppliers' Network* (Boulder, CO: Westview Press).

Powell, Walter W. and Paul J. DiMaggio (eds.) (1991) *The New Institutionalism in Organizational Analysis* (Chicago: Chicago University Press).

Prados, John (1986) *The Soviet Estimate. U.S. Intelligence Analysis and Soviet Strategic Forces* (Princeton: Princeton University Press).

Price, Richard (1994) "Interpretation and Disciplinary Orthodoxy in International Relations," *Review of International Studies*, 20:2, 201–204.

Price, Richard (1997) *The Chemical Weapons Taboo* (Ithaca: Cornell University Press).

Price, Richard and Nina Tannenwald (1996) "Norms and Deterrence: The Nuclear and Chemical Weapons Taboos," in Peter J. Katzenstein (ed.) *The Culture of National Security. Norms and Identity in World Politics* (New York: Columbia University Press), 114–152.

Prins, Gwyn (ed.) (1984) *The Choice: Nuclear Weapons Versus Security* (London: Chatto & Windus).

Prokosch, Eric (1995) *The Technology of Killing. A Military and Political History of Antipersonnel Weapons* (London: Zed Books).

Prunier, Gérard (1995) *The Rwanda Crisis: History of Genocide* (New York: Columbia University Press).

Pugh, Michael (1997) (ed.) *The UN, Peace and Force* (London: Frank Cass).

Quester, George H. (1966) *Deterrence Before Hiroshima: The Airpower Background of Modern Strategy* (New York: John Wiley).

Quester, George H. (1977) *Offense and Defense in the International System* (New York: John Wiley).

Ramberg, Bennett (ed.) (1993) *Arms Control Without Negotiation: From the Cold War to the New World Order* (Boulder, CO: Lynne Rienner Publishers).

Ramsbotham, Oliver and Tom Woodhouse (1996) *Humanitarian Intervention in Contemporary Conflict* (Cambridge: Polity Press).

Randle, Michael (1994) *Civil Resistance* (London: Fontana).

Rathjens, George W. (1973) "The Dynamics of the Arms Race," in Herbert York (ed.) *Arms Control* (San Francisco: Freeman).

Rattinger, Hans (1976) "From War to War: Arms Races in the Middle East," *International Studies Quarterly,* 20, 501–531.

Raudzens, George (1990) "War-Winning Weapons: The Measurement of Technological Determinism in Military History," *Journal of Military History*, 54, 403–433.

Ray, James Lee (1995) *Democracy and International Conflict* (Columbia: University of South Carolina Press).

Redick, John (1988) "Nuclear Restraint in Latin America: Argentina and Brazil," *PPNN*, 1.

Redick, John (1990) "Argentina and Brazil: An Evolving Nuclear Relationship," *PPNN*, 7.

Reiss, Mitchell (1995) *Bridled Ambition. Why Countries Constrain Their Nuclear Capabilities* (Washington, DC: Woodrow Wilson Center Press).

Reiter, Dan (1995) "Exploding the Powder Keg Myth: Preemptive Wars Almost Never Happen," *International Security*, 20:2, 5–34.

Renner, Michael (1992) *Economic Adjustments After the Cold War. Strategies for Conversion* (Dartmouth: Dartmouth Press).

Report of the Independent Commission on Disarmament and Security Issues (1982) *Common Security: A Programme for Disarmament* (London: Pan Books).

Report of the Secretary General (1977) *Economic and Social Consequences of the Armaments Race* (New York: United Nations General Assembly), A/132188, 12 August.

Report of the Secretary General (1985) *Study on the Concepts of Security* (New York: United Nations General Assembly), A/401553, 26 August.

Reppy, Judith (1990) "Review Essay: The Technological Imperative in Strategic Thought," *Journal of Peace Research*, 27:1, 101–106.

Reuters (1990) "UN Fears Iraq is Hiding Chemicals," *The Guardian*, 13 May.

Rhodes, Edward (1994) "Do Bureaucratic Politics Matter? Some Disconfirming Findings From the Case of the U.S. Navy," *World Politics*, 47:1.

Richardson, James L. (1994) *Crisis Diplomacy. The Great Powers Since the Mid-Nineteenth Century* (Cambridge: Cambridge University Press).

Richardson, Lewis F. (1960) *Arms and Insecurity* (Pittsburgh: Boxwood Press).

Roberts, Adam (ed.) (1967) *The Strategy of Civilian Defence: Non Violent Resistance to Aggression* (London: Faber & Faber).

Roberts, Adam ([1976] 1986) *Nations in Arms* (London: Chatto & Windus; Basingstoke: Macmillan), second edition.

Roberts, Adam (1994) "The Crisis in UN Peacekeeping," *Survival*, 36:3, 93–120.

Roberts, Adam (1995) "Communal Conflict as a Challenge to International Organization: The Case of Former Yugoslavia," *Review of International Studies*, 21:4, 389–410.

Roberts, Adam (1996) *Humanitarian Action in War*, Adelphi Paper 308 (Oxford: Oxford University Press for the International Institute for Strategic Studies).

Roberts, Brad (1992) *Chemical Disarmament and International Security*, Adelphi Paper 267 (London: Brassey's for the International Institute for Strategic Studies).

Roberts, Shawn and Jody Williams (1995) *After the Guns Fall Silent. The Enduring Legacy of Landmines* (Washington, DC: Vietnam Veterans of America Foundation).

Rogers, Clifford J. (ed.) (1995) *The Military Revolution Debate* (Boulder, CO: Westview Press).

Rose, Margaret A. (1991) *The Post-Modern and the Post-Industrial: A Critical Analysis* (Cambridge: Cambridge University Press).

Rosen, Stephen Peter (1982) "Foreign Policy and Nuclear Weapons: The Case for Strategic Defenses," in Samuel P. Huntington (ed.) *The Strategic Imperative*, 141–161.

Rosen, Steven (ed.) (1973) *Testing the Theory of the Military-Industrial Complex* (Lexington, MA: Lexington Books).

Ross, Andrew L. (1993) "The Dynamics of Military Technology," in David Desitt, David Haglund, and John Kirton (eds.) *Building a New Global Order. Emerging Trends in International Security* (Oxford: Oxford University Press), 106–140.

Rotblat, Joseph, Jack Steinberger, and Bhalchandra Udgaonkar (eds.) (1993) *A Nuclear-Weapon-Free World: Desirable? Feasible?* (Boulder, CO: Westview Press for Pugwash).

Ruggie, John Gerard (1997) "The Past As Prologue? Interests, Identity, and American Foreign Policy," *International Security*, 21:4, 89–125.

Rummel, R.J. (1996) *Death By Government. Genocide and Mass Murder Since 1900* (New York: Transaction).

Rummel, R.J. (1996) *Power Kills. Democracy as a Method of Nonviolence* (New York: Transaction).

Russett, Bruce (1983) *The Prisoners of Insecurity* (San Francisco: Freeman).

Russett, Bruce (1993) *Grasping the Democratic Peace: Principles for a Post–Cold War World* (Princeton: Princeton University Press).

Russett, Bruce (1995) "Correspondence: 'And Yet It Moves,'" *International Security*, 19:4, 164–175.

Russett, Bruce and Zeev Maoz (1993) "Normative and Structural Causes of Democratic Peace," *American Political Science Review*, 87:3.

Russett, Bruce and James Lee Ray (1995) "Raymond Cohen on Pacific Unions: A Response and a Reply. Why the Democratic-Peace Proposition Lives," *Review of International Studies*, 21:3, 319–323.

Saaty, Thomas L. (1968) *Mathematical Models of Arms Control and Disarmament* (New York: John Wiley).

Sabin, Philip (1987) *Shadow or Substance? Perceptions and Symbolism in Nuclear Force Planning*, Adelphi Paper 222 (London: International Institute for Strategic Studies).

Sagan, Scott D. (1993) *The Limits of Safety: Organizations, Accidents and Nuclear Weapons* (Princeton: Princeton University Press).

Sagan, Scott D. (1994) "The Perils of Proliferation: Organization Theory, Deterrence Theory, and the Spread of Nuclear Weapons," *International Security*, 18:4, 66–107.

Sagan, Scott D. (1996–1997) "Why Do States Build Nuclear Weapons? Three Models in Search of a Bomb," *International Security*, 21:3, 54–86.

Sagan, Scott D. and Kenneth N. Waltz (1995) *The Spread of Nuclear Weapons: A Debate* (New York: Norton).

Salmi, Jamil (1993) *Violence and Democratic Society. New Approaches to Human Rights* (London: Zed Books).

Sampson, Anthony (1991) *The Arms Bazaar* (Sevenoaks: Hodder & Stoughton), second edition.

Samuels, Richard J. (1994) *Rich Nation, Strong Army: National Security and the Technological Transformation of Japan* (Ithaca: Cornell University Press).

Sandler, Todd and Keith Hartley (1995) *The Economics of Defence* (Cambridge: Cambridge University Press).

Sarkesian, Sam C. (ed.) (1972) *The Military-Industrial Complex: A Reassessment* (London: Sage).

Sarkesian, Sam C. (1978) "A Political Perspective on Military Power in Developing Areas," in Simon W. Sheldon (ed.) *The Military and Security in the Third World* (Boulder, CO: Westview Press).

Sarup, Madan (1993) *An Introductory Guide to Post-Structuralism and Post-Modernism* (New York: Harvester Wheatsheaf), second edition.

Satoh, Yukio (1982) *The Evolution of Japanese Security Policy*, Adelphi Paper 178 (London: International Institute for Strategic Studies).

Schaerf, Carlo and David Carlton (eds.) (1995) *Transfer of Dual Use Technology* (Dartmouth: Dartmouth Press).

Scheer, Robert (1982) *With Enough Shovels: Reagan, Bush and Nuclear War* (New York: Vintage Books), updated edition.

Scheffran, Jurgen (1995) "Proliferation of Nuclear-Capable Missiles and International Control Measures," in David Carlton, Elena Mirco, and Paul Ingram (eds.) *Controlling the International Transfer of Weaponry and Related Technology* (Aldershot: Dartmouth), 69–88.

Schell, Jonathan (1982) *The Fate of the Earth* (London: Picador).

Schell, Jonathan (1984) *The Abolition* (London: Picador).

Schelling, Thomas ([1960] 1980) *The Strategy of Conflict* (Cambridge, MA: Harvard University Press), second edition.

Schelling, Thomas (1966) *Arms and Influence* (New Haven: Yale University Press).

Schilling, Warner (1981) "U.S. Strategic Nuclear Concepts in the 1970s: The Search for Sufficiently Equivalent Countervailing Parity," in Robert O'Neill and D.M. Horner (eds.) *New Directions in Strategic Thinking* (London: Allen & Unwin).

Schweller, Randall L. (1994) "Bandwagoning for Profit: Bringing the Revisionist State Back In," *International Security*, 19:1, 72–107.

Scott, W. Richard (1992) *Organizations: Rational, Natural and Open Systems* (London: Prentice Hall).

Scott, W. Richard, John Meyer and Associates (eds.) (1994) *Institutional Environments and Organizations* (London: Sage).

Sedaitis, Judith B. (1997) *Commercializing High Technology: East and West* (Lanham, MD: Rowman and Littlefield).

Segal, Gerald (1983–1984) "Strategy and Ethnic Chic," *International Affairs*, 60, 15–30.

Segal, Gerald (1985) *Defending China* (Oxford: Oxford University Press).

Segal, Gerald (1992) "Managing New Arms Races in Asia/Pacific," *Washington Quarterly*.

Sen, Gautam (1984) *The Military Origins of Industrialisation and International Trade Rivalry* (London: Frances Pinter).

Shambaugh, David and Richard H. Yang (eds.) (1997) *China's Military in Transition* (Oxford: Clarendon Press).

Shapley, Deborah (1978) "Technology Creep and the Arms Race," *Science*, 201, 1102–1105, 1192–1196; 202: 289–292.

Sharp, Gene (1973) *The Politics of Nonviolent Action*, three vols. (Boston: Porter Sargent).

Sharp, Gene (1980) *Social Power and Political Freedom* (Boston: Porter Sargent Publishers).

Sharp, Gene (1985) *Making Europe Unconquerable: The Potential of Civilian-based Deterrence and Defence* (London: Taylor & Francis).

Sharp, Gene (1990) *Civilian-Based Defense: A Post-Military Weapons System* (Princeton: Princeton University Press).

Shaw, Martin (1991) *Post-Military Society. Militarism, Demilitarization and War at the End of the Twentieth Century* (London: Polity).

Shaw, Martin (1996) *Civil Society and Media in Global Crises. Representing Distant Violence* (London: Pinter).

Sherry, Michael S. (1995) *In the Shadow of War. The United States Since the 1930s* (New Haven: Yale University Press).

Silber, Laura and Alan Little (1996) *The Death of Yugoslavia* (London: Penguin), revised edition.

Simpson, John (1983) *The Independent Nuclear State: The U.S., Britain and the Military Atom* (London: Macmillan).

Simpson, John (1994) "Nuclear Nonproliferation in the Post Cold War Era," *International Affairs*, 70:1, 17–39.

Singer, J. David (1962) *Deterrence, Arms Control and Disarmament: Toward a Synthesis in National Security Policy* (Columbus: Ohio State University Press).

Singer, Max and Aaron Wildavsky (1993) *The Real World Order: Zones of Peace/Zones of Turmoil* (Chatham, NJ: Chatham House Publishers).

Singh, Jasjit and Vatroslav Vekaric (eds.) (1989) *Non-Provocative Defence. The Search for Equal Security* (New Delhi: Lancer).

Singh, Ravinder Pal (ed.) (1997) *Arms Procurement Decision-Making Processes. China, India, Israel, Japan and South Korea* (Oxford: Oxford University Press for the Stockholm International Peace Research Institute).

SIPRI Yearbook. World Armaments and Disarmament (Oxford: Oxford University Press for the Stockholm International Peace Research Institute), annually since 1969.

Skolnikoff, Eugene B. (1993) *The Elusive Transformation. Science, Technology, and the Evolution of International Politics* (Princeton: Princeton University Press).

Sköns, Elisabeth and Bates Gill (1996) "Arms Production," in *SIPRI Yearbook 1996. Armaments, Disarmament and International Security* (Oxford: Oxford University Press for the Stockholm International Peace Research Institute), 411–462.

Smith, Chris (1994) *India's Ad Hoc Arsenal: Direction or Drift in Defence Policy?* (New York: Oxford University Press).

Smith, Chris (1995) "The International Trade in Small Arms," *Jane's Intelligence Review*, 7:9, 427–436.

Smith, Merritt Roe (1985) *Military Enterprise and Technological Change* (Cambridge, MA: The Massachusetts Institute of Technology Press).

Smith, Merritt Roe and Leo Marx (eds.) (1994) *Does Technology Drive History? The Dilemma of Technological Determinism* (Cambridge, MA: The Massachusetts Institute of Technology Press).

Snyder, Glenn H. (1971) "Deterrence and Defence," in Robert J. Art and Kenneth N. Waltz (eds.) *The Use of Force* (Boston: Little, Brown).

Snyder, Glenn H. (1984) "The Security Dilemma in Alliance Politics," *World Politics*, 36:4, 461–495.

Snyder, Glenn H. and Paul Diesing (1977) *Conflict Among Nations. Decision Making and System Structure in International Crises* (Princeton: Princeton University Press).

Snyder, Jack L. (1985) "Perceptions of the Security Dilemma in 1914," in Robert Jervis, Richard Ned Lebow, and Janice Gross Stein, *Psychology and Deterrence,* with contributions by Patrick M. Morgan and Jack L. Snyder (Baltimore: The Johns Hopkins University Press), 153–179.

Solingen, Etel (1994) "The Political Economy of Nuclear Restraint," *International Security*, 19:2, 126–169.

Sollenberg, Margareta and Peter Wallensteen (1996) "Major Armed Conflicts," in *SIPRI Yearbook 1996. Armaments, Disarmament and International Security* (Oxford: Oxford University Press for the Stockholm International Peace Research Institute), 15–30.

Sorel, Georges ([1908] 1975) *Reflections on Violence* (New York: AMS Press). Translated by T.E. Hulme.

Spector, Leonard (1988) *The Undeclared Bomb* (Cambridge, MA: Ballinger).

Spector, Leonard S. (1992) "Repentant Nuclear Proliferants," *Foreign Policy*, 88.

Spinardi, Graham (1994) *From Polaris to Trident: The Development of U.S. Fleet Ballistic Missile Technology* (New York: Cambridge University Press).

Spiro, David E. (1994) "The Insignificance of the Liberal Peace," *International Security*, 19:2, 50–86.

Spufford, Francis and Jenny Uglow (eds.) (1996) *Cultural Babbage: Technology, Time and Invention* (London: Faber & Faber).

Stanley, John and Maurice Pearton (1972) *The International Trade in Arms* (London: Chatto & Windus).

Stein, Janice Gross (1985a) "Calculation, Miscalculation and Conventional Deterrence I: The View from Cairo," in Robert Jervis, Richard Ned Lebow, and Janice Gross Stein, with contributions by Patrick M. Morgan and Jack L. Snyder, *Psychology and Deterrence* (Baltimore: The Johns Hopkins University Press), 34–59.

Stein, Janice Gross (1985b) "Calculation, Miscalculation and Conventional Deterrence II: The View from Jerusalem," in Robert Jervis, Richard Ned Lebow, and Janice Gross Stein, with contributions by Patrick M. Morgan and Jack L. Snyder, *Psychology and Deterrence* (Baltimore: The Johns Hopkins University Press), 60–88.

Stein, Janice Gross (1991a) "Deterrence and Reassurance," in Philip E. Tetlock, Jo L. Husbands, Robert Jervis, Paul C. Stern, and Charles Tilly (eds.), *Behavior, Society and Nuclear War*, 2 (New York: Oxford University Press), 8–72.

Stein, Janice Gross (1991b) "Reassurance in International Conflict Management," *Political Science Quarterly*, 106, 431–451.

Steinberg, J. (1965) *Yesterday's Deterrent* (London: Macdonald).

Steinbrunner, John (1976) "Beyond Rational Deterrence: The Struggle for New Conceptions," *World Politics*, 28, 223–245.

Steiner, Barry H. (1973) "Arms Races, Diplomacy, and Recurring Behaviour: Lessons from Two Cases," *Sage Professional Papers in International Studies*, 02–013 (Beverly Hills: Sage).

Stevenson, David (1996) *Armaments and the Coming of War. Europe 1904–1914* (Oxford: Clarendon Press).

Strategic Survey (London: International Institute for Strategic Studies, annually).

Studiengruppe Alternative Sicherheitspolitik (eds.) (1989) *Vertrauensbildende Verteidigung. Reform deutscher Sicherheitspolitik* (Gerlingen: Bleicher Verlag).

Sweeney, John (1993) *Trading With the Enemy. Britain's Arming of Iraq* (London: Pan).

Taylor, Philip M. (1992) *War and the Media. Propaganda and Persuasion in the Gulf War* (Manchester: Manchester University Press).

Thee, Marek (1986) *Military Technology, Military Strategy and the Arms Race* (London: Croom Helm).

Thomas, Caroline (1993) "The Pragmatic Case Against Intervention," in Ian Forbes and Mark Hoffman (eds.) *Political Theory, International Relations and the Ethics of Intervention* (London: Macmillan), 91–103.

Thomas, Raju G.C. (1993) *South Asian Security in the 1990s*, Adelphi Paper 278 (London: International Institute for Strategic Studies).

Thompson, John B. (1990) *Ideology and Modern Culture: Critical Social Theory in the Era of Mass Communication* (Cambridge: Polity).

Thompson, E.P. and Dan Smith (1980) *Protest and Survive* (Harmondsworth: Penguin).

Thompson, Mark (1994) *Forging War. The Media in Serbia, Croatia and Bosnia–Herzegovina* (London: Article 19 International Centre Against Censorship).

Thompson, Kenneth W. (ed.) (1991) *Negotiating Arms Control: Missed Opportunities and Limited Successes* (Lanham, MD: University Press of America).

Toffler, Alvin and Heidi Toffler (1993) *War and Anti-War. Making Sense of Today's Global Chaos* (London: Warner Books).

Tsipis, Kosta (1985) *Understanding Nuclear Weapons* (London: Wildwood House).

Tucker, Jonathan (1993) "Lessons of Iraq's Biological Weapons Programme," *Arms Control*, 14:3, 229–271.

Tucker, Jonathan (1994) "Dilemmas of a Dual-Use Technology: Toxins in Medicine and Warfare," *Politics and the Life Sciences*, 51–62.

Tunander, Ola (1989) *Cold Water Politics. The Maritime Strategy and Geopolitics of the Northern Front* (London: Sage).

Uekert, Brenda K. (1995) *Rivers of Blood. A Comparative Study of Government Massacres* (New York: Praeger).

Ullman, Richard H. (1989) "The Covert French Connection," *Foreign Policy* 75.

UNIDIR (ed.) (1990) *Non Offensive Defense. A Global Perspective* (New York: Taylor & Francis).

Van Creveld, Martin (1989) *Technology and War: From 2000 B.C. to the Present* (New York: The Free Press).

Van Creveld, Martin (1991) *On Future War* (London: Brassey's).

Van Creveld, Martin (1993) *Nuclear Proliferation and the Future of Conflict* (New York: The Free Press).

Van Evera, Stephen (1984) "The Cult of the Offensive and the Origins of the First World War," *International Security*, 9, 58–107.

Van Evera, Stephen (1990) "Wars of Intervention: Why They Shouldn't Have a Future, Why They Do," *Defense and Disarmament Alternatives*, 3:3, 1–4, 8.

Väyrynen, Raimo (1983a) "Economic Fluctuations, Technological Innovations and the Arms Race in a Historical Perspective," *Cooperation and Conflict*, 18, 135–159.

Väyrynen, Raimo (1983b) "Economic Cycles, Power Transitions, Political Management, and Wars Between Major Powers," *International Studies Quarterly*, 27, 389–418.

Väyrynen, Raimo (1992) *Military Industrialization and Economic Development: Theory and Historical Case Studies* (Aldershot: Dartmouth for United Nations Institute for Disarmament Research).

Virilio, Paul (1986) *Speed and Politics: An Essay on Dromology* (New York: Semiotext(e)). Translated by Mark Polizzotti.

Virilio, Paul (1989) *War and Cinema: The Logistics of Perception* (New York: Verso). Translated by Patrick Camiller.

Virilio, Paul and Sylvere Lotringer (1983) *Pure War* (New York: Semiotext(e)). Translated by Mark Polizzotti.

Von Clausewitz, Carl ([1832] 1984) *On War* (Princeton: Princeton University Press). Editors and translators Michael Howard and Peter Paret.

Wæver, Ole (1995) "Securitization and Desecuritization," in Ronnie Lipschutz (ed.) *On Security* (New York: Columbia University Press), 46–86.

Wæver, Ole, Barry Buzan, Morton Kelstrup, and Pierre Lemaitre (1993) *Identity, Migration and the New Security Agenda in Europe* (London: Pinter).

Wallace, Michael (1982) "Armaments and Escalation," *International Studies Quarterly*, 26, 37–56.

Wallander, Celeste (1988) "Coercion and Crises in Soviet Behavior," unpublished ms.

Waltz, Kenneth N. (1959) *Man, the State, and War* (New York: Columbia University Press).

Waltz, Kenneth N. (1979) *Theory of International Politics* (Reading, MA: Addison-Wesley).

Waltz, Kenneth N. (1981) *The Spread of Nuclear Weapons: More May Be Better*, Adelphi Paper 171 (London: International Institute for Strategic Studies).

Warnke, Paul C. (1975) "Apes on a Treadmill," *Foreign Policy*, 18.

Wehr, Paul, Heidi Burgess, and Guy Burgess (eds.) (1994) *Justice Without Violence* (Boulder, CO: Lynne Rienner Publishers).

Weiner, Myron (1996) "Bad Neighbours, Bad Neighborhoods: An Inquiry into the Causes of Refugee Flows," *International Security*, 21:1, 5–42.

Weiss, Thomas G. (ed.) (1994) *Collective Security in a Changing World* (Boulder, CO: Lynne Rienner Publishers).

Weiss, Thomas G. (1995) *The United Nations and Civil Wars* (Boulder, CO: Lynne Rienner Publishers).

Weiss, Thomas G. and Larry Minear (1994) *Humanitarianism Across Borders. Sustaining Civilians in Time of War* (Boulder, CO: Lynne Rienner Publishers).

Welch, Jasper (1989) "Assessing the Value of Stealthy Aircraft and Cruise Missiles," *International Security*, 14:2, 47–63.

Wendt, Alexander (1992) "Anarchy Is What States Make of It: The Social Construction of Power Politics," *International Organization*, 46:2, 391–425.

Wendt, Alexander and Michael Barnett (1993) "Dependent State Formation and Third World Militarization," *Review of International Studies*, 19:4, 321–347.

Wesley, Michael (1997) *Casualties of the New World Order. The Causes of Failure of UN Missions to Civil Wars* (London: Macmillan).

Weston, Burns H. (ed.) (1991) *Alternative Security. Living Without Nuclear Deterrence* (Boulder, CO: Westview Press).

Wheeler, Nicholas J. and Ken Booth (1992) "The Security Dilemma," in John Baylis and Nicholas J. Rengger (eds.) *Dilemmas of World Politics* (Oxford: Clarendon Press), 29–60.

Whiting, Allen S. (1975) *The Chinese Calculus of Deterrence. India and Indochina* (Ann Arbor: The University of Michigan Press).

Wilkenfeld, Jonathan, Michael Brecher, and Sheila Moser (1988) *Crises in the Twentieth Century. Vol. 2: Handbook of Foreign Policy Crises* (Oxford: Pergamon Press).

Willetts, Peter (ed.) (1995) *"The Conscience of the World": The Influence of Non-Governmental Organisations in the UN System* (London: Hurst).

Williams, Phil (1983) "Arms Control and European Security: Competing Conceptions for the 1980s," *Arms Control*, 4:2, 73–96.

Windass, Stan (ed.) (1985) *Avoiding Nuclear War: Common Security as a Strategy for the Defence of the West* (London: Brassey's).

Windsor, Philip (1982) "On the Logic of Security and Arms Control in the NATO Alliance," in Lawrence Hagan (ed.) *The Crisis in Western Security* (London: Croom Helm).

Wiseman, Geoffrey (1997) *On the Defensive: A Critical Examination of Concepts of "Non-Provocative Defence," 1980–1992*, D. Phil. thesis in International Relations, University of Oxford.

Wohlstetter, Albert (1974a) "Is There a Strategic Arms Race?" *Foreign Policy*, 15.

Wohlstetter, Albert (1974b) "Rivals But No 'Race,'" *Foreign Policy*, 16.

Wolf, Reinhard, Erich Weede, Andrew J. Enterline, Edward D. Mansfield, and Jack Snyder (1996) "Correspondence: Democratization and the Danger of War," *International Security* 20: 4, 176–207.

Wolpin, Miles D. (1972) *Military Aid and Counterrevolution in the Third World* (Lexington, MA: D.C. Heath).

Wolpin, Miles D. (1986) *Militarization, Internal Repression and Social Welfare in the Third World* (London: Croom Helm).

Woodward, E.L. ([1935] 1964) *Great Britain and the German Navy* (London: Frank Cass).

Woodward, Susan (1995) *Balkan Tragedy. Chaos and Dissolution After the Cold War* (Washington, DC: The Brookings Institution).

World Development Movement (1995) *Gunrunners' Gold. How the Public's Money Finances Arms Sales* (London: World Development Movement).

Wright, Quincy ([1942] 1969) *A Study of War* (Chicago: Phoenix Books), abridged edition.

Zeldin, T. (1994) *An Intimate History of Humanity* (London: Minerva).

Zhang, Shu Guang (1985) *Deterrence and Strategic Culture—Chinese-American Confrontations, 1949–1958* (Ithaca: Cornell University Press).

Zisk, Kimberly Martin (1993) *Engaging the Enemy: Organization Theory and Soviet Military Innovation, 1955–1991* (Princeton: Princeton University Press).

INDEX

ABOUT THE BOOK

What is the relationship between the arms dynamic and world politics? How has that relationship changed? Considering the entire set of factors that influence the nature of armed forces, this comprehensive book puts these essential questions into historical and analytical perspective.

Buzan and Herring focus on four themes. In Part 1 they discuss the ways in which the political and military impacts of technological revolutions spread. Part 2 surveys a range of explanations for arms-related behavior. Part 3 examines three ways of applying military power: the use of force, the making of threats, and the deployment of symbols. And Part 4 addresses military technology not primarily as a problem because it is in the hands of potential users, but as a creator of security problems in itself; in this section, regulatory approaches are discussed in terms of their political, economic, and military implications.

While the arms dynamic does not determine directly what happens in world politics, it does, the authors argue, shape in dramatic ways the context and possibilities of world politics; thus, an understanding of its influence is essential to a meaningful interpretation of international relations.

Barry Buzan is professor of international studies at the University of Westminster and project director of the European Security Group at the Copenhagen Peace Research Institute. **Eric Herring** is lecturer in international politics at the University of Bristol.